Trailer Life's

Guide To Full-Time RVing

Trailer Life's

Guide to Full-Time RVing

by Don Wright & the Editors of Trailer Life

Editor in Charge: Patrick J. Flaherty

Published by TL Enterprises, Inc.
29901 Agoura Road, Agoura, California 91301

Book Division TL Enterprises, Inc.

Art Rouse
Chairman of the Board

Richard Rouse
President

Denis Rouse
Executive Vice President/Publisher

Patrick J. Flaherty
Vice President/Editor-in-Chief

Composition by: Publisher's Typography
(A Division of TL Enterprises, Inc.)

Book Design: Robert S. Tinnon

Cover Design and Illustrations: Joe Cibere

Project Editor: Pamela Taylor

Editorial Assistants: Pat Kolb, Rena Copperman

Published by TL Enterprises, Inc., 29901 Agoura
Road, Agoura, California 91301. Copyright © 1982 by
TL Enterprises, Inc. All rights reserved.
Reproduction of this work, in whole or in part,
without written permission of the publisher, is
prohibited. International Standard Book Number
0-934798-05-2. Printed and bound in the United States
of America.

Contents

Chapter Nine

Young Full-Timers

Under-30 Full-Timers • Full-Timing With Kids •
On The Road At 39 • Working Full-Timers

Chapter Ten

Loners On Wheels

Free-spirited Single Full-Timers • A Trailer Built For One •
A Club For Singles • Romance On The Road •
Conversation With Some Loners

Chapter Eleven

'Til Death Do You Part

Widows And Widowers • Combating Loneliness •
Women Alone

Chapter Twelve

Work While Traveling

Jobs In Campgrounds • Finding Supplemental Income •
Good Sam Sambassadors • Freelance Your Skills •
Full-Timing Celebrities • RVing Vendors •
Cardtable Businesses

Chapter Thirteen

Winter Camping

Some Like It; Some Don't • Winter Destinations •
Adjusting To The Cold

Introduction

This book has evolved over the last five years as a sort of self-education process. First as a contributing editor and later as Midwest editor of the *Trailer Life* family of publications, I became more and more involved with and fascinated by the RVing lifestyle. As my family and I tested travel trailers and fifth-wheels, Class A's and mini motorhomes, vans and trucks, pickup campers and folding trailers for those publications, my attention gradually began to focus on a group of people who seemed to be enjoying the best of life possible: full-time RVers. They had, it seemed to me, truly found The American Dream. They were either retired or semiretired and were totally free to travel wherever they pleased, soaking up the riches of the world as they camped across this vast continent. They were independent spirits, unrestrained by anyone or anything except the limits of their own personal skills and their financial resources.

I wanted to join them. I wanted to be one of them. I wanted to follow the sun, as they did, spending my winters in Florida or Texas or Arizona or Mexico or California or South Carolina; my summers, on the coast of Maine or in the forests of Minnesota or atop the mountains of Colorado. But I knew all along that I'd have to wait. My children came first; they needed to be nurtured, loved, educated and prepared for the harsh realities of our world. I started preparing for the day, however, when the kids would be grown and my copilot and I could join the full-time RVing fraternity. I talked with other aspiring full-timers and with people who were already living The Good Life. I began to collect data and build files.

And then I realized that thousands of other RVers who hoped that some-day *they* would be full-timers were also trying to gather information in preparation for the time when they would be ready to sell their houses, give their antiques to their kids and hit the road on a full-time basis.

Sometimes it seemed that every RVer in America aspired to the full-timing lifestyle. But the fact was, only a small percentage of those people would ever actually do it. Why? Because they were afraid of it. They couldn't quite come to grips with the realities of leaving their homes, their friends, their families and their jobs behind them in order to pursue a dream. A dream that could lead nowhere and which seemed to have obvious economic perils associated with it. They couldn't know that their dreams were *real*—that their dreams were being lived, on a day-to-day basis, by thousands upon thousands of full-timers who had already re-jected the notion that a house and two cars are necessary ingredients of personal happiness. It became clear to me that most aspirants to full-time RVing simply gave up their dreams because no one could provide them with evidence that they—not other people, but *they*—could realize those dreams and live happily ever after.

What they needed was a book: a guide to full-time RVing. And I wanted to write it because I knew that by researching it, I would learn enough to enable me to more easily join the ranks of the full-timers when my own time came.

This book is the result of that research. Here, you will find a lot of space devoted to the economics of the lifestyle because, ironically enough, it is the economics of the lifestyle which worries most aspiring full-timers. Many would-be way-of-lifers are concerned that they might not be able to afford to pursue their dream; others seek to be full-time RVers because they can't afford to retire any other way. Be forewarned, however: the cost of full-timing soon becomes of secondary importance to anyone who does it for a while. Full-timers learn quickly to budget their expenditures, and soon they're doing it almost unconsciously. It is at that point that the pleasures of living become of primary importance to them.

This book is, in reality, about living. And enjoying it. It is about people so caught up in the pleasures of a unique, fiercely independent lifestyle that, for them, giving it up as long as they have their health is unthinkable. Unlike all other books ever written on full-time RVing, this one also is about people; it is not written from the narrow perspective of one person's, or one couple's, full-timing experiences. In preparing this book, I have probed the lives of dozens of couples who are engaged on a day to day basis with the full-timing lifestyle. This book is, more than anything else, *their* story—the story of why they're full-timing today, the story of how they prepared themselves for it, of how they're doing it, why they're enjoying it, of how they travel, where they go and why. It deals with their worries, their problems and their adjustments to a type of living for which there are no experts to advise them.

This book discusses the all-important RV rigs that they use as their homes and their modes of travel. It deals with expenses and budgets, with the practical problems of cashing checks and forwarding mail. It investigates the exciting phenomenon of widows, widowers and other single people RVing full time alone. It discusses working while traveling, saving energy, making repairs. It runs the gamut of the full-timing lifestyle from the practical aspects of trip-planning and cost-cutting while on the road to the more human aspects of making new friends, adjusting to a so-called "life of leisure" and keeping in touch with old friends and family.

Finally, this book was written for you, if you are not now a full-time RVer, but aspire to be one. It is truly intended as your "guide to full-time RVing" and is meant not only to enlighten you about how today's full-timers live and travel, but also to help you decide whether you, too, should be a part of the full-timing lifestyle.

DON WRIGHT

Chapter One

Making
The Decision

I f everyone who *talked* about becoming a full-time RVer would quit his job, hock his furniture, sell his house and join the annual snowbird migration, the nation's recreational vehicle industry wouldn't be able to build travel trailers and motorhomes fast enough to meet the demand. Each year a growing number of middle-aged and older Americans do hit the road as full-timers. But thousands of others merely talk about doing it without taking any definite, positive steps to ensure that some day they can join the RVing way-of-life fraternity. They can come up with dozens of reasons not to take the plunge—just yet. They can't do it until their children are grown, or through college, or married, or financially secure—they say. They can't do it until they start receiving their pensions or their social security benefits. Or until they strike it rich with their investments. They can't do it right now because they don't have the right RV rig. Or they're too young. Or too old. They're worried about the prices and supplies of gasoline. They feel tied to the house where they raised their family. They don't want to leave their children, their grandchildren, their friends, their neighborhood. They're not sure they can cope with each other while living together in the relatively small confines of an RV. They don't want to give up the possessions they've accumulated over the last forty years. They're worried about personal health problems. They're afraid they'll be bored.

Active full-timers have heard all the reasons people give for not going on the road themselves. And they don't have much sympathy any more for those who say they want to make the move but somehow never get around to doing it. Jerry and Betty Campbell, who describe themselves as "originally from Kentucky," have counseled dozens of aspiring full-timers—often unsuccessfully—during the seven years that they've been RVing way-of-lifers. "I'll tell you what it is," Jerry said. "People don't have enough nerve, enough guts to jump into something that's unknown."

But didn't the Campbells themselves have serious qualms when it came time for them to sell their house and get rid of their furniture?

Betty answered. "He didn't, but I did. I thought my heart would break. But I finally realized it wasn't breaking for the house itself, but because it was where we had raised our family. As for the furniture, we managed to give some to this kid, some to that kid and some to the other two, so we still see most of that furniture now and then. It was a big decision, but I would not go back into a house to live."

"I've asked her seriously about moving into a house or an apartment, and her answer's been negative each time," Jerry said. "Maybe she's just said that to appease me, though."

Betty replied, "No, I haven't. Whenever you express a desire for a house or an apartment, I know you don't really mean it. But I answer no because I know that I don't want to do that either."

DECISION: SELLING THE HOMESTEAD

The decision whether to sell the house and furniture is one that nearly every aspiring full-timer must face. And it's no simple decision, partly because of the memories that are in that house and partly because of the emotional security—the sense of belonging somewhere—that a permanent home provides. Frequently, external pressures come to bear, too. The children, although grown, look upon the house as a place to come home to, and it tugs at their heartstrings to realize Mom and Dad are considering getting rid of it. The home also represents familiar surroundings: friends, neighbors, favorite stores, a lawn that has been nurtured for twenty years. In addition, there is a solid sense of security in knowing that the house is paid for—or nearly paid for—and that it represents a good investment because its value will increase every year. A mortgage-free house could serve very easily as a home base for the full-time travelers, a port to return to whenever the sailing gets rough, when old age calls a halt to the wandering, when those almost inevitable health problems occur.

On the other hand, there are sound financial reasons for selling the family home. It probably is larger than it needs to be for Mom and Dad after they retire. It represents a huge chunk of cash that, invested wisely, could ensure financial security while providing the full-time travelers with a regular income. Unfortunately, if it is not sold, it also represents a constant drain on the couple's financial resources because, even if it is mortgage-free, upkeep will cost an average of $100 to $200 per month. And the taxes always have to be paid. And the insurance. And somebody must be appointed to check on it periodically and to mow the grass, prune the trees and weed the flowerbeds.

The Gaynors: "We've Built Another Home"

Like most aspiring full-timers, Hal and Penny Gaynor faced the decision of what to do with their home when they retired in 1972. For Hal, the decision was easy; he wanted to travel, and he didn't like the idea of worrying about a house. For Penny, the decision was more difficult. I talked with them about their decision one evening at a campground in central Connecticut. "For a man, going full-time is not usually a big deal," Penny told me. "He needs a shave and a haircut and a pressed shirt, and he's ready to go. But a woman has a lot of security wrapped up in her home. She looks around it and she sees the things she's had for years; things she's accumulated that she loves. A very, very smart woman told me many years ago, though, 'The only thing that possesses you are your possessions,' and I always believed that. So I wanted to sell the house and go full-timing and, at the same time, I didn't. I'll tell you what happened that finally made me say okay. Hal lost his parents and I lost mine, one right after the other. And I saw what happened to those two homes. The kids went in and took what they wanted, sold the rest and locked the houses up. Zing! It was finished. There was no one in either house any more. I thought about our family, our four children. They were gone and on their own, and I suddenly realized there were just the two of us, and we weren't honeymooning any more. I told Hal, 'I'm ready to go.' I've discovered since then that a home—a house—isn't really important. We lost another home last year when our trailer was destroyed by fire. It looked like nothing, but to us, it was a full house of furniture and clothing. Everything burned up, and I felt very badly. But little by little, we've built another home. This trailer. And as long as we are alive and in good health, that's all that matters."

Penny added, "I talk to a lot of other women who are full-timing. We can become good friends in three days, and we'll just talk our hearts out and tell each other things that I would never have dreamed of telling people I knew for years when we lived in a real house. We all agree that full-time RVing is a very nice way of aging and that the loneliest thing is when you're in a house, growing old in one room while you're watching the idiot box."

Hal offered, "If we lived in a house, we would not see our children and our grandchildren as much as we do because one lives in Florida, one lives in North Carolina, one lives in Connecticut and one lives in California. This way, we see them more often. If we were living in a house, we'd plan one trip a year—maybe to Florida or to California—because that would be all we could afford, especially if we had jobs."

"It works another way, too," Penny said. "We make very good in-laws, and we're very welcome visitors because we always stay in our trailer. The kids are glad when we leave so they can continue their happy lives, and we are very glad to leave too."

The Jennings: "We Have Old-Fashioned Parents"

For Harry and Juanita Jennings, leaving their family behind in North Carolina while they traveled the nation's highways was a traumatic experience. They had paved the way for an early retirement by paying off all their debts, and when Harry was thirty-nine they decided they were ready to make their move. "My sons were young—one eighteen and one twenty. We sat down with them and said, 'You have your own jobs, you have your own cars, and neither of you is married. Mommy and Daddy have raised you to this point, but now it's up to you. Here's what we want to do with our lives now. What do you think of it?' And, of course, they said, 'Go. Enjoy each other.' We told the boys that if they wanted to stay at home, fine. If they wanted to keep the place up, all right. They did that for a while—three or four months—but then they went their separate ways. All the rest of our family thought we were crazy. Especially our parents. We have old-fashioned parents. They live back in the mountains of North Carolina, and their idea of life is going to work every day and having a big house and a big car and that's it. It was hard for them to understand why we wanted to run the road like gypsies. We got a lot of flak from our parents, and that was kind of rough. They'd never camped, and they didn't know what camping was other than going out with us for the weekend. But I've been pretty independent all my life and I do about what I want to do as long as Juanita agrees, so we left home. And we haven't been sorry."

4

Full-Timers Alone: "I Sold My Farm And Took Off"

Jeannie Deyo is another full-timer who looked forward to an independent, traveling lifestyle after raising her children. She was a widow of fifteen years and was fifty-two years old when she made her move. She explained: "You know, when children get to be eighteen or nineteen years old, they leave home. But my four kids just stuck around, and I took care of them until I got tired of it. So I said, 'Hey, I don't have to do this any more.' I sold my farm to my son-in-law and I bought a trailer and took off. Like I tell everyone now, the kids wouldn't leave home, so I did."

Conway Tweedy, a native of Minneapolis, chuckled as he heard Jeannie's story. "That's the same reason I got into full-timing," he laughed. "I just ran away from home a week ago. I told my daughter she could have my place for at least two years. I've got one kid eighteen and one twenty-five, and I told them I wouldn't be back until they settled down."

Bob Woletz of Flint, Michigan, chimed in: "The same thing happened to me. When my daughter graduated from high school, I said to her, 'Hey, baby, I'm leaving you before you leave Daddy. Goodbye.' I hit the road in the summer of '74, and I've been going ever since."

Helen Duffessy: "I Was Ruthless About It"

Conway and Bob are widowers and members of a nationwide RVers' club called Loners on Wheels. Widow Helen Duffessy is another LoW member, and since May of 1977, she has been touring the country by herself in a 27-foot Empire travel trailer towed by a Ford station wagon. When she made her decision to travel full time, she faced the problem of what to do with her furniture. "It was hard to get rid of things that I had accumulated and bought and enjoyed," she said, "but it's something that if you have to do, you'll do it. I just made up my mind to get rid of everything and I was ruthless about it. I could have had a garage sale to end all garage sales but I was living in a condominium and couldn't do that. So I called a man from the nearest flea market to haul away most of it. He took three truckloads of stuff. I figured there was no point in putting my best furniture in storage because even if I would set up housekeeping again it would be in a mobile home in Florida, and I wouldn't want to use French provincial furniture. So when my daughter from New York visited me for Thanksgiving, I told her, 'You can have any of this stuff that's left if you'll take it back home with you.' She and her husband had just built a big house, and they needed all the extra furniture they could get, so they rented a U-haul and loaded it to the top. My other daughter, Rosemary, took some more. Some things, I saved—things that were monogrammed, I saved for my son—but eventually, I got rid of even that."

Ironically, Helen's decision to travel full time probably required as much adjustment by her family as by Helen herself. I talked with Helen and her daughter, Rosemary Hoff, while they were parked overnight at Eby Pines Campground in Bristol, Indiana, during the summer of 1980.

"When I started full-timing, I was living in Royal Oak, Michigan," Helen said, "but now the only address I have is Rosemary's, in Westland, Michigan. She's the only person who knows where Mother might be, where she is right now and where she was."

I asked Rosemary, "What's it like to have a mother who is a full-time RVer?"

"Well," she answered, "I have a map of the U.S. in my sewing room, and I just move pins periodically. That's the only way I can keep track of her."

"Does she write to you often enough?"

"Usually she does. She's good about keeping in touch."

I asked, "What is the family's attitude about Mom's taking off and traveling full time by herself?"

Rosemary said, "The original attitude was, 'She's out of her mind!' She wrote to my brother in Florida and my sister in New York to tell them what she was going to do, and the first thing they did when they received their letters was to phone me and ask, 'Is Mom crazy? What does she think she's doing?' But we never really tried to talk her out of it, did we Mom?"

"No, you never tried," Helen answered. "You knew better."

Rosemary said, "The biggest problem for the family now is knowing where she is. People ask us, 'Well, where's your mother this week?' and all we can answer is, 'How would I know? I knew where she was last week, and I know where she'll be next week, but I don't know where she is now.'"

The Coopers: "Don't Burn Your Bridges"

California natives Ken and Flo Cooper have been full-timing successfully for two years, but they advocate a conservative approach to the RVing way of life. They maintain a residence in San Francisco, and they advise aspiring full-timers to "very definitely, try it out, but don't sell your house before you try it. Don't make any rash moves. Go full-timing for one year, but don't burn your bridges. You might love it, and it might just be your cup of tea. But again, maybe not."

The Coopers started traveling almost immediately after Ken retired at age fifty-eight. But Flo emphasized, "We never really intended to full-time it. We intended to be on the road a good part of the year, but always with the idea that there was a home to return to. And I haven't changed my mind about that. We might spend only a month or six weeks at home each year, but I like knowing when I'm out on the road that there is a home somewhere. We have too many ties, too many possessions that I don't want to part with. We will never live entirely in our rig."

DECISION: HOW TO FINANCE FULL-TIMING

At the same time the aspiring full-timers decide whether to keep or sell their home and how to sever the family ties, they should consider how they will finance their travels. I've talked with single full-timers who are living on as little as $250 a month while on the road; at the other end of the spectrum are independently wealthy people who spend as much as $3,000 every month. The average full-timing couple, however, must keep to a budget ranging from about $800 to $1,100 a month. Thus, I think it is safe to say that if anyone is seriously considering joining the full-time RVing lifestyle, he should make sure he has a guaranteed income of between $200 and $300 per week.

There are several ways to structure such an income: through rental of real estate; investments such as stocks, bonds and mutual funds; pensions; Social Security; disability insurance; interest on savings, or by working at part-time or temporary jobs. Some full-timers operate their own businesses while traveling; others supplement retirement income by selling crafts, art work, paintings and even fishing lures that they have created. A few way-of-lifers have been able to prepare for their retirement travels by saving money and investing it wisely over the course of several years. Most aspiring full-timers, however, must depend upon income from the sale of their family homes, supplemented by Social Security benefits or pension funds, in order to live the life to which they'd like to become accustomed.

Ken and Flo Cooper believe that preplanning is critical to enjoyment of the full-timing lifestyle. Flo reported, "We made sure three or four years before Ken retired that we had channeled our money into investments so that we wouldn't have to be in California at any point and if we wanted

7

to be gone six or seven months at a time, there would be no problems."

Ken added, "We've both always been planners, and our retirement was planned very carefully. I actually started planning when I was twenty-five years old; my goal was to retire when I was fifty-five. I retired at fifty-eight with a modest income from our investments, and that income, coupled with our pension [from the City of Los Angeles, where he was assistant superintendent of parks and recreation], allows us to do all right."

I asked Helen Duffessy, "If you could offer one piece of advice to someone who is considering RVing full time, what would it be?"

She replied, "I'd say, 'Go ahead, but you've got to study your finances carefully.' I do. Maybe there are people who can say, 'God will look after me, so I'm not worried, and I can always get a job.' But I like to know that I've got enough money to do what I want and that I'm going to be all right. I'd say if you don't want to get rid of your house, rent it or close it. I opted to get rid of everything, but I was living in only a condominium that I wasn't all that crazy about. I had some reservations, so I thought I'd give myself a year, and, if I didn't like it, I'd do something different. But I'm still doing it! One of my friends asked me, 'Aren't you tired of traveling yet?' I said, 'No, I'm not tired of it yet.' She asked, 'When are you going to stop fooling around with those "Loners" and settle down someplace?' But I told her I'm just not interested. I figured at the beginning that if I were very careful with money, by golly, I could make it. And I've never regretted it. I've had a ball."

The Browns: "We've Bought An Education"

Jim and Mary Brown from Chesapeake, Virginia, wanted to start full-timing while they were young and healthy, so they began putting aside as much money as possible several years ago to finance their RV travels. They figured full-timing would cost them about $1,000 a month and, since they wanted to be on the road for at least two years, they saved $24,000. To cut expenses while traveling, they sold their house in Virginia and banked the proceeds against the day they would have to replace it. When I met Jim and Mary in July 1980, they had been on the road for almost 2½ years, and they were contemplating what to do with their lives after their travel money ran out. Mary told me, "We look at the last 2½ years this way. What we've lost is the money we might have saved during the time we've been traveling, and we've lost the money from the appreciation

of the house we sold, but what we've gained in experience, we couldn't buy for that money. We've bought quite an education."

The Browns began their two-year odyssey when Jim was only forty-eight years old. "We were encouraged by older friends who said, 'Do it. Do it now while you've got your health.' When other people realize that we're trailering full time at such a young age, they ask us, 'Were you born wealthy or did you retire from the military?' When I tell them we just saved our money and quit our jobs, they don't believe it."

Mary added, "But no one has ever told us, 'We think you're idiots.' They always say they give us credit for having the guts to do what we did."

Harry and Juanita Jennings also became full-time trailerists at an early age, but they finance their travels by working while they're on the road. Harry, at forty-one, is convinced that most people overestimate the cost of full-timing. "You can live, I'd say, on a quarter of what it would cost you at home. I've heard estimates that full-timing costs half as much as living in one place, in a house, but I think those estimates are high. A whole lot of people could live on one-fourth as much as they're spending now, even though they don't think they could. I've heard people admit they were interested in trailering full-time and then say, 'But I couldn't do it. I'd have to get by on $500 a month, and I couldn't live on $500 a month.' And then I've seen magazine articles that say it costs $500 a month to live on the road. I disagree with all that. If you have a suitable trailer and tow vehicle that are paid for and you don't have any outstanding bills, you can live on the road for a whole lot less than $500 a month. If you weren't obligated to travel, like we do, you could control expenses to the point where you could get by on very little. I could do it on $200 a month."

The Deans: "Retire As Early As Possible"

New Yorker Bert Dean agreed with that assessment as he sat in his travel trailer near South Padre Island, Texas, and talked with me about the full-timing lifestyle. In 1975 Bert took an early retirement from IBM, and he and his wife, Greta, began trailering around the country. He was fifty-seven years old and had to learn how to survive on income from a few real estate investments and a modest pension fund. After five years as a full-timer, Bert offered this advice to aspiring travelers: "I would recommend that people retire as early as possible—just as soon as they can work things out financially. But it doesn't cost very much to live this kind of life. I wish anyone who is contemplating retirement and has any reservations about their ability to live could realize how simple and inexpensive it is to live this way. It would remove their concerns, and they would go to it. There is no excuse any more, I feel, for anyone to hold back from retirement."

Jerry Campbell: "We Live A Beautiful Life"

Of all the people I interviewed about full-timing during the last few years, Jerry and Betty Campbell were probably the least financially secure but were among the happiest. Jerry retired in 1974 when he was fifty-five and Betty was fifty-two. They had operated a food store in Ohio which they hoped to turn over to their children in return for a retirement income. Jerry said, "All I wanted the kids to do was send me $100 a week to keep me on the road. But the kids didn't want the store, so we practically gave it away."

Four heart attacks during the next few years wiped out the Campbells' savings, but instead of sending them back to Ohio seeking help from their children, the health problems only intensified their determination to continue the independent RVing lifestyle. When I interviewed them in Florida late in 1979, they were working at the Outdoor Resorts of America campground near Orlando and living on $20 a day. Jerry told me that he and Betty had no income other than the modest amounts ORA paid them for helping clerk the campground office. When I expressed amazement at that, Jerry said, "Look at it this way. Do you see these two one-dollar bills?" He held up two dollars, then put one on the table in front of him. "Now that one," he emphasized, "is absolutely worthless."

"Why is that?" I asked.

"Because I haven't spent *this* one yet," he said, referring to the bill still in his hand. "I can't spend that one until I spend this one. Everything's relative to something else. I don't care about tomorrow because I haven't finished enjoying today yet. The second dollar bill has no value until I've spent the first one, and tomorrow has no living in it until I finish enjoying today."

Jerry said the heart attacks and the lack of financial security made him realize how important day-to-day life really is and how unimportant material possessions are. "You start out in life and work like a dog to acquire everything you can. You want a home, you want furniture, you want comfort and you want convenience. You get everything possible for your family, and by the time you get it paid for, the family's moved out! That's what happened to us. We ended up alone in an eight-room house. What were we going to do in eight rooms? Live in four and raise chickens in the other four and throw eggs at each other? I've also learned that although it's easy to make money and live high, it's hard to give up everything and live at a lower scale. Now that we've done it, though, it's not so hard; it's easy. We don't have anything—we don't *want* anything—that we don't need. And we don't need anything that we haven't used in the last six months. I would make this suggestion to any couple that is contemplating living full-time in an RV: if you can't walk away from what you own and what you've been without looking back, then don't go because you'll regret it. You'll never get along together. Betty and I never fuss; we never fight. We enjoy each other very much, and we live a beautiful life."

DECISION: GETTING ALONG WITH EACH OTHER

Before any couple decides to join the ranks of the full-timers, both the husband and the wife should determine whether they will be able to get along with each other over an extended period of time while living in relatively cramped quarters. Social scientists claim that most of the marital discord among retirees occurs because mates are unable to cope with each other. First of all, the wife regards the retirement home—or the RV—as her responsibility to clean and take care of, while the husband (who probably has not spent much time at home in the last forty years except to sleep and putter around the yard) tends to interfere with her and boss her around. Secondly, while the woman's adjustment from homemaker in a big house to homemaker in a travel trailer is relatively easy, the husband often has too much free time facing him, so he expects his wife to entertain or talk to him.

Unbelievable as it sounds, my research indicated that more couples become discouraged with full-timing because of their own incompatibility than for any other reason. Penny Gaynor probably said it best when she offered this advice for me to pass on to aspiring full-timers: "If you don't share compatibility and have great love and respect for your mate, don't do it. The test is knowing that you were able, in the past, to spend hours, days and weeks with your mate without need of anybody else because you were compatible. Then you're ready for full-timing. Also—and this is very important—make sure you have things to do that will make each day a more interesting, challenging and livable day. The worst thing when full-timing is to get up out of bed every morning with nothing at all to do."

Her husband, Hal, interrupted with twinkling eyes. "You're worse than my first sergeant in the army. You know what you want me to do for the next six weeks."

"That's right, dear," she admitted. "I've got it all mapped out."

"She pretty well decides every morning what she would like me to do," Hal explained. "But I'll admit it's always something worth doing."

Penny added, "I highly recommend full-time RVing. It's a great way to live. I count our blessings. I think Hal and I are very fortunate that we have weathered storm and hail, that we know what we want and that we're doing what we want. So many other people never reach that stage in their lives."

DECISION: HOW TO KEEP BUSY

A friend of mine worked for the same company for forty years. He had a very demanding, responsible job, and those of us who knew him agreed that he fit the description of "workaholic" perfectly. He retired at age sixty-five and moved to the Sunbelt where he could play golf and go fishing whenever he wanted. Six months after his retirement, he died. His doctor said he had a heart attack; his wife said he died of boredom.

For sociologists, what happened to my friend was not unusual. Retirees who once led active, productive lives often are unable to adjust to a life of leisure. They go into retirement with no—or few—interests outside of what had kept them occupied for the previous thirty or forty years—their jobs. They have no hobbies, no ambitions other than to catch a few fish or play a few rounds of golf. But fishing and playing golf can become extremely boring after three or four months of doing nothing else.

Hal Gaynor told me, "I have a very dear friend. He's earning more than $40,000 a year, but he could walk away from it tomorrow and have enough income—$12,000 a year—to full-time on. He's ready to chuck his work and go full-timing, and he's asked Penny and me for advice. It's hard for us, but we're going to throw every reason we can at him on why he shouldn't do it. That's what he wants us to do. He said if he can't answer all our arguments against it satisfactorily, he won't do it."

Hal added, "I see too many full-timers dying in their rigs out of boredom. They have no challenges, no hobbies, no interests. And I don't consider reading books and collecting stamps as suitable hobbies. They're okay when you're in a home, but in this type of life, hobbies are something that should have some physical aspects to them. Collecting rocks, for example. Polishing them. Making things of wood. Things a person can do to keep his hands and his mind busy. Many full-timers I know have a terrific existence because they have made contacts so that in the winter they can go south and get free campsites in return for a little work. And maybe they'll earn a couple of extra bucks, too. That's fine. But to retire and go full-timing just because you've got an income . . . that's not enough.

Helen And Chuck Mogg "We Just Love People"

Michigan retiree Chuck Mogg wasn't able to pursue physical hobbies following his open heart surgery two years ago, so he concentrated on becoming as active as possible in the Good Sam Club. He and his wife, Helen, attended Samborees in Florida, Texas, New York, Indiana and nearly every state en route during 1979 and 1980. For 1981, trips were planned to Samborees in California and Arizona. Chuck is now the public relations coordinator of the Michigan chapter of the Good Sam Club, and he takes that voluntary job seriously. "Attending Samborees and festivals is our hobby, I guess. We just love people, and we like meeting new people and helping them enjoy themselves."

Although Chuck realizes many full-timers would not be as interested as he is in Good Sam activities, he recommends to new way-of-lifers, "Try to figure out something to keep your mind occupied because if you're going to live in an RV, you've got to get involved with something that keeps you busy. Get into a club or a church group or a fishing group. Anything. Just get involved so you've got something to occupy your mind, or you'll go stir crazy. We get involved with different things in the Good Sam Club, and every day it feels as if we've accomplished something, even if we just meet one new friend that we know we'll never see again. There are so many wonderful people out camping that an active full-timer will meet more people and get to know more people in a year's time than he ever would staying at home. And you'll find that you get to know each of them better than you knew your next-door neighbor at home."

DECISION: WHICH RIG IS BEST?

Sometime before the final decision is made to hit the road full time, consideration should be given to the kind of RV which will fit your lifestyle best. Although a later chapter is devoted to full-timing rigs, I am mentioning it here because a rig is the largest single investment any full-timer has, and the aspiring full-timer should know how much his rig is likely to cost before he commits himself to all the other aspects of the RVing lifestyle.

No matter what you've heard, there are no perfect rigs for full-timing. They all have their drawbacks. On the other hand, any rig can be used for full-timing, depending upon the owner's living and driving habits, the amount of money he can spend and the degree of discomfort he's willing to accept. I've met couples full-timing in micro mini motorhomes, and I've seen single full-timers living in camper vans. I presume someone, somewhere, is making his or her home in a folding camping trailer, but I don't think I want to hear about it. Not that I'm an RV snob; I'm not. But I believe certain kinds of RVs are suitable for full-timing, and others are not. A folding camper isn't. Neither is a pickup camper. Nor a van. Nor a micro mini. In my view, there are only four kinds of RVs that should be considered as homes on wheels by aspiring full-timers: the Class A motorhome, the mini motorhome, the travel trailer and the fifth-wheel trailer.

Rig size is somewhat relative to the full-timer's needs and pocketbook, but the most popular Class A sizes for way-of-lifers are coaches between 27 and 32 feet. Minis 23 to 25 feet in length seem to have the most appeal. Full-time trailerists tend to choose units in the 26 to 32 foot range, while those preferring fifth-wheel trailers seem to like models that are no smaller than 30 feet but are as long as 40 feet. A solid bloc of full-timers insist upon compactness and therefore buy travel trailers 22 to 26 feet in length. Remember that size is not always a good indicator of how well an RV handles. Mini motorhomes are not necessarily easier to drive than larger Class A motorhomes; large motorhomes are easier for novices to handle than large travel trailers. And a small travel trailer is not necessarily easier to tow than a large one. When it comes time to choose a full-timing rig, I would offer this piece of advice to the new way-of-lifer: buy a bigger, longer and more luxurious rig than you think you'll need.

Not everyone agrees with that recommendation, of course. My friend Chuck Mogg, who himself tows a 40-foot Kountry Aire fifth-wheel trailer, recommends that beginning full-timers avoid buying rigs too large for them, reasoning that it is easier to move up in size if they make a mistake than it is to drop down in size.

On the other hand, here's the advice offered by Chris Moffett, a veteran trailerist who has lived full time on the road since 1970: "The most important thing," Chris said, "is to get a trailer that's big enough. There's a lot more comfort in a big trailer than in a little one, and that's important when you realize that you live in a trailer a lot more than you tow it. Besides, a big trailer is easier to tow. It doesn't bounce around, gusts of air from trucks don't bother it as much, and it's a lot easier to back into a campsite."

What are the best rigs for full-timing? That's difficult to say because individual needs and affordability have to enter into any decision involving purchase of an RV. However, I can tell you what kinds of rigs experienced full-timers seem to prefer.

Class A Motorhomes

Foretravel of Texas builds beautiful, large coaches that are quite popular among full-timers. The company's Travco units are very nice too. King's Highway motorhomes are among the best of the luxury motorhomes. Vogue, Apollo and Executive coaches are favorites of a large bloc of full-time motorhome owners. Sportscoach units have a good reputation among way-of-lifers, and the Airstream and Holiday Rambler coaches are tough to beat for quality construction and dependability. Barth motorhomes are considered among the best built in the country. For the buyer who doesn't consider price to be a factor, some of the best quality luxury coaches are produced by companies that convert buses: Blue Bird Wanderlodge, Newell Coach Corporation and Custom Coach Corporation. Price conscious full-timers would be wise to investigate the products built by Fleetwood (Jamboree, Pace Arrow and Southwind), Allegro, Beach-Craft, Coachmen, Georgie Boy, Champion, Titan, Midas, Winnebago, Travel Equipment Corporation, Journey and Sprinter.

Mini Motorhomes

There are dozens of mini motorhomes built in this country, but full-timers' favorites appear to be those produced by Georgie Boy, Beaver, Champion, Coachmen, Shasta, Fireball, Holiday Rambler, Winnebago, Jayco, Midas, Mobile Traveler, Kountry Aire, Skyline, Fleetwood, Travelcraft, Honey and Brougham.

Travel Trailers

Here full-timers appear to be more selective, concentrating on products built by a few companies that specialize in coaches designed with way-of-lifers in mind. The favorites are Airstream's 27- and 31-foot Excella models, Carriage's 31-footers, Holiday Rambler's 30- and 32-footers, Yellowstone's 32-footer and the big, luxurious trailers built by Silver Streak. After those units, full-timers tend to choose from among Fan Coach, Barth, Coachmen, Prowler, Kountry Aire, Globestar and Avion units.

Fifth-Wheel Trailers

Again, the full-timers are very selective. They choose fivers produced by Carriage, Holiday Rambler, Kountry Aire, Globestar and Nu-Way first. Then they consider those built by Yellowstone, Komfort, Prowler, Coachmen, and Jayco.

DECISION: WILL GASOLINE BE AVAILABLE?

During the summer of 1979, when the availability of gasoline was more questionable than it had been for five years, my copilot, Pam, and I were on the road constantly, researching articles for *Trailer Life* and *Motorhome Life* magazines. We left our home in Elkhart, Indiana, three days after angry truckers began boycotting fuel supply depots, shutting off the shipments of gasoline to thousands of the nation's service stations. Friends said we were stupid to begin a three-week, 4,000-mile trip in a motorhome knowing that we might not be able to buy gasoline. We left anyway, admittedly worried that we might find ourselves stranded somewhere without any fuel. We shepherded our gasoline supply carefully, making sure we did not let the gauge drop much below the half full mark, even though that meant stopping to refuel more often than we would have liked.

In Omaha, only one station in ten was selling gasoline, and those were limiting purchases to $5 or $10 per customer. Since we reached that city with our supply at its lowest ebb, we had to search out stations that were open and drive from one to another until we had enough gasoline to begin the next leg of our journey. We drove north into South Dakota and discovered that gasoline was a little more plentiful. There was an adequate supply of fuel in eastern North Dakota, but a few miles away in Minnesota, stations were closed. Over the next three weeks, we traveled extensively through the Dakotas, Minnesota, Manitoba, Illinois and Indiana without really ever coming close to running out of fuel. We learned either to top off our tanks every night before we camped, if possible, or to fill up early the next morning prior to hitting the road. We started driving early every morning and stopped early every evening. We went wherever we wanted on highways that were nearly empty of traffic, and we camped in parks where we were the only overnighters.

A week after we returned home, we hitched a 32-foot Holiday Rambler trailer to a van and traveled east toward Nova Scotia to cover the international rally of the Holiday Rambler Recreational Vehicle Club. To make sure we would be able to buy gasoline, we detoured north through Ontario, Quebec and New Brunswick where there were no fuel supply problems. After the rally, though, we returned home through Maine, Massachusetts, New York, Vermont, Pennsylvania and Ohio, always carefully watching our fuel gauge. While we were limited to $5 and $10 purchases a few times on toll roads, we felt relatively unrestricted by what was being reported as a contrived fuel shortage. Again, we stopped overnight in campgrounds that were almost totally empty. There were no tourists at the usual tourist spots, and merchants were overjoyed to see us. We stuffed ourselves with lobsters in Maine because seafood was practically being given away due to the slow tourist trade.

During the summer of 1979, we traveled more than 10,000 miles by motorhome and travel trailer and enjoyed ourselves tremendously. And when we returned home, we learned that the RV industry was in terrible condition because thousands upon thousands of Americans were so worried about the price and availability of gasoline that they had given up camping.

That fact distresses us, even today, not only because we know that travel—even extensive travel—is possible during periods when gasoline is in short supply, but also because we're convinced that energy-conscious RVers can use far less gasoline while they are camping and traveling than they would use if they stayed home. You don't believe that? Then consider that the average family owns at least two automobiles, and one or two of those cars are being driven somewhere almost constantly—to the supermarket, to and from work, to and from school, delivering children to the swimming pool, the playground and the YMCA. It is not unusual for a two- or three-car family to log more than 2,000 miles a month without driving more than fifty miles away from home. On the other hand, RVers—and especially full-timers—quite often drive their rigs to favorite vacation spots and park for a month, two months or three months at a time.

I feel strongly that no one should decide against joining the full-time lifestyle simply because of worries that gasoline won't be available or that the price of gas will be too high. Mac and Alice McGinley, a full-timing couple from Greenville, Mississippi, agree with me. I interviewed the McGinleys at Truro, Nova Scotia, in 1979 during the height of the fuel shortage scare. Mac reported, "When I tell people how much we enjoy

Like migratory birds, full-timers pack up and head for the temperate zones as soon as the first chill winds of autumn blow.

full-timing, a lot of them say, 'We'll talk to you in two or three years, and then you can tell us how much you enjoy it.' They're apprehensive about the price of fuel. But they don't realize that fuel cost is just one of our expenses, and we can control it better than we can control the cost of our food."

Alice added, "People who are not RVers have the idea that when we're on the road full-time we're running up and down the highway every day. They think we pull into a park every night to sleep and then get up and get rolling again in the morning. They don't realize that we spend at least several days, and sometimes several weeks, at most places we stop. They can't accept the notion that we're not wasting gasoline."

Ken and Flo Cooper faced a rather traumatic period in 1979 when they left California for a trip east representing the Good Sam Club as the organization's first Sambassadors. "It was a very interesting situation in terms of timing," Ken said. "We left Los Angeles about three days after the big gas crunch ended. For a while, we didn't know whether we were even going to be able to leave. We had no problems until we reached Wisconsin, and that's where the truckers were picketing the big tank farms. So instead of dropping down to Chicago and driving through Indiana the way we'd planned, we headed across the Upper Peninsula of Michigan and into Canada. Meanwhile, the West Coast gas crunch had reached the East Coast, and by the time we got to Maine, that state had initiated odd/even rationing. Still, we had no problems because of our out-of-state license plates. We stayed off the roads on Sunday, when most of the service stations were closed, and we were always careful to make sure we had a full tank of gas on the morning of the day we wanted to travel. We also stayed off the turnpikes and expressways as much as possible. We discovered that on the main U.S. highways, the secondary routes, the stations had all the gas we wanted."

Flo interrupted. "We also found that when we stopped at a campground at night, the people in the park generally knew where gasoline was available, and that helped. We talked with anyone we could to find out what experience they were having, and we got a lot of good information that way. We also carried a six-gallon auxiliary tank with us for emergencies, but we never had to use it. We still carry it, though."

Ken said, "I have two twenty-gallon tanks on my pickup, but even so, I seldom get into my second tank. I've learned that by carrying enough gas, such as forty gallons, it's amazing how I can always find less expensive gasoline. I can always pay the high price for fuel, but it's surprising how often I've been able to keep my price down on the lower side of the averages as we travel just by waiting to buy gas until I find an appropriate gas range."

DECISIONS, DECISIONS, DECISIONS

Traveling full time is quite different from taking a three or four-week vacation. It's a lot more fun. The sense of freedom is exhilarating. Most full-timers follow the sun, traveling north in the spring and south in the fall. But they are free to go anywhere, limited only by their interests and their finances. Grasping that freedom and running with it is not easy, though. There are decisions that have to be made beforehand. I've outlined the major ones in this chapter. But the decision-making process is endless. Health-related decisions have to be made, for example. The aspiring full-timer should consider how he will fill drug prescriptions while on the road; he should arrange periodic medical checkups; he should plan to see a dentist regularly. The aspiring full-timer should think seriously about how he will make new friends—should he join an RV organization such as the Good Sam Club or the club sponsored by the factory that built his RV? He should arrange for his mail to be forwarded to him. He should consider how he will cash checks while traveling, how he will keep in touch with his family. Although I can provide guidelines in this book to help the aspiring full-timer make some of those decisions, there is one decision he must make without help from anyone, and that is the decision to do it—to leave job, family, home, neighborhood and friends behind and become a full-time RVer.

One Piece Of Advice: "Go!"

One afternoon in Minnesota, I talked with three full-timing couples who were traveling together—Doris and John Lockwood, Dick and Helen Bright and Sam and Glenda Beaideme. I asked them the question that I always try to ask people who obviously are enjoying the full-time RVing way of life: "If you could offer one piece of advice to someone who is considering becoming a full-timer, what would it be?"

Sam answered simply, "Go!" Dick added, "I would say, 'Get a good tow vehicle and a good trailer and just enjoy yourself.' "And enjoy it while you can," emphasized Glenda, "if you put it off, you won't go."

"I know people who've done that," said John. "They think about it, but they will not make the move. Make up your mind and go. Don't have any designated point to be at, at any special time. Just stop where you want to stop, do what you want to do."

"We have a friend back in L.A.," Dick told us, "who owns an Airstream. He works for the government at one of the aircraft plants. We talk to him, and he just drools when he hears us tell about our traveling. He wants to do it so badly. . ." "But he can't cut the cord," Helen added.

John said, "We met a guy in Manitoba who wants to go camping full-time. But he has a big business and a big farm. He wants his kids to take over for him, but they don't want to give him as much money for it as he thinks they should. So I told him, "Well, give everything to them and tell them, 'Do with it what you want to—just send me 500 bucks every week. Remember, you can't take it with you.' He wanted to go in the worst way, but I've seen a lot of people like him who just won't give up their obligations."

Glenda added, "A lot of people are afraid of the gasoline situation, too. They'd rather sit still and do nothing than take a chance." Perhaps surprisingly, Sam stated, "Gas is one of the cheapest things a full-timer buys when you consider the price of a rig and its maintenance and the price of food." "And," Glenda pointed out, "by the time you pay property taxes in California, it's cheaper to buy gasoline and travel."

Sam said, "I have a mother who is ninety-two years old. When I was working, I went overseas once on a job assignment, and I'll never forget what she told me. She said, 'I'll never see you again. I'll be dead before you get back.' But she wasn't. When we left her three or four weeks ago, she said it again: "I'll never see you again. I'll be dead before you get back.' And she's still going strong."

"I think all old folks want you to be around when they pass on," Sam continued, "But we just made our minds up; we have to live our own lives. I'm not being selfish about it because we can always get back to California if she gets seriously ill. The airlines have plenty of flights to Los Angeles."

Chapter Two

Getting
Ready To Go

etween 1970 and 1980, the population of Americans sixty-five years
old and over grew from twenty million persons to twenty-four million—an increase of 20%. By the year 2000, our country will be populated
with twenty-nine million people who are at least sixty-five and fifty million people who are fifty-five or older. Most of those Americans, of course,
will not be attracted to the full-time RVing lifestyle when they retire.
They will, instead, choose to spend their retirement years in a variety of
other ways: living in a retirement community, in a senior citizens home,
in a cottage, in a mobile home, in their longtime family home, in an
apartment or condominium or with relatives. Ninety-two percent of them
will never leave the area in which they were born. They will spend the
rest of their years in safe, secure and familiar environments, surrounded
by people they know. They might make occasional vacation trips back to
sections of the country they visited when they were younger, and a couple
of times every year they'll probably visit friends or relatives who live a
few hundred miles away. They will live pretty much as they have always
lived.

That type of lifestyle just isn't enough for people who aspire to join
the ranks of full-time RVers. Full-timers are more adventuresome. They
want to visit places they've never been, see sights they've never seen,
meet people they've never known before. They don't want to be tied to
one place, their savings sunk into a house or tiny lot with a mobile home
on it. They don't want to be rocking chair retirees.

They have friends who are "retired" in the traditional sense, and
they don't like the way their friends are forced to live—the excitement

gone from their lives, the high point of a typical day being a winning hand of canasta or hard-fought game of shuffleboard. Sure, full-time RVers enjoy organized activities just as their friends do. But they treasure the freedom of being able to take part in a hobby show in Minnesota one week and enter a golf tournament in Arizona a week later. They like to break up the monotony of morning exercise classes and afternoon card parties with a bit of snorkeling in the Gulf of Mexico or some rockhounding in the hills of South Carolina. Maybe they, like their other retired friends, like to go fishing. But summers might find them netting walleyes in Ontario and winters, casting for bass at Lake Guerrero in Mexico. And no matter where they are, no matter what they're doing, they're at home. They take home—their RV—with them.

Full-time RVers believe that a home on wheels is more important than even a paid-up mortgage on the house where they raised their children and collected ten rooms full of furniture over a thirty-year period. They can live on less in their RV than they can in that house, considering the taxes they avoid paying; the cost of upkeep and maintenance that they don't have to worry about; the nonexistent utility bills, and the income that they're enjoying from their invested capital. As homeowners, they would have unavoidable fixed costs; as RVers, they can retrench whenever they need to reduce their expenses for a while and park in an inexpensive location while they wait for their budget to catch up with their spending. They can store their rig and forget it whenever they feel inclined to take an ocean cruise, fly to California or join a European tour group. They are truly free to enjoy the fruits of their previous years' labor.

TAKING THE PLUNGE

The hardest decision any aspiring full-timer has to make is not *whether* to travel full-time in an RV, but *when* to begin doing it. Most of us tend to wait until the kids are raised, we've become fully vested in a retirement plan at work and we're old enough—that is, age sixty-five—to qualify for full Social Security benefits. Ironically, 100% of the full-timers I've interviewed over the last few years told me they wished they had retired earlier. Some couldn't, of course, because their financial circumstances would not permit it. But most could have; they lacked only the courage to do it.

One of the best arguments I've seen in favor of early retirement appeared in *Trailer Life* magazine in 1979. Stan Christian, in a regular column called "Full-timing Handbook," proved that it is more financially advantageous for a working person to retire at age sixty-two than to wait until sixty-five in order to qualify for full Social Security benefits. Stan wrote, "It is my personal opinion that if you are considering going full time (or even serious part-time) in an RV upon retirement, you should give serious consideration to taking an *early, reduced retirement as soon as possible* [emphasis added]." He pointed out that if two individuals, both of whom earned an average of $8,000 a year for thirty years, retired three years apart, the person retiring at age sixty-two would receive $362.50 per month in Social Security income and the person retiring at age sixty-five would receive $453.10. But he noted that the later retiree's income would not match that of the early retiree for eighteen years—at which time they would both be eighty-three years old, nine years beyond the life expectancy for an American male (as of January 1978).

Not only would the early retiree have three more years of free time during which to enjoy travels with his wife, winters in the Sunbelt and summers in the forests or mountains, but he also would have collected $13,050 while his friend was still working every day so that he could earn approximately $90 more each month. Stan pointed out that if both men would die at the end of their seventy-fourth year, the early retiree would have collected $3,265 more than his friend in addition to enjoying three more years of retirement life. Stan's conclusion: "I consider these three extra years as the most important consideration. Whether you are accepting money from Uncle Sam or from an employer, money is only money, but those three years of 'extra' life are priceless. You can't buy time at *any* price."

"Don't Lose That Opportunity"

Maurice Parker, a Wisconsin welder, decided to retire in 1977 at the age of sixty-two. Friends tried to talk him out of it and urged him to wait until he was sixty-five so he could receive his full pension. I interviewed him three years later while he was soaking up sun at the Outdoor Resorts of America park near South Padre Island, Texas. "Well, now I'm sixty-five and I've had three years of this kind of life," he told me. "Maybe next year I'll get some kind of ailment that will take me right away. The only thing I would do differently would be to plan my retirement earlier. If I would have known earlier what I know now, I would have retired at around fifty-five to fifty-seven. I would have made plans so that I could handle it financially until I could get my Social Security."

His wife, Evelyn, added, "Then we could have traveled a little more when we could have afforded to go somewhere."

Don Klemczak, who retired as an engineer when he was forty-three due to health problems, said aspiring full-timers should join the RVing lifestyle as soon as they're able. "I don't care if you're 25 or 105, if you want to do it, do it. Don't let age be a factor. If you reach retirement age and you want to get out and see the country, that's great. But some people want to try it between jobs, and they should. Let's say you are an engineer and the job or program you're working on is gone and you have to look for a new job and relocate. Maybe you've saved a few dollars and you have an RV, so you ask yourself, 'Well, why don't we take a couple of years off and see the country while we can?' That, I think, is the key—while you're in the condition to do it. Too many people wait until they can't enjoy it because of their health. If you want to go full-timing, do it when you can—as soon as you can."

Walt and Charlotte Consider, former Ohioans who now call a Holiday Rambler travel trailer home, agreed. "Do it just as soon as you possibly think you can afford it" is the advice Walt always gives to aspiring full-timers.

His wife always adds, "The younger the better because you can't know that in another two years you won't have a medical problem that will prevent it."

Walt said, "We have been criticized severely by our family and friends for leaving everything and retiring when I was only fifty-nine. They've also been critical of the trips that we've taken to Spain, to Mexico and to Puerto Rico. But we have always said we're passing this way only once, and we're going to take full advantage of it while we're going."

Another early retiree, Frank Salerno of Illinois, offered this advice: "Go the first day you have the opportunity. Don't hesitate. Don't lose that opportunity, and remember that a day lost is just that—a day lost. I've talked with a lot of people who say, 'I'm thinking about retirement, but I hate to leave the job and I don't know what I would do.' Believe me, there aren't enough hours in the day to do the things you want to do, and yet when somebody asks you what you do all day, you're kind of hard put to tell them."

Martin and Taffy Day considered early retirement full-timing to be a dream—at least for them. But it was a dream they often discussed. Taffy wrote in a *Trailer Life* article ("Full-Timing Days on the Road," June 1979), "Our children were grown and we no longer needed to maintain a home in the city for them. Martin had undergone five major stomach surgeries over the past four years and faced two more within the next few months. He really needed to get away from the pressure involved in his job supervising high rise construction in Los Angeles. Although it meant we would be giving up retirement income, which would not be fully vested for another ten years, we also realized that Martin probably could not make it for another ten years without a nervous breakdown. So we decided to think seriously about it."

The couple quickly moved from thinking seriously about it to making definite plans. And it wasn't long before Taffy wrote her article and said, "We're full-timers now, have been on the road for three months, and we're delighted with our new lifestyle."

PLANNING FOR THE DAY

Planning for the time that full-time RVing will begin is a little like making plans for a special vacation that you know you'll never have to cut short so that you can return to work. It's possible, in fact, to let the excitement of planning sort of take over your life and control it. Mac McGinley, a full-timer from Mississippi who began his life on the road suddenly, without much prior planning, due to health problems, said he believes people tend to overplan their retirement. "Maybe we were fortunate that our circumstances turned out the way they did. I think if you do too much planning, you could talk yourself completely out of following this kind of life."

His wife, Alice, said, "I think that some people spend so much time planning a vacation that before they can actually leave they're tired of talking about it and thinking about it and all the excitement has been taken out of the trip."

But Mac added, "I think the beautiful part about this life is the lack of anxiety. We don't have to worry about getting back home for something. There's no pressure to be at work Monday or to get back so we can pay the bills."

"Believe it or not," said Alice, "we even forget the day of the week and the date of the month. We don't watch much TV in our trailer, so unless we buy a newspaper occasionally, we don't even know what's happening in the world. We forget all the cares and worries of the world, so to speak. Full-timing becomes strictly a life of rest and relaxation."

A Financial Inventory

Obviously, though, some preretirement planning is desirable, even necessary. Sidney Margolius, the late syndicated newspaper columnist, wrote about retirement planning quite often in his Women's News Service feature, "For the Consumer." He was a strong proponent of early planning and advised everyone to begin a preliminary financial inventory at least five years, and preferably ten years, prior to retirement. Among the items to be inventoried, Margolius suggested the following estimates:

1. How much income you'll need, based on an estimate of living expenses in retirement, plus an allowance for possible inflation of at least five percent a year.
2. How much you'll get from Social Security plus any private pension or other income from savings or property.
3. How much additional income you'll need to make up the difference between estimated expenses and present estimated income.
4. Where this additional income will come from.

Margolius said, "Especially important in planning for retirement is the timing of certain financial decisions with an eye on tax and other consequences. This strategy is based on the fact that usually your tax liability is lower after sixty-five because of extra exemptions, the non-taxable nature of much of retirement income such as Social Security, and other exclusions and credits. If you have a whole-life or endowment insurance policy on which you have been paying for many years, it probably has a fairly large cash-surrender value; when you are ready to retire, you probably will need income more than your heirs will need insurance protection. If so, you usually can convert this cash value into an annuity that will pay you an income each month. If you also arrange for survivor payments, or buy a separate annuity for your wife, this income can take the place of at least part of the insurance as protection for her if she survives you. Converting your insurance cash value to an annuity or other income-producing investment will reduce your living expenses by ending further payment of premiums. If you have an endowment policy, consult the insurance company about the tax effects of the optional ways of taking the proceeds. If you convert to an annuity before, or within, sixty days after the policy matures, you may be able to escape some or all of the tax on the difference between what you put in and what you get back."

You also should inventory your possessions in preparation of converting as much of it as possible to cash. If you are traveling full time, you won't need a lawn tractor, camping equipment such as tents and screenhouses, and heavy power tools. Inventory furniture, appliances, your second car, ski equipment, boats and hobbies such as stamp or coin collections. Consider how much use you've given to each item during the last few years and whether the minute possibility that you might use them in the future outweighs the value of the cash they can provide for your new traveling lifestyle. Sell the tractor, the camping equipment, the power tools and the car without hesitation. Some furniture with special meaning can be kept, either by storing it, carrying small pieces with you in your RV or lending it to relatives.

Mac and Alice McGinley divided their furniture among their children and relatives on what they called "a lend-lease" basis. They loaned valuable pieces of furniture—such as a solid cherry dining room outfit—to family members with the stipulation that the pieces must be returned if circumstances such as a death forces either Mac or Alice to retire from the road and set up housekeeping again.

Furniture with no emotional value should be sold along with household appliances. If a boat cannot either be towed behind or carried with your RV, it ought to be sold. Property should be sold also unless it is intended as investment real estate that is certain to produce significant income either through rental or sale after it appreciates. Most possessions, except automobiles, boats and real estate, can be sold profitably during a garage sale. Consult how-to books in your local library that tell how to set up, advertise and price items for garage sales.

The Beaidemes: A Five-Year Itinerary

Although preretirement planning is generally haphazard and unstructured, occasionally someone will plan his RV full-timing lifestyle down to the smallest detail. Sam Beaideme did just that kind of planning prior to his retirement from an aircraft company in California. He designed a five-year plan that was so detailed he was even able to distribute copies of an itinerary to friends so they would know where he and his wife, Glenda, could be found. I talked with the Beaidemes during the summer of their fourth year as full-timers, and they said that except for a few modifications, they had followed the five-year plan rather closely.

Sam said, "I was going to retire in December, 1976, but I decided to retire in July instead. So we put our house up for sale, held a garage sale and got rid of everything and then started living in our trailer in August. We spent four months in the trailer before we started out on the road."

"It's good we did," Glenda suggested. "We found out what we really needed to keep in the trailer."

"We sure did," said Sam. "I had sold all my electrical tools, including a jigsaw and a drill motor, and while we were spending those four months in the trailer, I realized I needed that jigsaw and drill motor, so I had to buy new ones. It was hard for me to get rid of some of the other things that I had carried around with me for years and years."

Glenda interrupted. "It hurt him more than it did me. We gave a lot of stuff to our kids, and what they didn't want we sold or stored. We have a small storage space filled with china and crystal, but no furniture."

Sam calculated he and Glenda could live on the road for just over $600 a month. The first year, they held to that budget rather closely, averaging about $650 a month in expenses, but double-digit inflation ate into the budget after that. The five-year plan called for them to spend their first winter in Florida, then travel to Nova Scotia, back through New England and across the country to California; they were to winter in Texas and Mexico in 1978, tow their trailer to Alaska that summer, then return to Texas and California; they planned to tour the country some more in 1979 and spend 1980 and 1981 RVing through Europe.

The first few months of their trip went as planned. "Then, after spending a couple of months in Nova Scotia, we were coming back through New England when we met some people on their way to Nova Scotia who convinced us to go on the Blue Ridge Mountain/Grand Ole Opry Caravan [sponsored by the Holiday Rambler Recreational Vehicle Club]. Then we met some nice people from North Carolina who insisted we had to attend a regional rally with them in October. We hadn't planned on going back to California that way, but they twisted our arms a little, so we went with them and had a lot of fun. We got back to California in November, eleven months after we left. We stayed there a couple of months and then took off again for Texas and the Central Mexico caravan."

Sam continued, "We were planning on going to Alaska our second year, but we heard that the Holiday club was going to sponsor a caravan there in 1979, so we postponed our Alaska trip until then." The Beaidemes traveled east again to visit family members and to attend the Holiday Rambler international rally in Nova Scotia, then pointed their trailer southwesterly toward Texas, where they spent part of the winter of 1978 before returning to California. In Alaska the next summer, they met John and Doris Lockwood of Maryland and renewed acquaintances with Dick and Helen Bright, whom they had met a year earlier in Mexico. The three full-timing couples agreed to rendezvous in Sarasota, Florida, during the winter of 1979/1980 and travel together awhile in the spring.

When I caught up with them in July, 1980, they had just arrived in Bemidji, Minnesota, after caravaning from New York. Sam and Glenda were already making plans for the last leg of their five-year trip—their two years in Europe. "We had originally planned on shipping our whole rig to Europe and touring over there with it," Sam reported, "but everyone we've talked to has told us the overhang of our trailer is so long that we would have trouble on most of the roads. So now we're planning on putting our rig in storage in North Carolina and buying a mini motorhome that we can use in Europe."

"Possessed By Possessions"

When Frank and Agnes Salerno began planning their early retirement, they realized they would have to get rid of not only their house in Illinois, but also their furniture and most of their belongings. "That wasn't easy," Frank recalled. "Some of it was very hard to let go because Agnes had formed such a personal attachment to her crystal, china and things like that. We sold all the furniture and gave half the crystal to my wife's sister. The china we gave to another sister. I gave my library and tools to our kids. Most of the furniture actually went with the house; we sold it fully equipped. The washer, the dryer, the TV, everything stayed right where it was because, fortunately, we found a buyer who needed furniture as well as a house."

Hal and Penny Gaynor believe that new full-timers should be free of debt and not "possessed by possessions" before they begin their life on the road. "We owed no one a dime," Penny told me in recalling how she and Hal began full-timing in 1972. "It's a very important thing to own everything and not owe anyone anything. Then you are the boss of your dollar, and that's one of the great parts of our way of life. If you're the boss of your dollar, you can either live it up or live it down. But Don, either way, it's a beautiful life. Even if we just go from here to another campground ten miles away, after we're all hooked up and we get into the truck, Hal will lean over and touch my hand and we'll look at one another. We both have—we share—that wonderful feeling of freedom. Freedom from pressures, freedom from phone calls. And it's a very good life."

Hal and Penny didn't really do much formal planning for their life on the road, though. "April 13, 1972, was my fiftieth birthday, and I came home and told Penny I had resigned from my job in management work. She said, 'Fine. What do you want to do?' She's always stuck with me like that. Less than a month later—on May 7, 1972, we went on the road full time. We had sold everything we owned, and we drove away and never looked back."

MONEY, MAIL AND MEDICINE

For practical reasons, it's almost impossible for a new full-timer to cut ties with his past completely. In order to travel, park his rig and eat, he needs money. And unless he's planning on RVing full time in an armored truck, he shouldn't consider carrying all his assets with him in cash. Obviously, then, the full-timer must develop and maintain a pipeline to the source of his funds, and it makes sense for him to establish that pipeline *before* he gets rid of everything he owns and hits the road. There are other steps that the aspiring full-timer should take, too, prior to joining the RVing lifestyle. Together they are part of a neat but troublesome little package of problems I like to refer to simply as Money, Mail and Medicine.

Channeling Your Income

Doubtlessly, every full-time traveler has some source of income, even if it is merely a monthly Social Security check. There are three primary ways for that income to be channeled so that, ultimately, the full-timer can get his hands on it.

First, the income check can be mailed directly to the full-timer. Unfortunately, full-time travelers are notoriously difficult to locate, and the U.S. Postal Service is not noted for its ability to track down Americans in need of their mail. So unless you have a foolproof scheme that allows the postman to know where you are at all times, forget this alternative. Even if, by some stretch of the imagination, you are able to communicate your whereabouts to postal authorities, this alternative is not recommended for most full-timers because, even after the check is received, it could prove difficult to convert into ready cash. Banks are hesitant to cash out-of-town and out-of-state checks for their own customers; transient full-time RVers have little chance of seeing their checks accepted and exchanged for currency. Some RVers have, admittedly, solved the check-cashing problem by opening accounts at banks in communities where they intend to camp for three or four months. Thus, when the bank teller asks the dreaded question, "Do you have an account here, sir?" the shrewd RVer can smile and answer proudly, "I sure do, ma'am." The full-timer can then deposit his income check and withdraw funds as he needs them.

The second alternative is for the income check to be mailed to the RVer's agent or representative. That person, usually a close friend or relative, can then deposit the money in a joint account on which both he and the full-timer can write checks. For the RVer, this method serves the dual purpose of allowing him to write both small- and large-denomination personal checks (a quick telephone call can reassure reluctant bankers that the funds are available), and it allows the RVer's agent to receive and pay bills for him. This system works for many full-timers, but others who have used it and discarded it claim it results in frequent check-cashing problems and bookkeeping errors.

The third alternative is for the income check to be deposited directly into an account, either at a designated bank or in a Prestige account at a participating savings and loan association. As with the second alternative, personal checks can be written on the bank account, but the intermediary is eliminated. Checks cannot be written on Prestige accounts, and money can be withdrawn only from savings and loans that participate in the Prestige program, but all the money in such an account has the advantage of drawing interest.

Bill paying presents another problem. The RVer can either pay his bills himself or have an intermediary do it for him, but no matter which way he does it, the success of his system ultimately depends upon the efficiency of the U.S. mails. The aspiring full-timer also should decide beforehand how much cash (or traveler's checks) he should carry with him and how he will replenish the supply. Although Chapter Five deals with this aspect of RVing in detail, the would-be full-timer should consider at this stage in his planning the desirability of applying for credit cards issued by Master Charge, Visa and American Express; such cards are invaluable in financial emergencies and can be used to supplement an RVer's ready supply of cash. Again, however, paying bills on charge accounts can be a problem unless a good mail forwarding system is used.

Forwarding Mail

Some RVers ask friends of family members to forward mail to them; others write out postal change-of-address cards routinely and depend upon the post office to forward mail from the RVers' last stops to their next ones; still others utilize mail forwarding services offered by the Good Sam Club, private forwarding agencies and a few of the factory-sponsored RV travel clubs. Ken and Flo Cooper, a full-timing couple who work as Sambassadors for the Good Sam Club, said they use the Good Sam system themselves and it works very well. "But," Flo said, "if you miss the forwarding, you've got to make sure your mail is forwarded again, and the post office may or may not do that."

Traveler's Checks

As for handling money, Ken has arranged for his monthly pension check to be deposited in a Prestige account from which he draws out between $200 and $600 in cash at a time. For emergencies, the Coopers depend heavily upon traveler's checks. "Usually when we start out on a trip, we carry $1,500 in traveler's checks which we figure we're not going to touch except in case of emergency," Flo reported. "We don't want any more money than that sitting and not earning interest. But there are some states that do not have many Prestige branches, and when I know we're going into one of those states and I figure we're starting to get toward the end of our trip, I will dip into the traveler's checks occasionally. Right now, for example, I know we're going to be on the road for only another six weeks, so I have reduced our $1,500 in traveler's checks down to $1,000. And we'll hold onto that $1,000 until, in the last month, I'll start working on the traveler's checks a little more."

Ken added, "There's one thing I'll always do with a traveler's check. If we stop at a service station that has a sign, 'No checks,' I say to the attendant, 'I notice you have a sign, but does that mean no traveler's checks?' The answer is almost always no. There are certain traveler's checks, however, that they've never heard of out in the boondocks, so we buy nothing except the kinds that everybody knows."

Credit Cards

Don and Audrey Klemczak frequently use bank credit cards to replenish their supply of cash, especially when they're in the Orlando, Florida, area, where they own a condominium campsite. Audrey said Florida banks and businesses are notorious for refusing to accept either personal checks or traveler's checks. "We've run into a lot of places in Florida that won't accept traveler's checks, and many of the places that will accept them don't want them in denominations of over $20. Business places will accept them as payment for a purchase, but they won't cash them, and even the banks refuse to cash them unless you have an account there."

Don said, "We've definitely found that traveler's checks are not the best way to go. I'd offer this advice: when you get into a town, open an account and deposit a couple of hundred dollars. Keep depositing money when you get it, or write a check on your personal, out-of-state account and deposit it; then you're able to write checks and get cash. We also get cash advances on Master Charge or Visa cards, but we try to make sure that, when our monthly statements come in on those cards we pay them right away and cut down on finance charges. Here's something else: a lot of service stations won't accept any credit cards or gasoline cards from other companies; they want their own name brand cards and nothing else. So when I start a trip I try to carry enough cash to cover our fuel, basic food and some camping expenses."

One warm summer day in Indiana, I talked with L. E. "Whitey" Whitesell and Dick "Shadetree" March about their full-timing lifestyles, and I asked them, "Have either of you solved the problems of getting mail and cashing checks?"

March answered, "I don't have any problem with the money part of it; it seems to me that most things can be paid for by either plastic or a personal check, and the things that require cash are so nominal that I just don't have any problem. I've got base stations in Fort Worth and in Missouri where I know people well enough that I can get $200 or $300 in cash at any time and live primarily on personal checks and credit cards. If I run short of cash between base stations, I just get cash advances on the credit cards and pay the few cents finance charges. Now, mail is something else. That is the worst part of full-timing, I guess. I just can't seem to get current mail. I leave forwarding addresses, and I almost always get my mail; it's just slow in arriving. I don't think I got my November phone bill yet, and here it is July."

Whitey said, "Money is not a big problem for me. I can always go into a bank and introduce myself to one of the officials and ask him to place a call to my bank so that, in a matter of minutes, I have my money. With mail, though, I do have problems. I'm just now getting mail back from Florida that was sent out last April; I don't know where it's been since then."

Medical Care

Coping with medical problems is considerably less difficult than handling money and mail. Aspiring full-timers should, however, prepare for their life on the road by undergoing complete physical checkups and making arrangements for important prescriptions to be filled in advance, if possible. Some drugs can be prescribed in large quantities, and physicians can provide prescriptions for others that can be filled periodically. Full-timers also should consider using the mail pharmacy of the American Association of Retired Persons, 1225 Connecticut Avenue, NW, Washington, D.C. 20036.

Full-timers approaching age sixty-five might also want to consider postponing some medical care until Medicare coverage begins. Some needs not covered by Medicare, such as dental work, eyeglasses and hearing aids, should be fulfilled prior to retirement if they can be used as tax deductions. The deductibility of such expenses sometimes is less after age sixty-five.

NOW FOR THE GEAR

Once the aspiring full-timers consider themselves ready for the road, they should make sure the RVing equipment is in equally good shape. RV and tow vehicles should be checked for problems with lights; windows; brakes; and tire tread, inflation and balance. Wheel lugs should be tightened, radiators checked for leaks, windshield wipers replaced if needed, windshield washer filled with fluid, towing mirrors adjusted, wheel bearings packed, LP-gas bottles filled, wheel chocks stashed and spare tires checked. Emergency gear should be packed, including fire extinguisher, first-aid kit, highway safety kit and jack and tire wrench. If the full-timing rig is a travel trailer, the hitch ball mount should be inspected for proper height and tilt and the ball and antisway device checked for wear. Inspections also should be made of trailer electrical connectors, the breakaway switch and the safety chains.

Remember that you're not going on a long vacation when you begin your full-timing expedition; you're starting a new life on the road. Obviously, you want to be as comfortable as possible without dragging too much equipment along with you. There are, however, extras that make life on the road more enjoyable, and you should consider equipping your rig with some or all of them. For example, the convertible gaucho that served admirably as combination seating and a bunk in your vacation RV probably will not satisfy you full-timing; most full-timers feel a permanent bed with an innerspring mattress is an absolute necessity for living in an RV. Likewise, air conditioning was perhaps an unnecessary luxury in your vacation RV; it is necessary equipment in a full-timer rig.

Necessary Comforts

With the price of food shooting ever upward, and the difficulty of preparing quick meals and leftovers in an RV considered, thought should be given to equipping the full-timer rig with a microwave oven. Many way-

Built-in microwave and countertop blender are luxury features in this Pace Arrow motorhome.

Photo courtesy Fleetwood Enterprises, Inc.

of-lifers even carry portable auxiliary freezers with them so that they can buy larger supplies of vegetables and meat when they find bargains and also so that they can carry regional delicacies such as lobster or fish for longer periods of time. For entertainment, take along a television set, and equip your RV with a TV antenna. Consider whether you need—and if you can carry—bicycles, mopeds, motorcycles or a boat. Pack a hydraulic jack, a hibachi, a vacuum cleaner, an electric heater, folding chairs, a fully equipped toolbox, a water hose "Y" connector and install an awning on your rig. If you're planning to do any wilderness or boondock camping where there are no hookups, consider taking along a generator—either one built into your rig or a smaller, portable one. Also, make sure your RV has large enough holding tanks to serve at least a few days without needing to be emptied; carry a water purifier, a tow chain, a battery charger and jumper cables.

When I interviewed Mac and Alice McGinley in their Holiday Rambler fifth-wheel trailer, I noticed that they carried a microwave oven, a 10-foot refrigerator, a 5.4-cubic-foot auxiliary freezer, a color TV and a power generator. "All the comforts of home," Alice admitted.

"More, really," said her husband.

"I usually carry my sewing machine," she added. "It goes everywhere I do."

Mac said, "You name it, and she'll make it on that sewing machine. She makes her own formal dresses, she makes clothes for the grandchildren, and she makes my leisure suits."

Most of the veteran full-timers I interviewed told me they had difficulty packing enough, but not too much, gear when they first hit the road. It's particularly hard for new full-timers to control the amount of clothing and cooking gear they pack. After three years as RV way-of-lifers, Maurice and Evelyn Parker have narrowed their cooking gear down to a few items. She is especially dependent upon a small, electric cooker called a Wee Fry that she uses for preparing everything from roasts and steaks to pancakes and fried eggs. She makes casseroles in it, and she uses it as a deep fryer to cook french fries and fish.

Maurice has one complaint about his wife's packing habits. "When we first started full-timing, she brought along a lot more stuff than she needed. She still does. When she gets home (to their home base in Wisconsin), she pulls out items that she has discovered she doesn't need, but then she replaces those with something else!"

The Right Tools

For the do-it-yourself traveler, carrying the right tools is extremely important. Perry "Steamboat" Van Osdol, a former LP-gas dealer who is now a Sambassador with the Good Sam Club, carries gas leak detectors, pressure gauges and other LP-gas equipment so that he can repair his rig and also conduct seminars on propane use and safety. "I have a pop rivet machine so I can repair the skin on my [Silver Streak] trailer, and I carry extra wheel bearings and extra grease seals so I can pack my own wheels. I always carry spare fan belts, an extra heater hose, another short piece of hose in case it's needed, and I have an extra rotor for the electronic ignition distributor."

Another of the Good Sam Club's Sambassadors, Ken Cooper, said RVers have a tendency to carry either too many or too few tools. "I carry a rather modest amount," he said. "I can take care of 99% of my needs and 99% of anybody else's needs if I happen to be in a caravan and someone needs repairs. I do all of my own maintenance myself. I carry electrical testing equipment with me so that I can help other people if necessary, and sometimes that's my role if I'm with a caravan."

"Too Many Clothes"

I asked the Coopers, "At first, did you carry a lot of unnecessary gear?"

Flo answered, "I still carry too many clothes. I can never figure it out because in six months of travel, we don't know whether we're going to hit a mild spring or a freezing spring or whether summer is going to be hot or moderate. So I throw in winter clothes, summer clothes and spring clothes and hope the closet stays together. And it hasn't always. The whole closet came apart once. First the bar fell off, so Kenny bolted it to the shelf. He said, 'Now if it comes down, it'll bring the whole closet with it.' And it did."

Ken said, "I come pretty close to packing for my needs. Maybe just a trifle on the heavy side. I quite often get to the point where I have to wear the same clothes two or three times during an occasion, though. A lot of times we'll come to a place where we expect to do our laundry, but the time element is not just right or the laundry is filled with people so we might have to wait another four or five days. So that has to be taken into consideration while packing."

Flo added, "I think clothes planning was more difficult for this trip because we had to carry clothing for a boat cruise, and that kind of clothing is completely different from what we use in our rig. The things I took on the cruise I normally would never wear in the rig; I'd leave them home. So we had two completely different sets of clothing. My great dream is that one day I'm going to throw away all the stuff that I always figure I can get just a little bit more wear out of. Then I'll go to a department store and buy two or three coordinated outfits that will be good for anything."

Frank Salerno also had a problem packing clothes when he and Agnes were beginning full-timers. "My wife and I looked at things differently. We both had worked in offices, and I had a wardrobe of twenty or twenty-five suits. She thought I should take five or six suits and some sports coats on the road with me, but I preferred to take three of four pairs of jeans, six or eight pairs of shorts and maybe one or two sports jackets. We compromised the first year, and I took along a lot more clothes than I needed, and so did she. But we realized after a year that most of the clothing just hung in the closet and took up room and was very seldom used. Some of it we just never used at all. In this kind of life, you hardly need one suit, not to mention three or four. So this year I'm down to three sports coats and one suit, and my wife's wardrobe has been reduced to nothing but sports clothes; she didn't pack even one long dress. All I need, really, are about four pairs of blue jeans and sweatshirts. I don't even own a tie any more; I gave those up completely."

PREPLANNING YOUR LIFESTYLE

Aspiring full-timing couples have some additional important decisions to make prior to joining the RVing way of life. They should discuss:

1. Whether they will have to work occasionally or part time in order to supplement their income.
2. Possibilities for their initial destination, and possibly even alternative second and third destinations.
3. Who will be responsible for keeping expense records and how the expenses will be logged.
4. How campgrounds should be selected.
5. Meal schedules while traveling and at destinations.
6. Whether to consider winter—that is, cold weather—camping and wilderness camping.

If supplemental income is necessary for your enjoyment of the full-timing lifestyle, discussions should center on what kinds of work should be considered and how to lay groundwork for that work. One full-timing couple I know recognized that their retirement income would not be enough for them to live on comfortably, so they attended classes in park management before becoming full-timers; that training enabled them to earn money everywhere they went by working in public and private campgrounds. Another couple took training in bartending and food service so they would be able to work together in restaurants. Still another couple created their own jobs by building a business around the sale of shoulder patches at RV rallies. Chapter Twelve will deal more completely with the wide range of job possibilities open to full-timers, but it is important that aspiring way-of-lifers include a discussion about work in their early preparations.

As for planning destinations, most full-timers do not plan their travels as extensively as Sam Beaideme did when he developed his five-year trip schedule, but some people do seem to need detailed, structured itinneraries. Experienced full-timers usually advise newcomers to plan their travels rather loosely, setting an initial destination where a large block of time can be spent, but keeping an itinerary flexible enough to allow for changes in direction. Most way-of-lifers claim that their freedom to travel wherever they want, changing their minds with a whim if they so desire, is part of the appeal of full-time RVing.

A certain amount of preplanning is desirable, however. For example, maps, brochures and guidebooks should be collected in advance and, if possible, filed in the RV where they can be pulled out easily. Ken and Flo Cooper have wall shelves packed with maps and travel books, and they told me they spend many pleasant evenings together poring over that material and discussing possible sights to see between Good Sam rallies. Quite often, full-timers discard their planned itineraries because they meet other RVers who convince them to take unusual side trips.

Logging Expenses

Anyone living on a limited income—and that includes almost all full-time RVers—should keep detailed expense records, at least during their first year on the road. One family member should take responsibility for keeping a regular, or even daily, log and recording not only expenses, but also gasoline prices, mileage figures and notes about special destinations or experiences. Detailed record-keeping has proved to be very important to Don and Audrey Klemczak, for example, because it enables them to know how much traveling they can do and still stay within their budget. "We keep very detailed records," Don said. "We write down the type of gasoline we buy, the price, and we check our mileage continuously. We know, because of that, that when we start changing gasolines we'll detect a sudden drop in mileage."

Audrey added, "The records enable us to plan better. We have only so much money to spend every month on gasoline, so we have to keep track of it. This summer we did quite a bit of traveling, and we know from our records how much we'll have to cut down this fall."

Meals: "We Don't Obligate Each Other"

Meal scheduling is not a critical problem for most full-timers, but experienced RVers advise novice couples to discuss the subject before embarking on their full-timing lifestyle in order to clear the air on when and how meals will be prepared. Maurice and Evelyn Parker said they follow an extremely loose meal schedule: "If I'm in the trailer and she's not, I'll make myself something to eat. If I'm at the rec hall at lunch time and I don't want to go back to the trailer, I'll just go the snack bar and buy a taco or a hamburger. We usually have supper together, though."

Evelyn added, "And our evenings are usually spent together."

Maurice said, "One of the biggest problems, right from the start, was this: she didn't know how to cook for two people. While we were living at home, we were raising a family, and we always had friends and relatives visiting, so she cooked large meals. There are just two of us now, but at every meal, we have enough food for four or five people. It's expensive, but it's hard for her to cut down."

Maurice reported, "Eating out is where a lot of full-timers run into financial problems. They try to eat the same way they used to when they had more money. Maybe while they were home, they and some friends would get together once or twice a week for a big dinner. When you're full-timing, though, you have to limit yourself on that kind of thing. We go out and have a good meal a couple of times a month now." "Usually we go out when a group does," said Evelyn.

"And that's frequently when a restaurant has a special meal offer," added Maurice. "For example, there's a restaurant not far from here that offers a prime rib dinner for $5.95 sometimes, and we'll take advantage of that. But a lot of people are accustomed to ordering big steak dinners, and those can get a little rough on the billfold. Here's another thing we do: if we're going out somewhere with some other people, we'll usually get together in their trailer or ours and have a couple of drinks before we leave. Then maybe we'll have just one drink at the restaurant while we're waiting for our dinner to be served."

Frank Salerno admitted that he and his wife have a "weird" meal schedule. "I eat at 2:30 in the afternoon, and that's it for the day. I don't eat breakfast or dinner. We used to eat a big dinner in the evening and a light snack at lunch, but relative inactivity has a tendency to put weight on, so we don't eat that way any more. Now I exercise or do some other things in the evening and, before we go to bed we might eat a little fruit or something like that."

Harry Jennings said, "Juanita and I have one good meal a day, and it's usually breakfast. The noon meal is up in the air. Sometimes she'll go all out and cook a little bit of everything. But I don't worry whether we're going to have dinner at twelve o'clock or not. We don't obligate each other; I don't obligate her to cook, and she doesn't obligate me to be here. Whenever we get hungry, we eat. If she has something cooked, fine. If she doesn't, we eat sandwiches."

The typical retired couple can find many parks, such as this one in the Finger Lakes area, Alaska, that offer inexpensive camping facilities.

Boondocking Or Bingo?

Pretrip discussions about campgrounds are important because the full-timing couple should determine beforehand which kinds of campgrounds they will park in and which they should pass by. They should concentrate on camping in parks that fit their needs. For example, if social events are important to them, they should search out parks that offer organized activities such as bingo contests, crafts classes, exercise programs and pool parties. On the other hand, the typical retired couple does not need extensive playground facilities and game rooms, so they should not camp at parks whose prices reflect those accommodations. The couple with a self-contained RV should also try to save a few dollars by not renting overnight sites with full hookups if full hookups are not desired. Full-timers should, however, invest in annual, updated versions of their favorite campground directories and, if they camp in KOA parks frequently, they should carry a copy of that franchiser's directory.

Preliminary discussions of cold-weather camping and wilderness camping are important only because conflicts can develop if one member of the full-timing team plans to camp in the snow or in the desert without hookups and the other member of the team doesn't want anything to do with any form of "roughing it." If boondock camping of any kind is contemplated, the aspiring full-timers should make sure they are prepared for it emotionally and with the right equipment. Free camping in wilderness parks is one method full-timers use to cut expenses while their budgets catch up with them, but some RVers may not be willing to pay the price of discomfort and inconvenience that often is associated with boondocking.

One final word: while experienced full-timers consistently offer the same piece of advice to aspiring way-of-lifers—"Do it as soon as you can!"—it is naive to believe full-time RVing will work for everyone. There does seem to be agreement among veteran travelers that adjustment to full-timing requires a minimum of three months. Not many beginners are able to make new friends during the first two months because they are simply too busy sorting out the problems of finally being retired and on the road, and they consequently are thrown together twenty-four hours a day with only a minimal amount of contact with other people. New friends and new interests after that initial adjustment period will allow the couple to develop routines apart from each other and make full-timing a more satisfying lifestyle. Thus, while I would echo the advice of the veteran full-timers—try it, you might like it—I would add this caution: try it for at least three months, and preferably for six, and if you don't like it, consider looking for a comfortable retirement home.

Chapter Three

A Rig For
Full-Timing

Full-time RVers are a fiercely loyal bunch. Once they determine that a specific type and brand of RV fits their own lifestyles comfortably, they're willing to argue with anyone that every other RV is second-rate. Their loyalty is, probably more than anything else, responsible for the Great Debate that has raged for years over which type of RV is best for full-timing—a travel trailer, a motorhome or a fifth-wheel trailer. I'm not crazy enough to take a stand recommending one type of rig over another, thereby incurring the wrath of every loyalist camping today, but for purposes of clarification, I do think it is important that the advantages and disadvantages of each type of unit be explored here. Hopefully, then, aspiring full-timers will be able to make their own choices of rigs more easily, recognizing that they should select RVs that fit their personal lifestyles.

Travel Trailers

Since the majority of full-timers choose to live in travel trailers, let's look at those first and outline their advantages. Trailers provide RVers with more comfortable living space than motorhomes of the same size simply because the front end of a motorhome is devoted to the driving compartment and its functions. Trailers also have more open areas and walking-around space, more interior storage compartments, and, frequently, more bunk space. There are other reasons, though, why RVers choose to buy travel trailers. Experienced trailerists claim a trailer is easier to park

Travel trailers are popular with full-timers like Ken and Flo Cooper.

on a narrow, heavily wooded campsite. The trailer and its tow vehicle can be maneuvered and angled around obstacles such as trees while a large motorhome, which will not "bend" in the middle, cannot. Thus, trailerists often are able to camp on secluded, rustic sites not accessible to motorhomes. The biggest advantage a towable RV has over a motorized unit, however, is that it can be parked on a campsite and unhooked from the tow vehicle, which then can be used for exploring, shopping and driving to entertainment. Since most full-timers park their RVs and leave them at campsites for weeks or months at a time, this single advantage of the trailer over the motorhome frequently overshadows all other considerations.

Trailer Or Motorhome?

Arguments by motorhome advocates that trailers are more difficult to maneuver in traffic are poppycock. Experienced trailerists can pilot their rigs through the heaviest of traffic jams and encounter no more difficulties than drivers operating motorhomes of comparable size. On the other hand, finding places to park a trailer/tow vehicle rig, outside of a campground or a shopping center lot, is more difficult than with a motorhome; a 32-foot motorhome is just 32 feet long, but a 32-foot trailer rig is closer to 50 feet long, including tow vehicle and hitch. A poorly balanced trailer may not handle well (sway). A motorhome also is easier to handle when passing and being passed by large vehicles such as tractor/trailer rigs. In addition, a motorhome has a more prestigious image among non-RVers than a travel trailer has, although that image is not really justified in today's marketplace.

Prevalent thinking among non-RVers—and even among some experienced RVers—is that a motorhome is considerably more expensive and luxurious (and thus more prestigious) than a trailer. Actually, a combination trailer/tow vehicle might be far more expensive and luxurious than a motorhome, particularly if the trailer is one of the large, high-line models and the tow vehicle is a plushly equipped van conversion or luxury automobile. Consider that a van or truck equipped for towing and comfortably furnished on the inside costs between $8,000 and $18,000, while a travel trailer designed for full-time use carries a price tag of from $10,000 to $30,000. A low-priced Class A motorhome, on the other hand, can be purchased for $20,000 to $25,000; a medium-priced coach for $30,000 to $40,000, and a top-line model for as low as $45,000 (at 1981 model year prices).

There are reasons other than financial ones for considering the purchase of a motorhome for full-timing, however. The biggest advantage motorhomes have over trailers is the ready availability of food, beds and bathrooms while traveling. Admittedly, such convenience is far more important to families with children than to retired couples. Even so, it's nice to be able to prepare snacks, or even meals, while traveling down the highway, and it's hard to argue against the convenience of having a refrigerator close at hand with cold food, fresh vegetables, drinks and even ice cubes. Travel in a motorhome is much more relaxing for the copilot than riding in the front seat of a tow vehicle; boredom can be combated by walking around, lounging and napping on a comfortable sofa or bed, and even watching television.

Motorhomes are excellent touring or sightseeing vehicles, not only because they are self-contained, but also because they allow travelers to stop nearly anywhere they want to and stay as long as they want to without having to return to a base campground overnight or for meals. While a trailer's solo tow vehicle is unquestionably easier to maneuver and park than a motorhome, touring and sightseeing are necessarily limited to a couple of hours' drive from the base camp where the trailer is

Photo courtesy Fleetwood Enterprises, Inc.

Many motorhomes have appealing features like the entertainment center in this 35-foot Pace Arrow.

parked. Additionally, unlike trailerists, motorhome owners can tow boats, offroad vehicles, small cars or trailers loaded with motorcycles or snow-mobiles behind them. And, since a large percentage of the motorhomes built today are equipped with their own electrical power generators, they can be driven into wilderness camping areas where there are no camp-ground-type hookups. Full-time trailerists are not limited to using full-amenity campsites, of course, but boondock camping is easier when the RV is equipped with a generator, and most travel trailers are not built with storage compartments for generators.

Fifth-Wheels

The full-timer who determines that a trailer would fit his needs better than a motorhome has one more choice to make: should he buy a travel trailer or a fifth-wheel trailer? A fiver has all of the advantages of a travel trailer, plus some of its own. It also has a few of its own disadvantages. For example, while a fifth-wheel is safer to tow on a highway because it is less affected by crosswinds than a travel trailer, it also has the decidedly troublesome attribute of cutting across the tow vehicle's track instead of tracking obediently behind the tow vehicle, in tight turns. Most long-time fifth-wheel owners do not feel that cutting across feature is troublesome; in fact, after they've become accustomed to it, they claim they prefer trailers that do that. A fifth-wheel also is easier to park than a travel trailer; it can be jackknifed ninety degrees and backed into a parking space, unhitched and hitched up again quite easily.

Many full-timers select fifth-wheels over travel trailers because the fivers provide them with four to six feet of livable space (above the truck bed) that does not add to the overall length of the RV package. Plus, the length of the fifth-wheel does not include the three feet of nonlivable space that is relinquished to tongue and A-frame in a travel trailer. Thus, a 35-foot fifth-wheel has approximately six feet more living space in it than a 32-foot travel trailer. That fiver and its pickup truck tow vehicle measure about 43 feet long, whereas a 32-foot travel trailer and a truck-type tow vehicle stretch out to nearly 50 feet. On the negative side, many full-timers do not like to tow with pickup trucks for various reasons—usually related to comfort and a lack of storage space.

During the last several years, some imaginative features have been added to fifth-wheels to improve their livability. While most fifth-wheel trailers have bedrooms built into the front sections, companies such as American Traveler, for example, have designed units with stand-up forward sections. Those trailers must be towed by special vehicles (usually modified chopped van chassis that were meant originally to be forward sections of mini motorhomes) with lowered truck beds. Instead of equipping their forward sections as bedrooms, then, the RV companies convert the space into practical, comfortable living rooms. Several other companies, most notably Pioneer, Carriage and Estate, offer fifth-wheels outfitted with tipout, slideout and rollout room extensions. Such features are especially appealing to full-timers who park their units for several months at a time in one location.

The Klemczaks: "We Like To Move"

With so many positive and negative aspects to weigh, selection of the right type of RV for full-timing is not easy. Perhaps that is why so many RVers, including full-timers, begin with one type of unit, switch to another and then sometimes even switch back again. Don and Audrey Klemczak did that. When he retired in 1977 at the age of forty-three, they began their full-time RVing in a 29-foot Sportscoach motorhome. Later, they tried a 31-foot travel trailer and gave that up after two years in exchange for a luxury 35-foot Blue Bird Wanderlodge motorcoach.

Don explained, "We started with a Sportscoach because that happened to be the unit we owned when I retired. It was brand new when my health forced me to quit working, and I certainly wasn't going to sell it; we felt we had to utilize it. We drove it to Florida and spent the balance of the winter living in it. It served the purpose, but the floorplan didn't suit our needs, so we started looking at trailers. We thought it would be great to be able to park the trailer and have a car to run around in. We knew we'd need a large car but decided to try the trailer anyway. When we shopped for trailers, we looked at those that could take all types of weather. We also were interested in quality construction, towability and fuel economy, since I was convinced there would be an eventual fuel shortage. So we chose a 31-foot Airstream."

Don added, "That trailer worked out very well. It had all sorts of storage space on the inside, but we lost the outside storage areas we had in the Sportscoach. We kept the Airstream for two years, and we were very happy with it. But we towed it with a van that proved not to be so good. It was comfortable, with a conversion by one of the top-brand companies, but it was overpowered, its suspension was too heavy and it was too costly to operate as a run-around vehicle. The second year we had the trailer, we switched to an automobile for towing. It had a smaller engine than the van, but it performed as well, if not better, and gave us better gas mileage.

"Then we decided to go back into a motorhome and buy a small car to tow behind it. We knew our mileage wouldn't be as good on the highway as it was with our car and trailer, but we figured that when we got to a destination, we'd have an automobile that gave us thirty miles to the gallon, so energy-wise, we'd be saving a lot. We really started getting the bug for a motorhome because Audrey likes to walk around in a motorhome while I'm driving; she can read, write and do other things that are difficult to do in a car. Also, when we stop in a rest area to have a bite to eat, we don't have to go outside and get into the trailer; with a motorhome, everything is conveniently right there with us. I also like the outside storage space I get with a motorhome. I carry a lot of equipment and tools such as power saws and a router."

Audrey added, "Also, it's a psychological thing, but we got to the point with the trailer that we felt we sat in it too much; we stayed in one area too long. We like to move, to travel to different places. I think that's

Motorhome owners can tow many types of vehicles, including a small car.

Traveling in their 35-foot Blue Bird Wanderlodge motorcoach was the realization of a dream for Don and Audrey Klemczak.

part of our gypsy blood and why we're full-time RVers. But we weren't doing that when we had the trailer."

They decided to return to motorhome living even though they realized that exploring in it, with its six mpg gasoline consumption, would be significantly more expensive than tooling around in an automobile. They balanced out that cost somewhat by buying a Chevette to tow behind the Blue Bird so they would use less fuel while the coach was parked semi-permanently in a campground. Purchase of the Blue Bird was the realization of a longtime dream, Don and Audrey said. "It's a great coach. It's quiet inside, and it's very stable. We don't need all the space; we could get by in a 19-foot trailer if we had to. But we love it!"

The Campbells: A "Feeling Of Security"

Jerry and Betty Campbell began camping in 1963 and by 1980 had logged an estimated 300,000 miles, accumulatively, with several kinds of RVs. "I trailered one boat more than 100,000 miles," Jerry said. And all that experience has convinced them that, for their own full-timing lifestyle, a motorhome is better than a trailer. "There's a psychological feeling of security when you're living in a motorhome," Jerry added. "You don't have to get out of one unit and into the other in order to be on the road and out of trouble. You don't have to get out and hook up in a rainstorm. You've got your own power generator so you can be completely independent of outside utilities. You can tow a car and you can tow a boat. I get better mileage with my Travco, even towing a car behind it, than a lot of trailerists get with their tow vehicles."

Betty said, "Here's something else about a motorhome: if you find yourself in an undesirable spot, all you have to do is start your motor and move."

The Considers: Trailering Since 1948

Walt and Charlotte Consider, on the other hand, full-time in a 29-foot Holiday Rambler travel trailer, and they prefer trailers to motorhomes. They've been trailering since 1948, when they towed a 24-foot mobile home for 2,000 miles during the summer "and thoroughly enjoyed it." Walt said, "Even if you buy a 35-foot motorhome, you'll lose six feet of that length in the cockpit. Now, I know that the two captain's chairs will swivel around, but even so, it's not as livable a space in that cockpit as the front of a trailer has. I also believe that the maintenance of a motorhome is more expensive than it is for a trailer and a tow vehicle. In addition, if you have a trailering rig and you need a new tow vehicle, you can go out and buy one and tow the same trailer with it if you don't want to change the trailer. But if you have to change any part of a motorhome, the whole unit has to go."

WHAT SIZE RIG?

For full-timing, the size of a rig is almost as important as its type. Unfortunately, many beginning full-timers select rigs that they later say were too small, and they make their selections based on their experiences as part-time or weekend RVers. Rigs that serve admirably as weekend and vacation camping units, however, are not always suitable for full-time living. Aspiring full-timers should consider their at-home living habits before they select their full-timing rigs. If they are comfortable living in a one-bedroom, three-room apartment, they can probably adjust easily to full-time RVing in a 24-foot travel trailer. If, however, they are accustomed to living in at least a five-room house—and they need that much space in order to be comfortable—they probably will feel cramped in anything smaller than the largest fifth-wheels, travel trailers or motorhomes.

The size of a full-timing rig should be selected after considering several factors, with special attention given to cost and storage space. A couple with a permanent home base or storage area, for example, does not need as much closet, cabinet or storage compartment space as a couple with no place to resupply and replenish seasonal clothing, tools, special equipment and even stocks of canned goods bought in bulk at bargain prices. If the RV must carry everything the couple owns, it must be large enough to hold everything and still provide the couple with living space.

On the other hand, the size—as well as the type—of RV selected for full-timing could be restricted simply by what the couple can afford. This is less true today than it was several years ago because several of the nation's leading RV manufacturers are now building their "economy" lines of units in larger models.

For comparison purposes, let's take a look at what typical full-timer units cost, at the retail level, when 1981 models were introduced. Since the majority of full-timers prefer travel trailers at least 30 feet long, fifth-wheels 35 feet long, and motorhomes at least 32 feet in length, I have limited my pricing analysis to those sizes.

Among the leading travel trailers for full-timers, the most expensive was the 31-foot Excella II by Airstream, at nearly $30,000. Silver Streak's 32-footer was $20,000, followed closely by the 32-foot Holiday Rambler Imperial at $19,000 and the 31-foot Carriage/Royals units at $18,000. Yellowstone's popular 32-footer retailed at $15,000, while its nearest competitor, Kountry Aire, sold its 31-footer for $14,000.

The most popular fifth-wheels for full-timers were the 36-foot Holiday Rambler Fifth Estate, $23,000; Nu-Way's 35-footer, $21,000; Carriage's 35-footer, $20,000; Kountry Aire's 35-footer, $19,000, and Globestar's 35-footer, $17,000.

Motorhomes selected most often by full-timers ranged downward from the $135,000 bus-type Blue Bird Wanderlodge to the 35-foot Pace Arrow coach at $35,000. Within that price range were the 35-foot Vogue, $80,000; 35-foot Foretravel, $68,000; the diesel-powered Airstream, $62,000 (gasoline power about $10,000 less); the 32-foot Travco, $55,000; Apollo's 33-footer, $55,000; the 33-foot Sportscoach, $50,000; the 33-foot Executive, $47,000; Holiday Rambler's 32-footer, $45,000; Beach-Craft's 32-

footer, $37,000, and Georgie Boy's 35-footer, $35,000. All these prices, of course, reflect a full range of livability equipment in each unit.

Beginning full-timers often are willing to compromise their space and livability needs in favor of smaller RVs than they want because they believe they can save money by towing shorter, lighter weight trailers or driving smaller motorhomes. The fact is, size is not as important a factor in fuel savings as most people believe it is. For example, a 32-foot travel trailer may weigh only a few hundred pounds more than a 27-footer built by the same manufacturer, and the fuel savings from towing the smaller trailer may not be significant.

Undue emphasis also is placed on vehicle size by beginners who mistakenly believe that the smaller the trailer, the easier it can be towed; the smaller the motorhome, the easier it is to handle. Those are unreliable assumptions. The best handling trailers I have ever towed in my job as RV auditor for *Trailer Life* and *Motorhome Life* magazines have been the large, 27- to 33-foot coaches. I have tested 32-foot motorhomes that handled like logwagons and 32-footers that handled like sportscars. In one weekend, I drove two different motorhomes—one a 28-footer and the other a 32-footer—and the larger of the two outperformed the smaller coach in every way.

In selecting a rig, the full-timer should balance a large unit's potential lack of fuel economy against its livability, recognizing that on-the-road towing or driving time is relatively brief when compared with the amount of time the vehicle will be stationary in campgrounds. And while parked, of course, the amount of living space inside the unit is of utmost importance because that RV will be utilized as a residence.

Full-Timers' Choices

Chuck Mogg, a full-timer from Michigan, has not had very good fortune in his selection of RVs. "First I bought a big, 11½-foot pickup camper that was huge and very heavy. I put it on a three-quarter-ton 1973 truck equipped with coil springs, and that rig was a nightmare. We took one trip in it and sold it. Then we bought an old motorhome that was actually called a housecar; it was a camper mounted on a 1958 GMC truck chassis. We sold that and bought a 16-foot Shasta trailer. Then I bought a 24-foot, 1975 Starcraft trailer; we hauled that out to Yellowstone and back and traded it in on the 40-foot Kountry Aire fifth-wheel that we own now. A year ago, I bought a little, 20-foot mini motorhome so that we could drive something to New Orleans and tow a small car behind it."

When I talked with Chuck, he was considering buying another pickup camper that he could put on his Chevrolet truck and camp in while on long trips and at Good Sam rallies. He said he wanted to be able to tow a Chevette behind the truck so that he would have a high-mileage vehicle to drive after arriving at his destinations. "The Kountry Aire fifth-wheel will be our home that we'll come back to and that we can take to Florida if we go there for the winter. But if we're going to drive 600 miles to a Samboree, we'll just take the pickup camper; it's just not financially feasible to haul the fifth-wheel that far. Not at six miles to the gallon with us on a fixed income. When we're not using the trailer we'll park it at my sister's house and use it as sort of a home base. But we're still going to be full-timers; we're not going to nail down a permanent address. It's just that we want to be able to take the Chevette with us sometimes so that we can afford to see the sights on side trips. And next fall, when we go out west to California and Arizona, we'll take the pickup camper and the truck and tow the Chevette. Here's another reason we want that size rig: we've met a lot of people through Good Sam who have invited us to park in their driveways or in their yards whenever we're traveling through, but we can't expect to park a 40-foot fifth-wheel in someone's yard. We can do that with the pickup camper, though, and just pocket the $6 or $8 that we'd spend every night for campsites."

Frank Salerno had never towed a travel trailer before he retired, but he bought a 28-foot Argosy eight months prior to leaving his government job at Chicago's O'Hare Field. He also prepared for the full-timing life by buying a mobile home in Wisconsin that he figures would serve as home base for him and his wife, Agnes. "Although I bought the Argosy in February of 1976, I didn't get a chance to use it until I retired in October. I had towed it around home a little to get used to it and to learn how to back it up. The first time I really had it out on the road, though, was when we left for Florida shortly after my retirement."

Why did he select the Argosy? "I knew we'd be in it most of the time, so I wanted a good, comfortable trailer, and the Argosy seemed ideal for us." But it wasn't ideal, the Salernos discovered, so in mid-1979 they traded it for a 31-foot Royals International trailer by Carriage. Frank explained, "Well, the Argosy was a 28-footer, and the Carriage was three feet longer and we needed more space. For a while, we also had our mobile home, so we didn't have to carry everything with us. But I wanted to get rid of the mobile home, and my wife said the only way she'd go along with that was if I bought the biggest travel trailer I could find. That's when we got the Royals."

Mickey and Laila Rutledge of Louisville are among the loyal Holiday Rambler owners who are full-timing in their rigs. They began camping in 1964 with a tent, moved to a Volkswagen Campmobile in 1967, then to a 27-foot Holiday travel trailer in 1970. They began their full-time life on the road four years later and, in 1977, upgraded to a new 32-foot Holiday trailer. "I guess I'll use that until it falls apart, the way prices are now," Mickey told me in 1980. He said their RVs have enabled them to enjoy parts of the world they would not have been able to see any other way. They've traveled through all of Canada and most of Mexico; they've caravaned through the Northwest Territory to Great Slave Lake, and they have explored every state except Rhode Island, Washington and Oregon.

Chris Moffett began full-timing with his late wife, Charlotte, in a 29-foot Holiday Rambler trailer during the fall of 1970. One evening in July, 1980, I talked with Chris about his first years as a full-timer, and his voice choked a little as he told me about that trailer. "It had a little different layout than this one," he said. "Charlotte had sort of a nest over there with cushions, and it was just a little too tough on me to see that vacant space after she died, so I bought this 30-footer in 1977. I'm towing it with a Chevy truck outfitted with an Alaskan Camper because I like to go places where I can't tow a trailer. I spent five weeks in northern British Columbia last summer, for example, going back rough roads that stopped abruptly at the shores of lakes. I wore out one Chevy truck with a 454 engine, so I transferred the Alaskan Camper, which was custom built for me, to another chassis just like the first one. I carry a 12-foot, resort-type boat on top of the camper. It's five inches wider and three inches deeper than a normal car-topper—a very sturdy, heavy boat. It takes big waves on lakes and in the ocean. I also carry a 9.8-hp Mercury outboard motor everywhere with me. I don't need a truck to tow this trailer. Any full-size automobile will tow it. I want the truck for other purposes. Most people don't realize it, but the reason so many full-timers tow trailers with trucks is that they want to be able to carry extra things that a car can't hold."

When Ken and Flo Cooper decided to hit the road as full-time RVers, they realized that their 21-foot Nomad trailer would not be large enough for them, so they began to research various kinds and sizes of RVs. "I wanted a quality-built unit, and I wanted one with certain things in it. I analyzed half a dozen trailers, went to as many RV shows as I could and took notes on everything I saw and heard, and I decided to buy a 30-foot Holiday Rambler fifth-wheel because of one or two features. The primary feature was water capacity. We seriously considered a 30-foot Kountry Aire model, but its water tank capacity was only 30 gallons and there was no way the dealer could add a larger tank. The same size Holiday unit had a 40-gallon tank, and we considered that a minimum requirement because we were used to having more than that in our smaller trailer. I also liked the Holland hitch, which was offered with the Holiday."

Flo added, "I was interested in the fact that it had two good size closets, including a three-door closet for my clothes. That feature was very important to me. I also liked the Holiday's bedroom layout because it had room for us to carry a little organ with us. There was space for a small freezer, and I found an area to keep some of my crafts. I have never felt the trailer has enough counter space, but I've had to learn to live with that."

Why did they choose a fifth-wheel instead of a travel trailer? Ken answered, "Flo wanted it. I preferred a trailer and a truck with a camper on it so I could carry a boat. But now that I've towed a fifth-wheel, after having towed three trailers of various sizes, I am convinced that a fifth-wheel is a much easier and safer trailer to tow. And, considering all the time our job (as Sambassadors) with the Good Sam Club takes, I wouldn't have been able to use a boat much anyway."

A FLOORPLAN FOR FULL-TIMING

Selection of an RV floorplan is not as difficult as most people make it. Admittedly, it is a process that can be somewhat complicated for families with children of various ages and both sexes, but for full-timing couples, the floorplan selection process should be rather simple. The keys to any RV layout are the location and size of the bathroom, and for RVs that are suitable for full-time RVers, there are only three types of bathroom placements: in the rear; against the center of the roadside wall, and split, on both sides of the RV, at mid-coach. For someone to whom a large bathroom is less important than open living space, a center bath layout may be suitable; couples who want their bathroom space and facilities to be as extensive as possible should consider either rear-bathroom or split, walk-through bathroom layouts.

Let's look at the advantages and disadvantages of all three types:

Center Bath

Although center (sometimes known as side-bath) bathrooms are smaller than those of either of the two other types of layouts, they offer RVers three very important features—a front or rear area that can be used as a full-time bedroom; bathroom and bedroom privacy, and a section of

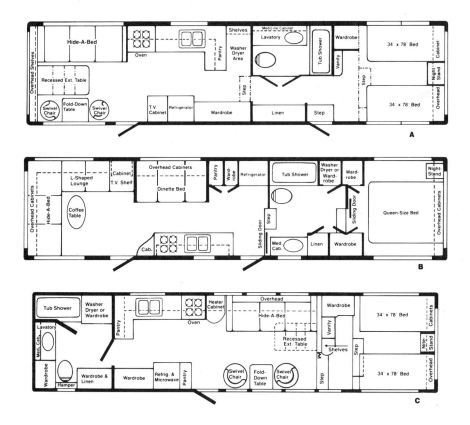

Three types of floorplans on 35-foot fifth-wheel trailers: (A) Center Bath, offering extra closet space on the curbside wall; (B) Split Bath, spacious enough to feature a full-size bathtub; (C) Rear Bath, a favorite among full-timers because it provides bedroom privacy.

curbside wall (opposite the bathroom) that can be utilized for closet and drawer space. Bedroom privacy can be especially important if one member of the full-timing team sleeps later than the other or if the couple occasionally invites other people (such as grandchildren) to travel with them and sleep in another part of the coach.

Split Bath

These bathrooms can be quite large, depending upon the size of the motorhome or trailer, and usually are spacious enough to include room for apartment-size washer/dryer combinations. Generally they are built so that both ends of the bathroom can be closed off to provide complete privacy. Split bathrooms also generally feature house-size bathtub/showers, something that is usually not available in center-bath RVs. Their disadvantages are that they can take up valuable closet space; they interrupt front-to-rear traffic flow by making it impossible for someone to walk the length of the RV when someone else has locked the doors to both ends of the bathroom, and because they are generally left open, they seem to be on display to visitors.

Rear Bath

Rear-bath models are the most popular of RV layouts among full-time RVers. Rear bathrooms are usually large and private; they have large bathtub/showers, and they have plenty of closet space. They are especially popular among fifth-wheel trailerists who are full-time RVers because bedroom privacy in the overhead section can be maintained, even with visitors. There is a distinct lack of nighttime privacy, however, in trailers and motorhomes that have rear bathrooms with convertible bedroom sections just forward of the bath area.

Floorplan selection generally comes down to trade-offs: if you want a permanent rear bedroom or, in a fifth-wheel, a formal rear living room, your choice is limited to split-bath and center-bath models, both of which have their own built-in disadvantages. If you want a large, rear bathroom, you might have to give up some nighttime privacy. In addition to those considerations, there are a few other features that can help determine RV layout: the availability of closet space, the type of eating space required, and the type of beds necessary for the couple to sleep comfortably while living on the road.

When considering closet space, aspiring full-timers should remember that they will carry considerably more clothing with them than they usually took on even a long, seasonal vacation trip; depending upon whether or not they keep a home base or a storage area for extra clothing and accessories, they might even carry all the clothing they own with them in their RV. Mealtime space is important not only because the full-timers will utilize it every day, but also because they probably will want to invite guests to share meals with them occasionally; thus, eating space should be of the type that serves two people routinely but which can be enlarged to handle two to four guests.

Selecting sleeping accommodations is largely a matter of personal preference, but convenience and living habits are equally important. For example, while aspiring full-timers might like the idea of a dinette section that converts into a double bed at night, most experienced way-of-lifers have learned that such convertible facilities are practical only for guests. Their living habits, formed over several decades, dictate that they sleep on permanent, full-time beds with innerspring mattresses that are considerably more comfortable than the four-inch-thick foam cushions of dinette/bunks.

ALL THE COMFORTS OF HOME

Non-RVers who have occasion to walk through fully equipped motorhomes, travel trailers or fifth-wheels usually feel obligated to exclaim, "Wow! This has all the comforts of home." That statement is usually spoken half in praise of the RV and half in jest; they don't really believe an RV can have "all the comforts of home," in spite of its full range of livability equipment.

RVs that are built for and bought by full-time travelers, though, must live up to that description. They *must* have "all the comforts of home" and maybe even more because the owners of those rigs probably will spend more time in them than they spent, proportionately, in the brick-and-wood homes where they raised their families. Truthfully, the key word to equipping an RV for full-time living is "comfort." A full-timer rig should have as much comfort built into it as possible, and that means it should contain the right kinds and sizes of accessories. An improperly equipped RV can make a new full-timer's life miserable and turn him against the RVing way of life forever.

Heating Systems

When full-timers buy their rigs, they don't give enough attention to RV heating systems, and that is a mistake. Even though full-timers generally are "snowbirds"—that is, they follow the sun seasonally so that they can live in warm weather all year around, a significant amount of their time is spent in moderate, not hot, climates, and they are forced to use their furnaces frequently. Small, direct-flow furnaces that are centrally placed and designed so that their heat is merely blown out of one or two vents in the sides of cabinets are just not adequate for full-time living. Most of those have output ratings of only 12,000 btu, and some are even smaller with less output.

A furnace for a full-timer rig should be a forced-air, ducted model, preferably with the duct work installed under the floor so that it not only frees up cabinet and closet space for storage, but also so that it provides a measure of heat for the RV's underbelly and helps prevent water tanks and plumbing from freezing. The furnace should be equipped with a solid-state, electronic-ignition system, not a match-lighted pilot. Although a furnace with a 20,000-btu output might be marginally adequate for small rigs, most full-timer RVs should be equipped with at least one, and possibly two, furnaces rated for 30,000-btu of output. The furnace should be regulated by a wall-mounted thermostat that is conveniently located but not placed near external heat or cold sources that will cause it to fluctuate erratically. Ducts should be directed toward every section of the RV for even heating throughout, and one duct should be installed in the bathroom.

Insulation

RV manufacturing companies that build the rigs which are most popular among full-timers also give special attention to insulating their products so that heat loss and cold bleed-through are reduced as much as possible. Although insulation systems vary slightly from manufacturer to manufacturer, the most common methods can be illustrated by looking under the skin of three brands: Carriage/Royals, Holiday Rambler and Escort products. Carriage's floors, sidewalls, fronts and rears are filled with two inches of R-7, house-type fiberglass insulation, and two thicknesses of fiberglass are used in the roofs. Holiday Rambler walls have cores of 1½-inch fiberglass insulation, a layer of craft paper vapor barrier and three-fourths inch of beadfoam. Escort units are among the best insulated RVs built. They utilize, in their sidewalls, an inch of Styrofoam, a layer of Monsanto Foamcore and two thicknesses of craft paper vapor barrier to prevent air infiltration. Escort fronts, rears and sub-floor areas are insulated with four inches of fiberglass, and the floors are covered with double carpet pads for added warmth. Suspended ceilings have three inches of insulation in them. Escort president Richard Murray emphasized that the most important insulation feature for full-timers to watch for is the vapor barrier. "Seventy percent of a unit's heat loss is by air infiltration, so that and condensation should be prevented by the installation of vapor barriers between the outer skin and the unit's steel or aluminum cage work."

Lightweight Styrofoam sheets form the cores of many of today's RVs.

The Refrigerator

Perhaps the most misunderstood accessory in an RV is the refrigerator. It seems at times that no one—even people who work within the RV industry itself—can ever agree on how large or small a refrigerator should be, how it should be powered and how it should be used. The most popular refrigerator installed in RVs in recent years is one that is commonly referred to as a seven-cubic-foot model but which, in reality, is actually about six cubic feet in size; a larger model, often considered the ultimate for an RV refrigerator, is generally described as a ten-footer, but it really has about eight cubic feet of capacity. I've talked with RV manufacturers who swear that the eight-foot model will not hold more food than the six-footer but that, admittedly, it does have a much larger freezer section. My feeling is that either size is adequate for RVing full time, but the larger model is preferable for couples who carry a substantial amount of frozen food.

A full-timer rig should, however, be equipped with a two-door refrigerator rather than a single-door model; it will cool more efficiently and be less subject to cold temperature loss in one section (the freezer, for example) if the door is opened to the other section. Controls should be on the outside of the refrigerator so that it can be lighted or switched from gas to electricity without opening the door, allowing the cool air to escape. The refrigerator should have, in addition to three or four shelves, space in its door for milk, eggs, butter and bottles; a vegetable crisper; a meat keeper, and ice cube trays in the freezer compartment.

RV refrigerators are generally powered in three ways: all-electric (AC/DC); propane/110-volt electric; propane/AC/DC. Proponents of all-electric refrigerators claim they are more effective coolers because they cool down faster than those powered by gas or battery. But they have one limitation: unless there is a generator on board, they need larger than normal storage battery capacity. A two-way gas/110-volt refrigerator has the advantage of an all-electric model except that it lacks the 12-volt battery power capability. A three-way refrigerator offers the most versatility, although both it and the two-way are slightly less effective when hooked to electrical power than the all-electric model because of the type of cooling units they utilize. Three-way refrigerators have gone somewhat out of favor with RVers and with the RV industry in general during the last few years, so it could be difficult to find a stock rig equipped with one of them. If your camping is limited strictly to campgrounds where hookups are accessible, or if you have unusually large battery capacity, an all-electric refrigerator is adequate for most needs. If, though, you like to camp in the boondocks where there are no electrical outlets, you should equip your RV with a two-way refrigerator; it offers the most versatility with the least amount of trouble for the money.

Some full-timers—such as the Coopers—carry auxiliary freezers with them so that they can buy larger quantities of meat and vegetables when they find bargain prices and also so they can stock regional delicacies found during their travels. Most full-timers, however, feel that electric freezers are too much trouble. Chris Moffett, for example, advises aspiring full-timers: "Under no circumstances should you buy a freezer. It ties you to electrical hookups; you've got to have electricity every night or your food will spoil. Of course, you can use a generator all night, but then all the other campers will hate you."

Accessories

Most RVs suitable for full-timing carry livability equipment that is absolutely necessary for survival on the road: a furnace, a four-burner gas range with an oven and broiler; a large two-door refrigerator; a six-gallon water heater; a double stainless steel sink; a combination tub and shower; dual holding tanks. Full-timers usually want more than those basics, though. An air conditioner that is mere luxury to weekend campers is a necessary accessory for full-timers. Special food storage sections such as slide-out pantries are very important, as are lighted closets, large medicine cabinets, floor-level courtesy lights, systems monitor panels (although many of those are unreliable) and AC/DC color TV sets.

While my copilot and I do not spend all of our time RVing, because we have not yet raised our family, we are on the road nearly as much as some full-timers, and we enjoy a rig that allows us to travel as comfortably as possible. Therefore, when we ordered a new 28-foot motorhome from the Holiday Rambler Corporation, we designed a coach laid out and equipped especially for our needs. Some of the accessories, I'll admit, were luxuries rather than necessities but we, like most full-timers, wanted them for the comfort and convenience they provided. We modified a Holiday Rambler floorplan slightly, adding a flat desk top and office chair to the roadside rear corner opposite a sofa/bed, and we replaced two swivel chairs on the front curbside with a flip lounge. Because we nearly always travel with at least one of our four children, we asked for a two-person "buddy" seat in place of the standard copilot's seat. We added a folding privacy door just ahead of the rear lounge/office/bunk area, and we had a swing-down bunk installed above the driving section. A hinged countertop extension was added to the galley area and a TV shelf was installed on a wall above the front living section.

For the outside of the coach, we ordered a hitch receiver and a Bargman electrical connector so that we can tow either our boat or a small car. A storage pod was installed on the roof; in it, we carry lawn chairs, a folding picnic table, fishing gear and other occasionally used equipment. We're considering adding a rack that will enable us to carry a moped with us.

The motorhome was equipped with a 6.5-kw Qnan generator, a 40-amp convertor, a three-way eight-foot Dometic refrigerator, a Magic Chef microwave oven, a Sony color TV set with a Winegard TV antenna, an AM/FM/8-track stereo sound system, a 13,500-btu Coleman roof air conditioner, Suburban's 30,000-btu electronic-ignition furnace, a Cobra remote control CB radio, LP-gasoline dual fuel system, an electronic-ignition water heater, hydraulic leveling jacks and a Thermasan II waste destruction system.

Most of today's luxury motorhomes have all that and more. Some coach manufacturers have even taken the guesswork out of figuring gasoline mileage, trip distances and other bothersome details by outfitting their motorhomes with trip computers. Such computers provide instantaneous readouts of time, fuel usage, distance traveled, speed, temperature, distance to destination, estimated time of arrival and the mile markers where speed traps were last reported. Popular options for towable RVs as well as for motorhomes include garbage disposers, food processing centers, entertainment centers outfitted with wine and cocktail glasses, and upholstery fabrics to match every lifestyle—from leathers and wools to velours and suedes. There are awnings, water purifiers, clothes hampers, diesel engines and fluorescent lights.

All the comforts of home? Certainly! And a lot more, too.

TOWING AN AUTOMOBILE

While there is one significant disadvantage to full-timing in a motorhome (and that is, the coach must be unhooked from utilities whenever transportation is needed), there are several important disadvantages to towing a small car behind a motorhome in order to avoid the hassle of breaking camp regularly. It is easier to unhook the car from the motorhome and drive to the supermarket or the theater than it is to break camp and then go through the process of leveling the motorhome and attaching water, sewer and electrical lines to it again. Also, it is simpler to drive a small car in heavy city traffic than it is to maneuver a large coach through narrow streets and in and out of parking lots. But full-timers who own motorhomes should consider whether those few advantages overshadow the numerous disadvantages of towing an automobile.

On uneven terrain, such as entering or leaving service stations and driving over rough roads, some cars will not track properly, and they can damage the towing equipment. Towing rigs which lift one end of the automobile off the ground will solve the problem, but the weight they add to the rear of the coach can cause instability in short-wheelbase motorhomes. When an automobile is towed without one end lifted off the ground, backing is virtually impossible because the car's wheels tend to turn in the wrong direction. Although a manual transmission car can be towed with its gearbox in neutral, it is necessary for the driveshaft to be disconnected on a car with an automatic transmission. Failure to disconnect the driveshaft could result in transmission damage. If the front end of the automobile is even slightly out of alignment, the car will drift from side to side and be difficult to tow.

Because the towed automobile is so much smaller than the motorhome, it is difficult to see, so the car must be checked frequently. Plus, it is easier to damage the automobile and create an accident situation when passing other vehicles and turning corners. The motorhome's large tires tend to pick up rocks and gravel and hurl them backward toward the towed automobile, thereby marring the car's finish, breaking head-lights and smashing the windshield. Acceleration and braking are some-times seriously affected when a car is towed behind a motorhome. Gasoline consumption can increase noticeably. Better towing usually oc-curs when a carrier that raises the car's wheels off the ground is used—particularly if that carrier is equipped with hydraulic surge or electric brakes—but such rigs are rather expensive. Often, reinforcement of the motorhome's frame extension is not adequate to bear the increased weight of a carrier and an automobile.

In spite of these drawbacks, many motorhome owners do tow au-tomobiles successfully, without incident, and insist they would not travel without small cars behind their coaches. For those persons, either an automobile carrier (which resembles a flatbed trailer), a rig that lifts one end of the car off the ground, or a tow bar connecting the motorhome with the automobile's frame (not its axle or bumper) is the best and safest bet. A carrier has the additional advantage of permitting a car with an automatic transmission to be towed. A lift rig can handle the same kind of vehicle so long as the drive wheels are off the ground. Both carriers and lift rigs also permit cars to be backed while attached to motorhomes, and they usually are equipped with auxiliary braking systems of some kind. Tow bars, on the other hand, are considerably less expensive, and most are made so they are easy to dismantle from the car. Some motor-homes must be equipped with frame or bumper reinforcements, however, to handle the push-pull stress resulting from towing with tow bars.

To make sure the hitch and towing device are properly leveled and mounted, with adequate reinforcements added, the work should be per-formed by a qualified hitch shop which installs load-leveling hitches for travel trailers because such shops understand the mechanics of towing equipment.

THE RIGHT TOW VEHICLE

Recommending a trailer-towing vehicle to an aspiring full-timer is a difficult task, if not an impossible one. Models and engine sizes have changed with nearly every new year recently, and the power plant that is available today for towing large travel trailers and fifth-wheels might not be offered next year or the year after. For example, a popular tow vehicle for many years was the Dodge three-quarter-ton pickup truck powered by a 440-cid V-8 engine; but production of that engine was halted by early 1980, forcing Dodge loyalists either to buy another brand of truck or drop down to a 360-cid V-8 engine. Similarly, although the 454-cid engine of General Motors and the 460-cid Ford power plant have been popular among full-timers for many years, they are being phased out.

It seems certain that the trailer towing vehicle of the mid-1980s will either be a General Motors pickup truck (or van) powered by a 350-cid engine and a 3.73:1 rear axle, or Ford's truck and van line powered by a 351-cid engine and a 3.73:1 rear axle. Some trailerists will insist upon buying trucks or vans with 4.10:1 rear axle ratios, but the demand for those will remain relatively small because of their lessened fuel efficiency capabilities. As this is written, in late 1980, the most popular towing vehicles on the road, according to veteran full-timers, are one-ton Ford pickup trucks with the 460 engine and GMC and Chevrolet Suburbans with 454 engines.

Jim Brown, the young man who quit his job in the late 1970s in order to spend two years traveling with his wife, tows his 32-foot travel trailer with a 1975 one-ton Ford Crewcab truck. He said he chose a pickup because of the storage space that is available in its bed, under a camper shell, and behind the driver. Walt Consider also drives a pickup—a Dodge 200 with a 440-cid engine and a 3.73:1 rear axle ratio. "I get better mileage with the 3.73 than I would with a 4.10 rear axle," he said. "When I'm pulling a hill, I don't climb it quite as well as I would with a 4.10, but I'm not too proud to shift down into second gear." Mickey Rutledge, on the other hand, chose a Suburban that he beefed up with stiffer suspension and equipped with an 80-gallon fuel tank. He logged 67,000 miles in it between 1974 and 1980—most of those in front of his 32-foot trailer.

Chapter Four

Customizing Your Rig For Full-Timing

T here is no such thing as the perfect full-timing recreational vehicle. Individual needs almost dictate that a full-timing couple shop around for an RV that closely fits their lifestyle and then either modify it so that it satisfies them, or modify their own needs to fit the layout and furnishings of the unit. Some full-timers, of course, have coaches custom-built for them, but it is difficult for everyone to do that because, first of all, only a few RV companies do extensive custom work and, secondly, custom building is usually—but not always—expensive.

Before Jim and Mary Brown began full-timing in the late 1970s, they were convinced they had a travel trailer that fit their lifestyle perfectly. Years earlier, they were attracted to an unusual floorplan that was offered in the largest trailers of the Holiday Rambler Corporation. Instead of either the usual double island bed or the twin beds in the rear, it featured a double bed whose side was flush against the roadside wall, with a dresser against the wall on the curbside. That layout was discontinued by Holiday Rambler, but when the Browns ordered their newest trailer in 1976, they convinced the company to build theirs that way. Jim, who was a regional director of the Holiday owner's club, wanted to be able to keep his club materials in the trailer, stored in a file cabinet just forward of the dresser.

Soon after the Browns began full-timing, they discovered that while their "perfect" trailer was fine for weekend camping, rallies and vacations, it had some shortcomings when it came to full-time livability. The rear bedroom, for example, did not have enough storage space to suit them; it was built with only two sections of overhead cabinets above the bed.

So within the first few months of beginning their full-time life on the road, the Browns installed more overhead cabinets on the curbside. Mary said, "Then I kept looking at the way his file cabinet was placed, with a chair in the open space beside it, and I thought, 'Why can't we put a piece of Formica over that open space on top of the file cabinet?' Jim did that, making that area into a desk that worked out fantastically. Now I can put my sewing machine there and, if we're parked, leave it there all the time if I want to."

Jim added, "It's become the most workable rear bedroom I've ever seen in a travel trailer."

Mary had even more ideas for customizing their trailer, though. She decided they did not need the large mirror above the bathroom vanity because it kept getting splashed with water from the sink, so Jim took it off the wall and replaced it with a smaller one. Like most Holiday Rambler trailers, theirs came with a shaded hanging lamp in the living section; Mary added a formal touch to the bathroom by moving the lamp to the ceiling above the bathroom vanity. She explained, "When you're away from home, living in a trailer that has become your home, you want to make it as homey as possible. A man might think that's silly, but I believe a woman has to do it to make a trailer feel like a home."

At the front of the trailer was a sofa/bed that the Browns decided wasted space. They never traveled with other people in their unit, so they did not need the extra sleeping accommodations. The sofa/bed, therefore, was replaced by a platform-mounted couch with full storage under its seat cushions. There, they stored Mary's sewing machine and typewriter and enough canned goods to last them during a long caravan through Mexico. With its back cushions on, it served as a lounge for seating guests or for afternoon naps. If necessary, the back cushions could be removed to convert it into a single bed for one overnight guest.

When I talked with Mary during the summer of 1980, she admitted she still wasn't completely satisfied with her trailer. "There isn't enough ventilation in the bathroom," she complained. But she had the answer: "The next time we're able to sit in one place long enough, I'm going to have Jim remove the little [ventilation] windows from each side of the trailer [near the front] and install them, one on top of the other, in the bathroom."

The Browns had special needs, and any trailer, to be right for them, had to be designed to fulfill their special requirements. But obviously, the Browns' coach would not be right for all full-timers. Still, the RVing lifestyles of most full-timers are so similar, it is accurate to say that the same basic principles in RV design apply to nearly all of them.

A full-timing coach must, for example, have enough storage space for keeping food; cooking utensils; plates, glasses, cups, bowls and pans; linens; clothing; blankets and pillows. There should be closets for carrying along clothes and coats on hangers, and there should be drawers or other storage space for folded shirts, underwear and socks.

The good full-timer rig also should have storage space for lawn chairs, a barbecue grill, tools, a vacuum cleaner, jacks and leveling blocks. The shape of the meal preparation area should be determined by space requirements and individual preference for L-shaped, split, in-line or front galleys and by the need for special accessories such as a microwave oven, an extra-large refrigerator, a spacious countertop or a pantry. Options that are most popular among full-timers include garbage disposers, food processing centers, motorhome driving compartment consoles with drink holders, entertainment centers outfitted with TVs and stereo sound systems, floor-level courtesy lights and luxury upholstery fabrics ranging from leathers and wools to velours and suedes. There are awnings, water purifiers, roof storage compartments, clothes hampers, icemakers, slide-out pantries and fluorescent lights.

THE IDEAS ARE LIMITLESS

Over the years, hundreds of RVers have written to *Trailer Life* magazine with details of their own customizing efforts. Some of those ideas can be used by most full-timers; others are so narrow in their range of appeal that only a few other RVers could possibly appreciate them. One full-timing couple reported how they outfitted their motorhome with a permanent dinette by removing a single bunk and replacing it with facing bench seats and a plexiglass-topped table. Another couple offered this valuable tip: indoor/outdoor carpeting cut to size and installed on cabinet shelves will prevent dishes and cans from sliding around.

Trailer Life's "Lady Alone" columnist Edith Lane always provided good customizing advice. She removed one twin bed/lounge from her motorhome and replaced it with a six-foot desk; she converted rear and front drop-down bunks, which she didn't need, into storage attics; she installed a catalytic propane heater so she wouldn't have to operate her battery-draining LP-gas furnace; she modified her closet so it would handle more clothing; she converted an open shelf in the rear of her motorhome to a seven-foot-long bookshelf, and she added magazine racks, spice racks, paper towel and napkin holders, cupholders and glass hooks all over her rig.

A few years ago Sandy and Walt Shipley wrote to *Trailer Life* about how they converted their 28-foot Avion trailer into a better full-timing coach ("We Made Our 'Cage' A Castle," November 1978). "We began by taking two single beds out and installing a three-fourths size bed," she reported. "This provided equal storage room under the bed and space for a full-length vanity along one wall. Inside [the vanity] were four large drawers, a sewing section and miscellaneous storage. We located a two-drawer file cabinet the exact size of one corner over the dresser. A lifesaver: one drawer is his, one hers." The Shipleys also installed a fireplace that Walt built which doubled as a gas heater and wood-burning stove and saved them considerable money for electricity and propane. They removed a "not-so-comfortable" daveno and replaced it with a huge cabinet which included a six-foot storage section along one side, a six-foot bookcase with top shelf across the front and a two-foot bookcase on the other side. Then they reupholstered two old office chairs to serve as both table chairs and living room furniture, and they added an electric piano and amplifier to their new shelf area.

Single full-timer Peggy Dell wrote in *Trailer Life* several years ago about her unique customizing efforts ("What's the Best Rig For Full Time?" September 1976). When she bought a rental motorhome as her private rig, she ordered the dinette table and seats, a closet, the gas stove and large refrigerator removed. The refrigerator was replaced by a smaller countertop model; the stove, by shelves and a storage cabinet (she used electric appliances and a small gas burner for cooking); the closet with a smaller one. The front of the motorhome, on the curbside, was converted into a combination work table, office and dining area utilizing a hollow door and some plywood for a wrap-around table. She added a rolltop desk and fashioned a storage area for books and out-of-season clothing from the motorhome's overhead bunk. Peggy wrote, "The feeling as you enter my motorhome is one of homey comfort. I love it!"

"Gorgeous On The Outside"

Hal and Penny Gaynor have lived in various travel trailers during their years as full-timers, but they don't have very much confidence in RV manufacturers' abilities to build coaches that satisfy the needs of their fellow way-of-lifers. The Gaynors have, in fact, either modified by themselves, or had custom-built, every RV they've owned. Hal, as a journalist and an experienced trailerist, has often been asked to critique new RV products, but he said his criticisms are seldom welcomed by manufacturers. "What they really want is praise, not criticism," he pointed out. "We feel we're not here to compliment a manufacturer, but to tell him what is wrong with his work."

Hal mentioned an especially beautiful fifth-wheel trailer that was introduced to the public by a company that is no longer in business and said he was asked to critique it. "The trailer was gorgeous on the outside; it had a smooth shape and lots of big, beautiful windows. But there was no place on it to install an awning because of the placement of those windows. Inside, you couldn't even put a can of soda into the kitchen cabinet without turning it sideways. The ceiling was beautiful, but it could not be cleaned. There was no place for storing pots and pans. The toilet was in the middle of the floor. The couch took up so much room that you couldn't walk around it or use the valuable space near it. We told the builder all that, but he brushed us off and dismissed our comments with a wave of his hand. The following year, we were asked to come back and offer our critique again. The manufacturer promised he'd listen that time. He greeted us and pointed to the rig and said proudly, 'See, I've got an awning rail up.' None of the other shortcomings were changed, though, and even the awning rail was installed all wrong."

As Hal and Penny travel around the country conducting their well-known "Trailering Safety Clinics" at RV rallies, they live in a 33-foot Century travel trailer that they customized themselves. "The first thing we did," Hal said, "was rip the arms off the couch and install two end tables so we'd have places for drinks and ashtrays. There was an extension table in front of the couch, but the couch itself is the wrong height for anyone who tries to sit on it and eat, and the couch is uncomfortable at mealtime because whoever sits there will sink into the upholstery. So we took out the table and replaced it with two chairs and a high-low convertible table. Over there was a swivel chair that matched the couch. It was very comfortable, but it occupied a quarter of this room. We sold it for $119 to some people who put it into their living room. We cut the galley down from L-shaped so that it is a straight-line layout. We replaced the under-range oven with a cabinet and installed an eye-level oven over the range. The bathroom had a three-quarter-size tub, so we enlarged the bathroom by just four inches and installed a full-size, steel, porcelain-coated tub there."

Hal added, "I could tell RV manufacturers a thousand things they ought to change in their units, but it wouldn't do any good. They're not building RVs for livability; they're building them so that when a person walks through the door he's so struck by the beauty of the furnishings that he loses his breath."

CUSTOM-BUILT TRAILERS

With a few exceptions, the dozen or so RV companies that build custom-ordered fifth-wheels and travel trailers are not very well known. They are generally small operations, each with just a single plant and a limited work force. They are, however, usually quite skillful at what they do, and they are justifiably proud of their own workmanship. They do not, as a rule, produce lightweight coaches; their products are often among the heaviest in the industry. But the trailers are generally solidly built, well insulated and equipped with the best accessories available. They are not inexpensive, but on the other hand, neither are they outrageously high priced. Among companies that build custom-ordered units, only Nu-Wa, Elkhart Traveler, Marathon, Franklin Coach and Carriage/Royals are widely known; those companies produce production-line RVs to compete with the nation's major manufacturers, but they still build custom units on occasion. For some of the other companies, custom-built trailers are more important. Those manufacturers include Escort RVs, Estate Manufacturing, Merrigan Brothers, Melody Coach, Royal Coach Manufacturing, Space Craft, Specialty Manufacturing, Thoroughbred Industries, Travel Units, and White Pine Campers.

One Custom Coach

Charles and Violetta Legler began full-timing in the mid-1970s with a 15-foot Phoenix travel trailer. They switched to a 22-foot Nomad, then to a 26-foot Fan and finally, during the fall of 1980, they ordered a custom-built 34-foot travel trailer from Travel Units—a small RV company on the outskirts of Elkhart, Indiana, that produces only about 100 custom-built coaches each year. The Leglers' trailer was built, from the ground up, to their specifications.

Charles insisted, for one thing, that the trailer's refrigerator be placed on the curb side of the unit. He explained, "With the refrigerator on the traffic side, every time a big truck goes by, it can blow out the flame of the refrigerator's pilot light. Another reason for having it on the curb side is that's the side the trailer's awning is on; when we've got the awning out, it shades the cooling unit on the refrigerator; therefore, the refrigerator performs better and it's less costly to operate. The sun shining on the outside of the refrigerator's air vent makes about a 10-degree difference on the inside of that refrigerator."

Charles and Violetta Legler customized their coach with cabinets and countertops scaled to Violetta's height.

Violetta felt strongly about another feature for their trailer: she wanted the coach longer than the usual 32-footer because she ordered a two-foot-wide rear clothes closet the entire width of the trailer. "There is never enough storage space in a trailer," Charles explained. "Never enough space to hang your clothes. This way, we have an eight-foot closet across the rear and a six-foot closet along the side. That gives us fourteen feet of closet space in which to hang our clothes. Violetta also wanted a laundry chute in the back, so it's on the floor of the closet, opening into the storage compartment in the trunk." Like many other large trailers, the Leglers' coach has a rear trunk area that is opened from the outside for storing tools, electric cords, water hoses and miscellaneous items. But unlike other rigs, part of the trunk was designed to hold a large clothes basket, and Violetta drops dirty clothes into that basket through a small door in the floor of the bedroom closet. When the basket is full, it can be lifted out of the trunk from the rear of the trailer.

"I couldn't stand clothes in my tub any more," Violetta said. "Everybody has dirty clothes in their tubs. Some people have so many clothes they even put rods across the bathroom and never use their tubs. But I like to use my tub every day, and I don't want to have to clean it out every time I use it. This way, there's going to be nothing in that tub but my body."

To gain even more storage space, the Leglers ordered their bed on a frame with large drawers built into the structure under it. Oversize wall-mounted cabinets were built into the front of the coach everywhere possible, and they were made extra-long so that Violetta, who stands only four feet, ten inches, could reach them easily. "We also had a space built into the bedroom for my sewing machine, with a light above it," she said. Kitchen countertops were built only thirty-three inches from the floor to compensate for Violetta's height, and she demanded that her trailer be equipped with an apartment-size range with a large oven instead of an RV range/oven because she likes to bake. She also ordered the largest RV refrigerator available and had it installed so that a large drawer fit under it and a large storage space over it. Her pantry, she had built with drawers instead of compartments with doors. "I like drawers better than doors," she said, "because you can just look into them and see what you have there; you don't have to reach all the way back in."

A special 20-by-20-inch cabinet on casters was built for the Leglers' TV set, and the living room couch was designed with pull-out drawers under it. End table-type cabinets with more drawers flanked the couch. A cabinet across the back of the couch provided more storage space in two additional drawers.

To conserve heating fuel, the Leglers asked Travel Units to enclose the area beneath the trailer with an aluminum underbelly. The floor was constructed of three-eighths-inch plywood, with a two-inch layer of block Styrofoam between each floor joist, then the main flooring, with carpeting laid to the outer edge of the flooring before the sidewalls were attached.

A Low-Profile Company

Sam Paolillo, whose company built the Leglers' coach for them, produces custom travel trailers almost exclusively. Travel Units has maintained a very low profile in the marketplace during its more than ten years in existence. The company advertises its services in *Trailer Life* magazine, but its address is almost a secret. Paolillo admitted to me: "I have made it very difficult for people to come to us without an appointment. Before a customer comes in to see us, we've talked on the telephone and corresponded by mail a couple of times. I have given them an idea of what we do, and they have given me an idea of what they want, so by the time they actually get here, both of us pretty well know in what direction we're headed. Then we sit down and draw up a very simplified floorplan." Early discussions focus on the size of the bedroom, placement and size of the bed or beds, the size and location of the bathroom, placement of electrical outlets and lighting, then a review of the available options. Customers are asked to select their interior colors, their carpeting and drapes, countertops, bathroom vanities, paneling and cabinetry, and exterior trim. "If someone is ready, and can make decisions quickly, we can come up with a layout and furnishings within three to eight hours of consultation," Sam said.

He added that cost is usually a major consideration "because my customers are mostly middle income people. I don't usually do business with people who can spend whatever they want to; most of the people who come to me have only so many dollars that they can spend, and they don't want a trailer with a lot of birthday cake. We do emphasize interiors very strongly; our interiors are second to none." Most of his customers, he said, are retirees who want to spend between $10,000 and $15,000 on their trailers. The typical Travel Units coach is 32 feet long with a rear bedroom, a side bath and a front living room. It is equipped with one roof air conditioner, the largest refrigerator available, an automatic-ignition furnace, a four-burner range, either a microwave oven or a cavity into which one can be placed, a full-size tub, radius windows, plenty of overhead cabinets and a generous supply of 110-volt lighting. Heavy insulation also is emphasized, both for full-timers who like to camp in cool weather and for those who park their rigs in hot climates such as in Arizona. Sam uses either fiberglass or Styrofoam, and sometimes, a combination of the two.

Interestingly enough, Travel Units has been relatively unaffected by the economic ups and downs which have plagued the rest of the RV industry. The little company has maintained a rather level production schedule annually since 1971. "Bad times don't seem to affect me," Sam said. "We just go on the same." The secret to his success, he said, is that the company will build a trailer any way a customer wants it.

Chapter Five

Expenses
And Budgets

A full-time life on the road is less expensive to maintain than a life that includes a house, one or two automobiles, a job and all the accoutrements of urban and suburban society. How much less does it cost? That's a difficult, if not impossible, question to answer. The U.S. Bureau of Labor says that retirees need between 70 to 80% of their working income in order to maintain the same lifestyle. Most full-time RVers admit those figures might be accurate—for retirees in general; but they claim those estimates are at least 20% too high when applied to way-of-life RVers.

The typical full-timing couple does not make house mortgage payments. Since they have no regular jobs, they do not spend money commuting to work, and they do not need a "second car." They spend very little money on clothing, and their wardrobes are relatively small. They do not eat in restaurants very often. They spend very little money entertaining friends and relatives. Their expenditures for electricity and telephone are minimal. Their LP-gas bills are quite low not only because their RV uses less energy than their home did, but also because they follow the sun seasonally and do not need large amounts of propane for heating. Their taxes are limited to whatever small amounts they pay on their incomes and for their vehicle license plates. They can control their gasoline costs by scheduling their travels carefully, and they can reduce campsite fees by camping without full hookups whenever they need to.

The U.S. Bureau of Labor has made an attempt to summarize the expenses of retirees, but its breakdown on retiree budgetary items bears little relationship to the budgets followed by most full-time RVers. Let's look at the bureau's summary anyway, as a point of comparison with

RVers' budgets. The Bureau of Labor figures that 40% of a retiree's income is spent for housing, including fuel, taxes, insurance and upkeep. Of the remaining income, 30% goes for food, 10% for transportation, 6% for clothing, 11% for medical care, and 9% for personal expenses. It is difficult to compare RVers' expenses point by point because "housing" costs are related to campsite fees, insurance and upkeep are more related to "transportation" costs, and fuel costs are "housing" (propane), "food" (propane), and "transportation" (gasoline) related.

Campsite Expenses

My investigations revealed that "lodging"—more accurately, campsite—costs among RVers range from a low of about 12% of a couple's income to a high of about 33%. This wide range occurs primarily because of two factors. One, a couple with a relatively low income naturally spends a proportionately higher percentage of that income for campsites than a couple with a high retirement income and, secondly, some full-time RVers do more "boondock" or wilderness camping than others, so the average fee they spend for campsites is smaller than couples who camp only in formal private or public parks. The average RVing couple, I learned, spends approximately 25% of their budget for campsites—but only up to a point. An interesting fact that I discovered about full-time RVers is that some of their expenses do *not* increase proportionately with their incomes. Campsite fees are one such expense. My research revealed that while full-time campers in general spend 25% of their income for campsites, that percentage drops significantly among couples with incomes of more than $750 per month. In other words, the average amount of money spent for campsites increases, along with income, until daily fees of $6-$6.50 are paid; then an average of about $6.25 per night is maintained consistently, regardless of the couple's income. Unexpectedly, this $6.25 figure held rather steady through the late 1970s and going into 1981, even though inflation pushed campsite fees ever higher. The reason is clear: full-timers on fixed incomes refuse to spend more for campsites than they think they can afford, and they are adjusting to higher campground fees by searching out free and less expensive campsites. On an average, full-time RVers spend 15% less of their income on campsites than other retirees do on housing, but as mentioned earlier, that lower amount does not include fuel, taxes, insurance and upkeep; those expenses are, however, absorbed by other areas of the full-timer's budget.

Food Costs

Like other retirees, full-time RVers spend about 30% of their income for food. Unlike some other budget items, food expense remains fairly constant among all RVers, with a rather narrow range between couples who spend a minimum amount of money for food and those who spend a maximum amount. Couples studied in my research spend between 20% and 35% of their incomes for food. Those whose food expense totals only 20% of their income nearly always have budgets in excess of $1,000 per month, and they follow lifestyles that do not include much eating out and liquor expense. Again, couples maintain a 30% food expense average until their monthly incomes reach $750 per month; then the percentage declines while the amount of money spent for food remains rather constant at about $7.50 per day and $225 per month.

Transportation

Obviously, full-time RVers spend less than other retirees on two important lifestyle items—food and housing. But they spend considerably more for transportation, according to my research. Remember that the Bureau of Labor estimates that retirees spend only 10% of their budgets for transportation. Full-time RVers spend a whopping 35%! This is not surprising, considering that the full-timing lifestyle is chosen primarily because of the travel opportunities it offers. And even though full-timers might not travel more actual miles in the course of a year than other retirees, their per-mile costs are higher because they are taking their homes—their RVs—with them, thereby increasing their fuel consumption figures. Transportation costs for full-timers are higher, too, because they must spend more money than other retirees to keep their RV rigs in a good state of repair; they must buy tires and batteries more often, and their license and insurance costs are higher.

My research into full-timer transportation costs revealed two startling facts: the percentage of income spent for transportation by way-of-lifers is within a very narrow range—between a low of about 32% of income to a high of about 40%; secondly, the actual dollar amount of outlay for transportation does not level out when income reaches a certain point, as do the outlays for food and clothing, but it continues to increase and hold at the 35%-of-income level as per-couple incomes increase. It may be simplistic for me to say that full-timers with higher incomes travel proportionately more than those with lower incomes, but that is an important fact that should not be understated; the freedom to travel and explore is the most attractive aspect of full-time RVing, and the more money a couple has, the freer they are to enjoy travel opportunities.

Clothing

Full-timers spend half as much money on clothing as other retirees—3% instead of 6% of their income. While their actual cash outlay for new clothes is consistently less than that, their laundry costs are higher than most other retirees because they are forced to use coin-operated laundries which charge up to $1 a load for washing and drying clothing. Clothing expenses hold at the 3% level only for full-timers who have incomes of $750 per month or less; for those with higher incomes, the percentage declines after cash outlay reaches about $20 per month, and full-timing couples continue to spend $20 per month or less for clothing and laundry no matter how high their incomes are. RVers claim they have lower clothing costs than other retirees because they wear more casual, and fewer dressy, clothes. Wash-and-wear materials are an absolute necessity when traveling in an RV, and jeans are the most popular item of clothing for both women and men full-timers.

Medical Expenses

Because RV way-of-lifers are, in general, healthier than retirees who cannot travel because of illnesses, their medical expenses are considerably lower than those of other retirees. My research reveals that full-timers average spending 3% of their income for medical attention and drugs as opposed to the Bureau of Labor's estimate of 11%. Full-timers probably should spend more than they do in order to safeguard their health and have regular physical checkups, and my research indicates that they spend more if they feel they can afford it. The 3% level is maintained rather solidly across all income brackets and does not seem to decline among couples with higher incomes. Thus, while a couple with only $500 a month of income spends $15 of it for medical attention, a couple with an income of $1,250 spends the same 3% proportion, but lays out $37.50 each month for medical care.

Propane

Propane expense is one item I researched separately even though the Bureau of Labor includes home utilities in its "housing" expense breakdown. I did this partly because the cost of propane is not included in the fee an RVing couple pays for their campsite and partly because, for full-timers, it is an expense that should be budgeted separately. Like medical expenses and transportation costs, expenditures for propane tend to maintain a rather constant percentage level of the couple's income. Full-timers spend approximately 2% of their budgets for propane, no matter how much income they have. In researching full-timers' budgets, I discovered that the most conservative couples spend 1.5% of their budgets for propane, while the most liberal users spend only 3%. There is some leveling out of propane use at the $20-per-month cost point, but increased use then continues relatively unabated at the 2% level among couples with monthly incomes of more than $1,000. My only explanation for this continued increase in usage is that couples with higher incomes might tend to travel more in cooler climates than couples with fairly restricted budgets due to lower incomes.

Personal Expenses

The most closely watched segment of full-timers' budgets is the area the Bureau of Labor calls "personal expenses." While the bureau figures the typical retiree uses 9% of his income for personal expenses, the range among full-time RVers can be pegged at as little as 2% for couples with incomes of less than $750 a month and as high as 20% for couples with incomes of $1,250 or more. The wide range of difference can be explained easily. Couples with incomes of under $750 a month tend to spend nearly all their money on things they consider indispensable to their lifestyle—campsites, transportation, food, clothing, medical care and LP-gas. They restrict their personal expenses to that extremely low 2% level knowing as they do so that if they can cut expenses in any of the necessity categories, they will have extra dollars for personal expenses. Couples with incomes of more than $750 a month realize very quickly that their campsites will not cost them more than $185 to $200 per month; that food bills will average about $225 at a maximum, and that expenditures for laundry and clothing level out at about $20 per month. Thus, money they have available to spend for those items often is not used, and it can be channeled instead into one of three other areas of their budgets: transportation, medical care or personal expenses. Most of the high-income couples opt for diverting the money into personal items, accounting for why some of them spend as much as 20% of their income on telephone, postage, photography, liquor, entertainment, personal insurance, supplies, books, tolls, fishing licenses and other miscellaneous expenses. Some couples use the extra money for more extensive traveling, and a smaller number put it into savings.

LIVING ON LESS

Mickey and Laila Rutledge live on about $800 per month—considerably less than they needed in 1974 when he was employed as an electrician. But Mickey figures that they get another $200 worth of free campsites each month because they work, seasonally, at parks owned by the U.S. Corps of Engineers and by Outdoor Resorts of America. I talked with the Rutledges while their trailer was parked in an ORA campground near Orlando, Florida, and they were working part-time as assistant park managers. They said they are able to live on less income than they did several years earlier because expenses in an RV are so much less than in a house. Even though their income was cut in half when Mickey retired, they told me they are able to enjoy full-timing without following a budget—something they could not avoid doing when they lived in a house in Louisville, Kentucky. "I don't set aside a certain amount of money for anything," Mickey said. "We pretty much go where we want to; we darned well eat what we want, and we do everything that we want to do."

Full-timer Chris Moffett also lives just as he wants to without pinching pennies, and when I asked him, "Have you ever figured what your daily expenses run?" he answered, "I hate to admit this, but no, I haven't. I'm fairly well off, and I have a ball park figure of what I can spend in a month, so I haven't bothered with a budget. I balance out living royally against dry camping in a state or national park, but I do that as much because I like it as I do to save money."

I asked, "Did you discover that when you went full-timing you could live on a lot less income?"

"Certainly. You can make this type of life cost you just as much or just as little as you want to. I have friends that live on a shoestring, so to speak, but they live quite comfortably. The two of them spend a lot less money than I do. They're very careful about their money; they do a lot of figuring and take advantage of grocery specials and sales that save them money. They're naturally the frugal type, though. He was a successful businessman, but he has no pension of any kind other than Social Security. He says there are a lot of corners that Rvers can cut."

Mac McGinley retired from a junior college teaching job in the mid-1970s. He and his wife, Alice, immediately began living full time in their travel trailer, supported by pensions totaling $1,100 a month. I met them in the summer of 1979 while we were attending an RV rally in Nova Scotia, and I asked them if they had to adjust their lifestyle downward to compensate for the reduced income. "No, we haven't," Mac said. "But you have to remember, when I was working, I had a lot more expenses—house payments, taxes, insurance, car payments."

"Have you been able to keep your lifestyle at the same level it was then?" I asked.

"I think so. I don't see where we're hurting."

Alice said, "I see what we have now as a *different* lifestyle—a more enjoyable lifestyle—than we had before."

Mac added, "We have to distribute our cash assets differently. We can't buy a new boat whenever we want one, but that's not our cup of tea anyway. We know how much money we have to spend every month and, sure, we can get extravagant with it and eat $25 or $30 dinners, but we just don't do that. We have our fun in less expensive ways. We like to attend rallies and visit friends."

Like most aspiring full-time RVers, Ed and Marty Eades worried about how much a life on the road would cost them. A year after joining the full-timing ranks, Ed recalled those worries in an article he wrote for *Trailer Life* ("How Much Does Full-Timing Really Cost?" February 1979) following their first year on the road. He reported that "we did not attempt to set a record for inexpensive living; nor did we throw caution to the wind and spend our money indiscriminately. We just lived, did the things we wanted and traveled to the places we had dreamed about."

Ed and Marty quickly discovered ways to cut expenses: "Most of the coach maintenance work I do myself, such as oil changes, greasing the vehicle, and changing filters. The equipment necessary for this is inexpensive and the savings are considerable. We found that our clothing needs and costs dropped to almost nothing. After disposing of the bulk of our clothing, we find we still have enough to last years with a minimum of replacement necessary . . . campground fees are mostly minimal since we are self-contained and do not require electricity, sewer or water hookups. The only time we use full hookups is when we plan to be in one spot for a week or more. Consequently, as our camping fees increase, our gasoline costs decrease."

Daryl and Ginny Johnson, a former Iowa couple who became full-time RVers when they were in their twenties, were somewhat surprised to discover how inexpensively they could live in a travel trailer parked in a condominium campground within shouting distance of the Gulf of Mexico. "We own our lot here, and we pay a condominium fee of $30 a month," Daryl said. "But our lot is paid for, so we don't have any payments to make on it. Our electricity in the summer runs $40 a month with the air conditioner running. Our sewer and utilities, garbage pickup and maintenance are included in our condominium fee. It's really an inexpensive way to go, and we don't feel we're pouring money down a rathole by paying rent or making a mortgage payment. Our money is freed up so we can do other things with it."

Blanche Shunk of Michigan has had to learn how to budget her expenses carefully because her only income is her $338 monthly Social Security check. And out of that, she pays nearly $100 to rent a mobile home lot in Florida. Blanche, a widow who began RVing full time in 1979, travels as much as possible each summer in her 23-foot Prowler travel trailer and soaks up the Florida sun by living in a mobile home between October and May. "I try to live on my Social Security, but once in a while I have to dig into my savings a bit. I'm a pretty careful spender, though, and I also earn a little—maybe $100 or so a year—with beadwork and wall hangings that I make and sell. I've thought about getting a job, but I don't know if I will. I enjoy the activities at the parks too much to take time out and look for a job. I don't do a lot of driving since the price of gasoline has gone up so much, and I had to draw out only $300 from my savings all of last year."

Suggested Income: $800 To $1,000 Per Month

In northern Michigan, I asked full-timers Glenda Beaideme and John and Doris Lockwood how much income they thought a full-timing couple should have before embarking on a full-time RVing lifestyle. They suggested between $800 and $1,000 a month. "Especially now, with the price of gasoline being what it is, if you intend to do much traveling," Glenda said. "Three years ago, when we retired, traveling was a lot less expensive."

I asked, "Do you travel as much now as you did when you started full-timing?"

She answered, "Yes, we do. We've found that it's cheaper for us to live in the trailer than it was to maintain our home in South Carolina, even though we travel a lot. Our property taxes, insurance and mortgage payments on that house amounted to $325 a month; we can park in a campground for $200. We figured it up, and when we were both working, we drove two cars and put at least 40,000 miles a year on them. Now, we travel all year, but we still don't put that many miles on our trailer."

"That's right," John said. "We'll travel a couple of hundred miles a day for eight or ten days; then we'll park somewhere for a while." "And maybe we'll sit there two or three weeks," added Doris. "This winter in Florida, we did very little driving. We actually saved money, even though we were still maintaining an apartment and paying rent on it."

John said, "It's not unusual for us to spend $50 or $60 a day for gasoline while we're making a long run. And we might spend $7 or $8 a night for a campsite while we're traveling. But once we stop in a place for two or three weeks, we can catch up with those expenses again before we move on.

"When I was working, we drove 60,000 to 70,000 miles a year. Now, I'm towing my trailer with a 1979 van. When we left home last March (sixteen months earlier), it had nine miles on it, and it has only 40,000 miles on it now. That's a reduction in driving for us of almost 20,000 miles a year."

HOW TO CUT EXPENSES

Veterans of full-time RVing are experts at saving money and finding bargains. They have to be; they want to travel as much as possible, and traveling is expensive. So they save money by buying food—especially canned goods—and toiletries on sale in large quantities. Way-of-lifers who have either home bases or centrally located storage facilities are particularly adept at buying groceries in bulk from warehouse stores and factory outlets and then restocking their RV's depleted stores from time to time. Full-timer Charlotte Consider discovered a catalog surplus outlet in Columbus, Ohio, that sells closeout items at bargain prices. In her travels, she kept watch for more stores like it and finally spotted another one in Atlanta. "It's amazing the things you can buy in those stores," she reported, "and the prices are just unbelievable. Sometimes, I can't find anything I want there, of course, and other times I might find something for my grandson and nothing for my granddaughter. My husband bought two pairs of shoes in the Atlanta store for $5 each. If you know about stores like that, it can help your financial situation a lot."

I asked Charlotte, "Are you more aware of that type of store now than you were before you started full-timing?"

She answered, "I definitely am. I never shopped before. I never paid any attention to prices, either. Now I do."

Best Bargains

Many full-timers—especially women—rather enjoy their new status as bargain-hunters, and they perceive the search for good buys as somewhat of an adventure. One full-timer who was formerly a buyer for a department store chain pointed out that bargains can be found more easily some months than others. For example, she said, the best bargains in January are usually tires, furniture, cosmetics, linens, television sets and radios. In February, she suggests shopping for women's coats and men's clothing. In March, housewares; in April, clothing advertised in clearance sales; in May, clothing, housewares and linens. She advises shopping for men's clothing and summer sportswear in June; outdoor furniture, linens, summer clothing clearances and tires in July; women's accessories, outdoor furniture, linens and stationery in August; tires in September; new RVs, model-end automobiles and women's coats in October, and women's coats in November and December.

There are several other ways of cutting expenses while RVing. Cook a steak on a charcoal grill instead of buying one in a restaurant. Eat fresh fish that you've caught yourself or that friends have caught. Carry a list of dealers and service centers that service your RV, and postpone repairs—if you can—until you are near one of those outlets. Buy gasoline at minor brand, self-service stations, and carry as large a fuel tank as you can. Consider a dual-fuel (LP-gasoline) conversion or diesel power, but only if you drive enough miles to justify the high initial investment. Take advantage of the 10% discounts available at campgrounds to members of the Good Sam Club and, if you are a member of the American Association of Retired Persons, look for businesses that offer discounts to AARP members. Attend movie theaters or stage plays during matinees or on evenings when special prices are offered. Some campgrounds lend paperback books to site renters without charge, and books also can be borrowed from public libraries and bookmobiles. Take advantage of free or inexpensive recreation such as attending community concerts, practicing hitting golf balls on a driving range, attending interesting lectures at colleges and universities, and participating in community and ethnic group-sponsored festivals.

Avoiding The Traps

Pat Kenoyer, who wrote an attention-getting article called "Rving on $200 a Month" in 1976 for *Trailer Life*, found penny-pinching to be rather difficult when she and her husband, Roy, embarked on an extended RV trip with a budget pegged at only $200 every thirty days. "It was rough,"

Pat wrote. "We wanted to eat out more, to use gasoline freely, to buy goodies to share with the folks we met along the way. But we couldn't do those things on our skinny wallet . . . we found the key factors to being happy on a slim income are to park near friendly people, where there are things to do that you enjoy. Just chatting a few moments each day with interesting neighbors can make you forget that you don't have much money to spend. And when you are busy at something you like, you are rich indeed, even if your pocketbook is empty."

Even sightseeing can be expensive, beginning full-timers learn when they visit popular tourist attractions. I talked with Mac and Alice Mc-Ginley about that, and Mac said, "One of the biggest transitions we had to make was ignoring the tourist traps. They want to sell you everything under the sun."

Alice added, "Two or three years ago, when we first started traveling full time, I felt like I couldn't go into an area without visiting every gift shop and looking at everything. But I soon discovered that every tourist shop has exactly the same thing. Now I can just look around and walk away, whereas before we started traveling full time I always had to buy something from every shop."

I asked, "Is that because you feel you don't need the items or because you feel you shouldn't buy them?"

She answered, "Basically, I feel now that I shouldn't buy them because we know just exactly how much money we have to spend. But a lot of that stuff is overpriced, and besides, we have everything we need in our trailer; we don't need all the odds and ends and junk that's offered for sale."

"Do you still find yourself buying gifts from shops like that?" I asked.

"Occasionally, yes, but I've cut that down considerably. I used to think I couldn't go home without spending an equal amount of money on everyone for gifts. Now, I don't do that."

CHECKS AND CREDIT CARDS

Handling money while on the road is one of the toughest problems facing full-time RVers. Nearly all full-timers, at one time or another, try using traveler's checks, with mixed results. A typical couple off on a seasonal trip will, for example, buy about $1,000 in traveler's checks for every $1,000 in cash they carry. They will divide the traveler's checks evenly between them, apportion out about half of the cash and hide the rest in what they hope is a safe place. Most never lose either their traveler's checks or their cash. But, they discover, in spite of assurances by friends, bank clerks and television commercials that the traveler's checks are acceptable everywhere, the checks are, at best, a nuisance and, at worst, difficult to cash.

"We tried traveler's checks," Mickey and Laila Rutledge told me while they were camped in Florida, "but getting a traveler's check cashed in a lot of places is just about as hard as cashing a personal check. Florida is one of the worst states about cashing traveler's checks *or* personal checks. Maybe they have more bad checks being cashed here than anywhere else. I don't know. It's particularly hard to cash traveler's checks in the Ft. Lauderdale area and on the West Coast."

"How do you adjust to that?" I asked.

Mickey replied, "We usually establish a bank account by depositing $100 in a local bank if we're going to be in that area a month or more. Opening that account seems to establish our credit, and then we have no problem cashing checks. I also carry two major credit cards, and I keep the limits at $1,500 because I can never know that I won't blow an engine or need major repairs of some kind. I use the credit cards about once every two months in order to keep the accounts open."

Individual reliance upon traveler's checks seems to depend upon whether the full-timer has ever had any problems, so they depend upon them heavily. "When we start out on a trip, we carry traveler's checks and cash," Mac reported, "and when those funds are exhausted, I just go into the nearest bank with a Visa card and get more cash. Then I can convert some of that cash into more traveler's checks. And as soon as I get the money, I send off a check to Visa so that my credit is kept at an excellent rating."

Alice reported, "We carry the Visa and a telephone credit card only for emergencies. Everything we do is on a cash basis, otherwise."

Most full-timers tend to use three or four money supply systems, including buying traveler's checks, opening accounts at local banks, carrying credit cards for emergencies and utilizing special services such as a check guarantee card (CGC) or Prestige account. Frank Salerno, for example, keeps open checking accounts both in his home state of Wisconsin and in the Rio Grande Valley of Texas, where he spends his winters. But on the road, he depends upon credit cards to resupply him with cash. "I've found the easiest thing is a credit card," he said. "I can stop at almost any little bank in any little town and get $400 or $500 quickly, and the cost is practically nothing. We always carry Master Charge and Visa cards, and I have never needed money, except on Sunday, that I couldn't get it."

Credit Buying

Since most U.S. banks participate in either the Visa or Master Charge system, holders of those cards can get cash advances of around $400 (and sometimes more, depending upon state laws). That money can be paid off either in monthly installments or at one time, with finance charges levied against the advance varying from state to state. Participating banks also cash personal checks of up to $100 to $150 for card holders. In addition, AMEXCO travel service offices cash checks of up to $500 for holders of American Express cards, but all but $50 of that money usually is in the form of traveler's checks. Many banks also honor CGC cards issued by the individual's home bank, although some full-timers have reported CGC cards are sometimes undependable tools for replenishing cash supplies. Finally, full-timers sometimes make use of letters written by bank officers on their stationery which state that the bearer is a valued customer who travels and that the bank will put a hold on any funds required following a telephone call.

Not surprisingly, the majority of full-time RVers do not use bank credit cards extensively; they rely on them primarily for emergencies because they are wary of "credit buying." Full-timer William Soule came to grips with that problem himself back in 1974 when he wrote one of the best articles on full-time travel financing ever to appear in *Trailer Life*. In his article, "Handling Your Money Away From Home" (February 1975), Bill admitted that he and his wife "make all possible purchases with our main bank credit card or, if necessary, with one of our other credit cards. For example, we normally even make gasoline and other service station purchases with our bank card. This procedure simplifies checking and paying bills each month."

But what about "the evils of credit buying"? To guard against it and also "to know where we're at, financially, at all times," Bill reported following an inflexible record-keeping system. "Each night, without fail, I post to a simple form all that day's purchases. I review our itinerary and activities against receipts, paid bills and jottings on a 3-by-5-inch card that I carry in my shirt pocket at all times. In this way, I make as certain as possible that we haven't overlooked any outlay. This regime is an acquired habit, and it takes real willpower not to skip one night's posting with the thought, 'Well, I'll do it tomorrow morning.' It is also extremely difficult to habitually accumulate some sort of record of each outlay during the day, especially when there is no receipt involved. This is where the 3-by-5 card is invaluable. Of course, it's not necessary to be accurate to the penny. If, after I review the day's sightseeing and shopping, a few unaccounted-for items pop up, I just make a reasonable estimate. The main consideration, to repeat, is the unfailing daily review and recording to each day's expenditures. Now, after long self-indoctrination, I post the day's expenses as automatically and conscientiously as I brush my teeth."

Bert Dean, a New Yorker who spends six months of every year in the sun of the Rio Grande Valley, established credit in Texas by opening a bank account in his wife's name. Her Social Security checks are then deposited in that account. But Bert said he does not depend upon bank checks for his money; he utilizes credit cards for most of his purchases, and he renews his cash supply by taking advances on his Master Charge and Visa accounts.

Walt and Charlotte Consider, who also travel extensively in the Southwest, handle their finances differently. "If we are going to be in an area for a month, two months or longer, I'll go to a local, full-service bank, open a savings account and write a check on my home bank account for the amount deposited in the local account. After that, I can write all the checks I want on my home bank account and get them cashed merely by putting my local savings account number on each check above or below my endorsement."

Walt reported, "Before we started full-timing, we heard a lot of talk about places where you couldn't get a check cashed and about other places where you had to wait five days after you deposited a check before you could make a withdrawal, and we've found places like those ourselves. But we also have been places where they would much rather take your personal, out-of-state check than to take Visa, Master Charge or a gasoline credit card."

"All over the Southwest," Charlotte added, "service stations would take personal checks before they would take bank credit cards."

I asked, "Do you try to use cash primarily and depend upon credit cards as little as possible?"

"We didn't last winter," Charlotte said. "We left the cash at home and used credit cards. Then we made one big payment at the end of each month." She said she and Walt do not use traveler's checks.

"I guess we have just a little advantage over everyone else because I'm retired from the Bell System," Walt said. "I have an I.D. card that gets us into any Bell System facility, and one of the benefits of being a Bell retiree is that we can go into any Bell commercial office and, by showing our I.D., cash a check."

Cashing Checks

Some full-timers run into quite a lot of difficulty cashing checks; others do not. I asked "Steamboat" Van Osdol, a Good Sam Club Sambassador, if he ever has difficulty. Steamboat was sitting just outside his trailer during the Connecticut State Samboree of 1980, and he replied, "It's funny you should ask that. I tried to cash a personal check here in Salem the day before yesterday, and they wouldn't even talk to me about it. Under no circumstances would they cash my check. This morning, I received my Good Sam check, and I went to a different bank to cash it; they didn't ask any questions; they just cashed it immediately. Earlier, in Virginia, I couldn't get a check cashed even with a lot of I.D."

Full-timer Jim Brown, on the other hand, said, "I have never run into a check-cashing problem, and I've had no problems with traveler's checks." Jim and his wife, Mary, were attending the international rally of the Holiday Rambler Recreational Vehicle Club in July, 1980, when a situation developed that they were certain would cause them financial difficulties. HRRVC director Howard Warren asked them to lead a late-summer caravan, and the Browns, who had intended to stop at a daughter's home after the rally in order to replenish their cash supply, were worried they would not have enough funds for the caravan. "I went to the bank here in Bemidji and told them who I was and what the problem was. I explained that I needed money for the caravan and asked if I could write a personal check for what I needed. I pointed out I would be here for a few days so the check would have time to clear my hometown bank. The banker said, 'That's fine,' and he gave us the money."

Cashing checks in communities where tourism is promoted or where RV rallies are held is generally rather easy, according to Don Rose, a retired oil company executive. But Don said cashing checks can be an adventure, and "I enjoy seeing what is going to happen." He reported, "On one Sunday before the opening of an NCHA rally in Florida, we had gone with many other couples to a local church where we were asked to stand and were welcomed. The next day, on our requesting to cash a check, the bank teller directed me to one of the vice presidents. He greeted me with: 'Didn't I see you in church yesterday?' Of course, I had no trouble. Another time we had stopped with another couple at a shopping center. I noticed a bank across the street and went over to try and cash a personal check. In all cases, the teller at the window will direct you to see someone at a nearby desk or office. In this case, the lady inquired, 'Are you here for the rally?' This was confirmed by my Holiday Rambler cap and name badge. 'What is your Holiday Rambler number?' was the second question. When I gave her the number, she looked it up in the Holiday Rambler Club member book and immediately okayed my check."

But ordinarily, cashing checks is a "big problem" to most full-timers, according to Hal and Penny Gaynor, a pair of former Connecticut Yankees who now travel all over the country conducting RV safety seminars at rallies. Hal reported, "There are two good systems, in my opinion—the Prestige account with a savings and loan association, and our system which involves a bank letter of credit. We've been with one bank in Connecticut for twenty-seven years, and even though we no longer live there, we still bank with that establishment by mail. In fact, our checks are even imprinted with our Pennsylvania mailing address. The bank provides us with a letter of credit—it's really a letter of introduction—which has the bank seal on it, and with one exception, our checks have been honored at any banks in the U.S. that have seen that letter. That one exception was a savings bank, and that was my own fault; I should have gone into a commercial bank.

"In St. Augustine, we stopped at a bank to cash a check for a couple of hundred dollars, and I gave the check and letter to a teller. She looked at it and said, 'Excuse me,' and she left with the letter. A few minutes later she came back and said, 'Follow me, please,' and took us into a vice president's office. He said, 'Welcome, Mr. and Mrs. Gaynor,' and he tried to sell us on the merits of St. Augustine as a good business city. Finally he asked, 'How big a loan do you need, Mr. Gaynor?' I said, 'I'm not after a loan. I just want to cash a check.' He was really impressed by that letter. He cashed our check, too."

The Prestige Account

The Prestige account mentioned by Hal is rapidly becoming the most popular bill-paying and check-cashing service among full-time RVers. Prestige savings account memberships are available through several thousand savings and loan offices around the country. No service charges are levied, and the memberships are free. Prestige accounts earn (as of late 1980) 5½% interest at most participating savings and loans, and deposits are insured by the Federal Deposit Insurance Corporation. Each member is given a Prestige card and assigned a number. Income such as pension and Social Security checks may be deposited automatically in the account and, by showing the Prestige card, a member can withdraw $200 (and sometimes more) from his account from any Prestige affiliate in the country. Several participating savings and loans also issue free money orders and traveler's checks to Prestige card holders. In addition, a full-timer can ask his affiliate savings and loan to pay his monthly bills and mail a check to anyone he designates on a withdrawal slip.

Ken and Flo Cooper of California are among full-time RVers who are using the Prestige account successfully. It helps them remain on "a cash basis for everything" while they're traveling around the country, Flo reported. When the Coopers retired, they asked Flo's mother to pay their bills for them, and Flo said, "We figured that it would be very difficult, if we charged a lot on the road, for my mother to keep up with the bills. Now, the only thing she has to worry about with charges are major things such as our repairs, tires or other large expenditures. The rest of the things we pay cash for. And the Prestige account enables us to do that."

Ken said, "My pension check goes into that account, and it draws interest all the time. What's unique about the account over a lot of other types of accounts is if you want money from other accounts, it costs you to verify that you have funds available. With Prestige, though, the affiliate savings and loan calls collect to your home branch, and it doesn't cost you a penny. Your savings and loan verifies who you are by getting on the phone with you and asking you a key question. For us, the question is Flo's mother's maiden name, which nobody else in the world knows; even I can't remember it. Once verification is given, the withdrawal is approved, and the bank writes us a check and then cashes it. We know about what it costs us each day to function, so if we feel we're going into an area that does not have a Prestige affiliate, we'll withdraw more money before we reach that area. We always draw out as little as possible so we can keep the account up and let it earn interest for us."

Flo said, "The Prestige account is designed to provide you with only $200 at a time. They will not claim to provide anyone with more than that, but some of the banks will allow more to be withdrawn; it depends upon the bank. We've been lucky. If I know we're going into an area where there aren't many Prestige branches and I ask for $400 or $600, most of the time I've gotten it."

Direct Deposit

Chris Moffett uses another kind of direct-deposit system that also is popular with full-timers. "I have a checking account at the Valley National Bank in Tucson, and my Social Security check goes right into it. I also have a brokerage account with Merrill Lynch, and its dividends and interest are automatically forwarded and deposited. I use Visa and Master Charge, and the bank pays those automatically and then notifies me every ten or fifteen days with an itemized list. Everything is sent to me in care of the mail forwarding service of the Holiday Rambler RV Club in Napannee, Indiana." Other full-timers use similar systems, but some have all income and bills sent directly to a friend or relative who has power of attorney to write checks on a joint bank account. Arrangements also can be made with banks to pay bills such as mortgage payments. Banks in most metropolitan areas give full-timers additional leeway in paying their bills by automatically depositing money for check overdrafts in increments of $50 and then charging those deposits against the individual's Master Charge account.

Trailer Life columnist Stan Christian has said several times that he opposes systems wherein the full-timer receives his funds through the mail from a relative, friend or forwarding service. "I consider this to be the least desirable method," he wrote in his column "Full-Timing Handbook," in June 1979. There are too many opportunities for these various checks to go astray, given the recent questionable performance of our postal service. Another problem is that you often have to stop traveling long enough for all of the checks to catch up to you. For folks who live 'close to the bone,' a lost or delayed check can be a mini-disaster, and the wear and tear on the nerves is just not worth it."

Like many other full-timers, Charles and Helen Mogg of Michigan have arranged for their income to be deposited directly into their bank account. "We have credit cards, but we're very, very careful with those because it's easy to overspend with credit cards. And it's just like borrowing in advance; if you don't pay it back next month, you'll start hurting, and it doesn't take very long until you're *really* hurting. I've found that nearly any bank will cash a check after a phone call to my home bank. I've also gotten cash by using a Penney's charge card and, with an Amoco Club card, I can get a check cashed at any Amoco service station. All of the Kroger stores will allow you to write a check as long as you have a Kroger check cashing card. Now, if you're in the South or you're passing through an area where there are no Kroger stores, you can go to the manager of nearly any supermarket and explain to him that you'd like to buy some groceries and write a check for the amount of the purchase. Nine times out of ten, he will let you write a check for your groceries. Montgomery Ward and Sears credit cards also are very good cards to carry. Most of those stores have auto repair departments in case you have any automotive problems, and you can be pretty sure those places aren't going to rip you off for work that they do."

Chapter Six

Structuring
A Budget

Mickey and Laila Rutledge have not held to a strict budget since they began traveling full time on the road in 1974, but Mickey keeps such a detailed log of their expenses that he knows exactly how much money they can spend from day to day. Mickey explains his insistence on meticulous record-keeping this way: "It's not that I resent what I spend. I just want to know where it went. Then if I have to cut $100, all I have to do is sit down and look at my books to know what we're going to cut." Mickey's records show him not only details such as money spent for groceries—he and Laila spent $1,207.70 for groceries in 1979, for example—but they also reveal how many miles he drives daily. They reveal his gas mileage, the amount of money he and Laila spend at restaurants, how much her hairdresser appointments cost and even how much they spend for stationery and postage stamps.

Most full-timers view detailed record-keeping as absolutely essential to their lifestyle, primarily because they live on fixed incomes and cannot afford to spend more than they have coming in. Also, by keeping ledgers, they are able to track subtle changes in prices rather closely and therefore avoid allowing themselves to get into unexpected financial binds. A ledger or log should focus primarily on such major expenses as campsites, food, gasoline, clothing, medical care and propane purchases. But records also should be kept on the following details: miles driven, fuel economy, telephone calls, postage, RV and tow vehicle repairs, photographic supplies, entertainment, liquor and soft drinks, tolls, tires and batteries, vehicle licenses and insurance, personal insurance, books and directories, laundry, gifts and fishing and hunting licenses.

The size, shape and structure of a ledger can be anything the individual using it wants it to be. We have, for example, adapted for our use a pocket-size "Auto Record Book" produced by Pratt & Austin Company of Holyoke, Massachusetts. It's an inexpensive little booklet only one-fourth inch thick inside a protective plastic cover. Inside the front cover are spaces for our names, address, telephone numbers, driver's license number, make and year of our vehicle, its engine identification number, the name and telephone number of our insurance company and our insurance policy number. Another page contains space for important information about our vehicle, such as its air filter number, fan belt number, tire size, tire pressures and spark plug gaps. Thirty-eight pages inside are blocked for recording gasoline purchases (both cost and gallons); oil purchases; lubes; tolls, and other travel related expenses. Two subsequent pages are provided for detailing "explanation of other costs," and two pages are provided for listing tax-deductible items. The booklet also includes space for an annual summary of vehicular expense, an advance planning calendar, numbers frequently called, accident report information and even a street intersection map for use in describing the scene of an accident. This log is kept in our motorhome and used when we begin a trip, when we make gasoline or other vehicle related purchases, and when we arrive at our destination. Entries are then lifted from the log monthly and recorded in an overall expense ledger.

One of the best and simplest expense ledgers I've ever heard about was designed by writer William Soule, who described his accounting system several years ago in a *Trailer Life* article ("Handling Your Money Away From Home," February 1975). He wrote, "I use a standard 12-column accounting form, easily obtainable at any stationery store, 8½ by 14 inches with 32 lines—one for each day of the month and one for totals. After I've labeled column headings and days of the month, I have some copies made and use one for the outlays for each month. I change the column headings from time to time as necessary, within the limits of twelve categories." His typical column headings are food, lodging, drugstore items, eating out, gasoline, postage and phone, propane, miscellaneous auto/trailer, miscellaneous operating expenses, miscellaneous travel expenses, periodic costs and nontravel costs. Under miscellaneous operating expenses, he lists items such as books, beer, haircut and laundry. Under miscellaneous travel expenses, he records photographic supplies, fishing license, museum fees and boat rental. Expenses recorded under periodic costs include hitch, tires, shoes and light fixtures; under nontravel items, gifts, contributions and jewelry.

Bill wrote, "One item I do not post each night is gasoline purchases. Instead, I record each such purchase when made, on a gas record form which I keep in the car. In the remarks column, or at the top or bottom of the page, I log anything else I do to the rig, such as oil changes, lubes, tires and other items purchased. As a result, in this one record I have a complete history of what and when since the day the car was purchased. I refer to it to see if it's time to change the oil or plugs, to see how long a tire lasted and to check gas mileage."

In addition to the above, you should know that *Trailer Life*'s Book Division is soon to publish the ultimate in ledgers for full-time RVers: the *RV Logbook*. This 250-page hardbound volume is patterned along the lines of the very popular yachting logbooks and contains every entry needed to keep a well-organized but simple-to-use record of life on the road . . . for three years running. You'll be hearing more about this invaluable book in the near future, and we urge you to obtain a copy when you do. For it is by far the best thing of its kind that I have ever seen.

BUILDING A NEST EGG

A full-timing couple that doesn't intend to work while traveling should count on having steady, dependable income from at least one of three primary sources: investments, pension funds or Social Security. Most early retirees, of course, cannot qualify for Social Security benefits, and those who can usually have to supplement that income with money from other sources. As for pension funds, those who have them are fortunate; those who don't . . . well, they just don't. Investments are another matter. They can be planned and structured rather quickly without the years of preplanning necessary for building pension funds. The base income for most full-timing couples is an investment portfolio built with funds from the sale of their house and possibly the sale of personal possessions such as furniture, tools and an automobile.

In today's real estate market, it is not unusual for a 55-year-old couple to own a house in which they have $50,000 or more worth of equity, even after real estate broker fees and capital gains taxes—if there are any—are paid. Add to that another $10,000 from savings and the sale of personal assets, and the couple has a tidy bundle available for investment in their own future. If those funds are invested in medium or short-term second mortgages, stocks, certificates of deposit or other money-market products that are, at that time, earning around 10% interest, the couple can realize an annual income of $6,000 a year from their nest egg.

That figures out to $500 a month in income, just in income, without touching the investment principal. Add to that another $300 or $400 a month from insurance policies and pension funds, and the couple has an income that is quite adequate for a comfortable RVing life on the road.

A Broker Talks To Full-Timers

Investment of a nest egg in order to earn maximum yield is something that should be done only after consultation with a financial advisor or stockbroker. Jay Wehr, a broker with the national firm of Merrill Lynch Pierce Fenner & Smith, Incorporated, addressed a group of aspiring full-timers on the subject of investments during the 1980 fall rally of the Jayco Jafari RV club, and some of what he told those RVers bears repeating here. He noted, "In the past, we were able to put our money into passbook savings, and it would accumulate so that, when we retired, it was a nice bundle that retained its spending power. I grew up with that type of philosophy, and it worked extremely well. Then around 1970, along came this animal called inflation. It has given us a lot of problems in that if you have a little more than 7% inflation annually for ten years, your dollar is worth only fifty cents. So you need to get 7% return on your investments to retain the spending power of your dollar."

Wehr said changes expected during the 1980s will provide better investment opportunities for individuals. "Some of the investments have been available for large institutions," he explained, "but the little guy had trouble. No one would pay any attention to his funds, and he couldn't get the high rates of interest that everybody else was getting." The 1980s will, for example, see a strong deregulation of the banking and savings and loan institutions, he said. "They have been very regulated, much to the detriment of the savings and loans because they've had a tough time keeping up. They'll be much more competitive with deregulation. So when that happens, check what the banks and the savings and loans offer. Their products are extremely safe."

Aspiring full-timers who need high returns on their investments should watch the cycles of the economy and tie their investments to those cycles. "The economy has a normal cycle every three to five years," he said. "Every three to five years, we see a recession, and in between, we have boom times when everybody makes a lot of money." He outlined for the Jayco owners several investment alternatives to consider.

"There are a lot of insurance products—very good ones at very low costs, and some at no cost at all—that can guarantee you a dollar amount for the remainder of your life or for a set number of years," he said. "There are a lot of newly created annuity products out; some cost nothing, and some cost something. But always remember: you'll never get something for nothing. The ones that cost you nothing to get into can levy a whale of a penalty when you want to get out."

As for the stock market, Wehr said there are definite bargains to be found for the diligent investor, and several good quality corporations consistently provide returns on investments that are significantly higher than prevailing rates of inflation. But he described the stock market as "a risk game" and said, "If you have funds set aside that you need a certain income from to support your lifestyle, I wouldn't take a risk with it." Utility stocks that yield 12% and increase dividends either annually or biannually are always available. "That's one way to fight inflation," he said, "but it's also risky. Back in the early '70s, utility stocks were trading for about double what they are today. They're paying more dividends than they were then, but if you have to sell them, you won't get out everything you put into them."

Real estate, he said, "has proven to be one of the best investments of all time. If it's providing you with rental income, terrific. If you know of bargain properties that can provide you with rental income for needy times, fine. As long as you stick with real estate, you'll know the value is going to keep up with inflation. It's a good investment. The only problem with it is liquidity. If you need money, you've got to move it at the going market rate, and in some areas, houses haven't been moving very rapidly."

On precious metals: "A lot of people are buying gold," Wehr noted, "but I have to say, up front, I'm not sure I understand the fundamental reasons why they're doing it. Forty percent of what is mined is hoarded, and there's no great commercial demand for gold. It used to be the standard of our society, and a lot of people believe it will be again. If you believe our economy is on a bad track and we will see another depression, you might want to consider buying some gold coins. Silver? With it, you're holding a coin that's not going to pay you any dividends or rental income, but there's only so much silver in the ground. It is 100% commercially used, with the exception of jewelry, and it is a commodity that has proven to increase in value quite a bit. Less than two years ago, it was $2 or $3 an ounce, and two days ago, it was $22 an ounce. It is precious, it most likely will retain its value and, considering inflation and the cost of goods ten years from now, it most likely will be worth more. It can be very liquid, very saleable, but make sure you buy it from a reputable dealer who will provide you with a market if you need to sell it and that you'll get a fair market value for it."

Regarding bonds and fixed-income securities, Wehr told us: "You can now buy six-month certificates of deposit, you can buy two-year CDs or four-year CDs or you have a multitude of other choices. You can go to any brokerage firm and buy any of nine different classes of bonds and even nonrated bonds that are okay but which have a much higher risk factor. Bonds, in the pre-1970s, were a good investment, just like passbook savings. You bought the bond, you hung onto it, it matured and you got your money back with a good rate of interest. In the mid-1960s, you could buy a bond that would give you a 4 to 5% yield. That was good. But along came high interest rates, and all of a sudden the people who spent $1,000 for some of those bonds saw them being worth $600 or $700. That can make you feel mighty nervous if you need to have that money. I believe you can lose as much money in bonds as you can in stocks."

He pointed out that in the spring of 1980, when interest rates were incredibly high, six-month certificates of deposit that paid 17% interest were offered. Those dropped rapidly as interest rates fell, however. With the economy back on track, CDs that yield 6 to 7% will be common, and that rate at least allows the investor to keep up with inflation, but Wehr said investors would be better off buying longer-term CDs—those termed at two or four years, for example—that yield higher rates of return. He also advised staggering investments so that one set matures in one three-month period, another matures the following three-month period and so on. "You won't get the top rates if you do that, but you'll be all around it, and you'll be doing at least as well as anybody else."

Before selecting a broker, he said, new investors should seek the advice of friends who have utilized the services of a broker successfully, and ask if they would recommend that person. Someone who just walks into a brokerage house and asks to be served could be assigned a broker who is inexperienced. "Any brokerage house will have tons of brochures lying around; pick them up and take them home to read; educate yourself and then go back with your questions."

The Deans: "We Supplement With Investments"

Investments can be the key to an active full-timing lifestyle, according to Greta and Bert Dean, who hit the road in 1975 after Bert took an early retirement from IBM. "The retirement income we get from the company is mediocre," he said. "It's something we have to supplement with investments in order to keep our heads above water." The Deans opted to invest in real estate, and when I interviewed them during the early part of 1980, they owned two rental properties in New York ("that we hang onto mainly as a hedge against inflation") and three condominium camp-sites at the Outdoor Resorts of America park near South Padre Island, Texas. They park their Silver Streak trailer on one site all winter and allow the ORA organization to rent out the other two to tourists. "When we leave here in June, our spot will be rented solid until we come back in the fall," Bert said. "Meanwhile, we're renting our properties back home to IBM World Trade people."

I asked Bert if he and Greta follow a budget, and I was surprised by his answer: "Yeah, but I'm probably different from most people you'll meet. I operate sort of like a government—we live on an overextended budget, and I use our investments to get us back out of the hole. Like right now, for example. I'm about $15,000 in debt, so I've got to sell a piece of property to pay that off. I've been doing that all my life. I've always had a knack for picking up investments and being able to make a few bucks here and there on real estate. I go in the hole as far as I can every chance I get to invest."

"Have you ever figured how much income you need to live the way you want?" I asked.

Bert answered, "I've always had everything I ever wanted. When I want something, I buy it, but most people don't operate like that. All I've ever had to have was the desire to get something, and I got it. I could figure out how much we spend, and it wouldn't be hard because I know the framework. I know how much it costs me to rent a campsite, how much it costs me for my RV and for my fuel, and I know about how much our food costs. But I've never really figured it out; never had to. We live very economically, especially here in Texas, where we can get some food at practically no cost. There's an abundance of fish, for example. The fishing boats go out into the Gulf and catch red snapper; they bring in bushels of snapper. If you know someone who's going, they'll usually bring you back some. But the boats bring back so much fish that they'll sell you what they don't want for almost nothing. And then there's gleaning. That's a popular pastime in Texas. The farmers harvest their crops—their onions, carrots and potatos, for example—with machines, and they let people go into the fields and pick up whatever vegetables are left, at no cost. That's called gleaning. I also fish off the bank (in a canal) behind the trailer and catch all the panfish I can eat. I always have a crab trap hanging over the edge of the wall into the channel, and it has three crabs in it now."

He added, "I don't know how much we're spending. Don't really care. But I know this: we're living high on the hog for peanuts. What we're doing is about the most inexpensive way possible to live, short of going out in the woods someplace and building a log cabin. Really, it doesn't cost me any money to live here (at the ORA park). This lot I'm sitting on cost me $9,000, and right now it's worth $25,000. I'm not living here for nothing; I'm being *paid* to live here."

Living On Less Than $1,000 Per Month

Jim and Mary Brown also did not follow a budget closely during the 2½ years they were on the road full time. (He is now business manager of the Holiday Rambler Recreational Vehicle Club). "I kind of just keep track of our expenses in our checkbook and use it as a sort of monthly statement," he told me just before ending his RVing adventure. "But I would say we spend roughly $1,000 a month. We could get by on a lot less than that if we didn't move around so much and camped in state parks more often. If we hadn't been so involved with the club (as an officer and caravan leader of HRRVC), we would have used the national and state parks more, and we could have saved some money and had more of an outdoor experience than we've had."

Frank Salerno said he and his wife, Agnes, also could get by on less money than they spend if they had to. "We spend about $1,300 a month, but only because we get $1,300 a month pension. If I got $1,200, we'd live on that; if we got $800, we could live on that. But I do not believe that, at this point in my life, I should be putting money away for a rainy day because this *is* my rainy day." Aspiring full-timers should realize, however, that they can live comfortably in an RV on less than $1,000 a month, he said.

Hal and Penny Gaynor, who have talked with hundreds of full-timers all over the country, agreed. "It can be done on a lot less than $1,000 a month," Hal said. "Someone camping in parks that don't cost $250 or more a month could get by on $700 quite easily."

Penny said, "But Hal, that depends upon how much socializing they do. A lot of people come into our trailer and ask, 'Penny, where do you keep your liquor?' And I show them a place where liquor could be kept, but we keep our files there. Don't misunderstand me; we have nothing against liquor. But it's something we don't buy. Then there is clothing. A lot of women dress very well, and they are constantly shopping for new clothes. Well, that's an expensive way to live, and I don't do that. I have a lot of clothes, but they're things I feel I can wear in the mud and rain if I have to; I wear them, wash them and wear them again. But even depending upon the differences of individual lifestyles, I'd say anybody can live full-time in an RV for $1,000 or less a month. I would say $1,000 is a lot of money."

HOW MUCH DOES IT REALLY COST?

The cost of full-time RVing is no secret. Magazines such as *Trailer Life* and *Motorhome Life* have carried articles regularly for several years detailing the budgets of active full-timers and illustrating how inexpensive the RVing way of life is. Full-timers themselves are also happy to share the intricacies of their budgets with other people who are considering joining the lifestyle. Unfortunately, I discovered when I began my research on full-time RVing in the mid-1970s that no one had ever surveyed a large cross-section of way-of-lifers in an effort to determine exactly how much money the aspiring full-timer should expect to spend. Aspirants, as a result, estimated they would need between $500 and $2,000 a month income in order to live comfortably in their RVs. I even talked with one couple who said they were planning to spend $3,000 a month.

Back in 1976, *Trailer Life* created a flurry of interest among its subscribers when it published a pair of articles under the banner, "Believe-It-Or-Not Budgets For Full-Time Rving." One article reported on how a couple from California tried—and apparently succeeded—to live on $200 a month in a 16-foot travel trailer. The other article was written by a couple who spent $450 a month in 1975 while living in a 22-foot trailer. Such budgets were, without question, difficult to follow in 1975 and 1976; today, they would be nearly impossible.

Notice that I said "nearly impossible." As unbelievable as it seems in this day of double-digit inflation and high-priced gasoline, I know of single RVers who are living on as little as $200 a month and enjoying themselves. And I've interviewed full-timing couples with incomes of under $500 a month. Those people are definitely not the norm, however.

The average full-time RVing couple, in 1980, lived and traveled in a 27- to 32-foot-long travel trailer, a 32- to 40-foot-long fifth-wheel trailer or a 28- to 32-foot motorhome. They spent between six and nine months of the year in the Sunbelt, most of that time in one or two parks where they rented campsites by the month. They drove considerably fewer than 20,000 miles a year, and they lived on incomes of between $800 and $1,000 per month. About half of them owned home bases somewhere; the rest lived exclusively in their RVs. A large percentage of them retired from their jobs early; 100% of them wished they had done it earlier.

That rather general profile of today's full-time RVing couple was compiled following my four years of research into the full-timing lifestyle. There are thousands of exceptions to that profile, of course, and I have reported various ones of those later in this book. But I think the portrait I've painted of the typical full-time RVer is accurate. These typical full-timing couples live by budgets that are rather simple, and so can be used as guides by nearly anyone who aspires to be an RV way-of-lifer. On the following pages, I have compiled four sets of budgets using representative figures provided to me by active full-timers. The budgets relate to incomes of $500, $750, $1,000 and $1,250 per month, and they follow, with some important modifications as you'll see, the itemized cash outlays reported in Chapter Five: 25% of income for lodging, up to a maximum of $6.25 per day; 30% for food, up to a maximum of $7.50 per day; 35% for transportation; 3% for clothing, to a maximum of $20 per month; 3% for medical care; 2% for propane to a maximum of $20 per month, and 2% for personal expenses.

NOTES ON $500 BUDGET

Although the $4 budgeted for campsites represents 25% of the $500-per-month income, translated to daily expenditures, it obviously is not enough to pay for campsites over a long term. Therefore, anyone attempting to follow this budget would have to keep his campsite fees as close to the $4 figure as possible and, meanwhile, be alert for ways to cut expenses in other budgeted areas. Couples who live on $500 per month told me they practice boondocking as often as possible; that is, they camp in wilderness areas or areas not designated for public camping where there are no overnight charges. They also trade off work for free camping space, and they camp on property owned by friends and relatives as often as possible.

The $175 per month budgeted for transportation expenses is adequate if the RVers plan their driving carefully. If their RV or tow vehicle gets 10 miles per gallon of gasoline and gasoline averages $1.20 per gallon, they can drive up to 1,000 miles each month and still have $75 or $80 left for repairs, tires, batteries, licenses and insurance. For every 100 miles under that 1,000 miles they drive, they can add $10 or $12 to their balance sheet for nontransportation items such as campsites, food, clothing or personal items.

The $5 per day budgeted for food is only marginally adequate for couples who do not eat out often and who watch grocery bills carefully.

$500 Per Month Budget		
	Per Day	Per Month
Campsites	$4.00	$125.00
Transportation	$5.83	$175.00
Insurance, Licenses		
Fuel		
Repairs		
Tires, batteries		
Food	$5.00	$150.00
Groceries		
Restaurants		
Laundry, Clothing	$ .50	$ 15.00
Medical	$ .50	$ 15.00
Propane	$ .33	$ 10.00
Personal Expenses	$ .33	$ 10.00
Phone		
Postage		
Photography		
Liquor, Entertainment		
Personal insurance		
Supplies		
Books, directories		
Miscellaneous		

That $5 can be increased slightly, however, by holding down expenses for budgeted items such as fuel, clothing and propane. On the other hand, the $15 clothing allowance is a somewhat generous amount for beginning full-timers because they will be able to use wardrobes built up over several previous years, and clothing replacement should not be an expensive item for them. They will have to schedule trips to the laundry so that they can stay within their budget. The $15 per month medical care allowance simply is not adequate. It presupposes that both members of the full-timing team are healthy, and it is intended as a fund to be built up in case of emergencies. The $10 per month propane allowance is adequate only if the full-timers spend all year in relatively warm climates so that they have to use their furnace just on cold nights. The $10 personal expense allowance also is not adequate; it can be increased slightly by reducing fuel expenses, but even so, it will remain a budget area without much flexibility. Purchase of a nonresident fishing license, for example, can blow a whole month's allowance.

NOTES ON $750 BUDGET

Years of research into full-time RVing has convinced me that nearly anyone can enjoy a life on the road if he is motivated strongly enough, even though his or her income might be extremely low. Low-income full-timers have told me that they are able to enjoy a more comfortable lifestyle RVing full-time than if they had tried to live on the same amount of money in a traditional lifestyle. Obviously, though, there is some income level at which strict economizing is no longer necessary and RVing becomes a truly pleasurable adventure. I believe that level begins with a $750 per month income. Why? A couple with an income of $750 doesn't have to scrimp to pay for campsites or food—two of the basic requirements of "the good life"—and they also have more money for travel.

Let's look at that $750 per month budget. Remember that earlier estimate that full-timers spend an average maximum of $6.25 per night for campsites? Well, 25% of $750 (25% representing the portion of income typically spent by full-timers for camping fees) is $187.50 per month, or almost exactly $6.25 per day for campsites. Finding campsites that average $6.25 a day over a long period is not difficult, particularly if the couple spends several weeks at a time in one park and rents their site at a lower-than-daily rate. Again, some adjustments can be made by occasional stops at free or very inexpensive places and by parking on property owned by friends and relatives.

$750 Per Month Budget

	Per Day	Per Month
Campsites	$6.25	$187.50
Transportation	$8.75	$262.50
Insurance, Licenses		
Fuel		
Repairs		
Tires, batteries		
Food	$7.50	$225.00
Groceries		
Restaurants		
Laundry, Clothing	$ .66	$ 20.00*
Medical	$ .75	$ 22.50
Propane	$ .50	$ 15.00
Personal Expenses	$ .50	$ 15.00
Phone		
Postage		
Photography		
Liquor, Entertainment		
Personal insurance		
Supplies		
Books, directories		
Miscellaneous		$ 2.25

*Maximum level reached, so $2.25 per month surplus assigned to miscellaneous expense.

As for transportation expense, a $750 monthly budget allows extensive travel, based on the formula that a typical full-timing couple lays out 35% of their annual income for transportation-related expenses (fuel, repairs, tires, batteries, vehicle licenses and insurance). As noted in the budget chart, $750 per month allows the couple to spend $262.50 for transportation. If $200 of that is used for fuel (average cost, $1.20 per gallon) and the couple averages 10 miles per gallon with their driving, they are able to travel 1,650 miles per month, or, 19,800 miles each year. Of course, if they reduce their driving below that level, the savings that they experience in fuel costs, repairs, tires and batteries can be assigned to other areas of their budget such as the Personal Expense section. A $750 budget, therefore, provides them with a degree of flexibility that the couple living on a $500 per month budget did not have.

Remember, again, that full-time couples average spending 30% of their budget for food—up to a maximum monthly figure of $225, or $7.50 per day. A $750 monthly budget allows them to achieve that maximum level naturally, without scrimping; the couple does not, in effect, have to worry much about where their next meal is coming from so long as they can stay within their budget.

The first surplus of funds—admittedly a very tiny one—appears in the clothing and laundry section of the $750 budget. My research has shown that full-timers spend 3% of their income for clothing and laundry, up to a maximum of $20 per month. Since 3% of $750 is $22.50, the clothing allowance fund has $2.25 more in it than is needed. In the budget chart, I have assigned that $2.25 to Miscellaneous Personal Expenses. The medical care, propane and personal expense sections of the $750 budget are inadequate, but only marginally so, and each of those funds can be supplemented at times with surpluses from the campsite, transportation or even food sections so that a style of life is significantly more comfortable than one permissible with only $500 a month income.

NOTES ON $1,000 BUDGET

This budget illustrates, I think, how comfortably an RVing couple can live on a moderately good income of only $1,000 a month. Actual surpluses are possible in two primary areas—campsites and food—as well as in the more minor area of clothing and laundry allowance. In all three cases, the surpluses have been channeled into the Personal Expense section, thereby hiking that fund to such a degree that a relatively gen-

$1,000 Per Month Budget

	Per Day	Per Month
Campsites	$ 6.25	$187.50*
Transportation	$11.66	$350.00
Insurance, Licenses		
Fuel		
Repairs		
Tires, batteries		
Food	$ 7.50	$225.00**
Groceries		
Restaurants		
Laundry, Clothing	$ .66	$ 20.00***
Medical	$ 1.00	$ 30.00
Propane	$ .66	$ 20.00
Personal Expenses	$ 4.75	$142.50
Phone		
Postage		
Photography		
Liquor, Entertainment		
Personal insurance		
Supplies		
Books, directories		
Miscellaneous		

*Maximum level reached; $37.50 assigned to personal expenses.
**Maximum level reached; $75.00 assigned to personal expenses.
***Maximum level reached; $10.00 assigned to personal expenses.

erous amount of money is available for the couple to spend any way they wish. The surpluses include $37.50 beyond the amount needed for camp-sites; a whopping $75 above a typical family's food costs, and $10 more than is usually needed for clothing and laundry.

With $350 budgeted for transportation expense, the couple could buy $275 worth of gasoline every month and still have enough money left to take care of repairs, tires, insurance, and other expenses. That $275 would enable the couple to travel approximately 2,300 miles each month—or about 27,600 miles a year—on gasoline priced at $1.20 per gallon. That should be enough driving to satisfy nearly any full-timer's wanderlust. With $1,000 of income every month, there also is enough money ($20 per month) for the couple to buy about as much propane as they want without restricting their travels just to warm climates, and the $30 per month medical care allowance is more realistic than the amounts budgeted with lower incomes.

NOTES ON $1,250 BUDGET

A monthly income of $1,250 ensures freedom, comfort and luxury almost beyond belief for the average full-time RVing couple. Couples that I have interviewed with incomes in the $1,200 or higher range claim they have more money than they need and that they save several hundred dollars a year which they either salt away in investments or allow to accumulate until they can take a special trip such as a boat cruise or a European excursion. RVers fortunate enough to have incomes in the $1,250 per month range can travel nearly as extensively as they want, since they have $447.50 each month to use on travel related expenses. The budget I have outlined here provides $225 per month for food, but such a couple could spend a fair amount more than that if they enjoy eating out frequently. The budget also sets aside an adequate, but rela-tively small, amount of money ($20 each month) for clothing, and couples who do eat out a lot probably would want to spend more than I've bud-geted in order to buy new clothes more frequently. Medical care funds are adequate but still assume both members of the full-timing team are in good health. The propane expense allowance is sufficient for nearly all needs, and the money allocated for personal expenses is exceptionally generous because it has been supplemented by surpluses from campsite, food and clothing allowances.

$1,250 Per Month Budget		
	Per Day	**Per Month**
Campsites	$ 6.25	$187.50*
Transportation	$14.92	$447.50
Insurance, Licenses		
Fuel		
Repairs		
Tires, batteries		
Food	$ 7.50	$225.00**
Groceries		
Restaurants		
Laundry, Clothing	$ .66	$ 20.00***
Medical	$1.25	$ 37.50
Propane	$ .83	$ 25.00
Personal Expenses	$7.25	$217.50
Phone		
Postage		
Photography		
Liquor, Entertainment		
Personal insurance		
Supplies		
Books, directories		
Miscellaneous		

*Maximum level reached; $24.00 assigned to personal expenses.
**Maximum level reached; $150.00 assigned to personal expenses.
***Maximum level reached; $17.50 assigned to personal expenses.

A WORKING BUDGET OF $803

Now let's take a look at an actual budget followed by a South Carolina couple who have been full-timing for seven years. When they began full-timing, they had an income of $660 per month, and they lived on that quite comfortably. Fortunately, as the cost of living increased, their income did too, thanks to some adroit reinvestment of capital by the husband. As of the summer of 1980, their monthly income totaled $803, and every dollar of that was budgeted, although not always spent. Their budget is very similar to the ones I have used on these pages except they have two additional areas of expenses budgeted under what they call Personal Costs; they put aside money every month for highway tolls and for fishing licenses.

They have learned by experience that they will spend, over the year, about $185 per month for campsites. Actually, they lay out a little less than that because they enjoy camping in very inexpensive state parks in Minnesota and Wisconsin every summer, but they budget $185 a month anyway. They do not travel a great deal, in comparison with some other full-timers, but they put between 12,000 and 14,000 miles each year on their Ford pickup truck, both towing their 31-foot trailer with it and driving it solo. So they put aside $150 every month for fuel and add $20 to a repair fund, $10 for tires and batteries, and $45 for vehicle licenses and insurance—a total of $225 per month for travel related expenses. They eat most of their meals in their trailer and seldom eat in restaurants except for the occasional hamburger the husband buys at noon from the snack bar at the campground where they spend their winters. Therefore, they budget $225 per month for groceries and $10 per month for the husband's occasional sandwiches. Their groceries usually cost closer to $200 a month, though, so they often have an extra $25 for eating out.

The couple puts aside $18 a month for clothes and laundry, but they told me they've never spent that much. Their trailer is equipped with an apartment-size washer/dryer, so their laundry expenses are minimal. The wife is a very well dressed woman, but she said she shops for her clothes at flea markets and at clothing manufacturers' warehouse outlets. Both husband and wife are in excellent health, so although they budget $25 per month for medical care, they've seldom used those funds, and their medical kitty now contains several hundred dollars, on which they're drawing interest because it is deposited in a bank in South Carolina.

The couple's propane expenses run rather high some months of the year because they like to spend their summers, and part of every spring, in Minnesota where the nights are cool. However, because their winters

One Couple's $803 Budget		
	Per Day	**Per Month**
Campsites	$6.16	$185.00
Transportation		
Insurance, Licenses	$5.00	$150.00
Fuel	$ .66	$ 20.00
Repairs	$ .33	$ 10.00
Tires, batteries	$1.50	$ 45.00
Food		
Groceries	$7.50	$225.00
Restaurants	$ .33	$ 10.00
Laundry, Clothing	$ .60	$ 18.00
Medical	$ .83	$ 25.00
Propane	$ .66	$ 20.00
Personal Expenses		
Phone	$ .33	$ 10.00
Postage	$ .17	$ 5.00
Photography	$ .33	$ 10.00
Liquor, Entertainment	$ .33	$ 10.00
Personal insurance	$ .33	$ 10.00
Supplies	$ .33	$ 10.00
Books, directories	$ .17	$ 5.00
Fishing Licenses	$ .17	$ 5.00
Tolls	$ .17	$ 5.00
Miscellaneous	$ .83	$ 25.00

are spent around Myrtle Beach and in Florida, they do not use much propane then. They budget $20 per month for LP-gas and sometimes have to supplement that with an extra few dollars borrowed from another part of their budget. One area of their budget that they watch very closely, however, is the Personal Cost section. They budget $10 monthly for occasional telephone calls to their children, $5 for postage to keep in touch with friends by mail, $10 for color film and slide processing, $10 for entertainment (neither drinks alcoholic beverages except for an occasional bottle of wine), $10 to replenish supplies in the trailer, $5 for paperback books and magazines and an annual *Trailer Life RV Campground & Services Directory,* $5 for fishing licenses, $5 for highway tolls and $25 for miscellaneous expenses (such as fishing lures, charcoal and gifts for the grandchildren).

TRY BOONDOCKING

Back in 1975, when Pat and Roy Kenoyer set out to RV full time on $200 a month (see "RVing on $200 a Month," *Trailer Life,* April 1976), they discovered that one of the keys to conserving funds while on the road was to park in either free or inexpensive campgrounds as often as possible. While most RVers today don't hanker for the spartan lifestyle experienced by the Kenoyers, some of the methods they used to save money in 1975 can be considered today by RVers who need to play catch-up with their money supplies. "We found the key factors to being happy on a slim income are to park near friendly people where there are things to do that you enjoy," Pat wrote in her *Trailer Life* article. "Just chatting a few moments each day with interesting neighbors can make you forget that you don't have much money to spend." While holed up in a free or inexpensive camping spot, Pat said, she and her husband tried to stretch their funds by eating fish they caught themselves and gleaning free food wherever possible.

She reported, "At Blythe, California, it was cantaloupe, and in the Yuma, Arizona, area we got lettuce and dates. Then there were other foods we purchased at very low prices. In Yuma we got walnuts for 29 cents a pound. Shelled and put into those free dates, the walnuts gave us a treat as grand as any millionaire could afford." Pat also reported, "Propane is another expense a person can save on. We used one five-gallon bottle per month. We didn't use our oven, made toast and baked biscuits in a cast-iron skillet on top of the stove, heated water in a kettle on the burner and stayed in warm areas during the winter months so we used little fuel heating our trailer."

Full-timers find adventure panning for gold in Colorado's fast-running rivers.

RVers quickly learn they can save money for emergencies by spending their spare time in free pursuits: fishing, hiking, rockhounding, painting, bird watching, playing games such as Scrabble, exploring museums and libraries and inventing unusual diversions. Few full-time RVers, except possibly those who are very well off financially, can travel and live as if they were simply on a short vacation. Charles and Helen Mogg, for example, have a good income that totals about $1,000 a month. "But," Charles said, "we don't have too much left out of that, especially if we do much of anything. We spent last winter in Florida and didn't travel much, and we gained on our money supply. But I don't believe anyone on a $1,000 budget can travel twelve months of the year, and I don't believe they can afford to stay all the time in the most expensive campgrounds. They've got to find something cheaper to stay in part of the time. That way they can put back enough money so that they can travel another two or three months."

Full-timers Maurice and Evelyn Parker search out free camping as often as possible while they're traveling the country. They bought a book that lists free and inexpensive campsites, and they frequently spend two-week periods camped in U.S. Army Corps of Engineers parks where, as senior citizens, they qualify for a pass entitling them to camp for $2 a night with electrical and water hookups. "There are no activities in those parks except for fishing, hiking and bike riding," Maurice said, "but they're good places to go when we want our income to catch up with our expenses."

Mickey and Laila Rutledge see other full-timers such as the Parkers every summer while they work as attendants at Corps of Engineer parks. "We see a tendency for full-time trailerists with big rigs to spend more time in those parks during the summer," Mickey said. "With the price of gasoline being what it is, people on fixed incomes have to cut somewhere, and they are cutting expenses on some of their overnight stops. We've seen people come in and spend two weeks at $1.75 a night. They pick up enough slack in their finances that they can move on and continue to travel."

Chapter Seven

Home
Base

No one has ever satisfactorily defined the expression "full-time RVer," although definitions have been debated around campfires for many years. Clearly, anyone who lives and travels permanently in a recreational vehicle is a full-time RVer. But is he a full-timer if he parks that RV in one spot and lives in it there, never venturing away from his campsite with it? Is he a full-timer if he lives in an RV half the year and spends the other half in a house? Is he a full-timer if he owns a mobile home lot in one place and splits his year between living there and traveling around the country in an RV? Is he a full-timer if he spends nine months of the year in a house and ventures away from home for three months every summer? The debate over which of these are and which of these are not full-timers probably will never be resolved completely, but I had to resolve it in my own mind before beginning this book because I wanted to limit my investigations strictly to individuals and couples who are bonafide full-time RVers.

I concluded there are four distinct categories of full-timers. First, there is the person whose only home is his RV; he lives in it all the time, and he takes it nearly everywhere with him. He is the purist among full-timers, and he tends to regard nonpurists with a little bit of disdain, as if they haven't the courage to pursue the total freedom that he sees himself as enjoying. He is a little like the fly rod fisherman who wouldn't consider impaling a worm on a hook in order to catch a trout, and who is contemptuous of anyone who would do that.

Second, there is the person who lives in his RV nearly all the time, but he has a home base that he visits once or twice a year in order to resupply his wardrobe, replenish his larder and tie up loose financial ends. He sees himself as a little more practical-thinking than the purist because he can avoid carrying all of his possessions with him all the time.

Third, there is the RVer who travels nearly the year around, but he has a permanent house or mobile home that he not only uses as a home base, but which he actually lives in for periods of time ranging from a couple of weeks to a few months. He considers himself to be the most practical of all full-timers because he has a home and furniture that he can return to if health, fuel or financial problems force him to give up his life on the road; he views the purist full-timer as being foolhardy and someone who will eventually suffer for sticking to the concept of keeping no possessions except his RVing rig.

Finally, there is the individual who owns or rents one or two pieces of property, and he travels back and forth seasonally between northern areas and southern areas. While traveling, he lives in his RV; while parked, he may either live in the RV or in a mobile home on one of the lots. Although most of his travel is on a straight line between the point south and the point north, he does explore outward in his RV, always using those points as bases to which he will return periodically.

There is a fifth group of RVers who live in a permanent home eight or nine months of the year and travel the other three or four months. This group also includes the breed of RVers who call themselves "snowbirds" because they spend their winters in the sunbelt, or "winter Texans" because they escape cold weather by journeying south to the Rio Grande Valley of Texas. They like to refer to themselves as full-time RVers, but they are not. They are RV vacationers. A man from Iowa who plants and harvests corn every year on his 300 acres and then travels south for the winter is not a full-time RVer; he is a full-time farmer who, because of his special circumstances, can take a longer vacation than his friends who have jobs in offices, stores and factories. A retired couple from Indiana who leave their friends, family and home every fall and tow their trailer to Florida certainly deserve the label of "snowbirds," but they are not full-time RVers; they are vacationing retirees—part-time RVers.

Obviously, then, my definition of a full-timer hangs very precariously by the thread of whether the RVer has a permanent, full-time residence; if he does not, generally he can be considered a full-time RVer. But don't confuse "permanent residence" with "permanent home base." Many full-time RVers—in fact, considerably more than half—have home bases. Often their bases are houses that once were their residences, but sometimes the home bases are simply apartments or small lots on which mobile homes or storage sheds are stationed.

Where Is Home?

The problem facing most aspiring full-timers is not whether they should have a home base, but rather, whether they should keep their home and use it as a base. Because the disadvantages of doing that are almost as great as the advantages, their decision is a difficult one. Here are some of the major advantages to keeping a home as a base: it is a good investment and will increase in value; it is a good place for keeping furniture and possessions that might be needed after a life on the road is no longer feasible; it is a familiar place to return to if full-time RVing has to end; it is an important link to old friends, relatives and familiar surroundings, neighborhoods and stores. But those advantages must be weighed against the disadvantages of keeping it: the equity in the home can be used to finance the full-timing lifestyle and make life on the road more comfortable; upkeep on a home is expensive and time-consuming; an empty house often is the target of vandals and burglars; taxes can be a drain on finances, and meeting mortgage payments if the house is not paid for can be difficult with the reduced income of a full-time RVer.

There also is no easy answer to the question of where RVers should maintain their home base if they decide to sell their home and utilize a storage shed, a house, a mobile home, an apartment or some other form of headquarters elsewhere. Location of a home base actually depends upon the travel habits and special circumstances of the individual RVer. Consideration should be given, however, to factors such as the state and local taxes that can be levied against the base; the local cost of living, and whether the location is within reasonable driving distance of the RVers' primary destinations. Tax information is compiled annually by the American Association of Retired Persons, 1909 "K" Street NW, Washington, DC 20049, in its booklet "State Tax Facts," while comparisons of living costs are prepared each year by the Bureau of Labor Statistics, Office of Information, Room 1539, GAO Building, 441 "G" Street NW, Washington, DC 20212, in its publication, "Budget Estimates for Retired Couples."

"Home Is The USA"

Experienced full-timers agree that a home base should be located in an area where the individual or couple would like to live permanently if and when The Good Life of traveling full time is concluded. But selection of such a locale is very difficult, especially for RVers who have traveled extensively and who have several—maybe even dozens—of favorite destinations. I discussed the problem one evening with Hal and Penny Gaynor, a couple of "purist" full-timers who write travel columns for several regional RV newspapers and who conduct RV safety clinics around the country.

"Our home is the USA," Hal told me. "We have one address—a son's address—that we file our federal income tax from. And, because we get so much mail related to our columns, we use a campground as our national mailing address. But we have no home except for whatever trailer we're living in."

Penny reported, "People say to me, 'Penny, you're getting older; you've been on the road for nine years now, and you *are* nine years older. You'll have to settle down some day. When and where are you going to do it?' But you know something, Don, I don't know where in these beautiful United States I would want to live. Every place we've been is special. Florida is great in the wintertime; I don't like it in the summer. The northeast is lovely in the summer; I don't want the snow in the winter. California is great at times, but . . . I just don't know where I'd want to settle."

Hal interrupted. "When people ask me that, I say, 'I want to settle in the United States.'"

"I don't know what is going to happen tomorrow," Penny continued, "but I know I am not ready to move back into a house. I have everything for comfort that I could want in this trailer, this 'house,' as I call it. I have some discomfort sometimes, of course. I have to do without water if we run out, for example. But what we have more than makes up for whatever little discomforts there are. At night we sleep with the windows open, and the breeze comes in with all those wonderful outdoor smells—the trees and the flowers and the grass. When I get up in the morning and I'm not happy with where I am, I can go to another campground. If I don't like *it*, I can go to another one."

"There are pros and cons to having a home base," Hal said. "One reason for having a base is, because of federal income taxes, you need an address. We have that; my son's home. Secondly, you need some place to receive your mail. Rather than have ours forwarded, I elected to receive ours through the Circle M Ranch campground in Lancaster, Pennsylvania, because I wanted to be able to give people a telephone number to call. We call the Circle M our base camp, but it's that only insofar as our mail is concerned. The people at the campground like the publicity they get from us, and they give us excellent service. Any of our family members or friends can call there and leave a message or say they want to get in touch with us, and the campground people will tell them where we are."

The Gaynors considered keeping their family home as a base when they decided to travel full time. "We lived in a college town," Penny said, "and it would have been easy for us to rent the house to a college professor. But we would have had to put our furniture and stuff into storage and maybe depended upon neighbors to help take care of the property, so I said, 'Hal, we have made up our minds to go full-timing; let's do it right.' And we did. We got rid of the house and stored some furniture. I won't say I wasn't worried about that decision. We were experienced campers, but doing it full-time was something else, and I convinced myself that if we didn't like it after a year or two we could always move into another home. So for five years, we stored things that I didn't want to sell, and finally Hal said, 'Penny, do you realize what it's costing us to store those things?' And we got rid of everything."

"It's A Nice Little Nest"

Dick and Helen Bright had been full-timing two years when I interviewed them in the summer of 1980, and they were still somewhat undecided about what to do with their home in Newark, Delaware. They used it as their home base during their first year on the road, and their daughter and her husband lived in it the second summer while their house was being built. "It was empty all last year when we were away," Dick reported. "The neighbors looked after it; we paid them a little to cut the grass and shovel the snow. It's a nice little nest for us to go back to, but I've been trying to convince Helen for a year that we should sell it."

"The mortgage on it is so low, now," Helen said, "and besides, I don't think we'd make enough by selling it and investing the money. It's in a very nice neighborhood, too, and this is the first time we've ever had a house where we could make close friends. We spent twenty years of our lives traveling with the army. When you spend a year here and two years there, you just don't make close friends. We've been in that home fifteen years now, and it's the first real home we've ever had. I always look forward to going back to it. I was glad to go back after we were in Florida all winter. And keeping it is not that big of an expense."

Harry and Juanita Jennings kept their home in North Carolina when they joined the full-timing lifestyle, and although they use it as a home base, they said they would prefer not to have it. The forty-year-old couple work while traveling, however, and Harry said business dictates that he maintain a home base. But he does not have time to keep up with repairs, so the house is a problem to him. He told me he was considering whether he should sell the house and use another property he owns as a home base or whether he should rent out the house. "If I weren't in business, we wouldn't bother to have a home base. We're there only twice a year. In October, when we head south, we stop there for about two weeks, and then we're off again. On the way back north in April, we stop again for a couple of weeks."

Although Mickey and Laila Rutledge have been full-time RVers since 1974, they have never quite decided what they should do about either keeping or selling their family home in Louisville. They discuss their options frequently. "It's a question that's always been with us," Mickey told me while I was camped near them in Florida in January, 1980. "We don't know what we'll do. The property is still increasing in value, but it's costing us money to keep it. On the other hand, there's no way we could replace it for what we have in it."

I asked, "Do you keep it primarily because it is a good investment?"

Mickey answered, "Not altogether. Last year we thought we were going to sell it. Then when we left Florida in the spring, we saw what was happening to the price and supply of gasoline. The stations were limiting purchases to $10 or ten gallons. Who knows where that's going to end? It may get so that gasoline costs $2.50 a gallon, and if it does, it will be impossible for us to move around. So we decided to keep our house as a place to go back to in case we have to get off the road."

I asked Laila, "When you do go back home, are you glad to be there or can you hardly wait to leave again?"

"I have mixed emotions," she admitted. "I love the house. But I never want to stay there very long."

"Is it just the idea of having that nest there, or do you miss the possessions that you've collected over the years?" I asked.

She said, "I think that's it. The possessions. I hate to part with things."

Mickey added, "We've talked with a lot of people who have gone full-timing, and it always seems to be the women who want to keep their houses; they tend to miss a home more than a man does." One valuable aspect of a home base, he said, is that full-timers can return to it period-ically to unload and resupply. "Even so, it's hard for us to limit what we carry. Invariably, we overpack and take more stuff on the road with us than we need. People get attached to things, and that's why it's a big decision to break away and get rid of everything. Having a home base has its tax advantages too. When I'm working here in Florida, I'm working away from home, and I can deduct my travel expenses to here and a certain amount of expenses while I'm living here."

"The Base Was A Nuisance"

Health problems, including open heart surgery, forced Mac McGinley to retire when he was in his mid-forties. Since their children were grown, he and his wife Alice sold their thirteen-room house prior to deciding to become full-time RVers. "We were camping every weekend, and the house was too much for her to keep up. I couldn't do the labor I used to do, either, so we sold it and moved into a townhouse. Then after the surgery I couldn't walk up and down the stairs there, so we divided the furniture among the children on a lend-lease basis and moved into our trailer."

I asked, "What do you mean, you divided the furniture on a 'lend-lease basis'?"

Mac answered, "We knew something could happen to one of us and that the other one probably would want to move into an apartment again. We loaned out the furniture until then because we had pieces we couldn't replace—like a solid cherry dining room outfit—and if we sold it, we could never buy it back again."

He added, "Now, we keep a lot in a mobile home park in Greenville, Mississippi. We have a storage shed there where we keep changes of clothing, equipment and a few other things, and we rent a post office box in Greenville. I pay $45 a month for the lot, complete with sewer, water and electricity, and the people who operate the park watch my equipment. We go here each year to harvest pecans, then we winter in Fort Meyer, Florida."

"Haven't you found it a handicap to travel without a house or an apartment as a home base?" I asked.

"No, we haven't," he answered. "Look at it in terms of dollars and cents and consider how much money it takes to maintain a house, a yard, a lawnmower and things like that. Maybe a house would need a new roof on it or a new water heater. Not only are we not able to do that kind of work, but we can find better ways to spend the money those improvements would cost. There also are certain taxes we don't have to pay, we don't have to buy insurance on the house, and we can save the money we would have to spend on the house in a lot of other ways."

When Jim and Mary Brown quit their jobs and began a 2½-year adventure in their travel trailer, they sold their house in Rochester, Minnesota, and moved as much furniture as possible into a mobile home, which they intended to use as a home base. They soon decided "the base was more of a nuisance than it was worth," though, so they sold the mobile home. "We bought the mobile home partly for our youngest daughter to live in, but then she got married and moved to Chicago. We rented the mobile home to a couple of Rochester policemen for a while, but finally we divided up some of our furniture, stored the rest and sold the mobile home." He waved at the inside of their 32-foot trailer and said, "So now, this is it; everything we have."

Mary said, "Some day I will want a base again, but for the moment we've found a base to be a nuisance. This trailer is set up for full-time living, but if we were going to live part-time in a mobile home too, we'd constantly be dragging stuff back and forth, and soon we wouldn't know where anything was. If I knew in the beginning what I know now, I wouldn't have had a home base at all."

"I could have gone full time all at once without the mobile home," Jim said.

"Not everybody can do that, though," Mary pointed out. "You have to be ready for it to be able to accept it. I just wasn't ready. I think most women need to go full-timing in stages."

Jim said, "I think people should do it however they, as a couple, feel most comfortable. If one feels they ought to have a base for a while and one doesn't, they should follow the feelings of the one that does. Neither one of us had any real emotional attachment to our house, though. It was the sixth one we had owned."

Mary added, "We liked our home, but we were never there to enjoy it, and it got to be quite an effort to keep it up to the standards we wanted it."

The decision of whether to utilize a home base or not could be predetermined by a couple's finances, Jim pointed out. "We know people who have two homes and a summer place and two RVs, but not everybody can afford to live like that. We also know a guy who has a mini motorhome that he uses for fishing and hunting trips and on caravans, and he has a travel trailer stashed in Mesa, Arizona. Most of the full-timers we know, however, have mobile homes somewhere as opposed to trailers that they live in all the time."

Mary said, "More and more people seem to be selling their homes in the north and putting mobile homes on lots in Texas, Florida or Arizona. They're changing their thinking that they had to have a home in the north because then they've got the problem of winterizing it and making sure everything doesn't freeze up while they're gone. They can live in the south in a mobile home for six months and then live in their RV when they want to travel in the north."

The Condominium Campsite

Don and Audrey Klemczak don't have a home base either, but they own two lots—one in Florida and one in Michigan—where they park their Blue Bird Wanderlodge motorhome on a sort of seasonal basis. I talked with the Klemczaks while they were wintering on their condominium campsite in the Outdoor Resorts park of Orlando, and Don told me, "We know we're going to spend our winters here, and that's why we bought this lot. We always go back to Michigan in the summer, so we have a lot there too. That way, we have two places—two home bases, in a sense—to operate from. We can leave here any time we want and rent our lot out, so the arrangement works out well for us. Rental sites in Florida cost so much in the winter that it's almost better to own a site than pay rent. Then too, when you're renting, sometimes you can run into availability problems because the parks are all full."

Don added, "People are a little concerned now about fuel availability, so a lot of people who ordinarily take their RVs to Florida every year are leaving them here all the time; they're just driving back and forth in a car and not towing a trailer. We don't do that because our coach is our home."

Daryl and Ginny Johnson, a pair of 30-year-old full-timers, also own a condominium lot. Theirs is in Texas, and they've lived on it in a trailer since they left Algona, Iowa, and joined the full-timing lifestyle in 1977. It is more than a home base; it's their permanent address. Daryl is a bartender and Ginny, a waitress, at the South Padre Island Hilton Hotel. Ginny was once a teacher and Daryl was a struggling actor. "We were both getting tired of our old occupations and wanted to do something different and travel at the same time," Daryl told me while we talked inside their comfortable 32-foot Holiday Rambler trailer not far from the Texas Gulf coast. "We figured this was the farthest point south in the Continental United States outside of the keys in Florida, so we felt it had to be warm here. We'd had it with the snow. So we gave up our old occupations, and I learned how to tend bar and Ginny learned how to be a waitress. We bought a 20-foot travel trailer and a station wagon to tow it, sold a bunch of household goods and headed south."

Warm weather and luxury accommodations attract thousands of full-timers to South Padre Island on the Texas Gulf coast.

Daryl added, "Our original idea was to work and travel. We wanted to work four months in an area, travel somewhere else and work another four months. We worked four to five months at the Island Hilton and set out on the road but ended coming back again. Then we bought a lot at this park, and we've been working and living here ever since. Now we have a seasonal job; we run the outside bar at the Hilton, and that allows us to travel for 2½ to 3 months of the year. We put a year's work into a nine-month period and use our trailer as our base and headquarters."

Ginny said the trailer is easy to keep clean and provides inexpensive living space that allows them to save money for their travels. "I wouldn't want to raise children in one of these trailers," Daryl said. "It's a little confining. But for people our age with no children, it's really the way to go. Living here, we have all the luxuries of tennis courts, jacuzzis, saunas, swimming pools, game rooms and other amenities that we wouldn't have in a home. We couldn't afford a home with a pool and have the time to maintain it. The only time we really spend in the trailer is when we're sleeping because we work between fifty-five and seventy hours a week."

129

A Mobile Home Base

"Steamboat" and Hazel Van Osdol felt a big house was too difficult and expensive to maintain, but they wanted a home base that they could retire to if they ever quit full-timing. So they bought a mobile home and put it on a lot in Hutchinson, Kansas. "It's kind of funny things turned out that way," Steamboat told me. "We sure wouldn't have planned things that way because I was one of those people who said he'd never live in a mobile home."

Hazel recalled: "We had shut off about half the house because we both were working at our business, and we had three rooms we just didn't use. We liked to camp, and we weren't taking care of the yard or keeping up the house like we should have because we'd rather go camping than work at home."

Steamboat chuckled. "Every time somebody suggested going someplace, we wanted to go. We'd take off and leave everything. Just forget about it. We'd try to trim up the outside of the house or work in the yard on Friday afternoon if I could get off work early just so we could go camping all weekend. Then we'd rush home from camping Sunday afternoon and work like mad around the house again before I had to go back to the business on Monday. Hazel told me, 'I just can't do it; I can't keep up this big house.' That's when we got rid of the house and bought a mobile home."

Hazel said, "There will be a time when we'll quit trailering full time, and we'll move into the mobile home."

"We decided that when that time comes, we wanted to be ready for it," Steamboat added.

When Frank Salerno retired from government work at Chicago's O'Hare Field in 1976, he and his wife Agnes bought a mobile home in Kenosha, Wisconsin, and sold their house in Illinois. "We were in it two months out of twelve, and we did nothing but work the two months we were there to clean up the yard and paint and maintain the property. So we figured we didn't need that, and we put it up for sale. We sold it and everything in it—furniture and all. Financially, it's been a boon. We saved a lot of money by getting rid of it; it's increased our retirement potential greatly. With it gone, our worries about it are gone.

"Even though our parents were looking after it, what could have been done if the temperature had fallen to twenty below zero and the electricity had gone off? Everything would have frozen, especially if my parents couldn't get there for a day or so. The water pipes would have burst and, by the time anyone would have known about it, there might have been water all over the place. Nothing like that happened, but there was always that little doubt in my mind about how things were working. When I got rid of that mobile home, it was just like a big load had been lifted off my shoulders, and we were just two people living very comfortably in a 31-foot travel trailer. Now, if somebody offered to give me a house free and told me I had to live in it, I'd tell them to keep it."

He added, "We're saving a lot of energy, too, by living in this trailer [a 1979 Royals International]. My heating bill at home was roughly $100 a month. When we're in Texas for the winter, it's something like $6 or $8 a month. My electric bill used to be $50 or $60 a month. Here [at the Outdoor Resorts of America Park near South Padre Island] it's almost nothing in the winter. Financially, full-time RVing is like living in heaven. When the first of the month comes, I feel naked because there aren't any bills to pay."

Renting From The Kids

Doris and John Lockwood not only turned over their house to their children, but they gave them the family construction business too, and the Maryland couple took an early retirement when John was fifty-eight years old. "I figured if I was going to do it, I should do it then," John recalled in the summer of 1980 while camped at an RV rally in Minnesota. "I was afraid that if I waited until I was sixty-five to travel full-time, I wouldn't do it. We're both about the same age, and we felt that if we're going to travel, we should do it while we can enjoy it. So we're going to travel this country and the rest of the world, and later on we'll let life worry about itself. We have enough income so we don't have to worry about money. The kids seem to be doing all right, so as long as they are and the bottom doesn't fall out of the country, everything will work out for us."

John continued, "We sold our house to the kids, but we have an apartment in it that we pay them for. I thought that would be a good way to give them a chance to get started on their own. We live in the downstairs and they live in the upstairs. Our apartment is 35 feet wide and 100 feet long, and the house sits on an acre of ground. I like gardening, and I miss doing that more than anything else. A tomato from somewhere else just doesn't taste like a tomato I've grown myself."

The Lockwoods have spent only a few weeks at their apartment since they began full-timing in May, 1979, however. "We went home in August and left again around the middle of September and headed down the road to Florida. When we went back, we stayed only a few days," Doris said.

John added, "I doubt if we'll get back there before the end of April next year."

The question had to be asked: "If you're home so seldom, why did you decide you needed a home base?"

John answered, "I personally feel—and I think Doris does too—that we need someplace to come back to. To cut all ties and say, 'No, I'm not ever coming back here.' Neither one of us could do that."

Doris said, "I think it depends upon where your family and children are. Three of our grandchildren are there within ten minutes of home. We've stayed in the same area since our children were little. My only brother lives next door to my mother, and one of my sons lives next door to him. So in twenty minutes, we could visit any one of them."

"I just felt we had to have a home base that was close to everyone," John said. "I wasn't willing to cut ties completely and say, 'I'm going to the West Coast and never coming back.' Also, I don't expect to be a full-timer all my life. There will be a time when I'll have to give it up. And when I do, I'll have someplace to live."

Doris said, "I'm sure there are a lot of people who don't have that option. But this way, we didn't have to sell all our furniture the way so many full-timers do."

Walt and Charlotte Consider still use their family house in Ohio as their home base, but their daughter has lived in it since they began their full-time RVing life in mid-1979. "That way we have an address for our mail, and our daughter just forwards it to us. That's one reason we kept it. But besides that, I'm just a simple old country boy, and that's where my home is. We've had a spot in the shade on a cement pad with full hookups for years, and part of our agreement with our daughter is that when we come home, we can have that place to park our trailer. When we go back, we generally sleep in our trailer, but we do eat meals with my daughter and her husband, and we share the cost of the food and electricity."

Walt added, "The house still belongs to us. They pay all the expenses such as insurance and taxes, utilities and the bills for any normal upkeep. If any major repair or improvement work has to be done, we share the cost of that."

I asked, "What will you do if you decide to give up full-timing? Have you talked with your daughter about that?"

He answered, "Yes, and there would be no problem. I've always said the best thing for a young couple to do when they get married is to move at least 100 miles away from their parents and in-laws. So consequently, if we decide to give up full-timing, we probably will move into a mobile home somewhere in the mid-South or the Carolinas."

A MATTER OF SECURITY
AND FREEDOM

I want to conclude this chapter by sharing with you the philosophy of Jerry Campbell, a Kentucky native who has definite opinions about RVing in general and full-time RVers in particular. Jerry and his wife, Betty, had been living full time in a 1970 Travco motorhome for six years when I met them in January, 1980, at a condominium campground near Orlando, Florida. Jerry and Betty have never had a home base. Not that they didn't want one; they did. The Campbells owned a beautiful house in Huntington, West Virginia, and a thriving food market just across the Ohio River in Chesapeake, Ohio. Jerry reported, "Back in 1960, my dream started. I was going to buy an acre of land in Michigan, an acre in Kentucky or West Virginia and an acre in Florida. I was going to travel from one point to another with the seasons of the year. That was my dream in 1960."

But four heart attacks interfered with that dream.

Jerry and Betty sold their house in Huntington and, because their children did not want the family food market, they sold their business for a fraction of its value. The Campbells began RVing full time without a pension to support them, and Jerry's heart attacks wiped out their savings and investments. By the late 1970s, it was clear to the Campbells that not only would they never be able to buy those three acres of land, but they also would never have the security of a home base that so many full-timers treasure. When I talked with Jerry and Betty in 1980, their only income was the money they earned by working wherever they were needed in parks owned by the Outdoor Resorts of America system. Financial security? Home base security? They had none.

But they had freedom. And they treasured it.

"There's so much freedom living in an RV that you don't feel if you're living in a house," Betty said. "I have the freedom to know that I don't have to stay in this spot all the rest of my life."

Jerry added, "Even though you may not be physically free or financially free—and no man is totally independent—there's always that deep-seated psychological belief that you *are* free."

In exchange for their campground work, the Campbells receive a free campsite from ORA in addition to their salaries. And they know that whenever they want to travel, they can find work at one or another of the ORA parks. "Everything we earn is disposable income," Jerry said. "We can use it for anything we want to because we don't have any bills to pay. We have never been harassed; we have never been touched by anything that would taint the RVing way of life. We have made friends, and we are close to a lot of people."

I was amazed by Jerry's outlook on life, his total absorption with "the good life" while disregarding completely the fact that his dreams had been destroyed and his future depended upon his ability to work at an age when his contemporaries were looking forward to retirement. I told him, "It really strikes me that if nearly anyone else had experienced four heart attacks—or even one—he would give up RVing so fast it would make your head spin."

Jerry answered, "Within the last five years, four of the wealthiest men in the world, whose total assets exceeded billions of dollars, passed away, and I'm still here. I don't take credit for that, of course. But you see, their money didn't buy them life, and even what's alleged to be a personal contact with the man upstairs didn't delay the passing of a pope. Somebody is dying right now while we're talking. All I was born with was time, and I don't intend to waste it. There's no way you can waste time unless you put it on a material gain basis. And money doesn't mean a thing to me. It's a commodity to be bought and sold just like any other commodity. If you've got enough for today, that's all that's necessary."

Jerry continued, "They pulled me out of this campground in an ambulance two years ago and gave me no chance to live. And when I came out of it, they gave me a 40% chance to stay alive even though I knew that I could give myself a 75% chance. Call it belief or faith or whatever you want. I just know I wouldn't be afraid to start out today in my motorhome stone cold broke because somebody, somewhere, some way, will let me help myself start over again. And it's all because of that psychological feeling of freedom that I told you about. But I'll repeat: nobody's free. People need other people, and the main thing is the relationship you have with yourself, your fellow man and, if I may say so, your God as you understand him. That, to me, is life."

Jerry said only one thing in life depresses him: "All you see in Florida is a bunch of old people, of which I am one. I would rather see a bunch

Jerry and Betty Campbell work wherever they are needed in one of the resort campgrounds owned by the Outdoor Resorts of America system.

of young people. But the young people went to California, and the old people came to Florida."

What effect have the heart attacks had on his outlook on life?

"They gave me a better insight into myself, and I know now that, in reality, I have no control over myself. Explaining that: can you stop your heart from beating? Can you keep from getting hungry? Can you keep from getting sleepy? Can you start and stop your lungs? If you can't, then you're not independent, are you?

"I found out the less greedy I am, and the more dependent I am on that which I believe, the happier I am. I can see the birds; I can see the water; I can travel from border to border if I want to. I can see the mountains. I can sit in the desert for hours and watch the changing of its colors and its beauty. It's all a part of the way of life we have."

"The doctor told my wife, "His heart can stop at any time, and there's nothing we can do about it.' I was in intensive care, and my heart was beating forty-two times a minute, and nobody can live with his heart doing that. I was slated to receive a pacemaker. I asked the doctor a foolish question: 'Doc, you wouldn't let an old fool have a cup of coffee, would you?' He looked at me a second or two and said, 'Yeah, you can have coffee.' The nurse brought me a cup, and that day I had two more, and the next day my heartbeat started up. It worked its way into the high sixties, and I didn't have to have a pacemaker. My heart is as good right now as anybody else's, but I wound up with blood clots in my leg. The medication I'm on is supposed to take care of it, and if it does, it does. If it doesn't, it doesn't. The ability to accept the things that I can't change is all a part of RVing to me.

"I don't wear a watch any more. I threw it away because I don't believe in time," he said.

I responded, "When I asked you if you had time for me to interview you, do you remember what your answer was?"

"No."

"You said, 'I don't have anything *but* time.' Do you find that people are envious of your outlook and your lifestyle?"

"Yes, but I don't feel sorry for them. Those that like it [RVing], should do it and not worry about the security of a home and furniture."

I asked him, "Based on your experience, what percentage of full-time RVers would you guess own homes?"

He answered, "I would say at least 50% still own a home or own property that they lease out or let their children use. The picture is changing, though. This campground is just one of several ORA parks, and there isn't a person who owns a lot here who wasn't already a camper, I would bet. The park is sold out, and the other parks are also either sold out or will sell out quickly. Now the owners are bringing park model trailers in—a tremendous number of them—and gradually each site is becoming a permanent address for someone. To me, that means those people are giving up one permanent address for another permanent address."

Chapter Eight

Keeping In Touch

"The most difficult things about RVing full time are keeping track of mail and cashing checks," a man who has been on the road trailering for ten years told me. "I have talked with dozens of people about those problems, and I have yet to hear a solution that sounds satisfactory to me." Unfortunately, he was right. Difficulties with mail and cashing checks are the two worst penalties people must pay for the freedom and adventure associated with RVing full time. In previous chapters I offered several alternatives aimed at improving check-cashing efficiency; here, we'll talk about the other problem: receiving mail.

There are four basic ways for mail to be forwarded to full-timers: (1) through RV clubs such as the Good Sam Club and through RV owners' clubs such as the Wally Byam and Holiday Rambler organizations; (2) by a friend or relative who receives the mail directly; (3) by commercial mail-forwarding companies, and (4) by post office forwarding. Each system has its advantages and disadvantages, and individuals should consider which system fits them best.

Club Services

Some owners' clubs forward mail to members without charge, except for the amount necessary to cover postage, and the forwarding service itself is included in the annual membership fee. Other clubs charge extra for the service, as well as for the postage. The Good Sam Club offers free forwarding with its $10 annual membership charge and, like the others, charges for postage. Most clubs, including Good Sam, forward mail once a week, which usually is adequate for the relaxed lifestyle of full-timers. I have not used club forwarding services, but those who have tell me they seldom have problems with them unless they are on the move so much that they miss receiving mail that is forwarded to a place they just left; in that case, they must make arrangements with someone to forward the mail to them again at their next destination.

Commercial Forwarding

Commercial forwarding services are more expensive than club services, but they have the advantage of daily mailings. Thus, full-timers who receive quite a lot of mail, some of it especially timely, probably ought to consider employing such a service. Annual fees generally range from about $25 to nearly $100 a year, depending upon the type of service selected and upon the volume of mail to be forwarded. Some services also utilize toll-free numbers, manned all the time, so that subscribers can call in changes of address. In addition, the services generally keep a card file containing a description of each subscriber's RV rig, license numbers and emergency addresses in the event the subscriber needs to be located by police officers due to an emergency. The only real disadvantage to a commercial forwarding service is its cost, but active full-timers often claim the extra cost is worth the peace of mind.

Some of the most popular mail forwarding services are MCCA, Inc., of Estes Park, Colorado; NATO, of Sarasota, Florida; Forwarding, Inc., of Port Angeles, Washington, and PBFWD, of Palm Beach, Florida. TOMA (Travelers Overnight Mail Association) of Sparks Nevada, and Texas Residents Association of Arlington, Texas, promote their systems as providing full timers with the opportunity to use their income tax-free states as home bases.

The Personal Touch

Admittedly, there is something a little too impersonal about utilizing a forwarding service to handle mail, and those who want a more personal touch often prefer to ask friends and relatives to forward their mail to them. Unfortunately, friends and relatives are sometimes undependable and usually do not forward mail as systematically as the professional services do; full-timers often complain, in fact, that they receive mail haphazardly from a son or daughter charged with that duty.

Writer and RV safety lecturer Hal Gaynor said, "Having children handle your mail is a terrific thing in the beginning; then it becomes a chore for them. As the old saying goes, 'One parent can take care of ten kids, but ten kids can't take care of . . .' They say things like, 'Oh, Dad, I'm sorry, I'll do it tomorrow,' so you say, 'Well I've been sitting here waiting for the mail all week,' and they say, 'I know. It won't happen again,' but it does. So I concluded it's just better not to have the kids do it. A full-timer should have a complete stranger handle all his mail. That's what to do. We never feel we're imposing on anyone, and it works out terrifically."

Walt and Charlotte Consider, however, have their mail forwarded by their daughters, with only minor difficulties due to pickup. "They know ahead of time the addresses for the rallies we'll be attending, and they forward our mail to us there," Charlotte said.

Walt added, "We always know—or at least have an idea of—where we're going to be either next week or the week after that, so we have our mail sent to that town in care of general delivery, or to the campground where we'll park, and we'll pick it up when we get there." He said occasionally they will arrive in an area later than they estimated and discover that their mail had already been returned. "In that case, one of the girls just has to send it to us again."

A friend or relative can be asked—or paid—to do something many people would not trust a commercial service to do, and that is sort through the mail and make judgments on which mail to forward and which to discard, based on his or her personal knowledge of the full-timer. The mail also can be packaged into a large envelope and sent out weekly or twice monthly under third-class postage, which is considerably less expensive than first-class postage. In doing this, the friend or relative can exercise judgment, if necessary, and send out single pieces of mail that seem to have some urgency. The full-timer's mail agent can receive his mail in one of two ways: either by picking it up at the full-timer's home base (or postal box) or by requesting the post office, through a change of address card with no expiration date listed, to send your mail to your agent's home.

The Postal Service

A change of address card also can be used to enlist the aid of the post office which handles your mail in forwarding it. First-class mail will be forwarded, without cost, to any address you designate, and second-class mail such as magazines can be forwarded along with first-class mail for periods up to three months, although you will have to pay the postage due on those pieces. Some full-timers make forwarding easier for their postmasters by providing gummed, pre-addressed labels that can be afixed to their mail easily. Bert Dean, whose home base is in New York, uses the post office forwarding service whenever he parks his trailer on his lot near Port Isabel, Texas. "I have a post office box in Woodstock and one here in Port Isabel," he said. "When I'm down here, and the mail goes to the Woodstock box, it's forwarded here. When I am in Woodstock, mail sent to Port Isabel is forwarded to Woodstock. If we're on the road for any period of time, and we're going to stay at one place for a few days, I'll fill out a change of address card so that the mail will be forwarded to general delivery at a small town where I can pick it up. I always designate a small town because it's easier to get into and out of a small town. When I pick up my mail at that post office, then, I'll leave a forwarding address from there in case any more mail comes in."

TELEPHONING HOME

Keeping in touch with friends, relatives and business associates by telephone also can be expensive and troublesome. California full-timer Flo Cooper told me, almost angrily, "As far as I'm concerned, the two worst things about traveling on the road are laundry and telephone calls. Telephone calling, to me, is the most awful thing in the world. The whole East Coast is full of mosquitos, and the mosquitos seem to wait until you get your party on the line, and the minute your party answers and you can't give any attention to the mosquitos, they call their friends into the phone booth with you and start dive-bombing. I hate telephoning on the road, as you can see. Also, time changes can be devastating. To call the West Coast from the East, you have to telephone very late at night in order to reach anyone at home after work, and that's when all the mosquitos are out in force."

Some full-timers have telephones installed in their mobile home bases and in their RVs while they park on their own condominium lots in resort areas, but most relish their ability to escape from the clanging of a phone. Full-timer Frank Salerno, for example, refuses to have a phone installed in his RV: "I wouldn't have a telephone if someone gave it to me free," he emphasized. "We call home every week, but we use the pay phone at the park's rec hall. And if my kids want to reach me, they can do it by calling the campground office."

Wyoming's magnificent Grand Tetons beckon full-timers.

Photo courtesy Wyoming Travel Commission.

Most veteran RVers are experienced enough in the use of telephones to know they should save money by making their calls on weekends and evenings and that they should avoid as much operator assistance as possible to cut down on the cost of calling. Whenever possible, the RVer should call direct by using coins at a pay phone, thereby eliminating at least some operator assistance. But there are other ways for travelers to keep in touch with their friends and relatives, too. One system is to pre-arrange for the RVer to receive the call, direct-dialed by the other party; then the RVer can reimburse the other person for the charges—or split the cost—on a monthly or quarterly basis. Another method is to use coins to call the other person, give that person the number of the phone from which you're calling and wait until he returns the call, dialing direct. We've figured out that it is rather inexpensive if the traveler reverses the charges when he calls his party, gives his party his number and waits for the return, station-to-station, direct-dialed call.

Some RVers circumvent the telephone altogether and keep in touch with friends and relatives by mailing postcards and cassette tapes on which they've recorded messages. Alice McGinley sometimes calls family members by telephone, but she usually communicates with them by letters and cards. Her husband, Mac, said he prefers to do his communicating face-to-face, so the McGinleys schedule their travels around visits to relatives and friends—and especially around get-togethers with other RVers at local, state, regional and national rallies. When I interviewed them in Nova Scotia in 1979, for example, they were making plans to visit a relative. "We were going to go back into Vermont," Mac said, "but I think we'll work our way down through Pennsylvania because I've got a sister there. We also have some friends in the southern part of the state. Then we'll go on back to Mississippi and see some more friends, then on to a regional rally at the top of Petit Jean Mountain [Arkansas]. From there, we'll take in a rally at Baton Rouge and then backtrack to Florida. We don't need a phone to communicate with our friends and family; at some point during the year, we'll probably see them while we're traveling."

Chapter Nine

Young
Full-Timers

Early retirement is a goal of many Americans and, thanks to the development of supplementary employee pension programs during the last twenty years, there has been a trend of people leaving the work force before they reach the traditional sixty-five-year-old retirement age. The pension funds, added to income from investments, have enabled men and women to retire from their jobs early and spend the remaining years of their lives traveling and enjoying leisure activities. Many of those persons were attracted to the unique lifestyle of full-time RVing. No statistics are available, but indications are, too, that increasingly larger numbers of very young adults—in their twenties and thirties—have for the past ten years been attracted to full-time RVing and a semiretired type of lifestyle.

In 1900, two out of every three men age sixty-five or older were either working or looking for work. By 1950, fewer than half were in the work force. And by the mid-1970s, only 20% of all men sixty-five or older were still working or looking for jobs. Obviously, Americans had come to accept retirement, and especially early retirement, as important to their idea of a full and rich life.

Futurists are now predicting a reversal of that trend, however, because of the severe inflation that has gripped this country since 1979. Following exhaustive studies of American consumer attitudes, Morgan Guaranty reported: "There is a good chance that the decade of the '80s will see a reversal in the historic pattern—a rising, rather than a falling, participation rate [in the work force] for older Americans." Inflation that Morgan predicts will cut the buying power of the dollar in half by the mid-1980s will force many American men and women to delay their retirement until age seventy, the nationally known insurance company said.

While Morgan could be correct in its predictions—at least, for non-RVing retirees—there seems to be a growing awareness among people thirty to sixty years of age that full-time RVing is the one intelligent method of enjoying early retirement, or semiretirement, and still beat the high rate of inflation. The experiences of men and women who already are living in their recreational vehicles prove that full-timers are not as susceptible to inflation as retirees who live in a more traditional manner. In fact, full-timers live so much more economically than other Americans with similar incomes that there seems to be a groundswell of interest in the lifestyle developing among young families, as well as among young couples.

Full-Timing In Their Twenties

Carl and Beverly Edwards hit the road full time in 1978 when she was twenty-six and he was twenty-eight because they wanted to realize their dreams of traveling throughout the United States while they were young enough to do it and before the price of gasoline made extensive RV travel prohibitively expensive for them. They hooked their 28-foot Jayco travel trailer to their converted Ford van and, after selling their house in Pennsylvania and storing their furniture, they left for California. "It seemed to our friends like a sudden decision," Bev, a small, pretty redhead said two years later, "but it wasn't. We had talked about chucking everything and just taking off for a couple of years before we actually did it. We had always gone on weekend camping trips—Carl and I are both from camping families—and we used our trailer every summer for our two weeks of vacation. Every year, it was harder and harder for us to go back to work after our vacations ended. Carl worked for a plumbing contractor, and I taught school and worked summers as a Manpower girl. We liked what we were doing, but we felt frustrated because we couldn't travel as much as we wanted to, *when* we wanted to."

Carl, tall and slim and always chewing a toothpick, said, "We really loved going places on weekends, but I hated having to rush home from work Friday evenings, pack everything in the van and trailer and then drive all night in order to go someplace new. We had to travel at night both going to and returning from our destinations just so we could have as much free daylight time as possible on Saturday and Sunday. We'd get home late every Sunday night, unpack and then fall into bed exhausted. And I had to get up the next morning at five o'clock and work all week so that we could afford to go out and do the same thing the next weekend."

"It got to the point where we even talked about giving up camping," Bev admitted.

Carl chuckled. "But those times didn't last very long. We'd get tired of our hectic weekend schedule by the end of summer, but when spring rolled around again, we were ready to do it all over. By then, I was ready to go crazy because of all the cold weather and the snow. Trouble was, we could never go camping when we wanted to. During the week, we both had to work, and I spent a lot of weekends fixing things around the house and fertilizing the yard. Or we'd plan a trip for a long time and, when the weekend came and we could leave, the weather would go sour, so we'd either have to stay home or camp in the rain."

His wife reminded him, "Don't forget how much you liked to shovel snow, dear."

"Yeah," he said. "In the spring of 1978, we planned a camping trip to a nearby lake, and eight inches of snow fell on Saturday morning and about buried the campground. I had to shovel us out with a flat piece of board."

Bev's face darkened. "What really made us decide to go full-timing was when we found out that Carl probably had an ulcer. It turned out that he didn't, but he had all the symptoms, and I was afraid he was going to have a heart attack, too. Can you imagine, a heart attack at twenty-eight years old? But that's what our lives seemed to be leading to. Carl was overweight and working very hard at his job. He worked for a big contractor in Pittsburgh, and I guess you could say he was in the process of climbing the corporate ladder. The pressures were unbelievable. Several guys were trying for the same supervisor's job, and they were all playing around with corporate politics. There was some real backbiting."

Carl recalled, "I came home one day with a bad case of the nerves. I had a headache, and my stomach was all knotted up. I told Bev I didn't care if I never went back to work again."

"And I said, 'Fine. Quit, then. I'll quit my job too, and we'll go full-timing in our trailer.' He thought I was kidding at first, but I wasn't. I pulled out a bunch of maps and books and some old *Trailer Life* magazines, and we started rehashing all the things we'd talked about for years—the places we could go, the things we could do. Then Carl got out a pen and notepad and started doing some figuring, and he estimated we could live six months on our savings if we were careful."

Carl said, "We had almost $5,000 in the bank. We'd planned to add to it and buy a new house in a couple of years. After reading in *Trailer Life* about other full-timers, I estimated we could get by on about $800 a month even if we didn't work, and I knew we could supplement that with jobs if we wanted to do it."

Bev laughed and said, "When he told me that, I really dropped a bombshell on him. I said, 'Let's sell our house and invest our equity in something that will add to our $800 a month.' That really shook him up! He sat there for a minute and then began figuring again. We estimated we had $20,000 equity in the house. Invested at 8% interest, it would give us another $130 or so each month to live on. When we sold the house, we actually got $22,000 out of it, and we picked up a couple of thousand more by selling some furniture and our lawn equipment."

"The way things turned out," Carl said, "we haven't needed very much of that money. I think we averaged spending $700 of it each month for about four months, and by then we were able to find enough work to support us. We haven't touched our savings for about a year, except to make a couple of repairs on the van and buy a new tire."

"We've Picked Tomatoes, Oranges And Apples"

The Edwards couple lived on a $700-a-month budget during the seven months of 1978 that they spent traveling. In 1979, partly because of inflation and partly because they were earning their own way, they averaged spending nearly $800 a month and actually saved $500 from their earnings that year. During the first few months of 1980, before I talked with them, they had reduced their expenses back almost to the $700-per-month level and were saving approximately $150 each month out of their earnings.

Bev explained, "Carl's very clever about finding places we can camp for free in exchange for a little work. Luckily, we kept his chain saw, and twice we've been given free campsites for a couple of months at a time in exchange for firewood that Carl cut up. And I haven't had any trouble at all finding jobs. I've worked in campground offices and in business offices all around the country, due primarily to my experience with the Manpower agency."

"We've also picked tomatoes, oranges and apples and worked on farms taking in hay and tobacco," Carl added. "I've been able to keep my hand in as a plumber by doing a little contracting work here and there, too. We just tell a few people what our talents are whenever we arrive

Farms and orchards often provide seasonal work for full-timers.

at a campground for a long stay, and the word gets out quickly. I've had several offers of permanent jobs—one, for more money than I ever could have earned back in Pittsburgh. And Bev has to turn down job offers everywhere she goes. We just tell people, 'Thanks, but no thanks.' It's nice to be in demand, but we're not ready to settle down to jobs again. I don't know if we'll ever do that again."

Beverly said, "We've discovered that the best places for us to stop are small towns. There, everybody knows everybody else, and once we make friends with a few people, it seems that everyone in town knows about us before very long. We make friends among other full-timers, too, although they are always much older than we are. Older couples who are full-timing have been marvelous to us. The women like to mother-hen Carl, and he just eats it up. We've made better friends since we've been on the road than we ever had back in Pittsburgh. Sometimes it's sad when either we break camp and leave or our friends do. But we know we'll probably see each other again, maybe in Florida, maybe in Texas or

Arizona or maybe even a year later at the same campground. There's one special couple we now call Mom and Pop. We've run into them about six times at various places during the last two years. When we see them, there's always a lot of hugging and kissing. They're like adopted parents to us, and no matter where we are, when we see them it's like coming home."

FULL-TIMING WITH KIDS

Like most young full-timers, Beverly and Carl Edwards do not have children. The presence of youngsters in a household probably prevents more people from joining the ranks of full-timers than any other single concern, including financial considerations. There are two schools of thought regarding full-timing with school-age children, and both are poles apart. One position is that children should be given the opportunity to interact with other youngsters and trained teachers in a daily class-room environment, where discussions of ideas, philosophies and theories are stimulated. The other position is that children who are members of a full-time RVing family can learn things not possible in classrooms and that widely traveled youngsters can become better rounded individuals because of their exposure to different locales, customs and people.

Let's examine more closely the negative aspects of full-timing with children. Children whose parents travel seasonally, or even just two or three times a year, face special problems if they have to change schools with every move. Most school courses are set up on an annual basis, with course credits based upon the full completion of a structured, nine-month program. Therefore, parents with school-age children face only three alternatives: argue with unsympathetic school authorities about incompleted courses and credit transfers before and after every move; spend every school term in only one or two locales and travel just in summer, or enroll the children in a correspondence school. Obviously, the correspondence school is the best alternative. But whether it is practical for everyone is questionable.

Children, unless they are extremely intelligent and especially self-motivated, must be taught correspondence school material by one or both parents. That alone can present insurmountable difficulties and severely strain family relationships. Most parents are not equipped with the education necessary for directing the learning process, and they usually do not have the time, patience or inclination to work with their children on a daily basis, forcing them to forget all the external attractions that

Full-timing youngsters gain new perspectives through a wide range of life experiences.

compete for their attention, and learn. Sometimes, children refuse to be taught by their parents, even though they might willingly accept direction from either a stranger or a trained educator. Furthermore, correspondence programs seldom afford children direct contact with other students that would encourage open discussion of subjects and lessons.

Aside from handicaps in the learning process, transient children frequently have a difficult time adjusting to strange surroundings and making new friends. Teenagers especially find it difficult to get acquainted with new people, although young children seem to make friends much easier. Since teenagers tend to socialize in groups and form cliques, the

Photo courtesy Florida Cypress Gardens, Inc.

Well-traveled full-timing children are known for their adventurous natures.

transient young person usually is in the position of an outsider at every gathering, and unless he is very self-sufficient and gregarious—willing to make the first overture in order to gain new friends—he will often be very lonely.

On the other hand, children who are well adjusted and enjoy a good, open relationship with their parents can usually reap valuable benefits from living on the road in an RV. Full-timing children boast that they are more independent and self-sufficient than their non-RVing friends. They claim they are less afraid to try new things and experience new adven-

First-hand learning experiences often replace classroom instruction for school-age full-timers.

tures. They say they know more about mechanics, geography, politics, geology and various ethnic groups than their peers. On balance, while some young people who have experienced the full-time RVing life say they regret not being able to make permanent friends, live in a house and attend school social functions, most feel they benefited from participating in a lifestyle that was broader and more enriching to them.

The world of full-time RVing is full of stories about children who learned history by seeing the actual places where history was recorded; who learned geology by climbing mountains, crossing deserts and exploring dark, deep caverns, the sea shores and the Great Plains; who learned biology by watching a butterfly extracting pollen from a flower. To full-time RVing children, a practical application of mathematics is figuring out how many miles per gallon the family tow vehicle achieved while being driven from Los Angeles to St. Louis. Or, in calculating the family's estimated time of arrival at the next campsite. To them, social studies means being able to talk with the coal miners of West Virginia, the hill people of eastern Kentucky and members of various ethnic groups in Cincinnati in a single week. They see, first hand, Americans in the grips of poverty and those enjoying a luxurious life of leisure. They observe farmers at work and movie stars at play. They are exposed to a wide range of language differences, racial minorities, art, music and scenery on a regular, routine basis.

Can any classroom take the place of all that? Maybe so, maybe not.

Correspondence Schools

Parents who insist upon taking their children RVing full time with them should at least check into the courses of study offered by some of the best known correspondence schools. Perhaps the best known program is available through the nonprofit Calvert Correspondence Courses of Baltimore. That school, founded in the early 1900s, has provided at least a partial education to more than 300,000 children worldwide. The school is especially popular among full-time RVing families and, interestingly enough, full-time sailboaters, too. While nine-month courses of study are set up by Calvert, the programs are arranged so that each child can progress at his own rate; lessons are designed so that parents without teaching experience can tutor their own children. Tuition fees range from under $100 for a kindergarten course to less than $200 per year for elementary grades. Calvert courses are not available to high school students, but some other correspondence schools offer advanced studies.

THE YOUNG FULL-TIMERS

During the fifteen years Harry Jennings was employed in a management position at a plant in North Carolina, he watched acquaintances wait until they could qualify for Social Security benefits before retiring, but then frequently die before they could enjoy the fruits of so many years of labor. While still in his twenties, he set a personal goal: he would retire at age forty. He and his wife, Juanita, began preparing for that day several years ago and, in February 1979, they began RVing full-time in a 20-foot Jayco travel trailer. Harry was thirty-nine years old.

"I had seen people work from the time they were fifteen years old until they were sixty-five, then drop dead, and I was determined that wouldn't happen to me," Harry told me from his campsite in central Connecticut some eighteen months later. "When our two sons were old enough to be out on their own, Juanita and I just took off, and now we're enjoying retirement as we go."

"We Call What We Do 'Retirement'"

Technically, Harry is not retired. He is a sales representative for Southern Emblem, a nationally known company that manufactures and distributes paraphernalia such as the shoulder patches worn by RV rallyists. Harry and Juanita carry their huge stock of patches, badges, buckles and signs with them to between nearly forty-five RV rallies and to several recreation and sports shows each year. They attend about 70% of all Good Sam state Samborees in the eastern half of the United States, as well as hitting rallies by the Jayco, Holiday Rambler and Winnebago sponsored clubs. "You're not really a retired full-timer," I told Harry. "You're a working full-timer."

"Right," he said. "But we call what we do 'retirement' because we enjoy it so much. If you retire at age forty, you've got to have some income, and this business has kept us going. Sometimes I think I'm the only person in the world that isn't living on a retirement fund of some kind."

Full-time RVing can be a very satisfying lifestyle, Harry said, but he cautioned, "Both the husband and the wife have to want it. If the man wants it and the woman doesn't, it ain't gonna work. Both of you have to prepare for it, too. Our preparation was to get everything paid off. We didn't want any obligations at home. We knew obligations could kill full-timing because we wouldn't be able to earn enough revenue to pay for everything. We were sitting on at least $20,000 of income each year. Well, cutting that down to $10,000 and being able to live on it took some doing. I don't care who the people are, the first year they're full-timing will be spent in adjustment before things start clicking. They can't have obligations at home worrying them while they're going through that adjustment period. I had been planning on our retirement for a long time, and

I was in a pretty good position to do it. I had already gotten my bills paid, and all our affairs were in order. When we hit the road, we weren't obligated to anyone."

Harry had quit his job as shipping director of a Southern manufacturing plant and taken on a sales position with Southern Emblem as a preparation to hitting the road. He and Juanita decided to keep their home so that their sons could use it, and so that they'd have a home base. Then Harry began building his list of contacts in the sports and RV fields and working "a sort of half schedule" in the region around North Carolina. Within a very short time, he and Juanita were following a full work schedule, attending state, regional and national rallies where they set up glass-top display tables and sold their merchandise. There were still adjustments to be made, though. "We had to learn to mix business with pleasure, whereas a fellow living on a pension doesn't have to do that; he can live any way he wants to. But full-timing can be a very flexible type of life, especially for someone with a retirement income, because you can spend about what you want to and you can save as much as you want to. If you have only $10 for gasoline one day, you don't have to use it; you can park where you are until more money comes in. After a while, a lack of money is something that never bugs you."

The North Carolina couple tows their 1972 trailer with a Chevrolet van, and Juanita said they are able to live rather comfortably in it, the only drawback being a bunk that must be converted into seating space every morning. "We've got our eye on a motorhome," Harry said. "I think it's the best kind of RV for us, considering the work we're in. We'll probably buy it and tow either a utility trailer or a little truck behind it to carry our supplies." Harry said he and his wife do not follow a strict budget but, unlike most RVing full-timers who save money by parking in one place for a long stretch of time, they cannot do that. "We have to move around—all the time, in fact. We have to live within our means, like anybody else, but I've found out I can live five times cheaper on the road than I could at home."

Surprisingly enough, Harry and Juanita don't spend nearly as much money on gasoline while full-timing as they did when Harry was working at a regular job. The year before Harry "retired," he recorded 23,000 miles on the station wagon he drove back and forth to work; the first year on the road as full-timers, they drove only 16,000 miles. "I get kind of angry when people talk about how much energy RVers use; they're critical of us without knowing what they're talking about. Last year, we drove 9,000 fewer miles than Juanita and I drove together when we lived at home, and we covered the whole East Coast in that year."

I had to ask: "When you're between rallies and have some spare time, what do you do with it?"

Harry responded, "I dream. I like to walk by myself, and I do my best dreamin' when I'm walkin'. I dream about the future and what can be done to help people. I feel like all of us have a purpose in life, and we should use every opportunity we have to help each other. As for recreation, we do paperwork for the business, I study books and read magazines about camping and we talk with a lot of people. I have yet to meet a stranger; I find people to be fascinating. I guess you could say work is my recreation. When we open our tables and people come around and start joking with us, that's our recreation."

Interesting destinations? "I've enjoyed it all," Harry said. "I enjoy seeing the country. We were riding through Connecticut the other day, and it was beautiful out in the country, away from the cities. We'll drive out to Iowa, where you can travel for fifty miles and not see anything but farmland. Oh, I love that! Juanita doesn't enjoy the countryside as much as I do. She likes going to places such as Hershey, Pennsylvania. But we both enjoyed New England last year. We had a rally in Vermont . . . then went up into Michigan, then down to Florida for the winter. We had never spent much time in Florida, and we were a little worried because we'd heard stories that you can't afford to live in Florida unless you're rich. But we found out we could live down there very reasonably."

He added, "We work rallies or shows eleven months out of the year, but if we go by a place such as Disney World and we want to stop, we stop. In Vermont, we were rolling along and saw a beautiful covered bridge, so we pulled over and looked around, shot some pictures and just enjoyed being at that bridge. We didn't plan our day around going there, though. That's the best thing about full-timing—not being obligated to do anything."

The Browns: "The Trips Were A Bonus"

Unlike Harry and Juanita, Minnesotans Jim and Mary Brown planned a full-time RVing adventure that they pictured as only temporary. Jim explained, "We had trailered since 1968, and we got involved with the Holiday Rambler RV Club in 1973. We decided that when the kids were on their own, we were going to take a couple of years off, travel and spend more time with the club. We thought we'd do it about 1979, so we started saving our money. Then, three years ago, I became a national director of the club, and we moved our time schedule up a year."

Photo courtesy Vermont Development Department.

One of Vermont's covered bridges provided an unplanned but pleasant stopping place for Harry and Juanita Jennings.

Mary was catering manager of the Golden Valley Country Club near Minneapolis, and Jim was employed in the customer service department of DeVac, a window manufacturing company. They quit their jobs January 1, 1978, intending to hit the road as soon as they sold their house. "We had hoped to sell the house before January 1 because that was actually our shove-off date. Well, the house didn't sell, so I went to the president of the company and said, 'Frank, our house hasn't sold yet, and I've already quit my job, but if there's anything around here I could do, like sweeping the floor, I'd like a job for a while.' He said, 'You stay as long as you want; I don't care when you leave. Furthermore, why leave at all? Why don't you just forget that nonsense about quitting?' I worked there three more months, and those were the best three months I'd ever had there. Before, I had always asked for help without getting it, but those three months, I got it whenever I needed it, and the company was so good to me I almost decided not to quit."

Finally, with $24,000 in savings to finance two years of RV travel, and with the proceeds from the sale of their house safely banked for future use, the Browns began their adventure. Jim was only forty-seven years old. They had felt the familiar frustration of vacationing RVers because they were unable to spend enough time at any one place, so they intended to travel leisurely, teaching themselves how to fish and seeing sights they had never had time to see before. They particularly wanted to travel through western Canada, Washington and Oregon. But they were sidetracked by the Holiday Rambler club. "We wound up doing more club stuff than we figured on doing, and we haven't seen some of the places we wanted to visit. Our fishing rods are in the truck where we put them 2½ years ago; we haven't had time to use them."

The Browns' trip was not quite the adventure they expected it to be, but it was an adventure, nonetheless. They joined a Mexico-Guatemala caravan sponsored by the club and traveled extensively throughout the eastern half of the U.S. in addition to journeying to Nova Scotia in 1979. During their second winter as full-time RVers, the club recruited them to lead three Mexican caravans and, the following summer, a western Canada caravan. They also represented the club at several state and regional rallies in various parts of the country. While they weren't paid for their club work, the organization did pick up the cost of their gasoline for the caravans they led, so not only were they able to visit exciting locales they wouldn't have seen otherwise, but they were able to extend their two-year adventure by nearly six months.

"The trips were a bonus for us," Mary said, "and they were good for the club because the club didn't have to pay out money for staff salaries during the caravans. Basically, we traveled and lived on what I had earned in my job and put away. I guess you could say we've lost the money we would have saved if we'd both continued working, and we've lost the appreciated value of the house since we sold it, but we couldn't have bought the experiences we've had for any amount of money."

Jim added, "Mary has always been a more outgoing person than I. I've always been an introvert. Getting involved with the club, first as a chapter president and then as a member of the state council, then state manager and finally as national director pushed me out in front of people. I've sort of come out of my shell."

The Browns did have to face a couple of temptations to cut short their travels, though. "One of the DeVac dealers called me the first winter and asked me if I'd had enough of this travel foolishness and was ready to go back to work," Jim reported. "He wanted me to manage the glass area of his business, and really, it was one heck of a good job offer. But I felt I had to run the route on this two years. We'd talked about it, we'd planned for it, and nothing was going to stop us from doing it."

When anyone asks the Browns if they would recommend either full-time RVing or a temporary, two-year travel adventure, Mary tells them, "Both of you have to agree that it's what you want. It can't be a situation in which one says, 'I'll go along if I have to, but I don't really want to do it.' Both the husband and the wife have to be 100% sure it's what they want. If there is total agreement, then do it. It's an experience you'll never forget. Lots of people have asked me how we can get along with each other in a 32-foot trailer, and I have to say that we've had fewer arguments and gotten uptight with each other less in the two years we've been on the road than when we were both working and the kids were around."

Jim added, "I thought this life would be great for a while but that we'd start hankering for our roots. We haven't, though. We run with an older group of people, and they have never criticized what we've done. They always say that people who are considering going full-time should do it while they have their health. I think the success of this venture of ours can be measured by what kind of life we have after we finish traveling. When we go out and try to find jobs again, we're going to be two or three years older and supposedly in a less hireable age group. If I wind up with a decent job, making a decent living, we'll consider that what we've done has been a success."

He continued, "The least favorable job for us now would be a typical one with two weeks vacation every year. I'm afraid I'm spoiled for that kind of job. We could go for jobs where we'd work six, eight or nine months of the year, do some traveling and then return to the jobs. Or, we wouldn't mind a seasonal job."

Mary said, "I'm going to be hard to get along with about a job too. I could go back to the country club because it's strictly a seasonable job, but I feel I would rather work in the South and be free to travel north in the summer if I wanted to. We would really like to find something with travel connected with it."

A couple of months later, the Browns got their wish. Jim was appointed business manager of the Holiday Rambler RV Club. And, although he spends most of his time working at the HRRVC office in Napannee, Indiana, he and Mary are free to attend club rallies and caravans all around the country.

The Johnsons: "A Little Bit More Security"

Two other young full-timers, Daryl and Ginny Johnson, began their RVing lifestyle in 1977 when they were in their late twenties. They live in a 32-foot Holiday Rambler travel trailer that is parked permanently on a lot they own at the Outdoor Resorts of America park near South Padre Island, Texas. For nine months of the year, they operate the outside bar at the nearby Island Hilton hotel, and they spend the other three months traveling in a specially equipped van camper.

Daryl and Ginny were natives of the same small town in Iowa, but did not know each other well. Daryl had always wanted to be an actor, so when he graduated from Iowa State University at Ames, he attended a Shakespeare festival in Oregon and then helped develop a theater in Garrison, Iowa. Ginny, who had landed a physical education teaching job at a nearby town, attended a production at the theater and became reacquainted with Daryl. After they were married, Daryl began a series of acting tours, and Ginny spent most of the money she earned flying to small towns to be with him. Gradually, they began discussing the possibility of quitting their jobs and looking for something new while traveling.

Since neither one was an experienced RVer, they began investigating various means by which they could travel and live while on the road. They considered buying a tent and living out of it, but Daryl said, "I don't think now we could have handled that for any length of time." They also looked at folding trailers that could be towed behind Ginny's small car, and they even considered towing a small utility trailer packed with their belongings. Fortunately, though, they were offered a good deal on a 20-foot travel trailer, and they bought a Plymouth station wagon to tow it. Daryl had never towed a trailer before, but he became experienced at it very quickly. "Within a year, we bought a 30-foot Terry, and a year later we bought our Holiday Rambler and a 1978 Dodge van to tow it from neighbors in the park. All we really did was tow it from their site to our site, and we haven't moved the trailer since. We converted the van into a camper by installing a refrigerator and building bunks into it, and now when we travel, we stay in the van."

To prepare for their unusual RVing life, they learned new trades—he, as a bartender and she, as a waitress. They picked up some valuable on-the-job experience at the restaurant of the theater where Daryl worked, and they began their new lives with the knowledge that they could at least tell prospective employers that they were experienced food and drink handlers. Leaving everything behind in Iowa was difficult, however. Daryl explained, "One of the reasons we got married was that we both liked antiques and art; we liked *things*. When we got married, we had no idea, of course, that we would ever live in a trailer. After a year in the trailer, we decided this was the way we wanted to go, so we had a large garage sale and got rid of a lot of things, although we kept some of our antiques and some other favorite things."

Concerned that their brief experience at serving food and drink might not be enough, they considered other alternatives of earning a living. "We thought at first we could stop somewhere and pick apples and then go on to another place and pick pears or work at construction," Daryl said. "But although there are people who do approach this lifestyle like that, we realized quickly that we needed a little bit more of a sense of security. Now, we've given up that whole idea of traveling and working in different places. We're trying to save money for later on in life, and having this lot and this trailer gives us something to come back to. We do need a certain amount of security in our lives. We're not that footloose and fancy-free any more."

How did they find jobs in the beginning? "We just started pounding on doors whenever we went into an area," Ginny said. "And we had a lot of trouble finding places that would hire both of us. Even the Hilton was a little dubious about hiring a husband and wife. But that was the only way we were going to work."

Daryl said, "At first, she was a waitress in the hotel dining room, and I was a bartender in another section, but at least we had the same schedules even though we weren't working together. After three seasons, we sort of fell into the outside bar setup. We ran a temporary outside bar during the 1978 sailboat races here, and the bar was so successful I was able to convince the hotel operators to let us open a new outside bar."

When I talked with Daryl and Ginny during the early part of 1980, they had just returned from their annual three months of travel. "Now we have to do our time [at work] again, get caught up on bills and start stashing some money away for next year's trip," Ginny said. She added that their lifestyle has both positive and negative aspects to it: "Although our jobs appear to be ideal, we work 12-hour days at a very hectic pace." But she said she and Daryl are able to earn more money in nine months than they did all year at their jobs in Iowa. "There's as much money being a waitress or bartender in the food and beverage business as there is in teaching. That's kind of a shame, but it's true."

While Texas does not have a state income tax, that was not one of the reasons the Johnsons settled on that state as a home base. Daryl said, "The main reason we're working here is that our jobs are seasonal, and we're fortunate enough to be working together. It's also an area on the move, but it's not overly developed yet. We can hop in our car and be at work in ten minutes. There aren't any traffic jams. We also have the positive aspect of city life in that a lot of people from Houston and Dallas come here during our summer season. So we have the advantage of living in a small town, yet drawing in business from the large cities."

The Johnsons do not follow a budget, Ginny said. "We should, but we don't. We manage to spend money quite readily. We eat out rather often, but I've started making meals in a crock pot nearly every morning for evening dinner because the island pretty well closes down at ten o'clock.

How long will the Johnsons continue to work their heavy schedules so that they can take their three-month trips? "As long as our legs hold up," Ginny said. "It's a year-at-a-time kind of thing." Daryl added, "When we're busy, we're on our feet eight hours straight, with no time for breaks. I would think we'll do this for ten years, but I don't know; it depends upon how much money we can save. We may eventually decide to get into our own business. We're trying to keep ourselves debt-free, and we don't want to plunge heavily into debt in order to get a business going."

Investing In A Campground

Their Texas campground lot has, in a sense, become an investment for them. "These lots are increasing in value quite a bit," Daryl admitted. "By the end of 1980, if we wanted to sell our lot, we could more than double our investment. We paid $8,500 for it, and lots like it are selling for $17,000 right now. We didn't really buy it as an investment, though; we bought it as a place to live and so that we could take advantage of all the recreational facilities of the park."

The campsite also serves as an excellent home base, as well as a residence, between the Johnsons' extended trips in their van. "We like to go new places, but we're always glad to be home, too," Daryl said. "This year we went to Big Bend for a few days, looked up old friends in Los Angeles, went to Vegas, took a three-week caravan into Mexico, and spent Christmas in Iowa with relatives."

One negative aspect of the Johnsons' lifestyle is that they are not able to associate with many people their own age. "We haven't run into many people our age who are doing what we're doing, although we hear comments from the older people that they wish they could have done their traveling when they were young and healthier. But then, they've raised families. Maybe one of the negative aspects to our lifestyle is that we won't ever have our own children, and maybe we'll regret that. One of the biggest positive aspects, though, is that we don't feel strapped down. We're not up against the wall for mortgage payments and, if necessary, we can pull out of here and go somewhere else."

Daryl said they usually plan their trips so that they're away from south Texas between December and March. "The wind gets to be too unpredictable down here," he explained. "A northern blowing in just wipes out the poolside business that we're involved in." While traveling, Daryl and Ginny rent hotel rooms only when the weather is too cold for them to sleep in the van or when they are in a hurry. "We'd rather stay in the van, even when visiting friends or relatives, so we don't upset their households," he said. "It's really nice in the van. We have all our clothes and everything we need there. We don't like to haul things into a motel and back out again."

Asked what advice they would give to other aspiring young full-timers, Daryl answered, "I'd say do it."

Ginny added, "I'd say try it out first."

"Try it with a small rig first and find out whether you're cut out to live in a trailer," Daryl suggested. "Not everybody is. It's claustrophobic for some people. And you have to cut down on your possessions; you can't have all kinds of pictures hanging around and three closets full of clothes."

Ginny said, "We're both packrats, and we have a rented storage area packed full of clothes, fishing gear, a boat and other things. Storage is a problem. We can't have everything with us that we would like to have, but we get along fine without it."

As for finding jobs while traveling, they said that is not difficult at all. Daryl explained, "Any area that's any size at all, if it has conventions or tourists, has lots of work available. There are always jobs open for bartenders and waitresses, and nurses also are in big demand everywhere. Sometimes it seems that bartenders and waitresses are a dime a dozen, but finding people who are responsible, honest and who can be counted on to show up for work on time is difficult everywhere. Our only problem in finding jobs was that we wanted to work at the same place at the same time. We were fortunate to find a place willing to hire both of us. There is really no problem going into an area and finding work, but the husband and wife might end up working on opposite sides of the city."

Surprisingly, Ginny and Daryl said they do not miss their acting and teaching careers. "I get quite a bit of opportunity to act in my job," said Daryl with a smile. "Working at that bar is like doing a theater in the round. I probably do more acting on this job, dealing directly with the public, than I did on the stage. Some day, perhaps, when I can afford to fail, I might get back into the theater. I figure I would have been miserable in either L.A. or New York. There are thousands of actors in both cities, and it's really a rough business. I don't have a need to compete like that."

Chapter Ten

Loners
On Wheels

The first time I saw Ruth Potter, she was riding through the trees of Eby Pines Campground in northern Indiana on the back of a motorcycle and threatening to nibble on the ear of the white-haired man who was steering the bike. She laughed uproariously at something he said, shouted, "You're a sissy," and hopped off the motorcycle before it came to a complete stop. Later, as we sat outside the 26-foot travel trailer that she lives in and tows around the country by herself, the vivacious sixty-year-old brunette told me that just a few years earlier she was a shy, withdrawn woman "afraid of my shadow." She said, "I was dependent on everybody; I never had the nerve to stand alone on my own feet."

She looked up and waved as the man on the motorcycle streaked by. Then she winked and confided in a conspiratorial whisper, "I just *love* to ride motorcycles!"

Ruth Potter is among the growing number of single women and men, primarily widows and widowers, who live in their RVs and travel around the country either by themselves or in caravans with other free-spirited "loners." They are people who have found full-time RVing so much fun, so adventuresome and so economical that for them, any other way of life is almost unimaginable as long as they are healthy.

Ruth began full-timing in 1978 at the age of fifty-eight. When I met her, she had been on the road for two years and was planning most of her travels to coincide with state and national rallies of the nationwide Loners on Wheels organization—a club of single RVers with 1,600 members scattered throughout the United States and Canada. A native Hoosier, she was back in her home state of Indiana for the annual Midwest rally of

Ruth Potter loves adventure and is extremely proud of her new-found independence.

LoW. Her late husband—a Portland, Indiana, farmer—died in 1964, leaving her with three children and a nearly crippling case of arthritis. Realizing she could not manage the farm, she converted it into a campground and operated it with help from her children until the late 1970s, when she sold it. Meanwhile, she had become interested in the activities of the new Loners on Wheels Club, founded in 1970 by *Trailer Life* columnist Edith Lane.

She bought an 18-foot travel trailer that she towed south to Texas every winter while her campground was closed. There, she camped with other LoW members who call themselves, simply, Loners. "There were 150 or 200 of us strung up and down the Rio Grande Valley near Harlingen," Ruth recalled. "I used that little 18-footer down there for three winters and, in the summer, it would become my office at the campground. Finally, my youngest kid got married, and that set me free. The campground had gotten completely out of hand, and I wasn't able to handle it by myself because of my arthritis, so I sold it. That meant I was *completely* free, but I needed a home."

Encouraged by the positive experiences of full-time RVing Loners, Ruth decided to join that lifestyle herself. And, if an RV were going to be her permanent home, she wanted one that fit her needs perfectly, so she asked an Indiana RV company, Travel Units, Incorporated, to custom-build a 26-foot travel trailer for her. She hooked it behind her 1976 Buick and began an adventure of traveling that few other RVers would deny envying. "I'll do anything, and I'll go anywhere for fun," she said. "I cannot just sit and do nothing. Sometimes the arthritis gets very bad, and I am completely helpless, flat on my back. But eventually I'm able to get up and go again, so I go!"

Ruth insisted upon showing off her trailer. She pointed to the bedroom and said, "Notice that my bathroom is just one step from my bed. Since I can't use a bathtub with my arthritis—I can't get in and out of it or lift my feet high enough sometimes—I had a shower put in. Since I don't spend much time in the bathroom, I have the smallest one I could get. I have switches for my lights and my catalytic heater placed where I can reach them without getting out of bed. My clock radio and my tape recorder are within easy reach too, and my bedroom windows are rigged so I can open them without getting out of bed." She walked forward a few feet and said, "I have a full-length closet here, and a drawer there. I have a linen closet here and a huge pull-out pantry right there. I have a closet I can hide everything in; I've got tape cassettes and eight-tracks and reel-to-reel tapes and all kinds of games that I just stuff in there."

She waved to the living section of the trailer. "I have room to put all this clutter away, once I get organized, and I can seat fifteen people. I've had the whole club [her Indiana chapter] in here for supper, and there's room for all of them. There I have my stereo and my TV and my sewing machine."

"Over the door, there, is my rifle. I know how to use it, too. I used to hunt a little, but I'm not able any more; I can't lift a big gun. I keep that little one for fun, for shooting targets. My only traveling companion is George. He's a gerbil. I have threatened to feed him to the cats because he makes so much noise at night. I gave this trailer a lot of thought before I designed it. I must have looked at a thousand trailers. I wanted something with enough room in it to handle my whole family when they visit me, and I want room for friends to get in. I cannot stand being alone all the time; I've got to have friends around. I stayed alone in a campground for two weeks this spring, and I nearly went crazy. But with a crowd like these Loners, I'm having a ball. I love it. As you noticed, if anybody comes by on a motorcycle, I'll climb on."

New-Found Independence

Ruth was excited because she was ready to embark on the first extensive trip she had ever attempted by herself. She grinned. "My family always sends a babysitter with me. Either my cousin drives my car to my destination and flies back home or I caravan with other people. But on this trip I'm going to visit a certain great big guy up in North Dakota, and I refuse to take along a babysitter! I've never had any problems on the road, and there is always somebody around in the campground to help me get hooked up. Once my car died while I was traveling, and I just picked up my CB radio and said, 'I'm having trouble with my car. Is there a mechanic in the area?' Somebody came on and said, 'Where are you and what's wrong?' I told him that I turned the key off, and it wouldn't start again. In about ten seconds, a big semi truck came wheelin' in, and the driver—who wasn't even the person I was talking with on the radio— found the problem and got me going again."

Ruth is extremely proud of her new-found independence. "When I was a little kid, I wouldn't get out of my sister's sight. She took care of me even after I was out of high school. Then when I got married, of course, my husband took care of me. Finally he started making me do things. He'd say, 'Go on. You can do it,' and after a while, I got a little more self-confidence. Even now, though, the people who have always known me just can't believe I have the nerve to travel alone in a big car and trailer."

I observed, "It must have been hard to adjust to things after your husband died."

Ruth answered, "When he died, I had two teenagers and an eleven-year-old, and I was flat on my back with arthritis. My teenage daughters and the boys they were dating helped until I was able to stand alone. Now, I think I have my financial affairs simplified about as much as possible. I gave my daughter power of attorney, and she takes care of everything while I travel on a Visa credit card and some gasoline cards. My mail goes to my daughter's home, and my income goes directly into the bank. If I'm going to stay in one place for some time, my daughter sends me a bank draft and I deposit it in a local bank. Then when I leave, I just draw out what's left. I don't worry much about money or budgeting."

One of Ruth's biggest regrets is that the days are not long enough to do everything she wants to do. She said no one should hesitate becoming a full-time RVer because he or she is worried about keeping busy. "Whenever another single woman asks me if I think she should full-time, I answer that question with one word: 'Go! Don't let anybody talk you out of it. If you don't have the nerve to go, ask somebody to give you a push.' It doesn't take a lot of money to enjoy this kind of life, and it's not really hard to leave everything behind once you make your mind up. I didn't store anything that I owned, so I don't have any ties holding me down. I either sold or gave away everything I had—antiques, keepsakes and a four-bedroom farmhouse full of stuff."

Asked about her recreational pursuits, Ruth returned to one of her favorite subjects: "I love to ride motorcycles, and I like bikes of all kinds. I never learned to ride even a bicycle when I was a kid, but a couple of weeks ago I bought a 26-inch, ten-speed bicycle. I was going to learn to ride it, but my feet wouldn't touch the ground. I dragged out my grand-daughter's little bike, and I could touch the ground on it, so I tried riding it. Well, I could go downhill all right, but I couldn't make it back uphill. I managed to fall off and bruised both ankles, so now I'm waiting for the bruises to heal before I try riding again."

She added, "Another favorite pastime of Loners is eating, and I suppose the next favorite is dancing. If the guys try to escape, we grab 'em and drag 'em onto the dance floor."

I observed, "Since the women outnumber the men [about 1,000 to 600 nationwide in the LoW club], it looks to me like it's a fellow's paradise."

"Oh, they pretend like they're running away from us, but they like for us to catch 'em," she said. Although the LoW membership is restricted to single people thirty years of age and older and members are constantly reminded that the organization is not a lonely hearts club, campground romances are relatively common, and occasional marriages result. "We have a very bad record for staying married, though," Ruth said of the Loners. "I think we're all too independent to stick with it. I went with the same man for two years, and we were talking about getting married. But it came to the point where he wanted to spend the winter in Texas and I wanted to spend the winter in California. Then I met this big guy from North Dakota, and we went to North Dakota and then to California while the other guy went to Texas by himself. That's what I mean about independence. There have been marriages [of club members] that have lasted for only one weekend. Lots of them have lasted for less than a month, although some of them have really lasted. But our average is bad.

Most of the women are like me. I've been a widow for sixteen years, and I'm financially independent. I am not about to let someone tell me what to do."

Enjoying the freedom and independence of full-time RVing is like being a teenager all over again, Ruth said. "But being a teenager the second time around is a lot more fun than it was the first time. We know so much more now than we did then. The arthritis and other ailments slow us down some, but they don't stop us!"

A CLUB FOR SINGLES

Loners on Wheels was formed in 1971 by Californian Edith Lane, a full-time RVer who for years wrote the monthly "Lady Alone" column for *Trailer Life* magazine. As this was being written, she was president and editor of the club's newsletter—a monthly sheet mailed to the organization's nearly 1,600 members. "Most of our members," she reported, "are widowers or widows who have traveled, or planned to do so, with their mates and, upon finding themselves alone, are uncomfortable in groups made up of couples and reluctant or timid about traveling completely alone. The club was formed to help these people find friends and groups with whom they can feel at ease."

By the end of the 1970s, membership in LoW had grown to nearly 1,800, but inflation, escalating gasoline prices and higher campground fees caused a decline in membership during 1979 and 1980. Membership was, at that time, made up of nearly two-thirds women and one-third men, predominently in their sixties and seventies. More than half were retired. Occupations ranged from former teachers and nurses (the fields most heavily represented) to retired military personnel, librarians, cooks, factory workers, doctors, secretaries and accountants.

Prospective members are told: "Loners on Wheels is not a lonely hearts club, a marriage bureau or a dating agency. If you are looking for such a club, please do not apply. We are interested only in those who wish to join in group camping and caravans."

The club does not consider unmarried persons sharing a rig to be loners, and if a member marries, his membership is terminated. Full-timer Bob Eavenson, a widely known LoW member for several years and president of the club's private campground in Missouri, even had to give up his Loner's insignia in 1980 when he married Rheta Maloney, a popular LoW member from Florida. Roger Roper, of Vallejo, California, called the club "the greatest thing for loners that ever existed," but he too had to relinquish his five-year membership when he married former LoW member Merilend Burns.

Interestingly enough, in an effort not to lose friendships that had developed through LoW, former members who are now married have organized a spin-off club called Friendly Roamers. Like LoW, it holds regular chapter-sponsored campouts. LoW itself has thirty chapters in forty-five states and Canada, and each chapter has its own rallies and special activities. Loners on Wheels national headquarters is at 2940 Lane Drive, Concord, California 94518.

Many of the chapters sponsor fund-raising events to raise money for guiding eye dogs for blind persons. The SoLows chapter in California, for example, has raised thousands of dollars by collecting and recycling aluminum cans and pop-tops found in campgrounds.

Occasionally, one of the active LoWs enjoys at least brief celebrity status by being the subject of a widely circulated newspaper or magazine article. In early 1980, for example, Knight-Ridder News Service published an article about the life on the road enjoyed by full-timer Helen Duffessy; that article was picked up by several major daily newspapers, including those in Dayton, Miami, San Francisco and Orlando. An April, 1980, piece in *Family Circle* magazine about LoW full-timer Dorothy "DeeJay" Jackson resulted in a flood of more than 2,000 inquiries to Edith Lane, whose address was published in the article.

Mrs. Jackson, a sixty-five-year-old widow when the *Family Circle* article hit the newsstands, logged more than 85,000 miles in her 22-foot mini motorhome between 1977 and the latter part of 1980. She personalized her motorhome with sea shell mobiles and handmade Navaho rugs, and she travels leisurely from adventure to adventure, preferring back roads and small towns to expressways and toll roads. *Family Circle* quoted her as saying, "I'm just a kid at heart. If someone tells me there's something interesting, I'm apt to swing around and see it. And if I enjoy a place, I stay until I see everything."

I met Helen Duffessy in 1980 not long after the Knight-Ridder article about her was published around the country. A tall, attractive sixty-five-year-old woman who looked more like a society matron than a full-time RVer, Helen credited Loners on Wheels with giving her the courage to strike out on her own and travel by herself. Widowed in 1966, Helen worked in Detroit as the office manager and executive secretary to a trial attorney for many years before retiring in 1977. "I joined Loners on Wheels before I was ready to retire, and it was my membership in that organization that gave me the inspiration to quit the job. I had done a bit of traveling by car and had run into difficulty several times in finding a place to stay the night. I traveled to the Upper Peninsula of Michigan during the summer of 1976, and in order to find a motel room, I had to stop at three o'clock in the afternoon. That really griped me. When I got back, I went to a meeting of Loners on Wheels. There, I saw women who could give me ten years who were driving motorhomes and towing trailers with pickup trucks. I thought, by golly, if they can do it, I can do it."

Helen continued, "I had been toying with the notion of buying a trailer, but I thought, 'Oh, come on, Helen. That's a lot of weight to pull. Do you really think you can do it?' And I found out I could, even though I wasn't mechanically inclined. You put a key in the ignition, and it goes buzz, and if it doesn't, you call a service man. I know a little more than that, but not much. Then I said to myself, 'Hey, you don't really have to stick with this nine-to-five work routine if you don't want to. You can travel around in your trailer.' I decided I had had it with organizing and directing and seeing to it that everyone in the office was where they were supposed to be. I decided it was time to worry just about Helen. I'd never been able to take a vacation when I wanted to. My boss would want me there to take care of things when he was on vacation, and he'd want me there to run things when he got back. The more I got to thinking about it, the more I became determined to get out and see the country while I was still able."

"The Legend of LoWzark"

After retiring and hitting the road in her 27-foot Empire travel trailer, Helen became more and more involved with Loners on Wheels activities until she was elected vice president and a member of the board of directors of the club. An occasional writer, she also allowed herself to be recruited to write "The Legend of LoWzark," a history of the club's unique, private campground in the Ozark Mountains of Missouri.

LoWzark, a 250-site park carved out of 90 acres of rolling land purchased by the club in 1973, is operated as a nonprofit enterprise intended to provide shareholding members with inexpensive camping space and, for full-time RVing members, a secure home base. Each shareholder pays a one-time fee of $250 in order to reserve a site that he can use for less than $2 a day. Other LoW members may also rent space at LoWzark, with written permission from a site-holder. Throughout the park, the high, level portions are developed into campsites and the rest of the property is kept in a natural state with wild flowers, trees and wildlife jealously protected.

In her booklet, "The Legend of LoWzark," Helen Duffessy wrote, "Once upon a time there was a group of people, well into their fifties and sixties, with many much older, who were friends. They had absolutely nothing in common to start with except they were all alone—single persons, widows, widowers and divorced people—and they loved to travel. Each one owned his or her own camping rig . . . and spent all, or most, of their time traveling about the country, following the seasons. They were the Loners on Wheels. They caravaned together when convenient or, if traveling alone, they would meet each other in prearranged campgrounds, where they visited back and forth. They held many rallies in places throughout the country, and boondocking held no terrors for them. The only thing they tended to avoid were the ordinary campgrounds which catered so frequently to families. It isn't that they don't like children, but this was their way of life, and while, on a brief vacation one puts up with a lot, when you have raised your family and seen them established and learned to enjoy the peace and serenity of silence, the eternal yelling and noises of small children do irritate! One night around a campfire in some remote spot during 1972, one of these people—Freda Griffith, according to Edith Lane and other memories of "those who were there"—made an offhand suggestion that a piece of ground be located and developed, on a cooperative basis, which would eventually become, at the least, a camping spot, or even a permanent refuge for any members of the organization."

Helen continued, "This was at first just an idea, but when it appeared in the newsletter, it fell on fertile ground, and the response was immediate and good. Suggestions for locations finally concentrated on the Ozarks, since it was felt land would be less expensive and regulations might not be as restrictive as elsewhere. At this point, the ringleaders of the project, which had progressed to actually searching for a prospective site, had narrowed down to Edith Lane, the originator of the Loners on Wheels organization, and Conley Grove, one of the members. After many miles of driving, searching, conversations with real estate men and all the other problems attendant to purchasing property, the present site, now named LoWzark, was located, decided upon and purchased."

LoWzark, situated about thirty miles northwest of Poplar Bluff, Missouri, was not created easily, though. The people who moved their rigs onto the rough, mountainous land had to clear the space first, and they generally were middle aged to elderly RVers without either skills or equipment for clearing land. Helen wrote, "They physically—not with bulldozers, but with picks and shovels and saws—cleared the trees and the brush and the rubble and laid out the first road onto the property. They cleared the area which is now the entrance so they could park rigs and get in to the rest of the land for more clearing. Like the founding fathers of this country, they literally pushed back the forest!"

Disputes were inevitable. "Straightening roads was a major source of difficulty," Helen reported, "as each tree was personally defended against the saw by someone. To hang a clothesline or not to hang assumed major importance. The individual who was actually doing a job assumed that he had the full right to state how he was going to do it, and there were as many other types of differences of opinion as there were people concerned." The LoWzark pioneers solved problems of road-building, well-drilling and power line installation. Work dragged on through 1973 and 1974. Neighbors to the budding park offered unexpected but valuable assistance, and Helen Duffessy wrote, "We have developed, over the intervening years, excellent relationships with the neighboring farmers. When a tractor is needed, someone will come along to help." The years passed: 1974, 1975, 1976. By April of 1976, the park's recreation hall and two dumping stations for use by guests were almost finished. Campsites already were taking on individual shapes, some well manicured with lawns and others left in their natural states.

In the fall of 1979, Helen reported, "Six years after the purchase of the property, we have now expanded to 250 sites, owned by 193 shareholders. It is half a mile from the community area to the end of the newest section, and if someone desired to walk over all the graveled roads, he would have a nice walk of close to two miles, including a stroll around our newly built lake, complete with dock and benches. Guests and visitors see a well-established development, with facilities available according to their desires. They see a nicely designed entrance, including LoWzark sign and orange mailbox, a flagpole, flowers, a neat office and a host to greet them and make them feel welcome; a community building, good roads and a place to rest from their travels for an overnight stop, a week, a month or, in some cases, a lifetime . . ."

They Call Him "Shadetree"

His name is Dick March, but the members of the Loners on Wheels organization refer to him affectionately as "The Shadetree Mechanic" or, sometimes, as just "Shadetree." Dick is a devilishly handsome Texan who tools around the country in the red, white and blue Winnebago motorhome that is his full-time home on wheels. I met him during a Loners on Wheels rally in Indiana just after he'd finished lecturing other LoW members about RV safety and mechanical troubleshooting during one of his popular "shadetree" seminars. Then fifty-nine years old and a member of the board of directors of LoW, Dick had been a full-time RVer for ten years following retirement from a 34-year military career. I had already heard about the "Shadetree Mechanic" from other full-timers because he is widely known not only for his ability to repair things, but also for his glibness and his dry sense of humor, inventing RV-related expressions such as "hitch itch," "dump date," "rig r mortis" and others.

Inside the special attic of his colorful Winnebago, he carries air compressors, spare parts, hoses, belts and tools so that he can deal with any emergency. At each rally, he conducts his morning mechanics seminars at no charge, and his only fee for rewiring a lady's convertor or unstopping her sink is a warm hug. He also carries a duplicating machine in his coach, and he unpacks it at rallies in order to publish a daily newspaper that he calls "Leaves from the Shadetree." LoW matriarch Edith Lane once wrote about him: "At every rally he attends, he *asks* for problems, sets up a work list and flies around on his motorbike from rig to rig, and I swear he can fix anything. The only way we can pay him for all he does is to hide money in his toolbox or buy him some little goodies and leave them in his rig when he is gone so he can't return them!" At the 1980 South Texas Rally of the Loners club, he received a more formal appreciation for his work—a large, black velvet sombrero braided with gold.

Dick said he was "hornswoggled" into joining the Loners club in 1978 while registering for a campsite in the Rio Grande Valley of Texas. "I was registering at the camp office and the man said, 'How many in your party?' When I said one, two women who were on either side of me grabbed me by the elbows and told me about the club." He became a LoWzark siteholder almost the same way: he stopped there to camp for a week and stayed a month.

In Indiana, I talked with Dick and another Loner, L. F. "Whitey" Whitesell, who at sixty-four years old was a relatively new member of the club following his wife's death. I asked Dick why he became a full-time RVer, and he said, "I'm fascinated by the idea of being independent, carrying all my stuff with me and traveling with the snowbirds. I drive that Winnebago and tow a utility trailer. I haul a Trail 90 bike on the back of the motorhome, carry a boat on top and an outboard inside."

I pointed out, "That *W* on your Winnebago looks like an *M*."

"You know what? They put a *W* logo on it at the factory, but since my last name started with an *M*, I said to myself, 'I think I'll turn it over.' So I did that and painted it in the same style as a Winnebago *W*."

Dick March, the "Shadetree Mechanic," fixes rigs at rallies and presents seminars on RV maintenance, "especially for the ladies."

What has Dick done with his life during the last ten years? "I like to go to rallies where there is a gathering of folks because I like to tinker around with the rigs and fix them. I also enjoy putting on the seminars. I talk to people about how to take care of their RVs, how to handle do-it-yourself service and maintenance, and I offer a few suggestions and techniques for preventing problems. I talk about tires and gas and oil and water pumps and johns and things like that—especially for the ladies who are not ordinarily oriented toward mechanical things."

Whitey reported that he retired soon after his wife died, and a sister who was an LoW member convinced him to join the group. "I realized I didn't fit in anywhere else, so I became a Loner and hit the road."

Dick interrupted, "Both of us have about the same problem, and many of the others have it too. Our backgrounds are a family, a business career, four bedrooms, three baths, two kids in college, a boat and cars and all the rest. In his case, suddenly his wife passes away, the kids are gone, and where is he? He's in that great big house all by himself. What's he gonna do? Invite his neighbor over to have coffee with him?"

Whitey agreed. "It doesn't work. If you visit another couple, you're regarded as a kind of broken spoke."

"So here," Dick emphasized, "is a very unique club. Very unique! We're all singles, and we have something in common—our RVs and our love of travel. Here, we're not broken spokes."

Off The Interstates

I asked Dick and Whitey if they regarded traveling by themselves as a lonely kind of existence, and Whitey replied, "Actually, I'm not as alone out on the road as I was in my own community. Most of the people you meet on the road are very nice, very congenial. They're more or less interested in you, and you can talk to them. Back in my own community, if a man raises a bushel of wheat more than you do, you're expected to speak first when you meet."

Dick said, "I sometimes surprise myself that I'm not lonesome. I had five kids, a wife, two dogs and a cat for thirty years. But it doesn't bother me one iota to be by myself for maybe a month at a time. Even if I stop at a roadside park overnight, if I'm outside my rig someone else will likely be outside his too, and we'll strike up a conversation. They're doing about what I'm doing—traveling in an RV—and we have something in common."

Whitey added, "Sometimes I'll spend two or three days in one county because there's so much to see. I travel off the beaten track quite often, too. I find it's a big help to go into county seats and chambers of commerce, ask for their literature and pick out what I want to see."

"I don't travel interstate highways unless I'm forced to," Dick said. "There are better accommodations, better restaurants, and more access to fuel and lodging off the interstates."

I asked the two men for their best estimates of how much money a single full-time RVer can expect to spend and still live comfortably. Whitey said, "I don't spend a great deal more than I would spend at home. Everybody thinks about the high cost of gasoline, and it's true that it costs a lot of money to travel extensively, but the other expenses are less. No matter where you are, you have to eat; you have to wear clothes. When you're on the road for a little while, you learn to be pretty thrifty. You learn to park where it doesn't cost very much or where it's free. I would say that two people could live very well full-timing on $1,000 a month."

Dick said that he spends about $250 per month, not counting insurance costs and gasoline expense. He estimated that gasoline costs him about $100 a month. He maintains two home bases which he uses alternately as resupply depots. "I have a residence in Fort Worth that I don't live in, but I have it fixed up so that I can park two or three rigs in the driveway and hook them up to electricity and sewer. I've also got a little shop there where I can tinker with my rig and do some repairs. My other home base is in Missouri at the club's campground (LoWzark), where I settle down and recover my energies and get ready for another migration back up north."

What advice would they give to other single men and women considering the full-time RVing life?

"I would advise them to join the Loners and go with it," said Dick. They can get a lot of advice from the Loners because they'll meet people that have been there, that are experienced full-timers. We have an awful lot of women full-timers in the club. The usual pattern is, they'll say, 'I camped for years with my kids and husband, and we had a campsite on the lake. We were retired one year, and the husband had a heart attack and died, and the kids are grown and gone, so now here I am full-timing by myself.' People like that are good sources of information for new full-timers and aspiring full-timers."

As my interview with Dick and Whitey was winding down, a woman club member approached Dick with a small electrical appliance and told him she had heard he could repair anything. "I don't know what's the matter with this," she said. "It just won't work. It's jammed or something." Dick rummaged in his toolbox until he found a small screwdriver, then began working on the appliance. Within a few minutes, it was repaired. She took it from him and beamed a bright smile. "How much do I owe you for that?" she asked.

"For that, I charge my usual rate," he said, and he pursed his lips for a kiss.

CONVERSATION WITH SOME LONERS

Grouped around a picnic table in a wooded section of a campground were six single full-time RVers—all members of the Loners on Wheels organization. There was Jeanne Deyo, a strikingly attractive fifty-five-year-old widow from Marshall, Michigan; Winnifred Fritsche, a shy, grandmotherly sixty-six-year-old native of Marietta, Ohio; comical Clara Siegle, seventy, a widow born in Holland; Conway Tweedy, a robust wid-

Winnifred Fritsche is a full-timing member of "Loners on Wheels," but "still a little shy where men are concerned."

ower from Minneapolis; Bob Woletz, sixty-seven, a retiree with so many things to do he couldn't talk very long; and Ruth Potter, a vivacious sixty-year-old who liked men and camping in equal measures.

They had joined me in order to talk about their lives as full-time RVers. They introduced themselves casually.

"I just retired a year ago," Winnifred said, "so this life is new for me. I've got a park model trailer in Texas, but I drove up to Oklahoma for a rally and then came up here to Indiana for this rally."

Clara said, "I'm from Van Nuys, California, but I sold my home in May of 1979 and bought a motorhome. I've been all over the West Coast, came east to Texas for a rally and then went to Florida."

"I'm from Flint, Michigan," Bob told us, "but I took my son's mailing address in Illinois. All I do is travel, and don't ask me where I'll be tomorrow because I don't know. I've got an 18-foot Trailblazer; it's all self-contained. I do very little boondocking, without hookups. A lot of the Loners do, but I don't care for it."

"I'm traveling in a van with a pop-top roof," said Conway. I figured on being away from my house for at least two years. I got mixed up with the Peace Corps, and if they gave me a job I like, I'll take it. I've been a widower for thirteen years, and I finally got my eighteen-year-old raised. When I got him through high school, I took off."

Clara said, "I left my kids behind too because I'm tired of being a built-in babysitter. I raised mine alone, so let them raise theirs without me. I still end up doing a lot of babysitting, but I escape whenever I get the chance."

"I belonged to the Loners for two years," Winnifred said, "but I just couldn't seem to find the time to get away. I run around in that high-top van that my son fixed up for me. I traveled a lot before I retired, but it seemed that I always had to hurry and get someplace so I could turn around and hurry back. I got tired of that. Now I want to just take my time."

Clara added, "Lots of us go on caravans. There might be anywhere from two to a dozen of us that get together and play follow-the-leader to wherever we want to go. We go wherever our hearts desire—usually to the next rallies or campouts."

Jeanne said, "I travel about half the time with caravans. If nobody's going my way or I don't want to caravan, I just go off on my own. I'm pretty independent. I figure if I have problems there will always be somebody around to help. I've gotten myself into some pretty wild places, but I just turn my rig around and get out of them."

"I've had a lot of problems," Clara said, "but mainly just with my rig. I had an accident in Miami, and then another one in Poplar Bluff, Missouri, that tied me up for 5½ weeks. I also was stranded in California with electrical trouble that nobody's been able to fix. Whenever my rig is being repaired, I just stay with it. I don't have any other home, and I'm not about to pay $25 a night for a motel room."

"I Don't Run Into Any Gold-Diggers"

How do full-timing Loners handle finances and mail?

"My pension checks go into the bank," Conway said. I have a checking account in my daughter's name, and she writes checks on it to pay my car insurance, my income tax and anything else. I have a post office box where my daughter picks up the mail, and she forwards it to me. I haven't been full-timing long enough to know just how my expenses are going to run, and if I continue the way I have, I'm going to be in trouble; I'll have to take a job somewhere. I'm trying to shoot for spending $20 a day, but I don't know if I can do it."

Clara reported, "A neighbor picks up my mail. I send her cards telling her where I'm going to stop so she can forward it to me by general delivery. My Social Security checks go into the bank. I have a savings and loan account that collects mortgage payments on a property, and some of that money also is put into a checking account. The savings and loan pays any of my bills out of that. I have only $600 a month to spend, and sometimes I have to save money by parking at a free spot and letting my finances catch up with me. It's the gasoline crunch that's killed me more than anything; $50 worth of gasoline is hardly a day's travel."

Winnifred said, "All my checks go into my checking account in Marietta, Ohio. My daughter-in-law collects my mail and sees that my credit card and telephone bills are paid. Then I reimburse her. While I'm in Texas, I just write checks and use Master Charge and Visa credit cards. The Fun 'N Sun parks there where I stay will cash $25 in checks a day, and they'll also take checks for anything you buy there."

"I don't have much money, so I don't have to arrange much," Jeanne said. "You won't believe how much income I have. Only about $250 a month! But this summer, I've been able to save money from that. I've always had to live on a little bit, ever since my husband died. I get a monthly check that goes into the bank, and I write checks on that. On my budget, I do a lot of boondocking and visit relatives in order to catch up with my gasoline expenses so I can go somewhere else. I was okay until the gasoline price increases came along. Now I do a lot of sitting in one spot. But I can just sit so long, then I have to go again."

I asked the group, "Why are you members of Loners on Wheels?"

Ruth answered for everyone: "Because we can be together. We're out of place in a crowd of married people. There, I'm an "extra" even though they are very nice to me. Here, we're all single. I can walk out there in that crowd of campers and speak to any man I want, and I know that he doesn't have a jealous wife sitting back someplace watching everything I do. I had that problem running my own campground; I had to be careful what I said to a man because I never knew which of those women was his wife. The first Loners rally I went to, I was still careful that way. The rally was almost over before it really sunk into my head that all those guys were single and I had a right to talk to any of them."

Jeanne said, "I never talked to men on the road before I joined the Loners. I still hesitate a little sometimes, but I find that I gravitate more toward the men because they talk about things I'm interested in. Like how to take care of things. I've always had to take care of the house, cars, and my rig."

Winnifred said, "I'm still a little bit shy where men are concerned. I don't know why, but maybe it's because I do have a fairly good income and I'm worried about men being after what I've got."

Ruth said, "I just tell them I don't have anything, that I gave everything I owned to my daughters before I started traveling and my daughters just give me an allowance to live on. So I don't run into any gold diggers."

Chapter Eleven

'Til Death
Do You Part

Chris and Charlotte Moffett were an ideal couple. He was a handsome, carefree Air Force pilot, and she was "an army brat" who was highly educated, talented and well traveled. They met in Puerto Rico, where Chris was stationed and Charlotte was working as head of the American Institute of Bankers Correspondence School after having graduated from secretarial college and the University of Michigan. People who knew them agreed: they had one of the world's great marriages. They began RVing in the early 1950s, moved into a kind of joint directorship of one of the first national RV clubs in the 1960s, raised two children and then hit the road together in the fall of 1970 for a life of full-time RVing.

Along the way, Charlotte was stricken with cancer in one lung.

Together, Chris and Charlotte fought the disease and, after twelve years, she recovered completely from its effects, only to see it reappear in the other lung. In 1976, Charlotte died, leaving Chris crushed and alone for the first time in the travel trailer that was his home. He's continued to live in a trailer, traveling from one favorite destination to another and making occasional detours to visit with old friends. But even today, when he talks about Charlotte, the wrinkles around his outdoorsman's eyes deepen, and his voice grows softer, quieter. "She was the love of my life," he says.

Chris, like so many other widowers and widows, had a difficult decision to make after his wife died: whether to continue alone, the kind of lifestyle that he and Charlotte had shared and enjoyed together, or give up his life on the road and settle down to living in a house or an apartment not far from his two children. It was a tough decision because Chris knew from his long acquaintance with other full-timers that he would have a constant battle against loneliness, and there would be many times when he would feel like an outsider and a fifth wheel among RVing married couples. But he chose to continue full-time RVing anyway.

I talked with sixty-eight-year-old Chris in the summer of 1980 while he was attending the international rally of the Holiday Rambler RV Club. He admitted, "It does get lonely at times. That's the biggest difference between traveling alone and with your mate. Charlotte and I got along so beautifully. I don't think we ever had an argument that was worth remembering. We had spats from time to time, but we usually agreed on the things we liked to do. She'd suggest something, and I'd think it was a good idea, so we'd do it. Now, I do as I please, more on the spur of the moment. Someone may suggest something I like, and I'll be gone the next day."

Chris learned to enjoy camping while he was a boy in Maine. "My wife, though, was an army brat and had always lived in the city," Chris recalled, "so she didn't know anything about camping. I bought a sleeping bag and an air mattress, and we camped in an umbrella tent the first few years we were married. She got pretty darned good at it. We made our own galleys to take along to make things easier for her. Then, in the early fifties we rented a 16-foot Delwood travel trailer in Wichita. She loved it. It had an icebox, a two-burner stove and a good bed, but that was about all. It didn't have a shower facility; in fact, we dumped water over our heads from out of a dairy can."

After the trip with that trailer, Charlotte kept me busy looking at trailers we could buy until she found another one identical to the one we'd rented. Later, we bought a 19-foot Holiday Rambler, and we pulled it all over creation—to the West Coast, Yellowstone and places like that— for four and a half years."

By 1967, Chris was ready to retire from the Air Force after thirty years. He and Charlotte had joined the new Holiday Rambler RV club a couple of years earlier, and when they heard the club needed a new executive director, Chris applied for the position.

For three years, Chris worked as director of the club while Charlotte served as his secretary and assistant, and their RVing experiences convinced them they wanted to be full-time trailerists. They bought a 29-foot demonstrator coach from Holiday Rambler late in 1970, Chris quit his job and they hit the road. "We found a place in Mexico we liked very much, and we went back there for four months every year until Charlotte became seriously ill. I haven't been there since, although I plan to go back. Funny, that place was not what you'd call a wonderful trailer park.

Chris Moffett, who with his wife Charlotte, began RVing together almost thirty years ago.

The electricity was crazy, and an awful lot about it left something to be desired. But it was on a beautiful bay. The surf was low enough that you could launch a boat and catch the Mexican dorado and, if you wanted, you could get marlin and sailfish."

Chris was silent, thoughtful for a few minutes. He smiled to himself as he remembered those early days of full-timing. Then: "Charlotte loved full-time trailering. She could clean a trailer in thirty minutes a week. She'd fix one honest meal in the evening, and we'd catch-as-catch-can for lunch, so I might go to the cantina and eat a bowl of shrimp or I'd go back to the trailer and we'd snack together. It was just a good, free, easy life. I'd get up early and go out to talk with the fisherman. She'd put on her bathing suit and join the other women in the bay. In the spring, we'd start back up into the U.S. and stop off in Tucson for a while before deciding where else to go. We both loved Alaska, so we went up there several times."

Time has eased Chris's pain somewhat, although he admitted he sometimes expects to find Charlotte waiting for him when he returns to his trailer after visiting friends. He has friends all over the North American continent due to his extensive travels and his continued association with the Holiday RV club.

He advises aspiring fulltimers; "The most important thing is to get a trailer that's big enough. Don't get a little one, for several reasons. There is more comfort in a big trailer, and you will live in it more than you tow it. A big trailer is also easier to tow; it won't bounce around, crosswinds and gusts of air from trucks won't bother it as much, and it's easier to back into a campsite. Next, prepare to cut yourself loose and forget about the things you've left behind. Also, don't go into parks and just sit inside your trailer. Get out and walk around and speak to everyone you meet. Just talk about anything that pops into your mind. If the other person smiles, that's an invitation to talk."

Chris added, "I stopped last night at a campground, and a fellow already camped there helped me park my trailer by holding some kids at bay so I could back in without hitting them. He came over later with a drink in his hand and invited me to sit with him. Pretty soon, we'd become friends. I might never see him again, but for a couple of hours, we were good friends."

During the ten years he has been a full-time RVer, Chris has cut back on his driving due to fuel costs and availability. "Last year I made a real contribution to gasoline conservation because I just left the U.S. completely," he joked. "But aside from traveling in Canada and Mexico, I think the answer to the fuel problems is that you can't make long runs. I've slowed down and shortened my trips considerably. More of us should drive every other day or every third day or wait a week and then drive somewhere. Also, sometimes it's not how far you drive, but how fast you drive that affects your expenses. We should all drive a little slower."

As for meals, Chris said, "I do most of my own cooking. I love gourmet food, and I like to go to gourmet restaurants, but I hate to go to those places by myself. If I can find a girl friend or another couple that wants to go, I'll do it. Eating in a greasy spoon restaurant, though, God forbid. I have a crock pot that I use in making my own stews—especially lamb stew—and I make oxtail soup in my crock pot; I make casseroles and I bake things."

I pointed out, "You mentioned girl friends. Do you have many lady friends?"

"There are some women that I've known for many years, and I'll stop by and see them and take them out to dinner if I'm near where they live. There are plenty of girls in the trailer parks in Tucson. They're pleasant to be with as long as they don't get too serious and act like they want to change my way of life. The worst thing about mature women is that they need a security blanket, and that security blanket is a house. They aren't happy unless they've got it. My wife, since she was an army brat, never had a house until we got married and bought one, and she didn't mind being without one at all. I can't find anybody else like that, and I'm not about to give up my way of life. I have had one or two traveling companions on occasion. I've got to be careful there, though. One of my traveling companions doesn't particularly care for the other one. I'm sold on this full-time trailering; there's so much to see in this country. And I'd rather see it alone than give it up and have a companion.

WOMEN ALONE

Widows frequently have a tougher time deciding whether to be full-time RVers than widowers. Our society expects men to be more adventuresome, more independent than women. An elderly man is respected and envied if he cuts loose from his family and friends in order to travel full-time in an RV; a widow the same age, on the other hand, is expected to settle into a quiet, grandmotherly role and spend her days rocking on the front porch with a warm blanket across her knees. Friends and relatives—and especially grown children—usually try to dissuade the widow from embarking on extensive RV adventures because they are afraid for her health and safety. Widows who depended heavily on their late husbands have a particularly difficult time convincing everyone who is concerned about them that they need—and deserve—their independence and freedom.

Edith Lane, founder of the nationwide Loners on Wheels organization, said, "One of our members who is in her eighties told me, 'My children have given me the greatest gift of all: the freedom to live my life as I see fit without interference or advice from them, and without making me feel guilty or selfish for doing so.' "

The Loners on Wheels club has probably been more responsible than anything else for hundreds of widows' decisions to become full-time RVers. By interacting with each other, traveling in caravans, camping together and simply commiserating about each other's problems, club members have opened up a whole new realm of travel and adventure for single women, and especially for widows. The club's outlook toward widowhood was probably best expressed by Helen Duffessy, a club director and a full-time RVer who admitted that enjoying life after her husband died was difficult. "But you have to realize that when the one you love dies, you still have the rest of your life to live. So go out and do it. You have to get over the shock; you don't go to the funeral and the next day start a new life. But eventually, you do come up, and every day it gets better. You realize that you don't have to please anyone but yourself now."

Aspiring single full-timers should not let others convince them to put their travel dreams aside with horror stories about robbery, rape, murder and mayhem. Edith Lane reported, "In over eight years of reporting the personal news set in by members of LoW, I have never heard of anyone being held up at gunpoint, robbed or molested while in their vehicles. And the few cases of a rig being burglarized while the occupant was absent were most often due to carelessness, overtrustfulness or just plain lack of forethought." Many a woman who depended on her husband to select destinations, map travel routes, choose campgrounds and campsites and then park, level and hook up their RV has discovered to her delight that she can do all those things herself, now that her mate is gone. Motorhomes are not difficult to drive; trailers are not hard to tow. Anyone can do it with a little practice, as hundreds of thousands of women have learned. People who claim otherwise just don't know what they are talking about. While there definitely is a mystique to RVing, there certainly is no mystery to doing it!

"I Seem To Manage Very Nicely"

Single full-timers even have one big advantage over full-timing couples: they don't require so much living space, so they have much more latitude in choosing a full-time RVing rig that suits them. Couples generally are limited to choosing from among rather large travel trailers, motorhomes or fifth-wheel trailers. Widows and other single travelers can select their rigs from among those, of course, but they also are more able to live comfortably on the road in small RVs such as camping vans, pickup campers, micro mini motorhomes, mini motorhomes and little travel trailers and fifth-wheels.

Remember Winnifred Fritsche and Conway Tweedy from the previous chapter? They live full-time in camper vans while on the road. Whitey Whitesell travels in a micro mini, as does another full-time RVing LoW member, Jack Underwood of Las Vegas. Mickey Newburn didn't want anything that small, though, so she taught herself to drive a full-size 24½-foot mini motorhome. Widower Paul Allison of California opted for a short, 21-foot travel trailer towed by a pickup truck, and he outfitted his rig with a fishing boat, a motorbike and a bicycle.

Jerry Griffin of Seven Hills, Ohio, bought a 25-foot Coachmen trailer and a propane-fueled Chevrolet truck to tow it in 1980, just before he retired from his chief electrician's job with the City of Cleveland and joined the ranks of the single full-timers. Jerry became a widower at the age of fifty-six, and I talked with him a few weeks later while he was attending a Loners on Wheels rally. "I was going to be a full-timer in April with my wife, but when she died I decided to continue working until the end of the year in order to get my feet on the ground. When I met the Loners, I decided I was going to join them and have a wonderful time with them. The other Loners have had some of the same problems and complications that I've had, and everything seems to have worked out for the best for them. They're all friendly. They know how I feel, and I know how they feel. I'm spending all the time I can at their rallies, and when I finally retire, I'm planning on traveling around the country with them."

Blanche Shunk, widowed in 1972 at the age of sixty-one, became a full-time RVer in 1979 and split her time between living in a 21-foot travel trailer and a mobile home in Florida. She retired from occupational therapy at the Michigan Masonic Home in 1975 and towed her little trailer to Florida and back three seasons before deciding to try full-timing. Then she bought a larger, 23-foot Prowler trailer that she could tow behind her 1970 American Motors Ambassador and spent most of her time since then traveling around the eastern half of the country by herself.

I met Blanche in Michigan when she was sixty-nine-years-old, and I observed that she was leading quite an independent lifestyle. "It sure is," she grinned. "I enjoy traveling, I enjoy people and I enjoy life. Some women my age don't like large crowds, but I do." She said she ignored warnings from friends and relatives that she might not be safe traveling alone and emphasized she has never had any problems RVing. "I seem to manage very nicely."

Blanche keeps busy, when other people aren't around, by creating beadwork and making wall hangings of carpeting and burlap. "I also can do crocheting, knitting, weaving, ceramics, and I make really different porcelain ware. I sell some of it at parks in Florida that have hobby and crafts shows, and I take some to a sale that is held during a church retreat that I attend."

In an effort to expand her horizons and meet more people, Blanche joined the Good Sam Club and began attending Samborees. "I really should take someone with me, though," she said. "Everyone is part of a little group of some kind, and it's easier to join a group like that if there are two of you. I'm learning to be more outgoing, however. I'm coordinator for the senior citizens at a state camp meeting in August. I've always been such a shy person that to get up in front of a group of people like that made me shake in my boots, but being coordinator last year was the easiest thing I ever did."

Blanche said she tries to encourage other widows who are RV enthusiasts to try full-timing too. "It would seem a little strange to them at first, but once they get a little confidence in themselves, they'll make it all right. I'd also advise anyone considering doing it to get rid of a lot of stuff, especially if they're going to sell their homes."

"Remain Flexible—That's The Secret"

Another widow who encourages single women to try the full-timing lifestyle is Helen Duffessy, who began her own full-timing adventures in 1977, eleven years after her husband's death. I met her in 1980 when she was sixty-five and traveling in a 27-foot Empire travel trailer towed by a specially equipped Ford station wagon. "I bought the trailer and wagon at the same time, and I had the car custom built on the inside for me. I like a big car. I'm big and tall and have long legs."

I asked Helen if she'd done any special planning before she became a full-time RVer, and she answered, "I did a heck of a lot of arithmetic, I can tell you that! I figured out that if Social Security set in at the appropriate time, as it did, I'd be able to make it financially. And things seem to work out right for me. For example, I wanted to go to Europe, and the day I went to the travel agent and found out what my air fare was going to be, I got a six-week job offer. I didn't hesitate taking it, but ordinarily I never would have taken a job for as long as six weeks. I thought to myself, 'Boy, some things are just meant to be.' But ordinarily, I watch my expenses very closely. I don't go to fancy restaurants, I don't do nightclubbing and I'm still wearing the same clothes I wore before I retired. I've changed my way of living; I used to live very expensively."

Helen said her preplanning arithmetic convinced her she could live on the road for $800 a month. "And I do. As with everybody else, when the money supply gets low, I sit in one place and spend as little as possible until more comes in on the first of the month. I don't even want to think about the price of gasoline. I don't spend as much time driving, and I don't go as far as some full-timers. I have discovered that the airlines have a beautiful 50% fare for senior citizens. I want to go to California for the tenth anniversary of Loners on Wheels, and I figured that if a friend picks me up at the L.A. airport, I can fly to California for less than it would cost me to drive."

She emphasized, "A full-timer has to remain flexible, however; that's the secret to successful full-time RVing. This is no kind of life for anybody who feels he has to be at a certain place at a certain time or for someone who must eat precisely at noon or six o'clock.

I wrote a good description of a "Loner on Wheels" once. I said an LoW is *very seldom*. Meaning, of course, that an LoW is seldom low. I said several things that we who are Loners would understand, and one of the things I said was that Loners can be depended upon to change their minds (about where they're going) between the time they hook up their rigs and the time they reach the main road. I said that the mating cry of a Loner is, 'Where did you come from?' You really, truly can never tell where we're going to show up. Somebody will say, 'Well, I was going this way, but all of a sudden I remembered I had never been down *that* way.' I have an expression: I say, 'I went down to Syracuse and turned left and ended up in Montreal instead of Massachusetts.' That's part of what I mean about being flexible."

Does an attractive woman like Helen meet many men friends on the road?

"Friends have told me that I slap down a man so fast it makes his head spin," Helen replied. "I've been out with men—with Loners and with other men that I meet here and there—but I'm just not interested! I think I'm just too used to being alone. I enjoy having my own place, my own choice of TV programs, and I enjoy being able to leave someplace when I want to go and not when somebody else is ready to go. I guess the truth of the matter is, I enjoy being alone. Maybe I'm too selfish. But for thirty years, I was a devoted wife and mother, and by golly, now I'm doing what I want to do!"

Like most Loners, Helen said she has had few problems with people while traveling. "I operate defensively. I don't use rest areas for over-nighters, and I am quite willing to pay the $5 or $6 fees, or even more than that, to park in a campground because I feel that is sensible. I never pick up hitchhikers. I don't think I have ever been ripped off by service stations, although I might have been without knowing it. If I do discover I have been taken advantage of, I'm a writer, and I can hit the typewriter and write a letter that will scorch the paper, and it gets results. I have had to write a couple of hot letters to oil companies about service stations, and I've gotten results from doing that."

"Helen And The Helpless Caravan"

Although Helen said she has traveled by RV caravan several times and "probably will again," she added, "I have traveled in caravans that have made me want to swear off caravans forever! The one I call the "Helen and the Helpless Caravan" was the worst. We were caravaning from The Slabs in California to South Texas for a rally in January, and on the way we encountered a snowstorm. Well, two of the people from California didn't know anything about snowstorms, and Helen, who was from Michigan, knew a thing or two and tried to persuade them to stop over at a little town in Texas. But no, they wouldn't do that. They didn't know how to drive in snow, but they were moving faster than I was, so they led the way, and they really got into trouble. One woman rear-ended somebody else because she was driving too close behind and too fast for icy pavement.

Either their CBs wouldn't work or they didn't know how to use them, and they got away from the rest of us; we lost them completely. When we got to camp, they weren't there yet, so we knew they were lost. I said to the others, 'I guess I'd better get on the CB and see if I can raise them so they know where we are,' and one of the men in another rig said, 'Can't we just let them stay lost?' I told him that wouldn't be the thing to do, but that we couldn't help it if they were unable to find us. I did what was necessary, though; I told them where we were, and finally they all came traipsing in. It's funny, now, and I guess as long as you can keep your sense of humor, you're all right."

Although Helen writes occasionally for newspaper and magazines, she does not do it to supplement her income, but for fun. "I am not sufficiently motivated to say that today I'm going to write on such-and-such a subject. I write when the mood strikes me." She does supplement her income with occasional office work. She usually finds work through agencies which hire people for temporary employment. "The hardest thing for me to do sometimes is stay out of work. I have turned down at least three permanent job offers—good ones. But I don't want them. For a good many years, I was the office manager and executive secretary to a trial attorney in Detroit—scheduling, and organizing him and making certain everything was done and followed up. I finally decided I'd had it. Now, when I go into an office for a temporary secretarial job, they point me toward the machine and I do what they hire me to do to the best of my ability, but when that job is done, I walk out."

Since Helen is a widely traveled full-timer, I was curious why she chooses to winter in a mobile home in Florida rather than in Arizona,

Southern California or Texas. "I much prefer the tropics to the desert or to Texas," she said. "In Texas, the wind blows constantly, and that really bugs me. I don't like the northers that hit Texas, either. They come on so fast that you can leave your trailer to walk to the rec hall and before you get there the temperature has dropped thirty degrees. And it's a *cold* kind of cold. Of course, in the desert, the climate is dry, and I prefer the moist climate of the tropics."

Asked about her travel habits, Helen replied, "When I'm by myself, I pull into a campground between three and four in the afternoon. Generally, about 300 miles is all I care to drive in a day. I've tried to go farther than that, but I get exhausted very quickly. Now I know my limits. If there is a restaurant conveniently nearby and I don't have to dress up, I might go there, but most of the time, unless I'm really beat, I'll cook my own dinner and either eat it in my rig or out on a picnic table. If I feel the urge to charcoal broil something, I walk through the park and, if I see somebody that has a charcoal fire, I'll ask if I might put my steak on it. I've always been welcome to do that, and I have even been requested to join them at their table. After dinner, I walk around the camp and gab with a few people."

In the winter, most campgrounds in Texas, Florida and Arizona have long lists of activities that appeal to single full-time RVers. "Fun 'N Sun in Texas is a big gathering place for the Loners in the winter," Helen reported. "Everybody's there. That's a place that maintains a schedule that could wear anybody out. Some people need that kind of thing. There are people who could start going with an exercise class at eight in the morning and wind up dancing until midnight. I never was one of those people."

Full-timers, and especially LoW members, are able to renew old acquaintances often while on the road, she said. "You can never tell when you're going to pull into a rest area or a campground and see an old friend. And, of course, the first thing anybody says is the mating cry of the Loner: 'Where did you come from?' And the next thing you know, you're in a caravan headed for someplace you never intended to go."

Full-time Loners are especially helpful to other single RVers, she said, adding that she remembers how patient Loner Marge Dickieson was in teaching her how to back up and maneuver her trailer when she first began RVing. Helen said she planned to meet a prospective LoW member in Florida to help the woman buy an RV. Another woman asked Helen to ride with her while she practiced towing her trailer and Helen, remembering her own early experiences with towing, agreed. "It's not my cup of tea—I already had to teach my three kids how to drive—but she says

I'm the only person that will ride with her. Somebody had to do it, I guess, and it didn't cost me anything except a few gray hairs."

Does Helen see the time coming when she will stop her full-time RVing and return to living in a house? "I can see the time coming, but not very soon, and not of my own volition," she answered. "I can see the time that the world oil situation or gas rationing will make driving a car that gets eight miles to the gallon with a trailer behind it prohibitive. Then, maybe, air fare will prove to be more economical. I think the intelligent person has to be prepared and flexible, to be able to roll with the punches."

Chapter Twelve

Work While Traveling

F orest H. "Frosty" Gehron tried to retire and travel a couple of times, but somebody always either offered him a job or a business opportunity he couldn't refuse. First he retired from a fifteen-year career as an antique dealer but didn't find the relaxation he sought in Florida because the property he owned on St. John's River there seemed like a perfect place for a campground, so he built one. He retired again a few years later when his son-in-law bought the park, and Frosty and his wife decided to travel the country in an RV. They went to California, where Frosty was convinced to work as manager of the Greenhorn Ranch Company; he took the job temporarily, but the weeks stretched into eighteen months before the Gehrons found themselves back on the road again. They trailered back toward Florida, intending to visit relatives, but were sidetracked in Tennessee by a request to help out the then-troubled Loretta Lynn Dude Ranch. Frosty managed the ranch for the last part of the season, then found himself agreeing to return the following year as full-time manager.

Frosty still isn't sure when he'll be able to enjoy the full-time RVing life that he's looked forward to for so long. He said, "Something always seems to come up . . ." But meanwhile, Gehron is making sure the dude ranch is among the growing number of private and public campgrounds that depend heavily upon the valuable skills and experience of active full-time RVers. Most of his thirty-five employees are full-timers who spend their summers at the ranch working.

He explained, "We work a short season—six months—and I know that to find competent people to work in a six-month span of time is a very difficult thing to do. I'd rather not use college and high school kids.

Frosty Gehron manages the Loretta Lynn Dude Ranch and campground with friendly efficiency.

You don't get the same kind of work ability and responsibility out of younger people and typical six-month employees that I need. I took the reverse attitude. I decided I needed the knowledge of older people—people who know *how* to work and can talk on the same level as our campers. They aren't college kids who simply don't know what the world is all about, and they are able to accomplish more and maintain a much friendlier attitude toward the campers. They get their work done without my having to stand behind them with a whip saying, 'You do this; you do that.' They're here in the morning on time and, after I give them directions on what work they should do, I don't ever have to check on them during the day. They're work oriented, and they know how to get the job done."

Most of the full-time RVers who work summers at the dude ranch are snowbirds who spend their winters in Florida. Frosty provides them with free campsites and small salaries that enable them to save enough money so they don't have to work during the winter when they trek back to Florida. The work is not easy, though, and the hours are long. "We work from seven o'clock in the morning until midnight," Frosty said, "but

The old grist mill on Loretta Lynn's Dude Ranch near Hurricane Mills, Tennessee, is now Loretta's museum.

these people seem to thrive on that schedule. The average person couldn't do it; he'd look at the clock in the morning and say, 'It's eight o'clock, time to go to work,' and then at five that afternoon he'd say, 'It's time to quit.' We can't run this place on that type of schedule. These snowbirds might be retired, but they still want something to do, and they do it well. We have a gentleman who works our recreation hall all summer. You couldn't find a cobweb or a speck of dust in that rec hall at any time, and the campers who go in there are always treated right. My campground manager—Sherbert Daniel—does an excellent job of visiting with the campers, making them feel welcome; he's a full-time RVer, just like most of the rest."

Work at Loretta Lynn's Dude Ranch isn't all drudgery, however. RVing employees are encouraged to lean heavily on their own experience in helping campers enjoy themselves. They handle horses, lead trail rides, schedule hayrides, put on campfire shows and square dances and take the "dude" campers on trail cookouts by horseback. In their spare time—and they always manage to find some—they have free access to the 6,000-acre park's facilities: shuffleboard courts, the rec hall, a swimming pool, tennis courts, pedalboats, canoes, bicycles, the horses and a mountain stream stocked with trout and smallmouth bass. As a bonus, they get to work with Loretta's husband, Mooney, and their children—all of whom have regular duties at the ranch—and sometimes, Loretta herself takes a break from her heavy schedule and returns home for a few days.

Working For The Park Service

While it would not be accurate to say the Loretta Lynn Dude Ranch is typical of the private parks and campgrounds that depend heavily upon full-time RVers for seasonal work, it is a fact that more and more campground operators are recognizing how they can take advantage of the work habits and skills of experienced campers. And a majority of the private and public parks in this country now employ at least a couple of retirees in their labor forces.

Public parks such as those owned by the U.S. Army Corps of Engineers and the National Park Service also hire full-time RVers for seasonal work. The Corps of Engineers began doing it several years ago in an attempt to cut its own expenses and, at the same time, put experienced campers in positions as employees where they could deal directly with the public. An experimental program which started when a live-in couple was hired to man the gates of the Whitley Creek Campground in Illinois has been expanded by the Corps to include nearly every district in the nation. By hiring full-time RVing couples to work at various jobs in the parks, the Corps discovered it could reduce its expenses tremendously, since the full-timers did not demand year-round salaries, vacations, sick leave and fringe benefits, and they were willing to accept free camping space as partial payment for their services.

Unexpectedly, the Corps also learned that camping employees were not only more skillful at explaining park programs and rules to visitors, but they also were enthusiastic supporters of the Corps' entire recreational and conservation system. In a sense, by hiring full-time RVers, the Corps also was employing a dedicated public relations staff and an invaluable network of goodwill ambassadors.

Mickey and Laila Rutledge are two of the full-time RVers who occasionally work in Corps of Engineers parks. During the years since they hit the road full-time in 1974 they also have worked in private, independent campgrounds and in parks operated by the Jellystone franchise and Outdoor Resorts of America. Their first campground job was with the

National Park Service after they attended classes in park management. They spend most of their summers working at parks in northern climates and their winters at ORA parks in the South. Some summers, they don't bother to find jobs, but travel instead. They joined the full-time RVing life when Mickey was only forty-nine and a semiretired electrician. "We'd thought about it for a while, and we had our trailer (a 27-foot Holiday Rambler that they replaced in 1977 with a 32-footer). We decided to try it a year to see if we'd like it. I guess we did because we're still doing it six years later," Mickey reported.

After they completed the park management training in California, they were offered several full-time jobs but turned those down because they didn't want to settle in one place. "But we knew we needed income from part-time jobs to supplement returns on our investments," Mickey said. "Any average person who thinks he can save enough money to retire and travel on should forget it, with the inflation rate going up the way it has. You make investments that you think are good, and today they are, but tomorrow they might not be. There's no way you can say you're going to live on *X* amount of dollars because you can't know that for sure. By working, we've been able to maintain our lifestyle at the same level."

When I met Mickey and Laila, they were working as park attendants at the ORA facility in Orlando. There, they helped supervise maintenance of the park and assigned rental customers to sites. The summer before, Mickey worked as manager of ORA's campground in Michigan. In addition to being paid wages for their efforts, the Rutledges also received a cost-free campsite with full hookups.

While the Rutledges were quite young for retirement, Mickey said they became full-time RVers "as young as we could because I've seen too many people wait too long to do it. I've seen more of it since I've been in the park business; people put off traveling until they're sixty-five and can qualify for Social Security, and by then they're lucky if both of them are healthy enough to travel. They're even luckier if they're both alive." The Rutledges maintain a home base in Louisville, but Laila said, "Last year, I think we were home only five days. We had a six-month contract last year with the Corps of Engineers that we had to fulfill. If we could work *only* six months a year instead of more than that, we'd like it better. Just so we could earn enough to pick up the slack. But is seems that as inflation goes up, we either have to work more often or do some cutting somewhere."

Mickey said he has hopes, however, of reducing his work schedule when he is old enough to receive Social Security benefits. He said most other full-timers he knows also "pick up odd jobs whenever they can find

197

them" in order to supplement their incomes. "And I'm sure there is going to be more and more of that as the prices and inflation keep going up. People on pensions and Social Security have only so much money coming in, and there is no way their fixed incomes can keep up with inflation."

The winter season was nearly at an end in Orlando, and the Rutledges already were planning their spring trek north. They said they would stop at their house in Louisville, resupply, and then probably work the summer at a Corps of Engineers park in Tennessee. "We've already inspected a couple of parks and bid on jobs, and we're waiting for our bids to be accepted somewhere," Mickey said. Each seasonal job is advertised in newspapers by the Corps, and interested couples and individuals must bid on the positions, declaring how much salary and what kind of fringe benefits they require. A combination of the lowest and most reasonable bids are usually accepted by the Corps, and six-month contracts are awarded. Anyone interested in seeking a position with the Corps should write to one of its thirty-seven district offices. A partial list of district offices was published in the January, 1978, issue of *Trailer Life*, and copies are available upon request, with a small fee charged for handling.

Working For Concessionaires

In most state and federal parks, facilities such as restaurants, campground stores, riding stables, boat and canoe liveries, recreational areas and sometimes even the campgrounds themselves are operated by commercial concessionaires that work on an annual or multi-year contract basis. Most concessionaires need seasonal employees to fill both full-time and part-time staff positions and, therefore, they frequently hire RVers. C. R. Madsen, a full-time trailerist who worked one summer for the concessionaire at Yellowstone National Park, wrote a very informative article about his experiences in a March 1978, issue of *Trailer Life* ("Get Paid For RVing This Summer"). Along with his article, *Trailer Life* published a list of national forests, national parks, monuments and some private campgrounds where full-time RVers can find seasonal work.

Madsen offered this advice: "Pick out the recreational area where you'd most like to spend a summer and whip off a letter to the concessionaire requesting an application for employment. Tell them you will bring your own trailer and live it it. January and February are the normal months for getting in your application for seasons beginning in June. But, a lot of concessionaires seem to have a perpetual problem with last-minute cancellations, no-shows, quitters and no-gooders. The result is that frequently there are job openings throughout the season for trailerists who are already on the road. These walk-on jobs don't always provide a lot of choice, so you should be prepared to accept anything from store clerk to dishwasher to janitor. Be sure to have a record of your Social Security number and if possible a recent health certificate including a TB test certificate which is sometimes required for food handlers or for insurance purposes."

About his own experience at national parks, Madsen wrote, "The biggest frustration [encountered] is lack of time to enjoy the surroundings, but that's an obstacle that can be overcome with wise planning of free time. And the benefits of seasonal park employment are many. Rose and I have acquired some very valued friendships with other trailerists and some wonderful young kids who still write to us. So why not let a concession company pay your vacation bills this summer? It can be a truly unique and memorable RV experience."

Jeane V. Baldner and her husband opted to try the work-while-traveling life when they were only fifty-two-years-old. Four years later, she reported, "Semiretirement is fun and very gratifying. We meet some of the nicest people in the world, see some of the most beautiful sights in America, and we've had the happiest four years of our life."

She added, "Semiretirement is a good time to start doing things you've always wanted to do but never quite had the guts to do. My husband was in the men's retail clothing business most of his life, but had always wanted to drive a semi truck or charter bus. The first summer we were retired, he qualified to drive a bus, got his ICC permit and used his experience driving a tour bus in Yellowstone National Park last summer. He also had a job last summer working at a trailer park where we were living. He loves working outdoors, and that was a great place to do it. I helped at the office during peak periods."

FINDING SUPPLEMENTAL INCOME

Experienced full-timers in need of extra funds have learned that the easiest way for them to earn money is to take temporary—or even seasonal—jobs in areas where they intend to spend a few months; for example, near their winter retreats in Florida, Arizona, California or South Texas. Since most mature RVers possess developed skills or talents that they used in their preretirement days, they have less difficulty finding jobs than one might think. Experienced nurses, for example, are always in demand in nearly every locale. So are accountants, product demonstrators, salespersons and cooks. Someone with solid skills and clerical experience can usually find work, and tourist areas usually need dependable bartenders, cashiers, waiters and waitresses. Nearly any talent can be put to use, from square dance calling to Tupperware sales.

Matching skills to the existing job market can be done by checking the yellow pages of the local telephone directory in order to glean a list of businesses that might need such talent, and then writing letters and making telephone calls to the personnel offices of those businesses. Job-seekers can place ads in the classified sections of newspapers and answer help wanted ads. Experienced people might even find work by telephoning directly to business executives in fields of their own expertise. A writer, for example, would not be out of line if he called an editor of the local newspaper and inquired whether substitute reporters or copy editors are needed for ill or vacationing staff members. An experienced chef could offer to help with the lunch traffic at a local restaurant. An experienced secretary could make her services available to a law firm.

Of course, local offices of Manpower and Kelly Girls are nearly always in need of temporary or seasonal workers, especially if such people have easily marketable skills. Senior Citizen Council offices in most major cities are quite helpful, assisting senior citizens in finding work, while offices of the Temporary Job Service are open to anyone, regardless of age. If the job-seeker is not extremely choosy, some kind of work usually can be found for him through the area's state employment service; fortunately, placement in such jobs is free.

One full-time RVer I know was a retired factory worker, and the area of Florida he visited every winter had no demand for his skills. Undaunted, he enrolled in a school for referees, and now when he winters in Florida he is in demand to officiate at high school and junior high school basketball games. Each summer, he picks up extra money in the north by umpiring at softball and Little League baseball games. A lady full-timer could not find a job that took advantage of her experience as a former stockbroker, so she convinced a community college and an adult school to let her teach classes in financial planning and investments. A former longshoreman found his niche at a combination campground and marina, where he supervises the riding stables and rents canoes and boats to guests. A retired teacher from Ohio earned certification to teach in the Arizona public schools, and now she earns money as a substitute teacher for three different school districts; her skills are in so much demand that she could work every day during the school year if she so desired.

The First Sambassadors

I've always been particularly intrigued by the small army of full-time RVers who travel around the country inspecting parks for the national campground directories. In that vein, one of the best jobs I've ever heard of is the position of Good Sam Sambassador, created a few years ago by *Trailer Life*'s Good Sam Club. Ken and Flo Cooper, a couple of full-time RVers from Los Angeles, were the first Sambassadors. Here's how the jobs were created.

"I had just retired and was working on some special projects for the Good Sam organization," Ken reported, "when I realized that there was a lack of communication between the international headquarters in California and the Good Sam chapters in different parts of the country. It seemed to me from my special viewpoint that no one from headquarters was really working directly with the chapters to help them solve their problems. I suggested to the organization that there should be some kind of structure implemented to assist the chapters."

Flo interrupted. "Meanwhile, Art Rouse [Chairman of the Board of TL Enterprises, parent company of the Good Sam Club] had been thinking along those lines himself."

"When Sue Bray became Executive Director of the club," Ken continued, "she said she was very much in favor of the concept of an ambassador program. We talked about it, and she asked us to become the first representatives of a new Sambassador system, on a sort of trial basis. We left California right away, went to Montreal, then to Nova Scotia and over the next couple of months hit about ten Samborees. Our job as Sambassadors is to represent Good Sam however we can—communicating with members and chapters, in a sort of public relations capacity. I also do things like working as a consultant to the New York Samboree, helping interpret policy."

Flo added, "We also take Good Sam groups to specific places, like leading a Samboree by Sea through the Panama Canal or to New Zealand. One of the other Sambassadors and his wife will take a group on a Princess Line cruise in September, and apparently we'll be asked to take groups on trips like that. Besides being the host on the Panama Canal cruise, Ken also worked in the capacity of official photographer."

Ken's own professional background enabled him to fit easily into the Sambassador's role. He was employed for thirty years by the parks department of the City of Los Angeles and retired in 1977 as assistant superintendent of recreation and parks. "I had a lot of professional experience in organizing big recreational activities and things that lent

Ken and Flo Cooper, the Good Sam Club's first Sambassadors, put professional experience to work in helping fellow RVers.

themselves to the same concept of the Samboree program. I've also been an RVer since 1942, and Flo and I have owned four different trailers."

Flo said, "Our lifestyle has been one of preparing for this kind of work for years. We've always loved to travel. I was even in the travel agency business, and we did a lot of traveling even while we were working. One of the reasons we retired was that every time we went on a trip, we had to go back to work too soon; we wanted more time to travel."

"The most interesting thing about the Sambassador job, though, is the people we meet," Ken said. "We find people to be fascinating, and the Sambassador program opens doors for us to be exposed to more cultures around the country than the average person sees while he's traveling. I also feel that the Good Sam concept is a terrific concept that is meeting the need of a certain segment of the RVing public for communication and socialization with each other. They are able to go to a Samboree and meet new people, then go to another one and meet some of the same people again and develop friendships that they couldn't have otherwise. It gives me a lot of self-esteem and satisfaction to know that I can put my past professional experience to work in an area that is so effective in helping people."

Ken and Flo's second year as Sambassadors was a busy one. "We ran the Knott's Berry Farm Samboree and the Rose Parade Samboree on the West Coast," Ken recalled. "I was the wagonmaster of the trip to Baja and the International Samboree in Tucson. An emergency came up, and we took over the Mardi Gras Caraventure to New Orleans, brought that to a successful conclusion and then went to Miami, where Flo and I hosted 150 Good Sam members on the twelve-day Panama Canal trip. Then, on our way back, we went to the International Samboree at Eustis, Florida, and now we're following a pattern of hitting the state Samborees."

What does he see as the future of the Good Sam Club? "The state Samborees are going to thrive; they actually are increasing in attendance because the price of gasoline and the cost of traveling are causing families to shorten the lengths of their trips, and they are giving more of their support to activities that are closer to home."

As Sambassadors, the Coopers travel about 20,000 miles a year. What do they do when they aren't on the job for the Good Sam Club? Ken answered, "We become tourists! We like to research the area we're in in terms of interesting sights. When we were finished with the Miami trip, for example, we had almost a month to ourselves, so we spent a week in the Keys resting, unwinding and taking it easy and then eased our way up through Florida, seeing the sights as we went and visiting friends along the way." They travel in a Ford pickup truck and tow a 30-foot Holiday Rambler fifth-wheel trailer. They keep a daily log of their travels, including their expenses, and figure their lifestyle costs them about $1,000 a month. They maintain a condominium in San Francisco as a home base but live most of the year in their rig.

Motels? "We don't stay in them unless we have to," Flo said. "When we went to Florida for our cruise, for example, we had to store our rig, and we couldn't stay overnight in it so we had to go to a motel. Originally, our plan. . ."

Ken interrupted, knowing what she was going to say: "Not *our* plan, dear. *Your* plan!"

His wife smiled. "Okay. Originally, my plan was . . . I felt it would be very nice to break up the traveling if we'd stay a couple of nights occasionally in a nice little inn or someplace special by the ocean where there was a beautiful view or special seafood dinners were served. That was the original plan, but we haven't done it. Actually, I'm so comfortable in our rig that it's more trouble to go to a motel now than to just stay in the trailer."

The Van Osdols: "It's The Only Way To Go"

A few months after the Coopers became Sambassadors, full-time RVers Perry "Steamboat" Van Osdol and his wife Hazel joined them on the road in that capacity. They don't make much money in that role, but the Good Sam Club covers most of their travel expenses and campground fees. "And at the same time," Steamboat emphasized, "we are able to go on very nice trips—the 'love boat' cruise to Alaska that ordinarily costs $3,500— that we'd never have been able to afford on our own. We also wouldn't be able to see so many different areas and meet so many nice people on our own. We'd still be traveling, of course, but we wouldn't go as often and as far."

Like Ken Cooper, Steamboat considers the Sambassador job a kind of intermediary position between the Good Sam chapters and the international headquarters. "We also promote the Good Sam tours a little, but we don't push them very hard. We might just tell a gathering that we have applications for the Franklin Samboree and the Alaskan trip at sea and the Mardi Gras and Baja Samborees or the Alpine country tour, but we do it rather casually. This whole Samboree program has caused us so much pride, I can't understand how we were so fortunate to be involved with it. It seems to me that there are a lot of other people who are better versed at camping and touring than we are. We're just a couple of jokers. But until the international headquarters catches up to that fact, we'll keep going as long as we can; we're having a great time."

Why should RVers join the Good Sam Club? "It's the only way to go," Steamboat answered, "basically because of all the wonderful people you meet. To me, that's the payoff. Good Sam gives you the vehicle for meeting those people. Their ideas about things are close enough to each others' that every time they see one another, they meet a friend. The principle of Good Sam is another key to it—that you should help your fellow traveler down the road. If you joined Good Sam strictly for the discounts that you could get at campgrounds and for some of your services and equipment, I think you'd be missing the boat. When I sell a membership, the last thing I talk about is the discount program; I talk first about the friends we make and the fun we have at campouts."

Steamboat added, "When you're a Good Samer, you're accorded a different treatment when you go through an area. Monday night, for example, we pulled into Connecticut, and we called the state director just to say we were coming through. Well, he insisted that we park our rig in front of his house. We have the same thing at our home base in Kansas. When a Good Samer we know comes through, we want him to park at

"Steamboat" and Hazel Van Osdol, trouble-shooting Sambassadors for the Good Sam Club, make friends while promoting the RVing way of life.

our place, plug in to water and electricity and stay a day or two. Good Samers also caravan together a lot. Three weeks ago, we traveled with the state director from South Carolina and a couple of regional advisors. You have to get to know other people well when you live close to them like that for a few days."

As Sambassadors, Steamboat and Hazel quite often also find themselves troubleshooting for other Good Samers and for RVing in general. During their travels through the northeast, they met three women at a rest stop who complained that although a campground nearby was displaying a Good Sam sign, the owner would not honor their membership with the usual 10% discounts. Hazel and Steamboat paid a visit to the campground, and the owner admitted he had let his franchise agreement expire, but Steamboat was unable to convince him to renew it. At Steamboat's urging, he took down his Good Sam sign. Steamboat also discovered that visitors to that area could make reservations through the local chamber of commerce for hotel and motel rooms, but not for campsites, so before he left, he complained about that policy to the chamber and suggested that it be changed.

In Salem, Oregon, Steamboat and a group of other Good Samers were visited by a non-RVing newspaper reporter who wrote a very negative article about what he called "the gas-guzzling RVs." Steamboat said, "Of course, we wrote a nasty letter in return, and everybody got on the phone and started to call him. One lady on Social Security said, 'Look fella, I saved all my life to buy this rig, and then you come in here and tell me I shouldn't travel in it. I came in here on half a tank of gas. I have been sitting here with it all week, and I won't put any more gas in it until I leave.' The reporter got so many calls, he didn't stick around; he left town for the weekend. But the chamber of commerce and the city officials came out and apologized. They said, 'He forgot that we're geared to tourism in this area and that you people brought in more than a quarter of a million dollars into our community. We need people like you; without you, our area is in trouble.' "

Steamboat said, "Our own little town of Hutchinson, Kansas, is geared to hotel and motel people, and the town was considering an ordinance against parking RVs. I took some Good Sam literature on the subject to City Hall, and now the town fathers have changed their thinking about RVs. I think they're finally realizing that RVing is a way of life."

FREELANCE YOUR SKILLS

Truly a whole world of money-making opportunities is open to full-time RVers, even those without special talents. An enterprising RVer could, for example, pick up enough work to keep himself in pocket money simply by performing services in the campground where he parks his rig. After asking the permission of the campground operator first, he could canvass his fellow RVers and find out how many would hire him to repair or service their RVs, seal their roofs, flush their water and holding tanks and wash their windows, their trailers and their tow vehicles. An experienced baker could sell his or her homemade bread and rolls; an outdoorsman could lead nature walks or conduct classes in birdwatching for a small fee.

An RVer with a background in electronics could repair television sets for his fellow campers. A former accountant could serve as a financial consultant and prepare tax returns. Someone who keeps himself physically trim could help other RVers be more healthy, and pick up a few extra dollars, by supervising morning exercise classes. And nearly anyone could earn money by buying and selling used paperback books at campgrounds and flea markets.

Connie Buffett, a widow who spends her winters in Florida, has developed a regular route of campgrounds that she follows a couple of days each week in order to sell paperback books to other RVers. She buys each book at either half its cover price or $1, whichever is less, and she resells them for $1.25. She also takes books in trade, accepting three used books for one of those she carries on shelves built into the rear of her van. She earns enough money in a winter to pay for her campsites all year.

A former newspaper photographer and his wife (a retired commerical artist) earn more than $10,000 every year with their combined skills, working at a leisurely pace and accepting only commissions that interest them. She paints portraits of other campers and does sketches of their RVs parked in scenic places, while he shoots portrait-type photographs of individuals and their rigs and prepares advertising brochures for campgrounds and other tourist attractions. They also photograph and paint landscapes that they sell at campground art and crafts shows and at community flea markets.

Jason Phillabaum, a retired corporate public relations man from Detroit, earns several thousand dollars each winter in Arizona and California by writing news releases and publicity promotions for businesses such as automobile dealerships, restaurants and department stores. He charges his clients only for the items that are published by local newspaper and magazines, but he reported, "I have an excellent percentage of success. At least eight of every ten news releases I write are published at least once. And some of them are published in three or four daily and weekly newspapers. I do news spots for the radio and TV stations too, and I charge my clients a little more when those are used. My work—and I suppose my face, too—became so familiar to one of the leading daily newspapers in the San Diego area that I was hired last year to put together the paper's annual automotive supplement. I made a nice bundle of cash from that project, and I'm going to do it again this year."

Gerald Gaver, who RVs with his wife, Clara, full-time in their Jayco mini motorhome, has valuable experience as a retired Methodist clergyman. While traveling, Reverend Gaver sometimes fills temporary church vacancies, officiates at weddings and funerals and conducts Sunday morning services at campgrounds. He also gives inspirational talks to business and civic clubs and charges $25 for narrating his own color slide show about RVing. A few years ago, he was written up in several national publications because he held nondenominational worship services every Sunday morning during the summer for fishermen on the shores of Missouri's Lake of the Ozarks. Hundreds of anglers—some of them taking time out from competing in fishing tournaments—attended his services while seated in their boats. "I think I provided a good service to those people that summer," he said, and then he grinned. "But I will have to admit it got a little distracting when one of the fellows would hook a bass right in the middle of one of my sermons." He winked and reported that he is formulating plans to hold Sunday morning services on the greens of a few Florida retirement community golf courses.

FULL-TIMING CELEBRITIES

When Hal and Penny Gaynor joined the ranks of the full-time RVers in 1972, they worried whether they would be able to keep busy, and they were concerned that they might not be able to find enough work to supplement their income. They needn't have worried. During the first summer they were traveling, the director of the Connecticut Good Sam Club asked Hal to give a talk on RV safety at the state Samboree. "It was supposed to last an hour, with questions and answers," Hal recalled several years later. "But 2½ hours later, I finally had to say, 'I give up. It's time to eat.'" That clinic led to an invitation to speak at the Good Sam international rally in Quebec, and that engagement led to three more which, in turn, resulted in several others. Now, Hal and Penny travel all around the country, concentrating on the eastern and midwestern states, conducting their unique "Trailering Safety Clinics."

The clinics are admission-free, and at each one Hal shares his nearly forty years of trailering experience; demonstrates techniques for towing, hitching and weight balancing, and warns about the improper use of LP-gas while Penny gives tips on equipping, organizing and packing an RV. "It's not a money-making venture," Hal reported. "The clinics haven't made money for us since the day we started. If we didn't write our columns [for nine regional RV newspapers] or I didn't have an outside income, we could never put on the clinics. It costs us more money to keep them on the road than we earn from them."

The Gaynors do, however, pick up extra cash by selling RV equipment and accessories that they've tested and endorsed, and even Hal admits that the clinics enable him to draw crowds and increase his chances for sales of his supplies. The clinics also have enabled Hal and

Hal and Penny Gaynor's popular columns and "Trailering Safety Clinics" have given them well-earned celebrity status in the RVing community.

Penny to achieve a measure of celebrity status and led them into writing their safety columns for RV newspapers such as Southern RV, Camp-A-Rama, Camper Ways, Northeast Outdoors and Trails-A-Way.

The safety clinic idea evolved over a period of years from when Hal first became involved with trailering in 1937. "I've always had a love affair with trailers," he said, "and I've always been a safe driver. I spent many years on the road before going full time—traveling up to 50,000 miles a year—and I never had an accident or even a parking ticket. In order to achieve that record, I think, my driving principles and practices must have been very good. I always practiced what is now called defensive driving. When Penny and I got our first trailer, I'd be a wise guy around the campfire and tell a few of the others what they were doing wrong. Sometimes, you can lose good friends that way—like the fellow who set his jacks and had his wheels off the ground—I told him he was wrong, and he said, 'I've always parked this way, and I've never had any trouble. It's none of your business anyway. I own the trailer.' "Well, things like that started me thinking, and I realized there was a need for some education of RVers." When circumstances allowed Hal and Penny to begin their safety clinics, they channeled their energies and their financial resources into the concept and became so widely known that they are booked up to attend rallies for several months in advance. "We've underwritten this work personally from our own pockets," Penny said, "and we're the only people in the country doing what we're doing."

Their celebrity status has resulted in pressures and a notoriety that they never imagined when they first began the clinics, though. Hal said, "We always used to run with our CB on, but it's gotten to the point now that we can't make our appointments if we travel with it on because we're hailed whenever someone has a problem. If we left the CB on and answered all the hails or helped all the people who asked us, we'd never make another rally; we'd be too tied up. Consequently, when we have goof-off time, as we call it, we'll turn on the CB, and every time we do it, we have an adventure. Maybe we'll wind up on the side roads at some farm, parking on the farmer's property and visiting him in his home while we help him with his problems."

He added, "Another form of pressure is that people will come knocking on our door any time of the day or night. But, as I tell Penny, to that person his problem is big, even if it's a small one to me. So I can't say no. I know that if something were bothering me, I'd go out looking for help to get rid of the problem, and that's what they are doing. A woman came to me just today and said, 'I've been smelling propane since the day we bought our rig. It makes me dizzy, but if I say anything about it, my husband gets angry and the dealer who sold us the rig gets angry.' Now I know from my experience, for some reason women can smell propane faster than most men. So I walked over to her trailer and found the leak for her."

The Gaynors said they truly enjoy people and they like camping in a crowd of RVers. "The only time we want to camp by ourselves," Hal said, "is when I have procrastinated with my writing, and Penny will say, 'We've got six days to get your column out.' So I'll say, 'Let's find a dinky campground and hide out in it.' We'll pull into a camp, and 99% of the time the other campers will recognize us and start asking questions. And the camp manager wants to talk with us: "Where have you been? What do you know? What have you been doing around the country?' I'll say, 'Look, we've got an article to get out—a deadline to meet. But when we're finished with it, you can come over and have coffee and visit.' That usually does the trick."

Penny added, "But there's been no real pressures, because we enjoy doing what we're doing. We receive between 150 and 200 letters a week, and we answer every letter personally." I asked her if she wouldn't rather get away from attending so many rallies and enjoy a little recreational camping once in awhile. She answered, "For us, our work is attending rally after rally, weekend after weekend. And there's no such thing as a mini-rally, so far as we're concerned. We give a full measure of effort at every one, no matter what its size. Sure, it gets a little wearing when we don't have any breaks; we're going to twelve rallies in a row this summer, for example. But Don, it's a wonderful thing, and very gratifying, to be able to make a contribution, particularly when people walk up to us and say, 'We almost had a fire, but I remembered something that you said at a rally, and we were safe because we listened to you.' "

Hal interrupted. "If we're not *trying* to get away from people and I pull into a campground, roll out the awning and someone doesn't come over to talk right away, I wonder what's wrong. Are we in a strange place where they don't read RV newspapers? We like people. I'm convinced you can't enjoy being a full-time RVer unless you also enjoy your fellow man."

On the general subject of working while traveling, Hal had this to say: "There's plenty that can be done by people who are full-timing and want to supplement their incomes. There are many ways to do it, from taking jobs in national forests and state parks to taking pictures of businesses and selling them to storekeepers. Over the years, we've compiled a list of unusual ways people earn money. We talked with a schoolteacher, for example, who wanted to retire but said he couldn't because his pension was too small. But he moonlighted by cleaning carpets while he was teaching, and I told him that since he needed less money to live on while RVing, he could charge less for cleaning rugs and supplement his pension by doing it. He started doing that, charging $10 for cleaning the carpet in an RV whereas he charged $20 a room for houses, and he said now he's putting money in the bank, and he's cleaning only three or four rigs a day, and only when he wants to work."

Hal and Penny aren't the only writers who live in their RVs. RV writer Kay Peterson has traveled full time in her rig for several years and even wrote a book about her experiences. Loners on Wheels founder Edith Lane also supplements her income by writing magazine articles and columns, while noted paperpack book novelist Janet Dailey (she writes Harlequin romances) lives with her husband, Bill, in an Airstream trailer.

The Jennings: "We're Part Of The Entertainment"

Harry Jennings isn't a writer, but he uses his Jayco travel trailer for one of the most unusual occupations I've seen: he designs and sells badges, shoulder patches and similar items for Southern Emblem. At thirty-nine, he left a plant supervisor's job in North Carolina so that he and his wife, Juanita, could travel full time to RV rallies selling his goods. "We hit between forty and forty-five rallies a year, meet with the leaders of all the clubs and advise them on designing their patches," he said. "We do approximately 70% of the state patches for the Good Sam Club, and we also make Good Sam jewelry."

Harry said money-making opportunities are wide open for someone in his field who wants to work hard to get it. "If a young guy really wanted to work, he could probably stop fifteen times between here and the next town at campgrounds, marinas and lodges like the Masons, the Shrine and the Moose. We don't push that much, and we don't answer to anybody. We are in the process of expanding, though. We put on another man last year, and we hope eventually to blanket the U. S. with sales representatives. There are so many people that want this merchandise! There are two or three states holding rallies right now that we can't get to."

The North Carolina couple doesn't consider themselves "venders" in the traditional sense of the word—that is, salespersons that set up tables at rallies. "We feel like we're part of the entertainment, and I think most of the state directors would agree with us on that. We have approximately 450 emblems and patches on display, and if you come in here ten times during a weekend, you'll see a different one every time you come. We draw a crowd every time we open for business, and we really get involved in the rally. We don't just open in the morning and close at night; we're out there enjoying ourselves with everybody else."

The Board Meetings

While doing that, Harry became a member of a sort of ad hoc committee to form a loose-knit organization that has since become one of the fastest growing phenomenons in RV rallying. It all started a few years ago during a state Good Sam rally in Ohio. The club directors and their friends, tired from a long week of events, decided to cap the rally by going to an ice cream parlor at midnight of the last day. They jokingly told everyone they were having "a board meeting." Quickly, word spread among other state directors, and by the spring of 1979, rally-ending "board meetings" at ice cream parlors were starting to become part of the weekend events. In July of that year, Harry and Juanita were talking with other rallyists about the "board meeting" popularity while they were eating ice cream at Amish Acres in northern Indiana. "With us were Frank Wagner of the Indiana Good Sam clubs, Dick Stoner from Connecticut and Chuck Mogg from Michigan. We decided that we ought to make up a little patch that could be worn by people who attend the board meetings." Further discussion led to the design of a board meeting patch featuring a delicious looking ice cream sundae with a red cherry on top.

Then at the week-long Ohio Good Sam rally, someone suggested that a "board meeting" be held on Tuesday night. There was one the next night, too, and the next, and the next. "Finally, on Saturday night, there were 120 people at the ice cream parlor. And it started growing from that. At the New York rally, even before I could make up the patches, sixty-four people showed up for the board meeting, and then the states started getting competitive about it. At Vermont, seventy-nine showed up, and at Michigan, 220 people went to an ice cream place that was only big enough to hold fifty. Campers were standing in line for two hours waiting to place their orders, but no one was upset; everyone was as happy as a lark. I had ordered just a couple of hundred patches, but by the end of the Michigan rally, we had 400 board members. So I upped production to 1,000 patches. Then we went to Eustis, Florida, for the international rally, and suddenly there were 1,300 members; I had to increase production again."

By the fall of 1980, more than 2,000 RVers had attended the midnight get-togethers, sharing ice cream and conversation. The unique "board meetings" have been expanded to include people attending National Campers and Hikers Association rallies and campouts of the factory-sponsored Winnebago, Jayco and Holiday Rambler RV clubs. "Now we're planning a board member rally," Harry said. "We'll have just a fun weekend, without any business being conducted—just a place to go and have a good time and maybe pass around a little ice cream." He added that although the special board member shoulder patches cost $1 each, Southern Emblem has agreed to furnish them for nothing, and proceeds from the patches are being donated to a children's home.

Harry said, "It's fine to earn money to make a living, but you can't make a profit all the time. I'm not bragging, but in a weekend at a rally, I'll give away $30 to $40 worth of merchandise to kids. I do it because I want to; I give them something they can remember the rally by. A kid will walk up to my table with fifty cents in his hand, and he'll want to buy a $1 patch. Nine times out of ten, I'll let him have it for fifty cents. I'm a firm believer that something, no matter how small, should be given back to the people."

CARD TABLE BUSINESSES

Hundreds of full-time RVers have learned that they can supplement their incomes by operating what are referred to generally as "card table businesses." They set up card tables either in front of their rigs, at roadsides, at campground hobby and crafts shows or at flea markets and sell items that they have made. The profits are small, sometimes ridiculously so if the craftsman's time is considered, but some RVers claim they can earn enough money from their work to pay for their gasoline and their campsite fees. On the other hand, RVers who have tried card table businesses with the intent of earning a great deal of money are almost always disappointed.

Full-timer Charles Mogg once told me, "I've been trying to figure out a job for my wife that would stimulate our budget. We've looked into trying the flea market things, selling arts and crafts, but, most of those things are pretty well covered. I thought once maybe I could buy an engraver and have my wife take orders that I could fill, but I took a look at the people that were doing that kind of work and it was obvious that they're not getting rich, and they're working a full-time schedule. They're working as hard as they would if they were at home, but they're doing it out of their trailers. I've concluded that in order to go full-timing and enjoy it, you've got to rely on actual income that you can lay your hands on every month.

A woman from Iowa who travels in her Prowler trailer full-time with her husband, however, says she earns several thousand dollars every year with her sewing. She makes dresses and socks that she sells at flea markets and to other campers; she alters discount clothing that other RVers buy at bargain prices, and she makes children's sweaters and jackets that her fellow full-timers buy for their grandchildren.

A retired fishing guide from South Carolina not only continues to pick up extra money by taking tourists fishing occasionally, but he earns about $3,000 every year by making and selling fishing lures and other tackle, including hand-wrapped graphite rods. Another woman who sews for a hobby adds money to her cookie jar from the sale of handmade gathered net hats and doll clothes. Hobbyists also make and sell macrame hangers for plants, knitted afghans, jewelry such as necklaces and belt buckles, decorated stones and pieces of wood, and frames for photographs and paintings. The types and number of products that can be made by hobbyists are limited only by the individual's imagination—and by his ability to sell them. Information on card table businesses is available to anyone sending twenty-five cents in postage to the National Snowbird

Association, 21100 Highway 79, Space 266, San Jacinto, California 92383.

Even persons who think they do not have the skills to operate a card table business can make money from them. A full-time RVer from Illinois who winters near Harlingen, Texas, discovered his own way to earn cash. He leases ground near a busily traveled highway, erects large, rented tents and then sells flea market space to hobbyists who want to display their merchandise. During the winter of 1979-80, he cleared $18,000 from his venture and worked only on weekends.

Chapter Thirteen

Winter Camping

Energy costs and other economic considerations have forced most full-timers to give up cold-weather camping and travel and seek solace from winter in the sunbelt. Still, some RVers like to spend part of every winter parked in the snow so they can ski, go ice fishing, snowmobiling, sledding, ice skating and tobaggaining. For other full-timers, winter camping is the only way they are able to spend Christmases in northern climates with their children and grandchildren.

Two free-spirit full-timers, Jerry and Betty Campbell, don't let either snow or heat deter them from traveling where they want to go. "We've lived in our Travco motorhome in temperatures that were 115 degrees above zero and 35 degrees below zero with a chill factor of 75 below," Jerry reported. To keep warm one winter, he packed the underside of the motorhome—from the ground to the undercarriage—with house ceiling insulation, duct-taped the corners shut and put an electric radiant heater under the coach to keep that area warm and prevent water and sewer lines from freezing. "I kept my water hose inside, and when we wanted water, I'd take it out, fill the water tank and bring it back inside so it wouldn't freeze. I ran a separate electric line into the coach and operated two small electric heaters off of it. We also heated with propane, but we filled a 96-pound LP bottle on the first of February and didn't use all of that until the end of March. We stayed just as comfortable in that sub-zero weather as we do while we're parked in Florida."

Chris and Charlotte Moffett also used to do a lot of winter camping, but Chris has cut back on his cold-weather traveling since his wife died a few years ago. "I don't mind the cold; I just much prefer the sunshine,"

Some full-timers thrive on the excitement of RVing through snow country.

he said. He added, "We used to take off between Christmas and New Year and go up to Timber Shores Campground in northern Michigan. One particular winter up there, it was fifteen below zero with a 30-knot wind, and we got eight inches of snow in one night. We'd rent a snowmobile to use the entire time we were there, and it was great fun! I'd run our sewer line across the top of the snow and hook it up, then pile about a foot of snow over it so the temperature in the hose was right at thirty-two degrees instead of being below zero. When we wanted to take a shower, I'd hook up the water hose, let it run and then unhook it immediately following the bath and we'd switch back to using water out of our water tank."

As for traveling in the snow, Chris said, "I've run around on icy roads and through deep snow and everything else, and I honestly believe you're safer towing a trailer in bad weather than you are driving a car by itself. An American-built car has heavier braking on the front wheels, and most people get in trouble either by putting on the brakes and losing steering control or by spinning their wheels going up a hill. With the trailer behind, you never use your car brakes; you use the trailer brakes. You can wiggle the hand control of the trailer brakes faster than you can pump your foot. The only time I ever had a problem on ice or snow was once coming across Michigan when the roads were very, very slippery. As soon as the other drivers would see a break in the traffic, they'd come charging around me and then slam on their brakes, go out of control and slide into a ditch. I kept having to stop because of those crazy drivers, and finally I figured it was just a question of time before I was going to broadside somebody, so I pulled off the road and quit driving. It wasn't that I couldn't control my car and trailer, but the drivers without trailers couldn't control their cars."

ADJUSTING TO THE COLD

Just as there are tricks to enjoying other kinds of specialized camping, so too is there a system to camping comfortably in the snow. No matter how well insulated they are, RVs are not designed for winter use. They can, however, be adapted for cold-weather living if a few common sense tips are followed. Because water tanks and plumbing lines will freeze up in all but the best-insulated coaches (and even those must be heated constantly to prevent freeze-up), winter campers should count on either using bottled drinking water or carrying water from the campground's bath house. Park shower and toilet facilities should be used, too, instead of those in the coach. LP-gas furnaces in most of the RVs owned by full-timers are large enough to heat a unit's interior, but experienced winter campers sometimes supplement that output with electric heaters. Even so, the motorhome or trailer should be parked in a wooded area, if possible, with the entry door opposite the prevailing wind. The exhaust fan over the range should be operated frequently to help vent out the moisture that collects in the unit and to prevent condensation. Carpeting and throw rugs should be added to the floor for warmth and insulation.

Most RVs do not have storm windows, but the winter camper can provide his own. First, the windows should be sealed with stick-on rubber weatherstripping. Then, clear vinyl plastic can be attached to the windows with duct tape; some RVers even prefer to use two layers of the vinyl sheeting—one on the inside of the windows and one on the outside. Water and sewer pipes should be wrapped with heat tape and then covered with packaged fiberglass insulation, and snow can be piled up around the perimeter of the RV to protect its underside from the cold. If any cool air leaks into the unit around vents or through seams, they can be sealed with either caulking compound or insulation materials. A catalytic heater can provide adequate warmth for a small area and help reduce the drain on the RV batteries through use of the vehicle's forced-air furnace. Holding tank freeze-ups can be prevented by dumping antifreeze into them, but for added precaution, experienced winter campers also take portable toilets with them into snow areas so that the RV's toilet does not have to be used at all.

The winter camper should be aware that his LP-gas system might perform differently during cold weather than it does in warm weather because the vaporization rate of LP-gas decreases in a direct relationship to a decrease in temperature. Also, the greater the amount of liquid gas in a tank, up to the recommended 80% level, the greater the amount of LP-gas vapor generated. A tank at 80% capacity, for example, will generate 64,400 btu at zero degrees. But at 50% capacity, it will generate only 50,400 btu, and at 20% capacity, only 33,000 btu. Since nearly twice as many btu are available from a full tank than from one three-fourths empty, it is to the advantage of the winter camper to keep his tank filled as closely to the 80% level as possible.

Winnebago Industries, the nation's leading manufacturer of Class A motorhomes, provided additional tips on how RVers can make themselves more comfortable while camping in the winter:

- Cover vinyl seats and cushions with towels to absorb cold air.
- Place newspaper under the entrance door throw rug to soak up melting snow.
- Position throw rugs against the bottom crevice of the entrance door to cut off cold air blowing in from the outside.
- Place an old rug outside the RV and another inside to prevent snow and moisture from being carried inside.
- Carry an adequate supply of LP-gas. A partially filled tank may last only a short time.
- Carry a can of lubricant or graphite to protect against frozen locks and latches.
- Try to keep a window partially open to prevent carbon monoxide buildup inside the RV and help prevent condensation from forming on metal and window surfaces. Remove snow from roof vents and open them for short periods of time.
- For added warmth, insulate the window side of the drapes.
- Make sure all heating ducts are clean and lint-free. Clogged ducts can restrict air flow and, in some cases, are a fire hazard.
- To help eliminate low battery and difficult starting during cold weather, place a thick rubber pad under the batteries. This will help prevent cold temperature transfer from the steel support plates to the base of each battery.

Snowmobile trails cut through the woods adjacent to campgrounds in many snowbelt states.

WINTER DESTINATIONS

A surprisingly large number of campgrounds in northern states plow campsites free of snow every winter and offer cold-weather activities to suit all tastes. Ponds are cleared for ice skating; trails are blazed for cross-country skiers; paths are laid out for snowmobiling, and rental equipment is provided for ice fishing, sledding, snowshoeing, skiing and even snowmobiling. A park in central Michigan provides a heated outdoor swimming pool for campers who want to take a warm swim while snow falls on their heads. An Indiana campground attracts thousands of RVers to its 50-mile-long snowmobile trail and its midnight cookouts in the woods. In New York, RVers set up camp in a park where the toboggan runs draw crowds of thrill-seekers. An Ohio campground not only boasts of several hills that are perfect for sledding, but it provides free transportation to a popular ski center nearby. The Great Smoky Mountain National Park in Tennessee now attracts RVers from all over the South—from Atlanta, Nashville and Louisville, particularly—each weekend as a new interest in downhill and cross-country skiing builds south of the Mason-Dixon line.

Campground owners in the upper Midwest compete particularly hard for winter campers and the off-season revenue they provide with their motorhomes, travel trailers, fifth-wheels and snow equipment. At one park in northern Wisconsin, winter campers can participate in nighttime skiing, sledding or snowmobiling activities on courses that are lighted by bonfires and torches. A competing park on the other side of the county offers its campers saunas, campfire cookouts, a huge game room and evening sing-alongs around a wood-burning fireplace in the campground's rustic lodge. At Houghton Lake, Michigan, droves of RVers—many of them full-timers—arrive in town for the annual ice fishing Tip-Up Festival every January. They set up shanties all over the lake and participate in a parade, snowmobile races and dozens of other events when they're not huddled warmly inside their RVs at campgrounds around the lake's perimeter.

The whole state of Michigan, in fact, is a paradise for winter-loving RVers. A favorite locale of skiers and snowmobilers is the area around Gaylord, where several private campgrounds provide snow season camping, and local LP-gas companies willingly deliver tanks full of propane for heating and cooking. The Gaylord Chamber of Commerce is quite helpful in providing information about its attractions, but the most popular ski slopes are at Sylvan Knob, just east of town. Cross-country skiing and snowmobiling trails are well marked in the area of the Pigeon River State Forest to the northeast. Other snowmobiling trails closer to town are open, as are a couple of privately operated ski trails. Topnotch skiing facilities also are open weekends at Boyne Mountain and Thunder Mountain—both within an hour's drive of Gaylord. Full-timers often choose to try the slopes at Boyne Highlands because skiing there is not very difficult. Winter resort areas near the town of Grayling also offer good snowmobiling and both daylight and nighttime skiing. Michigan has an impressive history of supporting skiing: the U.S. Ski Association was founded in Ishpeming in 1904, and the National Ski Hall of Fame was established there half a century later. Copper Peak, near Ironwood, is the only ski flying hill in the western hemisphere, and cross-country skiing has been popular in the state since it was introduced by Scandinavian immigrants in the 1800s.

Annual ski events are held in Michigan at Calumet, Iron River, Thompsonville, Marquette, Boyne Falls and Ishpeming. For snowmobilers, there is a poker rally at Grand Marais each February, the annual I-500 race at Sault Ste. Marie, the Thunder Bay 250 race at Alpena, an annual marathon and winter festival at Gaylord and the Gladwin 150 each December at Gladwin.

Vermont Development Department

The hills of Vermont offer full-timers winter camping and snow sports.

Other states which emphasize both winter camping and snow-season sports are Vermont, Minnesota, Indiana, Wisconsin, North Dakota, New York, New Hampshire and Maine. Northern Indiana offers full-time RVers the opportunity to combine winter camping and ice fishing. Favorite places in the Hoosier State to catch fish through the ice include Flatbelly Lake, just west of the Noble-Kosciuszko County line, where bluegills and redear sunfish are quite plentiful; Carr Lake, south of Warsaw, with a good population of big bluegills; Lake Wawasee, southeast of Elkhart, which has a lot of big bass and perch in it; Shipshewana Lake, northwest of Shipshewana, for bluegills and bass; Oliver Lake for winter trout; Lake James, north of Angola, with a big population of bluegills, yellow perch and northern pike; Clear Lake, near Fremont, perch and rainbow trout, and Snow Lake, in Steuben County, bluegills and crappie. The Indiana Department of Natural Resources has established both cross-country skiing and snowmobiling trails in various sections of the state. The four best known snowmobile areas are the Salamonie, Gateway, Miami and

223

Potawatomi trails. The shortest is the seven-mile Miami trail near Goshen; the Gateway trail is ten miles long and the other two twenty miles.

Jemstar Wilderness Campground near Park Rapids, Minnesota, is a good example of the parks in that state that attract RVers all year. The campground features a heated bathhouse with hot showers and acts as a sort of way station where snowmobilers can refuel and refresh themselves with hot food and drinks. The campground is close to the snowmobile trails of Paul Bunyan State Forest and the Heartland Snowmobile Trail as well as being only a short distance from the Val Chatel ski slopes and the three grades of cross-country ski trails at Itasca State Park. While not ordinarily thought of as a top skiing state, Minnesota has thirty-four downhill ski areas and more than 300 downhill runs, with 2,000 miles of formal cross-country ski trails. Snowmobiles, which were invented in Minnesota, can be run over more than 7,000 miles of marked and groomed trails.

In northwestern Minnesota, heart of the state's ski and snowmobile area, popular ski slopes are at Detroit Mountain, Buena Vista, Eagle Mountain, Powder Ridge and Ski-Gull. Favorite cross-country ski trails include Pine Lake Ski Trail in the Tamarac National Wildlife Refuge, Maplelag in western Becker County, private trails at Cedar Crest Resort, and the public trail system under development by the city of Detroit Lakes. Becker County's 412 lakes dot some of the finest snowmobiling terrain in the north country; more than 200 miles of state-approved, groomed trails were laid out by the Northwestern Minnesota Resort Association and the Detroit Lakes Sno-Fari Club. Some 160 miles of snowmobile trails are also open at Chippewa National Forest, and literally dozens of trails are marked near virtually every community in the northern half of the state. For a free guide to skiing and snowmobiling facilities, write to the State of Minnesota Department of Development, 480 Cedar Street, St. Paul, Minnesota 55155.

Chapter Fourteen

Follow
The Sun

Full-timers possess a freedom of movement and a freedom of ultimate destiny that eludes the rest of our modern society. While most Americans are locked into jobs, communities and a routine, day-by-day style of living, full-timers are experiencing—not *pursuing*, mind you, but *experiencing*—the American dream of living exactly as they want to live. Sure, they are hampered somewhat by constraints of various kinds: health, finances, gasoline prices, weather, and the limitations of the recreational vehicles in which they live and travel. But even with those constraints, they are *free*. They have freedom to go wherever they want and do whatever they decide on the spur of the moment that they want to do. They worked hard, in their younger years, so they could achieve that freedom, and they deserve it! At last, they can live today and let tomorrow take care of itself. And if, because of the unpredictability of the future, they have to give up their free, wandering lifestyle and settle into a more conventional mode of living, they know they will have had the opportunity and the courage to experience adventures that the rest of society can only dream about.

For the full-timer, adventure can be found everywhere, whether it's panning for flakes of gold in Colorado, fishing in the Gulf of Mexico for speckled trout, enjoying the Mardi Gras at New Orleans or camping in the middle of Utah's panoramic splendor. Full-timers like to follow the sun. They spend their winters where they don't have to operate the furnaces of their RVs very often; summers are spent in generally northern climates away from the scorching heat of the desert and the overbearing humidity of the tropics. Where they go, what they do, though, often de-

Photo courtesy Arkansas Department of Parks and Tourism.

Chris Moffett and other full-timers turn their RVs into houseboats for Camp-A-Float trips on Lake Ouachita.

pends upon their whims. While some full-timers like to return to the same areas year after year, others prefer to travel widely. Charles and Violetta Legler are one full-timing couple who never know where they'll be from one month to the next. "We're always going someplace between the Canadian border and the Mexican border and someplace between the Atlantic and Pacific Oceans," Charles said mischievously.

Chris Moffett is another person who enjoys the spirit of freedom that full-time RVing provides. Chris is a modern adventurer and travels around the country alone with his Holiday Rambler trailer and Chevrolet pickup truck. I met him in Minnesota one summer when he paused in his journeys to attend the international rally of the Holiday Rambler Recreational Vehicle Club, which he headed at one time. I asked him where he'd been lately and where he was going, and he said, "I spent the winter in Tucson, as I usually do, but I left early this year and went back to my home town in Maine to attend the fiftieth reunion of my high school graduation class. I wanted to go to the Holiday Camp-A-Float rally, but the rally was full, so I went to Arkansas later and rented one of the Camp-A-Float barges for a week by myself. Although it would have been a lot more fun with other people, I really enjoyed myself and had some exciting moments trying to moor that rig by myself. After that, a friend and I set up a trip we're going to take down the Mississippi River on the Delta Queen. I went on to Wright-Patterson Air Force Base, where I was stationed when I retired from the military, and I parked there for about a week. I spent a lot of time in the Air Force Museum and renewed acquaintances with a lot of old military friends."

He continued, "I needed some work done on my trailer, so I went to the Holiday plant in Indiana and had a nice reading light put in before coming up here to Minnesota. Next, I plan to park the trailer here and fly a few places to visit some relatives. After that, I don't know whether I'll head out to Seattle or go over to Cody, Wyoming, to see some good friends. I may drift down south if the weather is good, but if it's too hot, I'll go on out to Seattle to visit my son and then start down the West Coast after seeing my daughter in Oregon. Then I've got some back-and-forth running I've got to do between the mountains and the coast, and I'll probably stop in San Diego for a while.

I asked Chris, "What are your favorite destinations?"

"I hate to say this, but I don't like to cross the Mississippi heading east. The minute I cross the Mississippi, the visibility seems to disappear, and nine times out of ten, it rains on me on the eastern side of the bridge. Everyone seems to be heading toward me like they're trying to kill me, and they don't give me room to move over. I can't seem to get a deep breath until I get back on the other side of the river. So once I'm in the eastern half of the country, I try to touch all the bases that I should because I know I won't be back for a while. I have to go back where the air is clear and the sky is blue and you can see for fifty miles.

"I like Cody, Wyoming, very much, and British Columbia is one of my favorite places in the summertime; I think the Dogwood Campground southeast of Vancouver is one of the best campgrounds anywhere. Mexico is my favorite place to spend the winter, but I haven't been there for a few years and I've lost all my contacts. I like the ocean, too. Tucson is my favorite terminal for staying in one place a while. I like to go places where I can shoot photographs, especially of birds and animals. I enjoyed a field trip I took through the Arizona-Sonora Desert Museum to the lagoons at Baja where the whales calve and mate; I actually got to touch one—rubbed him on the jaw. Then we came back up through some rather remote country in four-wheel drive vehicles, and I got some good pictures of that country. Last summer I made a thirty-day trip to England, Scotland, Wales and Ireland with thirty-six Canadians. Those are things I do all the time; I try to keep busy."

Clockwise, a forest of Saguaro cactus presents an intriguing desert landscape on Tucson's west side; native American crafts are featured at the replica Cherokee village of Tsi-La-Gi; and Montezuma's Castle, Arizona, a national monument, contains ruins of prehistoric Indian cliff dwellings.

"Sunbirds" Flock To The South

Full-timers are often called "snowbirds" because they follow the sun and escape from the harsh cold of winter. I think the word "snowbird" is not quite accurate, though; RVers who follow the sun should be called "sunbirds." Like robins, they flock to the south in the late fall and return to the northern climates every spring.

Gene Woods, author of a column, "Full Time on the Go," in *Trailer Life* magazine, described the whole phenomenon very adroitly a few years ago when he wrote, "The neighbors I see at Flathead Lake in Montana in July or in New England or northern Wisconsin, I quite often see again in some park in Baja, California, or Mesa, Arizona, or San Diego in January. As the migratory birds, as soon as the first chill winds of fall blow, they just strike their awnings, load up the patio furniture, cast off hookups, hitch up and are on their way to another pleasant destination. I have talked to several stay-at-homes who say they prefer to see the seasons come and go, see the leaves turn in the fall and the first snow arrive soon after. But, Luisa and I have seen New Hampshire in autumn; it was great. And right after, we headed south for another visit to Washington, D. C., on our way to some other place that would have shirt-sleeve golf on New Year's Day and where the poinsettias and bougainvillea would bloom around our trailer space."

Don and Audrey Klemczak follow the sun in a different way. They spend four or five months in Florida, their Blue Bird motorhome parked on the campsite they own at the Outdoor Resorts of America park in Orlando, and most of the rest of the year they spend at another condominium lot in Michigan. "We've been here as long as five months," Don said from their Orlando campsite. "Most of the time, we come down here the end of October, but it depends upon when the snow flies. As soon as the days start getting cold up north, we'll leave. We love the fall, but not the cold weather. We've arrived here as early as the first of October and as late as the end of November. We've been doing that three years now, and it seems as if we've done it forever. We still call Michigan home because we have our home base there, and we always head north before Easter. Our travels, therefore, are basically between Michigan and Florida. We tried heading west two years ago, but we got into a storm, so we turned around in San Antonio and came back. Wherever we've gone, though, we've met very nice people camping—people who will help anyone however they can. We've met people here in Florida and established with them what we think will be lifetime friendships no matter whether we see them every year or once every five years."

The Klemczaks said that although they are happy with their system of traveling between two campsites at opposite borders, that style of full-timing would not be suitable to everyone. RVers who prefer to travel widely probably should rent, not own, campsites, Don said. "If you're going to use a lot only a couple of months a year, you might be better off renting because then, you're more flexible if you decide you want to move to another locale. You might decide you'd be happier in some other part of Florida; you might even want to try the East Coast, the West Coast or Arizona. You shouldn't own a campsite unless you plan to spend some time there every year. On the other hand, if you do own a lot and you don't go there one year, rental fees on it should pay for your maintenance fees and electricity and help build your equity. And rental fees in Florida are going up drastically."

Why did the Klemczaks buy a campsite in central Florida rather than on one of the state's coastlines? Don answered, "We've been to a lot of coastal areas, and it's difficult to find an open campground. You've got to have a campsite reserved for the next hundred years. If you go into a campground on the west coast north of Clearwater, the people at the registration office will tell you, 'Okay, you are number 280. Considering our death rate, you can expect to get a site in two or three years.' If you are fortunate enough to find a site to rent and you like it, you have to put a deposit on it a year in advance to make sure you can get it the following season. In central Florida, campsites are a little easier to find, and that's why we started coming here."

Bert and Greta Dean also own a condominium campsite, but theirs is in south Texas, not Florida. "We came here by happenchance," Bert told me from his trailer space near South Padre Island. "We were headed for Arizona, but we stopped in Texas to visit an old buddy of mine. Where we stayed, there were so many people on their way south that we had a chance to talk with some who were going to the Rio Grande Valley. So we diverted from our original course. We stopped at Fun 'N Sun Two, signed up for the square dance program and we were hooked for the rest of the winter. That was probably the worst winter weather south Texas has ever experienced; it rained every day. But we were so involved in the program of square dancing and round dancing that we didn't care what the weather was like. We were probably as busy that winter as we've ever been in our lives. We'd get up in the morning and go to a class at eight or nine o'clock, and we'd have dancing activities of some kind going all the time, with special dinners scheduled every night." After following the sun to south Texas and renting campsites there for two years, the Deans bought their campsite both as an investment and to save rental fees.

"This is our fourth winter down here," Bert told me during the winter of 1979-80. "We go home to New York in the summer. I say 'home,' but it's not really home any more. We have some property in the Hudson River Valley that we rent out and have to take care of, and we also have four children and grandchildren there, so we have to go home. When Outdoor Resorts started this campground project, we looked it over. We had had experience with Outdoor Resorts at Nettles Island, and we were impressed by the way property values increased there. Plus, we thought this would be an ideal place to live in the winter, being right on the water and with recreation of all kinds—especially tennis, my favorite sport— available. Just about anything we could want to do is right here. In fact, being here is like being on one long vacation."

In the south Texas sun, the Deans find plenty to keep them busy. "This year I took over the tennis instruction program because there wasn't anybody else to do it, and Greta got involved in Spanish lessons and an exercise program. I like to work on my car and my trailer, and I'm building two boats. To tell you the truth, we have so much to do, we just don't have time to do everything. We have *lists* of things to do." The Deans enjoy south Texas so much that during the first four years there they gradually shortened the time they spent in the north and lengthened their stay in the Rio Grande Valley. "We've left here as early as May and returned as late as November," Bert said, "but last year we left Texas in June and returned the first of September." He said more and more full-timers who once considered themselves "Winter Texans" are becoming three-quarter-time Texans.

Bert added, "The summer is a nice time of year because a breeze blows off the ocean constantly. I think there's a tendency among full-timers to leave here too early in the year. They're leaving right now [March 1], and the good weather is just starting. From now on, it's going to be beautiful."

A SUNBIRD'S CALENDAR

Texas is one of five states which attracts huge flocks of "sunbirds" every winter. The others are Arizona, Southern California, Florida and New Mexico. Full-time RVers in increasing numbers also are being attracted to the coastlines of Louisiana, Alabama, Georgia and South Carolina. It's anybody's guess how many RVers migrate into the sunbelt annually, but a study by the marketing research class at Pan American University indicates that as many as 100,000 families—mostly retired

Clockwise, contestants from as far as Nevada enter their stew recipes in the "Old Miners Stew Cook-off" at Calico Ghost Town; Sanibel Island, Florida, is a haven for winter travelers; and horseshoe pitching at the Calico Hullabaloo, San Bernardino, California.

couples—pour into the Rio Grande Valley of Texas each winter. In general, they arrive before the end of November and leave after April 1, and while they're there, they spend an average of $105 per week per family on food, drink, and entertainment. Sixty percent of them claim to be natives of Minnesota, Iowa, Missouri, Michigan, Illinois, Kansas and Indiana, according to the Pan American study, although they represent a total of forty-seven states and six Canadian provinces.

Full-timers gather at campgrounds not far from South Padre Island and all around the friendly communities of Harlingen, Brownsville, McAllen and Weslaco. There they meet new friends and renew old acquaintances. They go square dancing, fish the blue waters of the Laguna Madre and sunbathe on white sand beaches. They take up snorkeling, sailing, surf fishing, collect seashells and go beachcombing. They participate in arts and crafts exhibits, dine on fresh seafood and shop in Mexican border towns. "The Valley," as regular visitors to the area refer to it, boasts of more than 200 campgrounds. The largest ones schedule activities constantly for their Winter Texans, including exercise classes, bridge lessons, craft classes, blood pressure tests, Bible studies, movies, crocheting lessons, art workshops, shuffleboard tournaments, bingo contests, flea markets and pig roasts. Four huge commercial flea markets attract out-of-state shoppers every Saturday morning during the winter season. McAllen's huge civic center auditorium is reserved nearly every week for special gatherings of Winter Texans from the Midwestern states and Canada. A highlight of every winter, in fact, is the annual picnic attended by thousands of Iowa natives.

The November Migration

The annual migration of Winter Texans to the Rio Grande Valley and of sunbirds to Arizona, Southern California, New Mexico and Florida begins to pick up steam about the middle of November, just as the beautiful fall colors on trees in the north start turning to brown. The west coast of Florida is one of the first areas of the sunbelt to experience a return of the adventuresome RVers. They arrive in St. Petersburg and Tampa in large numbers, filling campsite spaces reserved many months, or even a year, ago. Full-timers who select Tampa and St. Petersburg for their winter quarters are generally rather cosmopolitan in their lifestyles; they are natives of large cities in the north, and they like the nightlife, the concerts, the dances and unusual attractions such as the jai alai games and the greyhound and thoroughbred races of the Tampa Bay area. Baseball fans can attend Grapefruit League games of the New York Mets and the St. Louis Cardinals, and anglers can catch fresh fish from either the bays of St. Petersburg or by renting a charter boat for a trip out into the Gulf. Other beautiful west coast areas are Sarasota on the Gulf a short drive south of Tampa, and Sanibel Island, where bird-watching and shelling are popular pastimes. Sanibel Island is not as tourist-oriented as some of the big Florida cities, and Sarasota lacks the rush-rush atmosphere of Tampa while having several special attractions of its own, including the Ringling Museums and the Circus Hall of Fame. In early November, northwest coast seaport Apalachicola holds its annual seafood festival, attracting hundreds of seafood-loving full-timers who are on their way south for the winter.

On the other side of the country, Southern California has plenty to offer those who like to combine beach camping with extended stays in the desert. Daytime November temperatures average about 75 degrees along the coast, but plenty of days are still warm enough for swimming and surfing. Beach camping is allowed in many areas by the California Department of Parks and Recreation, and some of the beach sites have RV hookups. For extended camping, full-timers head for the state-operated desert parks, such as the one at the Salton Sea or the huge Anza-Borrego Desert Park. In the Palm Springs area, hot mineral springs and a large number of golf courses are the big draw, although reservations are generally needed at the campground there. The state's second largest city, San Diego, is regarded as having the best year-around weather in the nation, and the community's famous San Diego Zoo and Sea World offer good diversions for full-timers. There also is plenty to do in the Los Angeles area—Disneyland, Mann's Chinese Theater, walking along Hollywood Boulevard, driving through Beverly Hills. The annual RV and manufactured housing show is held at Dodger Stadium during the first half of November. For sheer relaxation, a lot of full-timers prefer to park at one of the many campgrounds near smog-free Hemet, located 90 miles east of Los Angeles.

December: Arrival In Florida

With fall weather gone and the first snowflakes already falling in the Midwest, full-timers in ever-larger numbers follow the sun south into Florida. For most of them, their destinations are Orlando, Tampa, St. Petersburg, Sarasota and Fort Myers on the west coast and West Palm Beach, Fort Lauderdale and Miami on the east coast. RVers who want to

Disneyland by night is an enchanting spectacle for visitors of all ages.

Photo from ©Walt Disney Productions.

escape the crowds of those big cities, however, should consider north-eastern Florida south of the Georgia line. There, the beautiful, wide beaches between Fernandina Beach and Daytona Beach are relatively empty of tourists in December. There are enough diversions to keep any full-timer busy, too. Treasure-hunting, for example. Pirates buried treasure in the sands of Fernandina Beach hundreds of years ago, and occasionally a few doubloons show up, uncovered by the wind and tide. Or, there are shopping and cultural attractions in the bustling city of Jacksonville. Legend says that Ponce de Leon landed in the area in 1513 looking for the fountain of youth, and the legends about that undiscovered spring still are kept alive by the residents of St. Augustine. That town is in the middle of a full-scale restoration effort, and the shops and homes on St. George Street are said to be among the most beautiful anywhere. Some of the houses are open at times for tours. St. Augustine is said to be the oldest city in America; it was founded more than 415 years ago. There, RVers can visit terraced gardens of the 95-year-old Ponce de Leon Hotel or stop off at commercial attractions such as Ripley's Believe It or Not Museum, a "fountain of youth" and a beautiful old fort. Northeastern Florida also boasts of the original Marineland; picturesque little seaside towns; the auto racing capital, Daytona Beach, and Ormond Beach, site of the widest stretch of beach in the nation where an annual antique car show is held on Thanksgiving weekend.

January: Parked For The Winter

By the first of January, most full-timing sunbirds have arrived at their winter destinations, have parked their rigs and are ready to begin exploring attractions within a short drive of their campsites. For those camped in southeastern Arizona, there is Old Tucson, a Western town built in 1940 for filming the movie "Arizona" and maintained as a tourist attraction since then as well as serving as location for additional Western movies. Stagecoach, frontier train and antique car rides are featured. RVers also should visit the Arizona-Sonora Desert Museum at Tucson; there, desert animals and plants are shown in their natural environment. Tucson also is the location of the Kitt Peak National Observatory and winter home of the Cleveland Indians baseball team. Southeast of Tucson is Tombstone, site of the famous "Gunfight at the OK Corral," where life-sized figures represent Doc Holliday, Wyatt Earp, his brothers and the infamous Clanton gang, all participants in the shootout. Nearby Boot Hill Graveyard is a popular spot for visitors—almost as popular as Tombstone's classic Western saloon, the "Crystal Palace."

St. George Street, in the heart of St. Augustine's restoration area, is a charming setting for an afternoon stroll.

Photo courtesy St. Augustine Chamber of Commerce.

In central Arizona, you can view Montezuma's Castle—a national monument cliff dwelling abandoned in the 14th century, 300 years after it was built by the Sinagua Indians. Nearby, on Alternate Rt. 89 near Cottonwood, is Jerome, a former ghost town that is now an artist's colony. There, you can also see the magnificent panoramas of Oak Creek Canyon—an area often featured in photographs by the respected "Arizona Highways" magazine. Due south is Phoenix, the state's largest city, where the best shopping and cultural diversions are found. The city also has an excellent art museum, thoroughbred and dog racing tracks and plenty of golf courses and tennis courts. Mesa, a Phoenix suburb, is winter home to thousands of full-time RVers. The Mesa area has twenty-two parks, fifteen golf courses, seventy-six tennis courts and several fishing lakes. A big draw is the hiking or horseback riding in the nearby Superstition Mountain Wilderness Area. In January, Mesa is the scene of the annual Apache Junction Gem and Mineral Show. Full-timers also are attracted to Tucson in January for the Southern Arizona Square Dance Festival.

Another area that is becoming increasingly popular among sun-seeking full-time RVers is the Panhandle of Florida—a relatively undeveloped section of Florida that consists of a 150-mile arm northwest of the state's main body. While January temperatures in the Panhandle are a little cool for swimming in the Gulf, thousands of RVers are willingly trading off that pastime in favor of the Panhandle's other attractions. White sand dune beaches that are thinly populated by tourists stretch eastward along the Gulf from Pensacola. Another attraction is the Seville Square Walking Tour of Pensacola—a route of 100- to 200-year-old restored houses. The town also boasts of quaint old restaurants, art galleries and shops. Surf fishing from the nearby dunes is popular among RVing sportsmen, and it is quite productive. Fort Walton Beach is the cultural and commercial center of the Panhandle. There are lots of good seafood and steak restaurants, too, with fish supplied by local anglers, and beef coming from the nearby cattle ranches. Destin is the jumping-off point for deep-sea fishermen seeking sailfish, marlin, mackerel, wahoo and amberjack. Panama City, the most popular community in the Panhandle, boasts of a dog racing track and lots of seashell and souvenir shops. Santa Rosa Island has miles of empty beaches and a preserved fort dating back to 1839, built by slave labor.

On January 6 each year—the "Twelfth Night" after Christmas—full-timers who are within driving distance of southeastern Louisiana should consider taking part in the opening of the nation's biggest festival—the Mardi Gras at New Orleans. Mardi Gras begins with a series of elaborate debutante balls and continues with parties until the Tuesday before Lent begins on Ash Wednesday. Week-long Cajun carnivals celebrating Mardi Gras also are held in Lafayette and other nearby towns. Participating RVers can savor the popular Cajun delicacies such as crawfish stew, boiled shrimp, gumbo, jambalaya and oysters on the half shell. New Orleans itself is an exciting town to visit—especially the famous French Quarter, where artists display their work along Jackson Square, where walks can be taken past historic brick buildings that were erected early in the 19th Century, where the famous French Market is open twenty-four hours a day and where there are dozens of cafes, vegetable markets and flea markets. You can shop for jewelry along Royal Street while you watch performances of strolling musicians, or you can gather with the crowds of sightseers on Bourbon Street and listen to the sounds of Dixieland bands performing at the nightspots. You can ride a trolley through the Garden District, where mansions are surrounded by beautiful gardens, or float the Mississippi River and nearby bayous on a paddle-wheel steamboat. The big attraction of New Orleans, though, is its food because, in that town, a great chef is an honored man who counts a good sauce as his proudest achievement.

February: Winding Up Winter

For many full-time RVers, February is the last full month they'll spend wintering in Florida, south Texas, Southern California or Arizona before beginning a slow trek northward. Those camped on the eastern coast of Florida certainly will want to stick around for the Daytona Speed Week in February, though. There are events that even people who aren't auto racing fans can enjoy, but for speed freaks, the week is really a fun time. Daytona Beach is a good place for RVers all through the winter, with its famous wide beaches whose sands are so firmly packed they'll accommodate an RV. Swimmers frequently use RVs as surfside dressing rooms, in fact. In Daytona Beach, racing fans can visit the Daytona International Speedway, where races are now held—including the 24-hour Pepsi Challenge and the seasonal climax event, the Daytona 500 National Stock Car Race. Grandstand seat holders can park RVs overnight in the west parking lot, or space can be rented in the infield. Other diversions include nightly entertainment in town, dog races and jai alai.

Farther south in Florida, winter sunbirds are still snorkeling, collecting conch shells and starfish, catching lobsters or fishing for grouper, snapper, redfish, bonito and other species in the waters off the Florida Keys. Not far away, RVing visitors are attracted to the famous Everglades

National Park—a huge, 2,120-square-mile subtropical wilderness still shrouded in mystery, with its secrets hidden from public view. At the park, well marked wilderness canoe trails are available for exploring the marsh, or visitors can hike along the elevated boardwalks above the swamp. There's good fishing for redfish, snapper and snook, or RVers can just relax and watch the colorful herons and egrets or look for tropical plants or hope to spot either a graceful porpoise or an ugly manatee (the sea cow around which the mermaid legends were originally built). Rental canoes are available to the most adventuresome and, while canoeing, you might spot a black bear, a panther, a bobcat or a wild turkey, and you'll almost certainly see several alligators and crocodiles.

There is plenty to see in the central region of Florida: Disney World, Cypress Gardens, Sea World, Circus World, Busch Gardens and Stars Hall of Fame. At Cape Canaveral, space rockets are on display at the Kennedy Space Center. And boating fans shouldn't forget about the Southland Hydroplane Regatta at St. Petersburg.

California winter visitors who are golf and tennis fans can take in the Andy Williams $250,000 Open Golf Tournament at Torrey Pines Golf Course and the Pacific Coast Sectional Men's Doubles Championship at LaJolla Beach and Tennis Club. Another February athletic event is the Open Celebrity Golf Tournament in Tucson. Visitors to Tucson should also attend the annual Tucson Rodeo and, if interested, stop off at the annual gem and mineral show at the Tucson Community Center. The annual Quartzite (Arizona) Pow Wow in early February is one of the largest gatherings of RVers anywhere—upward to 750,000 persons show up for the yearly tailgate parties, gem and mineral displays, craft exhibits and sales of equipment needed to engage in rockhounding. Fifteen private parks open their sites to the RVers during that period, and the Bureau of Land Management provides camping without hookups at the nearby LaPosa Recreation Site.

March: On The Edge Of Spring

As the warm March winds begin to blow, the sunbird migration northward starts, gradually, with the first restless full-timers spending less time parked in their winter quarters and more time exploring farther afield. Locales such as South Carolina, Georgia, Alabama, Louisiana, Oklahoma, Arkansas, Nevada and northern Texas come in for a share of attention from the sunbirds. With the first hints of spring come the pre-

The four-tiered pyramid is the grand finale to America's best-known water show at Cypress Gardens, Florida.

Photo courtesy Florida Cypress Gardens, Inc.

season baseball training sessions of the American and National Leagues. The moist air and warm climate of Florida assist players in their efforts to work themselves into shape prior to the opening of their regular seasons' activities. Eighteen of the twenty-six major league teams hold their spring training in Florida, and they compete against each other in the Grapefruit League before the traditional season-opening games in Cincinnati and Washington, D. C. There is always some non-game practice going on at the various training parks: morning calisthenics, practice batting, fielding, pitching and baserunning. And the parks are generally open to the public, sometimes free and sometimes for a small fee. Here are the cities in Florida where the pros train: Toronto Blue Jays, Dunedin; Pittsburgh Pirates, Bradenton; St. Louis Cardinals and New York Mets, St. Petersburg; Detroit Tigers, Lakeland; Chicago White Sox, Sarasota; Cincinnati Reds, Tampa; Boston Red Sox, Winter Haven; Philadelphia Phillies, Clearwater; Baltimore Orioles, Miami; Atlanta Braves, West Palm Beach; Texas Rangers, Pompano Beach; New York Yankees, Fort Lauderdale; Minnesota Twins, Orlando; Los Angeles Dodgers, Vero Beach; Houston Astros, Cocoa; Montreal Expos, Daytona Beach, and Kansas City Royals, Fort Myers.

March is a good time for fishermen on their way north from South Texas to stop at the famous Toledo Bend Reservoir on the Texas-Louisiana border. The largest man-made reservoir in the South, with 1,250 miles of shoreline, is an early spring hot spot for crappie, bass and bluegills. An exploratory trip into Louisiana is in order for the final migration north. Try Cameron, a fishing village on the Gulf Coast where you can buy fresh shrimp and oysters or visit the nearby Rockefeller Wild Life Sanctuary—wintering ground for snow geese and other waterfowl. Visit the 1765 plantation at the Longfellow Evangeline State Commemorative Area, near St. Martinville, or take in the 19th century architecture of the town itself. At the waterfront restaurants of Henderson, order crawfish pie dinner. Taste more Cajun cooking and visit the antebellum homes of Baton Rouge, and don't fail to drive through Natchitoches, the oldest permanent settlement in the Louisiana Purchase Territory; the striking French Colonial architecture of the town is truly beautiful. No trip to Louisiana, either, would be complete without a walk through the magnificent Hodges Gardens, a 4,700-acre parkland landscaped with spectacular roses, berried shrubs, camellias and dozens of other flowers and flowering plants.

From Louisiana, head north into Arkansas and stop at Eureka Springs, where water from the famous springs there are said to have restorative powers; the water was originally bottled by the man who discovered it and was sold as "Dr. Jackson's Magic Eye Water." Now visitors are drawn to the town that grew up around the spring by other attractions: beautiful Victorian homes, bluegrass music, small shops which sell antiques and glassware, and by nearby Beaver Lake, where the fishing in March is usually excellent. On your way to Eureka Springs, stop at Hot Springs National Park for a hot mineral water bath, and while you're there, take your RV rig out on a Camp-A-Float raft for a fishing trip on Lake Ouachita.

If you've spent the winter in Florida, particularly in the northwestern Panhandle region, drift over into Alabama for some Deep South cooking and hospitality. The baked catfish, pan-fried chicken and hickory-smoked barbecued beef and ribs there are second to none. March is the time for taking part in the state's annual Azalea Trail Festival and Mobile's Jubilee Time Historic Tour of Homes. In mid-March, a huge arts and crafts show is held on the eastern shore of Mobile Bay, and folk dancing, parades and southern cooking are offered. Hundreds of antebellum mansions built between 1820 and 1860 are on display throughout March and into early April. The Rattlesnake Rodeo, featuring square dancing, snake racing and other unusual events, is scheduled annually at the town of Opp. And March is a good time to visit the Bellingrath Gardens near Mobile; built early in the century by the founders of the Coca-Cola company, the gardens are in bloom all year and open to visitors.

At the Alabama Space and Rocket Center in Huntsville, the world's largest space and missile collection is on display. Several underground caves, such as Sequoyah Caverns at Valley Head and Manitou Cave near Fort Payne, are top attractions in Alabama. Near the city of Florence and at Moundville can be seen the historic earthen temples left behind by the ancient Mound Builders. Also near Florence is the log cabin birthplace of William C. Handy, father of the blues. Or, at Suscumbia, visit the birthplace of Helen Keller. Lake Joe Wheeler has marvelous camping, fishing and boating facilities, or visit George Washington Carver Museum at Tuskegee National Park; it honors the man who discovered the commercial value of the lowly peanut.

Before sunbirds leave California, they should drive north to the wine country of Hecker Pass, south of San Jose, and sample the vintage wines produced by the family-owned vintners there. Most Hecker vintners operate out of their farm homes, so don't be surprised to have to drive down long lanes, through vineyards, in order to stop at a cozy wine-tasting room. More adventuresome RVers can then head east into the Feather River country of northern Nevada, near Quincy, to pan for gold in the streams and gravel bars, or on dry creek beds.

April: Northbound Again

Experienced full-timers usually report that while they aim at leaving their wintering sites in March or April, they like to wend their way through areas where the days are still quite warm and the sun is bright. Their favorite haunts during April are usually in Kentucky, Tennessee, Oklahoma, North Carolina and Louisiana. Another favorite early-spring locale is Washington, D. C. where, in April, the Japanese cherry trees are in full bloom. More than any other American city, Washington belongs to everyone, and cherry blossom time is a perfect time to visit the nation's capital. The famous cherry trees there are the result of a gift of several hundred trees in 1912 from the people of Tokyo. The trees usually bloom for ten days during the first of April, and the blossoms are celebrated in an annual Cherry Blossom Festival with dinners, parades, balls, concerts and street dances, and everyone eats cherry pie. Stopping in Washington during cherry blossom festival time also is an excellent opportunity for revisiting the Jefferson and Lincoln Memorials, the Smithsonian and any of the dozens of other historic and cultural attractions.

About the same time Washington is having its Cherry Blossom Festival, RVers in the area around Wilmington, North Carolina, are taking part in the parade, garden tours and other attractions at the annual Azalea Festival. Meanwhile, across the country at San Bernardino, California, the annual Calico Hullabaloo is being held at the Calico Ghost Town; events include three days of horseshoe pitching and an activity called "The Old Miners Stew Cook-Off and Tobacco Spit." Not so far away, at San Diego, judges are trying to select the best dressed men and women during four days of the area's annual Easter promenade. At San Jose, several dozen exhibitors are taking part in the annual Woodcarvers and Crafters Show, and in Manchester, New Hampshire, RVers gather for fun and instruction during the annual New England Square and Round Dance Convention.

Devotees of deep-sea fishing sometimes prefer to hang around the Gulf of Mexico coastal areas a while longer, particularly since April is regarded as the best time to catch white and blue marlin, yellowfin tuna, bluefin and sailfish from charter boats operating out of Grand Isle off the Louisiana coast. Shore and surf fishermen on the narrow spit of land catch redfish, sheepshead and speckled trout. One bluefin caught a few years ago weighed 859 pounds; it was the largest gamefish ever caught in the Gulf on rod and reel. Freshwater fishermen point their RVs northward until they reach Tennessee and Kentucky, then stop and fish for bass and crappies at Cordell Hull, Kentucky Lake, Lake Barkley, Lake

Cumberland, Dale Hollow and more than three dozen other reservoirs built by the U.S. Corps of Engineers.

Winter Texans headed north often are distracted by the eastern Oklahoma lakes region around Muskogee. There, they have their choice of Lake Tenkiller, Robert S. Kerr Reservoir, Eufaula Lake, or Fort Gibson Lake. All are clear, deep lakes in the wooded hills of Oklahoma; all offer fine fishing opportunities, and all offer excellent camping to RVers. A replica Cherokee village, Tsa-La-Gi, and the Cherokee National Museum are nearby attractions. In Tahlequah, capital of the Cherokee nation, RVers can stop at the Restaurant of the Cherokees and a tribe-operated arts and crafts center. Side trips can be taken to restored Fort Gibson, a 155-year-old military outpost, and to the inland seaport of Muskogee.

The Midwest In May

May is one of the best times of the year for touring the Midwest because of special attractions it offers. RVing epicures are well advised to travel to northern Michigan in search of the delicious wild morel mushroom. The three or four most sought-after species of morels grow in the hard-wood forests there only for about three weeks, commencing just prior to the middle of May and lasting until about the second week of June, depending upon the amount of sunshine and rainfall and other more mysterious natural factors. Popular areas are the forests near Gaylord, Grayling, Traverse City and Cadillac. Boyne City even holds an annual May mushroom festival, awarding prizes for the biggest, smallest and most mushrooms found.

The two other big events in May are the Indianapolis 500 race and the Kentucky Derby. The Indy 500 is more than a one-day race. Fans begin their annual trek to Indianapolis a month before Memorial Day in order to watch time trials and soak up the flavor of this nation's most popular single spectator event. More than a dozen campgrounds are within a short driving or walking distance of the motor speedway. Other attractions: a re-created 19th century drugstore that boasts it has the best chocolate sodas in town; Conner Prairie Pioneer Settlement; Speedway Museum and Hall of Fame with its antique touring cars and famous racing machines; historic homes, museums and art galleries. The old drugstore is actually Hook's Historic Drugstore and Pharmacy Museum, where ice cream treats are dispensed from an 1875-vintage soda fountain and where shelves are lined with cork-stopped bottles that once were "guaranteed to cure every ailment." The Conner settlement at Noblesville is a restored and working 18th century frontier village.

The Kentucky Derby period in Louisville is actually a ten-day festival climaxed by the annual race of nation's best three-year-old thoroughbreds. There's always a hot-air balloon race about a week prior to the Derby, and top amateur bicyclists from around the country compete in the Kentucky Derby of Cycling race. Other highlights of the pre-race days are an annual horse show, a thirteen-mile street marathon, the Derby Trial horse race and a steamboat race, a parade and a special race for thoroughbred fillies. Post-race activities include the Kentucky Colonels Barbecue, a downtown chuckwagon lunch with entertainment; a fashion fair; a watercolor exhibition, and square dancing in the street.

May also is the time for the Kentucky Guild of Artists and Craftsmen Fair at Berea—an annual show with more than 100 artists and craftsmen participating with help from musicians, dancers and puppeteers. May is a good time for visitors to the state to tour horse country; 150 horse farms operate under the auspices of the Kentucky Horse Council, and many of the farms are open to the public at times. Kentucky Horse Park near Lexington opened in 1979. A former working horse farm, the park even has a campground with full hookups for RVers. Using the park as a base, full-timers could plan short trips to private horse farms, Fort Boonesborough, My Old Kentucky Home State Park or stop at the cemetery in Frankfort where Daniel Boone was buried. Other attractions include dozens of beautiful, clear lakes for boating and fishing; the spectacular Cumberland Falls and several caverns, including Mammoth Cave.

Travelers through Virginia—perhaps those either leaving or on their way to Washington, D. C., could stop in Virginia Beach at Fort Story, which marks the spot where the Jamestown colonists landed in 1607. At Hampton Roads, Virginia, the historic battle of the Monitor and Merrimac is commemorated. Norfolk is another historic town; it has a lot of beautiful old buildings and a museum devoted to the memory of World War II hero General Douglas MacArthur.

Farther west, in Missouri, the Truman Week celebration is held in Independence. It includes a multi-media presentation, "The Man From Independence." A library and the museums schedule regular programs about the life of Harry Truman, one of our most colorful presidents.

June: Arrival Of Summer

Full-timers who are chasing the sun north can experience an unusual adventure by stopping off in the thinly populated southern Indiana cave country. It's within an hour of Louisville. Most popular of the three caves there is Squire Boone Caverns, with its mirror-like pools, its unusual rock formations and a 48-foot natural tower, called the Rock of Ages Column, which took millions of years to form. Squire Boone, Daniel's brother, was buried in another nearby grave. Wyandotte Cave not far away has the world's largest underground mountain, and Marengo Cave features a huge underground passageway and a miniature volcano. Several dozen caves in the region that are not state or commercial ventures are open for exploration by experienced spelunkers.

June also is a good time for touring the Hudson River Valley of New York and revisiting Niagara Falls. In June, the apple orchards of the Hudson Valley are in bloom, and visitors can combine wine tasting at the valley's famous wineries with sightseeing in the small, historic towns where stone houses built by early settlers still stand. One of the most famous of those houses is Phillipsburg Manor in North Larrytown; the restored house is surrounded by flower gardens and fruit trees. Other beautiful restorations are at Garrison-on-Hudson, Poughkeepsie, New Paltz and Newburgh. While you're in the area, visit the U.S. Military Academy at West Point and the famous Black Bear Trading Post.

Niagara Falls is one of the most popular tourist attractions in the country; it is visited annually by nearly fourteen million people. Europeans who heard of the falls through reports by a Jesuit explorer a couple of hundred years ago called Niagara one of the seven wonders of the world. Southern aristocrats journeyed there 100 years ago to escape the summer heat and gave it the reputation it still enjoys as a honeymoon resort. Even today, 25,000 honeymooning couples visit there each year.

North of New York is the state that is literally a seafood lover's paradise—Maine. Quaint, picturesque fishing villages seem today just as they appeared years ago in Currier and Ives prints. Along the coast on U.S. Route 1, antique shops are even more numerous than seafood restaurants, and most of them are beautifully restored residences. Stop in Ogunquit, just after crossing into Maine from New Hampshire, for your first taste of antique shopping. Eat lunch at one of the lobster pounds in Rockland. Plan a few days at Acadia National Park, driving the narrow road that winds along the coastline, sometimes hundreds of feet above the ocean and other times at the water's edge. Don't forget Bar Harbor, one of those tourist towns where you'll want to spend hours walking around. Take side trips north to the interior for great freshwater fishing. Catch salmon and trout in the Moose River just below famous, 40-mile-long Moosehead Lake, or explore the back country using maps provided by the Scott Paper Company.

June travelers in the Northwest can stop off at a certain hill in

Montana overlooking the Little Bighorn River. There, in June 1876, General George Armstrong Custer made his "Last Stand." Or visit Washington's Mt. Ranier, the Northwest's highest mountain, located southeast of Seattle. In the summer, flowers bloom all over the slopes, sometimes even before the snow has melted. At Paradise, pause at the visitor's center to learn about the geology and history of the park and about the recreation programs available. A popular diversion is hiking the ice glaciers. Paradise is, however, particularly crowded during summer weekends, so full-timers should plan their visits for weekdays.

July: Continuing North

From the Custer battleground, forays can be made to Beartooth Pass and Grasshopper Glacier near Yellowstone National Park. During one day in July—and no one knows which day because it depends upon the weather—residents of Red Lodge put up a serving bar along the road and serve soft drinks and beer to tourists. Their "snow bar" is called the Top-of-the-World Bar, and it's an effort by the Montana natives to show their visitors how much the tourist dollars are appreciated. One rather unnerving sight is the area of glacier in the Beartooth Range where millions of locusts were caught, frozen and preserved 200 years ago. Travel in or with RVs to the glacier is not recommended, though, because the roads are rocky and rough. South of Yellowstone National Park in the Grand Teton Mountains is Jackson Hole, Wyoming, one of the nation's most popular recreation areas. Activities include horseback pack trips along 245 miles of trails into the high country; sailing and canoeing on Jackson or Jenny Lake; float trips on the Snake River; fishing the streams for rainbow, cutthroat and brown trout. Jackson Hole also has a symphony orchestra, a swimming pool, a golf course and several tennis courts.

RVers in the middle of the country should consider escaping the summer heat by taking a loop trip around Lake Superior—the largest of the great lakes. The trip north of Superior is especially fun for RVers who like to go the fishing camp route while they're sightseeing. On the trip around Superior, you can gather blueberries in the forests north of Sault Ste. Marie; catch the Algoma Central Railway Excursion to Agawa Canyon; take in the riverfront redevelopment area of Sault Ste. Marie; search for gold just off the "Gold Mine Road" near Wawa, and buy hand-carved wood souvenirs at White River, the little community that bills itself as "the coldest town in Canada with the warmest heart." At Lake Nipigon Provincial Park, you can sift through black granite sand on the shoreline

Float trips down the Snake River in Grand Teton National Park give rafters a close-up view of wildlife and spectacular scenery.

and walk through two preserved cemeteries—one for white settlers and one for Christian Indians not far from the site of the old Sand Point Trading Post. Or, explore Old Fort William, the amethyst mines and Kakabeka Falls near Thunder Bay, Ontario.

For an unusual summer adventure, explore the beautiful Lake Erie islands. Take a ferry cruise from Catawba Island Peninsula to the village of Put-in-Bay on South Bass Island; if you take your RV with you, you can camp in the state park there and either rent bicycles or use your own to tour the romantic and peaceful little island, its wineries, its caves and its spectacular scenery. Hop over to Kelleys Island, then, for a relaxing stay. There's not much activity there—mainly just walking, biking and loafing—but the people are friendly and the wineries and shops are interesting. The finest beaches in the Sandusky region of Lake Erie are found on the Marblehead Peninsula. There are also several interesting attractions nearby: Danbury Pioneer Village (a replica frontier street where craftsmen make boots, barrels, guns, square nails and buggies);

Fort Firelands (featuring a huge model train exhibit); Mystery Hills, and the famous Cedar Point amusement park. While in the area, drive through the towns of Sandusky, Port Clinton and Vermilion and look at the beautiful New England-style homes.

Full-timers who aren't much bothered by the heat of mid-summer can point south again and attend two outstanding annual events: a country music show in southern Ohio and the "Highland Games and Gathering of the Clans" in North Carolina. The music show is a two-day outdoor festival, Jamboree in the Hills, at Brush Run Park, St. Clairsville—just across the Ohio River from Wheeling, West Virginia. The "Gathering of the Clans" is an annual event during the second weekend of July for people of Scottish descent; they come to MacRae Meadow on Grandfather Mountain—a terrain that resembles northern Scotland—for traditional dancing, piping, athletic events and other activities associated with the Gaelic culture.

August: Last Days Of Summer

Nauvoo, Illinois, near the shore of the Mississippi River, is just one of many small river towns that can be toured leisurely in late summer before it's time for a trek down south again. Nauvoo once had 12,000 residents and was the most populous city in Illinois—it was even larger than Chicago—but that was 1840, and Nauvoo now has only 1,000 residents. The original Mormon settlers moved west to Utah, but their descendants are now restoring the old town. Homes are once again taking on their 1840s appearance, and the town draws in travelers with the home-style meals served at the Hotel Nauvoo and its famous wine and bleu cheese.

Summer visitors to Colorado can take in the Royal Gorge area before the days turn cool. Ride the incline railroad to the bottom of the gorge; take a white-water raft trip down the Arkansas River; trail ride the mountains on horseback, and camp overnight at the timberline. RVers traveling farther west can drive along the beautiful coastline of Oregon and soak up the spectacular views at overlooks on U.S. 101. Continue along the spring-fed rivers and clear lakes of the Cascades; at Crane Prairie Reservoir, osprey and eagles can sometimes be seen. Near Bend, Oregon, an interpretative trail leads through an area of lava flows. Sights in that area also include famous Crater Lake, the Old West appearance of Jacksonville, and Mount Hood viewed during a scenic loop trip. Ashland is famous for its summer schedule of Shakespearean plays, while the town

From left to right, Nashville struts its stuff for country music lovers at Opryland, and visitors to Silver Dollar City, Missouri, can watch Ozark craftsmen at work.

of Newport is a marvelous little fishing village that specializes in serving clam chowder to visitors. Take a dune buggy ride at the Oregon Dunes National Recreation Area or dig for clams on the tide flats near Florence.

September: Just A Hint Of Fall

Extended-period camping is a good idea in areas where beautiful fall colors tend to attract large numbers of tourists. Many full-time RVers prefer to reach a favorite color tour spot two to four weeks early, park there and explore and await the changes in the weather that turn green leaves to red and gold. While waiting for the colors to appear in the 1,000 Islands area of New York, you can stock your larder with fresh fish from either the St. Lawrence River or from the beautiful lakes that pockmark the upper Northeast. Cross over into Canada and catch bass, northern pike, walleyes and musky from the lakes of the Rideau area. Or prepare for autumn in the Ozarks by visiting Silver Dollar City in southern Missouri. Consider spending a week in the Smoky Mountains, but go there early and take a side trip to the Franklin, North Carolina, area first in search of gemstones that are found there every day. The North Carolina mountains produce about 100 different varieties of gemstones, including rubies, emeralds, sapphires, amethysts, garnets and aquamarine. Wash buckets of rock and mud in flumes for a fee at the commercial gemstone mines, and count on finding at least some small stones suitable for making into jewelry. Tiffany's 13.14-carat emerald—the Carolina—was found at Hiddenite, North Carolina; it is valued at more than $100,000. And more than a dozen diamonds have been found in the state.

Lincoln, Illinois, also attracts RV travelers during September. The national railsplitting contest is held there in the middle of the month. The most famous railsplitter of all, Abe Lincoln, grew up in nearby New Salem, and the town of Lincoln was named in honor of the beloved president. The annual September festival features—in addition to railsplitting competition—square dancing, a parade, tomahawk pitching, cow chip throwing and tobacco spitting. If you want your "country' atmosphere a little more subdued, stop in Nashville and watch live country music performances at Opryland.

Farther west, adventuresome travelers can ride miles to the bottom of the South Rim of the Grand Canyon or they can take a river float trip on the San Juan River near Lake Powell. At Pendleton, Oregon, an annual rodeo—the Pendleton Roundup—is scheduled during the second week of September. During the rodeo, there are street shootouts—without live bullets, of course—daily, a carnival, stagecoach races, bareback Indian races and a wild cow milking contest in addition to all of the regular rodeo events. Before and after the rodeo, visitors can tour the nearby Umatilla Indian Reservation and attend a nightly pageant called "Happy Canyon" performed by the tribe during the Roundup. Farther southwest, RVers driving through Utah can visit Park City, a 100-year-old silver mining town that is now a popular resort community. The southwestern part of the state offers splendid colors in the rock formations of Zion and Bryce Canyon National Parks—Zion with its 2,000-foot deep gorge; Bryce, with its amphitheater-like chasm of pink and white spires and pinnacles. Visit cosmopolitan Salt Lake City's famous granite temple where the 375-voice Mormon Tabernacle Choir rehearses on Thursday evenings. Museums in Salt Lake City that are maintained by the Church of Jesus Christ of Latter-day Saints include former residences of the Brigham Young family. Utah also offers anglers great fishing in September: for rainbow, brown, brook and cutthroat trout or for largemouth bass, white bass and catfish. Take the Alpine Scenic Drive over State Route 80 across the Wasatch Range. Visit Promontory Summit and see the reenactment of the spike-driving ceremony that marked completion of the all-important Central Pacific Railroad line, and be sure to take part in the annual Melon Days at Green River. Explore the high plateau country of eastern Utah,

Photo courtesy Oregon Department of Transportation.

Travelers along US-101 enjoy panoramic views of the Oregon coastline.

where fantastic sandstone formations have been sculptured by the wind. Hike into the canyons of Arches National Park for close-ups of the natural arches which are now a national monument.

There's Vermont, of course, where fall color tours can be combined with a gigantic craft display at the "Fall Festival of Vermont Crafts" in Montpelier. There's the Kentucky Guild Fall Fair—an outdoor harvest festival featuring Appalachian music and dancing—at Berea. There's the Apple Butter Boil in the heart of the Pennsylvania Dutch country at Quarryville. There's the Paul Bunyan logging show at Nelsonville, Ohio, and the Fall Foliage Festival at Cohocton, New York. RVers can take color tours of Maryland and, at the same time, attend the Chesapeake Appreciation Days at Annapolis. They can enjoy the red and gold foliage of the Ozarks while they're on a trout float trip at Roaring River State Park near Branson, Missouri, or while attending the annual antique show at Rogers, Arkansas. They can motor along scenic Skyline Drive in northern

253

Virginia or park and hike through the colorful forests of Shenandoah National Park. They can also tour Arizona, Oregon, Michigan, Pennsylvania and northern California and watch summer change to fall.

What it all comes down to is that full-time RVers can go wherever they want and do whatever they please while they follow the sun. This beautiful country offers them an endless supply of destinations. That, along with the spirit of independence that full-timing encourages, was emphasized to me time after time as I spent hour after hour talking with the full-timers who are really living The Good Life today. Yet, without exception, every full-timer I interviewed expressed a heartfelt awe that he was able to participate in the unique, adventuresome full-time RVing way of life. If they had one common complaint about their lifestyle, though, it was this: not enough time in the day to enjoy the rich bounties of the world. Full-timers Dick Bright and his friend, John Lockwood, probably expressed it best while I was interviewing them in the summer of 1980 at Bemidji, Minnesota. Dick said, "Since we've retired, we have been busy doing the things we *wanted* to do *before* we retired. But even so, we don't have time to do everything we want to; there are many places we want to see, but we don't have time to go see them all."

John added, "When I was working, I did everything in a damned rush. Now I do everything at my leisure. If I want to sit outside the trailer here and talk, I can do it whether or not I've got something else to do. What I've got to do can always be done later. I'm occupied by something every minute of every day, and even though I don't get to do half the things I expected to do, I'm happy, and I'm never bored."

Chapter Fifteen

Familiar Faces

For Chris and Charlotte Moffett, camping and RVing was an enjoyable kind of experience that enabled them to get away from the everyday pressures of their home and jobs. They cherished the solitude camping provided, and while they shared that solitude with their children, they didn't consider traveling with other campers or joining groups of RVers at rallies. Then, in the mid-1960s, the Moffetts bought a Holiday Rambler travel trailer and, simply because it was available, accepted a membership in the new Holiday Rambler Recreational Vehicle Club. Fifteen years later, Chris recalled his early thoughts about the club: "We started getting literature promoting the club's first national rally. Well, I had heard about rallies and things like that, but had never considered getting involved. I told Charlotte, 'I just can't imagine why anybody would spend ten days and his hard-earned money and drive to Ohio just so he can park in a cornfield with a bunch of people he's never seen before in his life.' So we missed that rally. Then, the following year, our own Chapter Eighteen in Pennsylvania was to sponsor the next national rally. Since it was going to be close to where we lived, I volunteered to help park trailers. That alone should show what I knew about rallies because that's the toughest job there is. Thank God, they already had enough people for those jobs, though, and they elected me to be the hospitality chairman."

Chris continued, "A local RV dealer by the name of Brubaker loaned me a trailer with an awning to use. Keebler Cookie Company sent me a truckload of cookies—I never saw so many cookies in my life! We got a lot of chocolate from the Hershey candy company nearby, and we made the best lemonade I've ever tasted. Somehow, I allowed myself to get into the spirit of the rally, and I had a lot of fun." A year later, Chris found himself accepting the full-time job of national director of the club, and although he resigned that position three years later so that he and Charlotte could become full-time RVers, he has kept his membership and maintained a close relationship with hundreds of Holiday Rambler owners.

As much as Chris and other full-time RVers enjoy traveling and seeing new sights, they consistently report that a large share of their appreciation for the full-timing lifestyle comes from the friends they've made and the people they've met. Mac McGinley of Mississippi, for example, said, "We have friends scattered all over the country." And his wife, Alice, added, "Most of our traveling revolves around the rallies of our RV club." One of the primary pleasures of their way of life, they said, is renewing acquaintances with other full-timers that they've met in other parts of the country, perhaps even years earlier. "It's a special feeling when we see old, familiar faces," Alice emphasized.

During their 2½ years as young full-timers, Jim and Mary Brown collected enough memories and friends to last them a lifetime. Jim said, "Whether it's attending an RV club rally or spending the winter in the Rio Grande Valley, the part we always remember best is meeting new people and developing friendships with them and then running into them again somewhere else. To us, the importance of a rally is the opportunity it provides for seeing people that we haven't seen for a year."

Mary added, "Once you get hooked on club rallies, you don't go to a national rally for the programs and activities, but because it may be the only time that year you can see people you haven't seen for a long time."

Like Chris and Charlotte Moffett, Ohioans Walt and Charlotte Consider were RVing loners. They had camped all their lives by themselves and with a few friends, but without any intention of joining an RV club. In the early 1970s, though, they became Good Sam members primarily to qualify for the 10% discounts at participating campgrounds, and a friend who was Ohio state director for Good Sam suggested they also should join the Holiday Rambler club. "We debated about it for a while," Walt said, "and finally decided we'd try it for a year and, if we didn't like it, we'd quit."

The Considers met so many friendly people at the first rally they attended, though, that they began attending more. Now, as full-time RVers since 1979, they plan all of their travels around national, state and regional rallies of the Good Sam and Holiday Rambler clubs. "We have friends from all over the country now," Walt said.

I talked with the Considers during the summer of 1980 while they were attending the HRRVC international rally in Minnesota. They were especially looking forward to the arrival of full-timing couples from Missouri and from Philadelphia. "We meet them at different places all the time," Walt said. "For example, last year we all attended the rally in Nova Scotia, and we met them while we were parked in the same campground after the rally. We struck up a conversation and learned that we were all retired from the same company. Later, we saw them in Sarasota, Florida, and we ran into them again in Las Vegas."

Walt added, "We've attended six other rallies this year so far, and we went to each one because of the people we knew we'd meet, not because of the places the rallies were held. We've been to Sarasota; Harlingen, Texas; Costa Mesa, California, and Las Vegas, then stopped off in Canton, Ohio, for a weekend Good Sam Samboree. We stopped to visit friends in Alexandria, Minnesota, on our way here and they talked us into going back to see them after this rally. So you can see, we've got a very stiff schedule."

Walt said, "We don't meet people by sitting here under this awning. We get out and participate in activities and talk with everyone we meet. A lot of times, we'll just be walking along the roadway and we'll smile and say 'good morning' to some other campers. Often, we'll have to stop and talk. And before we've gone too far, we've talked with ten or twelve people. A smile and a 'good morning' go a long way.

CARAVAN SCOUTS

Two of the most familiar faces at rallies of the International Coachmen Caravan Club belong to Paul and Delphia Blizzard. The retired Illinois couple scout and lead the caravans sponsored by the club, and since 1971 have logged more than 300,000 miles—equivalent to twelve trips around the world—as caravan scouts and wagonmasters. It's no exaggeration to state that literally thousands of RV owners know the Blizzards and that the former Illinois Bell sales manager and his wife are among the most recognized RVers in the country.

Paul and Delphia became Coachmen owners when the Middlebury, Indiana, company was struggling along in 1964, just after being founded by brothers Tom, Keith and Claude Corson. The Blizzards bought the thirteenth travel trailer built by Coachmen and immediately began converting other RVers to the brand. "In those days," Paul said, "there were practically no Coachmen on the road, so it was easy for us to keep a list

Familiar faces to thousands of RVers across the country, Paul and Delphia Blizzard have been caravan scouts since 1971.

of owners, which we did. Whenever we saw a Coachmen unit on the road or at a park, we knew immediately who the owners were." By 1966, Coachmen had become one of the best selling brand names in the country, and the International Coachmen Caravan Club was founded. Five years later, Paul retired from his job with the telephone company and was recruited to lead club caravans.

Now, although they maintain an apartment in Greenville, Illinois, they travel nearly all the time in their trailer. "We are seldom home more than a couple of weeks at a time, and we like it that way," Delphia said.

After the club's international office selects a caravan destination, Paul and Delphia plot an outline of the expedition on paper, concentrating on scenic spots and attractions along the way. Then they scout the trip by driving the route personally. And by doing that, they avoid problems for themselves later when they are actually leading the caravan. "I remember one time," Paul said, "when we'd gone a couple of hundred miles only to come to a portion of road that even a van couldn't manipulate. Back we went to the starting place and mapped an alternate route that even the biggest RV could travel easily. It does get frustrating sometimes, but it's better for Delphia and I to backtrack than to run into a problem later when we're leading fifty or more rigs."

Delphia takes notes on campgrounds visited, landmarks at intersections, rest stops, miles between stops and unusual sights. That information is cataloged for later publication in the caravan itinerary. A typical itinerary said, "Turn left at the intersection of roads 23 and 8. There's a green shingle house on the corner with a big oak tree in the front yard with a rope swing suspended from the branches. Our campground for tonight is just four miles down the road on the right." A second campground is always checked out and held in reserve in case its facilities are needed.

Coachmen public relations director Betty Schreiner reported, "Places along the way are scouted with the same care. When a caravan trip describes the activities and highlights of any specific tourist attraction, it's because Paul and Delphia were there and they know!" Every fifty to sixty-five miles, a rest or refueling stop is scheduled, and the breaks are always taken in a leisurely fashion to allow for socializing. The RVs arrive at each night's destination with plenty of time left for the caravaners to set up camp and chat with each other before dinner. Sometimes, evening dinners at restaurants are scheduled, with reservations already made and confirmed.

While Paul and Delphia try to limit caravan sizes to fifty units, they once led 106 RVs on a fall excursion to New England. "It was really too big," Paul said. "We felt we couldn't do justice to that large a group." Which trip was their favorite? "They are all our favorites," Paul said. "This last one—the western sunset [caravan]—was wonderful; beautiful country, perfect weather and marvelous traveling. Our trips through the Smokies for the spring flowers, our color tours in the fall, the Nova Scotia trips—they've all been great. We love them all."

HARROWING EXPERIENCE

Before Paul and Delphia Blizzard retired to a life of full-time RVing, they had one of the most harrowing experiences ever reported by campers. Occasionally now, while caravan club members are enjoying the flickering flames of an evening campfire, someone will talk Paul into telling the story of his 1960 campout at Yellowstone National Park. Paul, a master storyteller, begins his tale in a slow, deliberate drawl calculated to build suspense and keep his listeners on the edges of their lawn chairs. Paul's words on one of those nights were passed on to us by the staff of the Caravan club's magazine, "Coachmen Capers."

"I hate to shave, and I'll clutch at any excuse not to," is how Paul always starts his story. "Well, Delphia and I were leaving on a western vacation trip to Yellowstone Park on Friday right after work. I shaved on Thursday, and on Friday I decided I could get by—we were leaving right after lunch, and a little five o'clock shadow wouldn't matter. The campgrounds we stayed in on Friday, Saturday and Sunday did not have electricity hookups, so of course I couldn't shave—not that I would have anyway. By the time we got to Yellowstone on Monday, I had a pretty good stand of whiskers. It was late in the day when we arrived, and we built a big fire, cooked supper and were eating in our trailer when I heard something thumping on my ice chest which we'd left outside next to the trailer.

"Now, wildlife is pesky sometimes in the park; any sign of food will often attract it. I wasn't about to lose my ice chest, so I went out to the fire to investigate, clapping my hands to frighten any wildlife away. Sure enough, I caught a fleeting glimpse of something as it lumbered away after knocking the chest into the woods. It looked like a bear. It was too dark to go looking for it without a light, so I went back in the trailer to get my flashlight. I couldn't find it immediately—doesn't it always happen that way?—so I told Delphia to look for it while I went back to the fire to make sure the bear or whatever didn't come back and destroy the chest. Because of the layout of our campsite, we had built our fire behind our trailer, next to the side without the door. I charged out, circled the side and ran smack into a huge, terrifying grizzly bear.

"What happened next is hazy to me. It all happened so fast, but I'm told this is what went on. The grizzly took one swipe at me with his long, sharp claws, slashing me down my face, my chest and my abdomen and knocking me about fifteen feet through the air. I let out a bloodcurdling scream, heard throughout the campground, and immediately Boy Scouts camping nearby started banging on pans and kettles. Delphia and I didn't know at the time that the Scouts and their scoutmasters had been warned that a rogue grizzly was in the area. They had been told to arm themselves with noisemakers to keep the brute away. The bear, which had 'gone bad' some time before, had been captured once and transported to the high country but had wandered back into the camping area and was even then being hunted by rangers.

"Because of the layout of our campsite, we had built our fire behind our trailer. . . . I charged out, circled the side and ran smack into a huge, terrifying grizzly bear."

"Well, as my scream rent the air, I picked myself up and, blood streaming from my wounds, dashed into my trailer. Scouts and their leaders rushed to our campsite, banging away on their pans. Stopping the flow of blood as best they could with towels, they hustled me into a car and headed for the nearest aid station. After quick emergency treatment, I was immediately taken from there to the nearest hospital, some fifty miles away. I was lucky. The bear missed my eyes and my jugular vein. My face and lips were mangled and the flesh of my chest and abdomen hung in ribbons. A wide leather belt I was wearing was cut through in three places as though it had been sliced by a sharp razor. I was lucky, too, because of those banging, noisy Scouts. Rogue grizzlies do not hit and run. Usually, a grizzly will not stop until he has killed his prey, and I was the prey. I'm convinced those young lads saved my life with their noise.

"After several hours in surgery, I was taken to my room, looking like a mummy—head and body swathed in bandages. Because of the healthy crop of whiskers I was sporting, the doctor could not sew up the cuts on my face. He cleaned them, treated them and drew the raw edges together with tape before covering them with dressings. The doctor who treated me was in Yellowstone doing research for a paper on bear wounds. The day after the attack, when he came to change the dressing, he asked me what I did for a living, if I dealt with the public in my job. I told him I was sales manager for Illinois Bell and yes, I deal with the public all the time. Sadly, he informed me that I would probably be horribly scarred. Bear wounds invariably became infected, he told me, and because he wasn't able to suture the wounds on my face, it would no doubt be even worse.

"Days passed with me looking like that mummy. Only my ears, one nostril and a corner of my mouth were visible. The merthiolate used to disinfect the wounds stained the dressing a brilliant red. And coffee, spilled as Delphia spooned it into the one corner of my mouth that was exposed, added another color to the gory looking bandages. Of course, I wouldn't allow my picture to be taken. How I regret that now—I'd give a million dollars for a picture today.

"Anyway, each day I got a little better. I was in good general health and I healed quickly. To the amazement of the doctor, no infection developed, and as the healing progressed, it was apparent that scarring would be minimal. The doctor kept many notes, and somewhere in the annals of medical lore, my grizzly attack is a case history. I credit my whiskers. Today, I still have vivid memories of that day in Yellowstone. There's a tender spot yet, inside my lower lip that is affected sometimes by too cold or too hot food that keeps the memory alive. The bear? He was tracked down and destroyed. The Scouts, bless 'em, went on to their Jamboree. And me? Well, I ended up handsomer than ever, just as you see me here."

Chapter Sixteen

Full-Timing In
The Energy-Conscious Eighties

Today's full-time RVers—and those aspiring to be full-timers—are understandably concerned about the cost and availability of gasoline and propane during the Energy-Conscious Eighties. But there is good news! Energy concerns should not dissuade anyone from joining the RVing lifestyle. Full-timers are among the most conservation-minded people in the world, and the evidence is clear that they consume far less energy while living and traveling in their RVs than they did while living in houses and working at jobs. In addition, the RV industry has already made some significant breakthroughs in energy conservation and is on the threshhold of so many others that full-time RVing during the 1980s should prove to be very satisfying for even the most fuel-conscious travelers. Some experts in the energy field are even predicting an oil glut on the world market during the decade ahead and forecasting an easing of gasoline price increases, coupled with some revolutionary successes in the development of new fuel sources.

One of the leading producers of RVs for full-timers—the Holiday Rambler Corporation—embarked on an all-out effort in 1979 to make its vehicles more fuel efficient and, that year alone, reduced the weights of its most popular travel trailers by 15%. The company matched that weight reduction in 1980 and then trimmed off pounds again in 1981. HRC engineers estimated that each year's weight reduction resulted in improved fuel economy of 2 to 3% for the average tow vehicle.

Other major RV companies followed Holiday's lead with their full-timer-type rigs. Coachmen RV Company produced a new line of lightweight, more aerodynamic Citation motorhomes. Executive Industries reduced both weight and lengths of its most popular model motorhomes, while Champion and Georgie Boy and then Honey designed new, lower-profile coaches that borrowed the best ideas of a mini motorhome and those of a widebody van. Escort RVs introduced a 40-foot fifth-wheel trailer featuring aluminum framing that was not only lighter in weight than previous models, but was also one of the most aerodynamic fivers ever built. Winnebago offered a low-profile motorhome of its own in 1981 that was dramatically different from anything ever built in the RV industry before, while Esquire converted a mini motorhome-type chassis into front-wheel drive and built a full-size motorhome shell on it.

Dozens of energy-conscious RV manufacturers entered the 1980s with improved insulation packages for their rigs. One builder of trailers for snowbirds and full-timers announced achieving a remarkable R-16 insulation factor in the ceilings of its units through use of five inches of insulation and a foil vapor barrier. Several companies offered thermal-pane storm windows on units—some as standard equipment. Sensitive to criticisms that household gas appliances were equipped with wasteful pilot lights, several RV companies switched their attention to appliances equipped with momentary electrical sparks instead. A motorhome builder, conscious of the fact that the fronts and rears of large coaches sometimes could not be heated efficiently with a single large furnace, discovered waste could be reduced by equipping each coach with two furnaces so that the temperature needs of different areas could be met more efficiently. Another manufacturer discovered a way that a motorhome's hot water tank could be heated using warm air from the coach's engine.

Designing The Energy-Efficient RV

Weight reduction of RV units became the first priority of America's travel trailer and motorhome producers as the 1980s began, due to widespread acceptance of the National Highway Traffic Safety Administration's estimate that, for heavy vehicles, a 10% weight reduction can result in a 2% improvement in fuel economy. Full-time RVers did not, at first, see much evidence of the RV industry's weight reduction efforts because initial concentration focused on building small trailers that could be towed by Detroit's new family of downsized automobiles, and those small trailers were not generally suitable for use by full-timers. Technology developed in 1979-1981 for the lightweight trailers has already begun making its way into the full-size RVs that full-timers buy, however.

Full-time RVers of the eighties can expect to see rigs equipped with hollow or foam-filled cabinet doors, bathroom doors, tabletops and countertops; high-density foam cushions; plastic drawers and shelves; foam-filled laminated sidewalls; acrylic windows; high-strength, low-alloy steel undercarriages; smaller, lightweight appliances. Wood and fiberboard will be replaced by reinforced plastics and honeycombed corrugated paper. Lightweight materials covered by woodgrained vinyl will replace hardwood paneling. Plastic will replace decorative metal hardware, and polybutylene tubing will be used for plumbing everywhere. Floors will be covered with lightweight vinyl or with carpeting that is light in weight with less depth than that used today. Knobs and faucets in bathrooms and kitchens will look like metal but will be made of plastic. Water and sewage tanks will be smaller and lighter. Lavatories and bathtubs will be made of acrylics, while acrylics and thinner, high-strength glass will replace plate glass in the RV windows. Seat frames will be made of reinforced plastic or aluminum, not steel. Upholstery fabrics will be both lighter in weight and easier to clean; foam padding blown full of air bubbles will be used for seating.

In the mid and late 1980s, a technique known as sandwich-panel construction, wherein layers of sidewall materials are bonded together to form one solid, nearly impregnable structure, will be used to build most travel trailers. The technique is already widely used in the RV industry to build Class A motorhomes. Laminated sidewalls are considered stronger than conventional stick-and-staple walls and, although they are more expensive to build and harder to repair, they also are considerably lighter in weight. Use of laminated sidewalls is only one step in the evolving process to produce lighter travel trailers, though. The most important research being done in the RV field today involves the use of high-strength composite materials similar to fiberglass but much lighter and immeasurably stronger. Using composites, a company could mold a complete shell of a travel trailer that would, itself, be load-bearing and would need no steel framing for reinforcement. Interior walls, countertops, cabinets, floor and ceiling could be created of composite materials at the same time and could be bonded to the inside of the shell so that very little interior finishing work would be necessary. In theory, a 30-foot travel trailer made primarily of composite materials would be lighter in weight than a conventionally built vehicle half its length, and its structural strength would be considerably greater.

Lightweight construction techniques (such as sandwich panel sidewalls) will have a snowballing effect on motorhome building. Lighter chassis will permit the use of lighter engines and transmissions, smaller brake systems and lighter axles. More emphasis will be placed on improving pulling power, allowing motor sizes to be reduced dramatically. Vari-speed transmissions or axles will become commonplace, thereby allowing the owner of a van, for example, to use his vehicle either for towing trailers or for markedly more efficient fuel consumption without the trailer. Motorized vehicles, including motorhomes, will begin to utilize five-speed manual and automatic transmissions with overdrives.

By the second half of the 1980s, and perhaps sooner, the typical full-time RVer will expect his motorhome or tow vehicle to give him at least twenty miles per gallon of fuel. That improved fuel consumption will be due partly to better engines, transmissions and drivetrains and partly to lighter weight components, but equally important will be the improved, more aerodynamic shapes of the vehicles. The front ends of Class A motorhomes and travel trailers will be swept backward and wedge-shaped to provide for smoother air flow and lessened wind resistance. Sidewalls and roofs will be smoother and rounded. The vehicles will ride closer to the ground on air suspension systems that will enable the coach's road clearance to be adjusted with the flick of a switch for either highway or offroad travel. All RVs will be built with enclosed underbellies that will not only improve their aerodynamics, but also give them a lower center of gravity and lessen road height.

Advances in high-strength glass will enable RVs to be equipped with thermal windows that are actually lighter than single thicknesses of today's safety glass. Improved acrylic windows that will not scratch easily will be installed in many types of units by 1985. Increasingly, thicker sheets of plastic foam will be added to the sidewalls, roofs and floors to improve structural strength and provide better insulation. As the RVs become better insulated, furnaces, air conditioners and refrigerators will become lighter in weight and more efficient because they will not have to engage in a constant battle against external temperature variables. Insulated RV underbellies will enable furnace and air conditioning ductwork to be channeled to various sections of the vehicle so rooms can be heated or cooled more efficiently. At the same time, water and sewer lines can be run through the underbelly, thereby opening up valuable storage space inside cabinets and closets, and the lines will be protected from freeze-ups in cold weather due to their proximity to heating ductwork.

According to Vernon Wamsley, vice president of engineering services for Coachmen Industries, RVers of the 1980s would make a mistake confusing the term "lightweight" with the word "small." Tomorrow's lightweight trailers and motorhomes will not necessarily be small, he said. "We have developed, and are currently using, construction methods which

Photo courtesy of the Verticel Company.

From top to bottom, corrugated paper is a lightweight, high-strength RV material; foam-core motorhome sidewalls help reduce weight to save energy.

will give us under 100 pounds per foot of length of travel trailers." That means a 30-foot travel trailer weighing only 3,000 pounds is capable of being produced, whereas a typical trailer that length, using current construction techniques, would weigh more than 5,000 pounds. Noting that automobiles will be built in 1985 that are capable of towing 3,500-pound trailers, Wamsley said, "At 100 pounds per foot of trailer, we can build a trailer more than thirty feet in length that new cars can still tow in 1985 and which would satisfy nearly anyone's size requirements."

Wamsley predicted that tomorrow's larger-but-lighter travel trailers and fifth-wheel trailers will be towed by vans and pickup trucks similar to the ones being used today. "The auto manufacturers will continue to build those vehicles, at least through 1990, and probably beyond. The new Ford pickup truck has an actual increased payload of more than 600 pounds, increasing the load it can carry. Also, we're going to see a new generation of mini-pickups and vans manufactured in the U.S. which will appear in 1982 or 1983. Those will handle the small, lighter weight travel trailers and fifth-wheels and give us a smaller chassis on which to build a new generation of micro minis. We're already designing products needed for this emerging market."

Wamsley predicted, "In the RV industry, we will be taking a close look at every component on the vehicle and rethinking it either for new materials or for new usage. RVs will be using new composite materials, new plastics, aluminum for structures and chassis, laminated plastic windows, new laminated walls systems, and honeycomb hollow-core laminates for tabletops and counters. Each manufacturer of Coachmen components is currently being asked to evaluate the product he supplies to reduce weight. Components such as refrigerators and stoves will be either redesigned or downsized. Our objective will be to provide maximum cube with minimum weight by using higher strength materials."

While the RV industry is concentrating on weight reductions, however, it cannot lose sight of the fact that fuel efficiency is affected drastically by aerodynamic drag, Wamsley said. "While weight will be reduced and some sizes will be reduced, the big change will be in the shape. Aerodynamics will dictate the shape of your RVs. The efficiency of a moving vehicle is affected by how easily it flows through the air. Reducing the frontal area or streamlining the shape will minimize the aerodynamic resistance. Tomorrow's RVs will cut through the air like a laser beam. The outside skins will be smooth. Flush-mounted windows and the elimination of molding and projections will characterize the exterior surfaces. Underbodies will be smooth with everything enclosed. Roof racks and exterior air conditioning units will be self-contained within a clean, aerodynamic shape."

Innovations For The Future

Energy efficiencies can be achieved in other ways, Wamsley said: through improvement of motorhome and tow vehicle drivetrains and transmissions; through improved differential assemblies; through improved lubricants with friction modifiers and lower viscosity; through the increased use of front-wheel drive systems; through use of more efficient engines such as the V-6; by designing air conditioning, power steering and other power-assisted features to operate only when needed, and by the development of tires which reduce rolling resistance while providing sufficient traction and a soft ride.

Overall operating efficiency also can be achieved by replacing a standard engine with a smaller one equipped with a turbocharger, he said. "General Motors recently made some analyses of various driving conditions to determine how often the turbocharged engine is operated in an activated condition. One test indicated turbo activation only 5.8% of the time. In another test, turbo activation was used less than 3% of the time. This illustrates the advantage of a turbocharged engine; 95% of the time, the turbocharged small engine will provide better fuel economy because of its small displacement. A turbocharged small engine can also have a significant weight advantage over a larger engine of comparable power. By using a small-displacement, turbocharged engine in a vehicle, there should be improved overall fuel economy while at the same time providing the performance that the customer demands. Turbocharging has some problems which need to be resolved in RV applications, but the potential seems great."

Diesel engines also have excellent potential for fuel savings, the Coachmen engineer said. Referring to the light diesel engine GM introduced in the late 1970s, Wamsley said, "That engine has a fuel economy advantage of about 25% when compared to a gasoline engine of similar size. Assuming emissions problems with diesels can be resolved, many more passenger cars and trucks could be powered by diesels by 1985, and RVs will be included in that future."

Wamsley revealed that Coachmen engineers in 1979 became interested in applying solar energy to RV use. "The ability to heat water for cooking, bathing and space heating through the use of solar collectors on the RV roof is of considerable interest to us," he said. "We see a breakthrough in the cost of solar cells which generate electricity from the sun and store that energy in batteries. We would then run a pump to circulate water for heating and bathing, providing a closed loop system. Our research into energy-efficient systems for RVs is leading us to some very interesting possibilities and could alter our approach to heating and cooling interiors, heating water, providing electrical power for overnight use. Heat storage batteries which absorb heat from an RV engine while it is traveling—or, from solar roof panels—and dissipate it overnight, either through heat exchangers or the use of a heat pump, might provide overnight heating, cooling and a hot water supply. Such experimental systems are now being tested at Coachmen's research facility. We have developed an experimental inverter system using nickel-zinc batteries and an electrical inverter; our objective is to power a coach, with air conditioning, overnight, which would thereby eliminate the need for a dual 12/110-volt power system."

The general feeling among RV industry leaders and engineers is that when it comes to downsizing and reducing weights, RVs will follow the lead of the automobile industry. What direction will that take? Well, some insights into that were provided by James G. Endress, an automobile engineer at the Ford Motor Company. Referring to Ford's initial, most dramatic downsizing efforts in 1979, Endress said, "We literally started from scratch on every one of those vehicles. Nearly every component of every one of those cars was redesigned, rethought, reengineered. We're doing things with materials on today's cars that we wouldn't have considered ten years ago. Just as we examined every part and every component in our redesign stage, we also looked at every conceivable material alternative."

Endress cautioned, however: "You don't necessarily have to substitute a lightweight material to save weight. An example of saving weight with heavy materials involves the use of thin glass; we have proved that we can maintain safety and function while reducing glass thickness by 20%. Zinc also is considered a heavyweight material, but weight reduction is possible with thin-wall molding designs." Such materials, he suggested, can also be used in RVs to reduce both weights and costs. On the other hand, significant weight savings can be achieved with lightweight materials such as plastics, aluminum and high-strength, low-alloy steel. "Magnesium and fiber-reinforced plastics have good potential, but cost may keep them out of the picture for a while."

On the other hand, he said, Ford's successes in weight reduction were closely tied to an increased use of plastics. There seems to be no end to the possible applications of plastics, he added. "Plastics offer us the greatest potential for cost-effective weight savings at this time. As weight savings become even more important, plastics will appear in the structural components and body panels where they are not necessarily cost savings." He predicted increased use of a plastic called polypropylene that is lightweight, will never rust and has strength and high density, along with flexibility and toughness. Because polypropylene can be molded to shapes not possible with steel, it will be used to lighten work-horse-type vehicles such as light trucks.

Production problems still must be overcome with plastics, though. "A shiny, jewel-like surface finish has become a requirement throughout the automobile industry, and that's one thing we have to resolve with plastics," Endress said. "Another is that plastic components not only must be strong and durable, but they must maintain their size and shape in order to fit on assembly. There also is the problem of productivity; cycle times to produce plastic parts are much slower than car production rates."

While steel undoubtedly will be used less and less in the production of RVs, Endress predicted it will continue to be the primary material used in automobiles and trucks in the future. He said that in 1979, 64% of an automobile was built with steel, and that percentage will hold at 63% in 1985. But he noted, "This continuing reliance on steel is due partly to the several families of new steel called high-strength steels that are emerging." Such materials, he said, allow significant reductions in thicknesses, providing weight savings of 20 to 30% at about the same costs of conventional steels.

BETTER AERODYNAMICS AHEAD

Lighter weight is only one factor affecting RV fuel economy. Another factor that is even more important is vehicle shape. Unfortunately, aerodynamics was practically ignored both by the automotive industry and by the RV industry until recently; fortunately, both industries have learned a great deal about aerodynamics during the last few years and are working hard to integrate improved shapes into their products. The 1980s should see some dramatic improvements in the aerodynamics of motorhomes, travel trailers and tow vehicles.

Fleetwood Industries, a leading producer of full-timing RVs, embarked on an intense investigation of aerodynamics prior to introduction of its new line of lightweight travel trailers a few years ago. Using wind tunnel testing, Fleetwood engineers discovered that up to 45 mph, shape had no relationship to how well a trailer towed or a motorhome performed; weight was all-important. A Fleetwood spokesman told me, "After 45 mph, though, shape makes *all* the difference. You could have a five million pound sled behind your car, and if it were aerodynamically shaped and you could get it going 45 mph, it will tow just fine." Fleetwood's tests revealed that at 55 mph, a box-shaped vehicle required 45 horsepower just to overcome air drag. The company's aerodynamic trailer, however, required only 30 horsepower, and a 15% fuel savings could be achieved at the same time.

An engineer with a major automobile and truck company stated flatly: "If you can reduce aerodynamic drag by half, you can reduce the required horsepower by half." He noted that the best way to achieve aerodynamics in an RV is to reduce the overall height and width of the vehicle, but he said packaging requirements and the demands of RV owners limit those reductions significantly. He claimed that by reducing aerodynamic drag by 10%, a 3% improvement in fuel economy can be achieved during combined city highway driving, a 7% improvement during highway driving at a steady 55 mph. He added, "If you reduce the weight of a typical RV 10%, you can expect only a 2½% improvement in fuel economy. And to achieve that 2½% economy, you'd have to reduce the weight of an 11,000-pound motorhome, for example, by 1,100 pounds." Obviously, it makes more sense to achieve fuel efficiencies with aerodynamics than with weight reductions—*if* shape changes can be put into production as easily as weight can be reduced.

The Detroit engineer said, "On today's RVs, reducing the aerodynamic drag 10% is extremely easy. It can be done with rather little pain, without changing the aesthetics or the requirements of the RV customers. Up to 20% drag reductions can actually be expected, and that would yield a 14% fuel economy gain on the highway." An RV whose shape already is streamlined also will yield fuel economy improvements, but at a lower rate, he said. A 15% drag reduction of an already-streamlined shape would result in a 4½% fuel economy improvement in city driving and 10½% on the highway. Shape can be improved, he said, by adding underbellies to RVs; by reducing the 2 to 4% penalty of rooftop air conditioners; by reshaping and relocating exterior mirrors and reducing thier 8% penalty to 1 to 2%; by eliminating roof racks; by relocating roof vents, and by changing grill area openings.

The Challenge: Performance And Economy

Gordon C. Cherry, director of truck planning for Chrysler Corporation, warned a group of RV company executives and dealers just as the 1980s started: "You can expect higher fuel costs, continued inflation, more urban problems and further government regulation during the decade ahead. Energy and conservation will be the watchwords of the decade. The average RV will become smaller, just as the average car is smaller. Your task is to provide the maximum amount of living room with a minimum amount of vehicle bulk. The furnaces, stoves, refrigerators and furnishings can be made smaller, and we can have the same amount of living and storage space in a smaller package. Our job as chassis makers is to make the drivetrains smaller and lower so overall height can be reduced. Better aerodynamics is the most effective way to improve fuel economy, and it's mostly under the control of the RV builder. His task will be to reduce drag and provide an attractive appearance."

Cherry indicated a domino-type chain of fuel economies can be achieved with improved aerodynamics and weight reductions combined because more mobile RVs can permit smaller engines to be used, and smaller engines can then be coupled to lighter, more efficient axles, chassis, brakes and other components. He told the RV manufacturers: "Each component will have to be examined and analyzed. These investigations will lead you to different materials for many applications—things such as high-strength, low-alloy steel, more aluminum, more plastics and composite sandwich structures. You'll be demanding more from these new materials than just weight reductions—things such as better corrosion protection, more design flexibility, increased durability and, in some cases, even a permanent finish."

But he warned, "There will be less product variety in the marketplace. Continuous innovation and product change have been the hallmark of the RV industry, and many of us in Detroit have envied you [the RV manufacturers] because of your simplified tooling and great flexibility. With new emphasis on sophistication and the more demanding materials, however, you will require greater research and development expense. Tooling costs will be much higher. Production time will lengthen considerably, with more attention being given to fuel/product relationships. For the full-time RVer and other camping consumers, the warning is clear: RVs of the 1980s will be more expensive. The convoluted logic of the 1980s will state, "If you want economy, you've got to pay for it!"

According to Cherry, Detroit engineers will concentrate on making power trains more efficient. "We can make important gains," he said, "by applying light truck technology to motorhomes. We can use lock-up torque convertors, lower axle ratios and smaller size engines to improve fuel economy with no loss of performance. Lower weight also means lower rolling resistance, especially in conjunction with radial tires. Cooling systems' losses can be reduced by declutching the vans, and many other hard-won efficiency gains that we have developed in light trucks can be applied to motorhomes if they are lighter. Eventually, we may have to sacrifice some vehicle performance to get more fuel economy and lower operating costs."

As for tow vehicles, Cherry said, "Fewer vehicles will be able to tow full-size, full-frontal-area travel trailers, and maybe drivers will just have to go slower up some hills. Our challenge will be to achieve a power train/vehicle match that is the best compromise of both performance and fuel economy."

WILL GASOLINE BE AVAILABLE?

Hardly a day goes by that someone does not make a dire prediction about the availability and cost of fuel in the decade ahead. Each such prediction is usually followed by an opposing view that gasoline is and will continue to be plentiful and the prices will either stabilize or decline in the near future. Who should the aspiring full-timer believe? If, on the one hand, he believes the doomsayer and stays home, insulated from potential fuel shortages and price hikes by the safe cocoon of his protective environment, he will lose the opportunity to enjoy a lifestyle that he has worked and saved for years to achieve. On the other hand, if he believes that shortages and high prices are nothing but the creations of Arabs who soon will see the errors of their ways, he will be sorely disappointed when he is unable to buy cheap gasoline anywhere.

Listen to David J. Humphreys, president and general counsel of the Recreation Vehicle Industry Association: "When all is said and done, the truth is that no one fully understands the energy problems that we are faced with. The more you read, the more likely you are to become confused. The conclusion that I have reached after careful study and much listening is basically this: it just seems that no matter how hard you work at it and how much you worry about it, fully understanding the energy problem is not one of our options."

According to futurists at the Hudson Research Institute of New York, those who claim the world will soon run out of its supply of energy, and particularly oil, are basing their predictions on the false assumption that energy use will increase rapidly until the world depletes its supplies. The Hudson Institute was commissioned by the American Recreation Coalition to study energy availability and its use for recreational purposes, and the institute's conclusions were quite positive in tone.

"Future energy requirement projections show a surprisingly moderate increase in energy demands, especially in the automotive sector," the institute reported. "Indications are, in fact, that automotive petroleum demand may be close to peaking, despite the projected increase in the numbers of cars on the road in future years and the anticipated growth in the use of recreation vehicles of all types. Increases in efficiency mandated by the government, if met, will almost certainly bring this about. Even if the targets are not met, the most pessimistic scenarios show a marked slowing in the rate of increase of automotive fuel consumption. This, coupled with the anticipated increase in U.S. and world fuel supplies, should assure adequate energy for recreational and other automotive uses in the near and mid-term future . . ."

Prior to release of the Hudson study, institute physicist William M. Brown in early 1980 addressed a gathering of Coachmen RV dealers in Orlando and told them, "Unless we have the maximum demand (for oil) that's projected by pessimists today and have the least production in supplies, the worst that will happen is that our need for OPEC oil will remain approximately level. But if we get anywhere near the minimum of projected demand and the maximum of supplies—and I think that's the most likely case, especially with the recent rise in prices—then the demand required from OPEC over a time essentially will shrink to zero in just over ten years. The implication of that statement is very simple: OPEC will rapidly get into trouble as an organization."

In its report, the Hudson Institute emphasized that short-term fuel shortages could develop in the U.S. in the early 1980s because the nation will be dependent upon OPEC for oil, and both deliberate withholdings of supplies and political upheavals among the Arab states could result in new lines at gasoline service station pumps. The institute added, "With the passage of time, however, we should become increasingly independent of OPEC, which should have the effect of lowering excessive OPEC prices. The increasing supply of natural gas, its relatively low cost, and its desirability as a clean-burning, efficient fuel have already resulted in some degree of substitution of gas for liquid petroleum products . . . and this trend is expected to continue. As new construction takes place, it seems reasonable to assume that gas will be the fuel of choice instead of oil. Development of domestic shale oil, tar sands processing and coal-based synfuels industries should begin to lower our dependence on OPEC oil in the next decade. Even if none of these developments takes place, the present trend in oil and gas production in non-OPEC areas of the free world, if it continues as expected, will reduce our present dependence by a significant degree within the next ten years."

The Hudson report added, "This is not to say that the price of energy will return to its pre-1973 levels, however. Energy will cost more because the methods used to produce it cost more than previously. Capital investments in unconventional hydrocarbon and synfuel production are enormous. Development of these industries will be largely dependent on the price of energy continuing at a level which will allow a reasonable return on investment . . . OPEC clearly does not intend to lower its prices voluntarily, and the high expense of exploration and exploitation of new oil and gas fields assures that energy from those sources will be more than they were before 1974. Nevertheless, the cost of fuel could return to about its 1978 level with adjustments for inflation and dollar valuation."

Six months after the Hudson report was issued, news reporters in Washington asked oil ministers from Mexico, where vast supplies of oil had been recently discovered, for their evaluation of the world market situation. Secretary of Finance David Ibarra answered that he believed oil prices and supply problems would ease by the end of the century as new sources of energy are developed. He said fuel problems "will diminish at a fast rate" once alternates are found to fossil fuels.

THOSE ALTERNATIVE FUELS

It is clear that the alternatives for fueling tomorrow's recreational vehicles are quite limited. Motorhomes and tow vehicles can be operated on propane or alcohol today, after some relatively minor adjustments and conversions. But there are problems with both types of fuel which thus far have restricted their use. Technology exists, too, for utilizing solar energy to power an RV's appliances; but again, significant problems must be overcome before solar power will be even partially feasible for over-the-road vehicles. As a long-term solution to the energy problem, hydrogen power seems to be the best alternative, and there is evidence that hydrogen may, indeed, be America's motor fuel of the 1980s.

Propane

Propane already is a relatively common motorhome fuel, thanks to the dual-fuel programs initiated since 1979 by such RV companies as Winnebago, Holiday Rambler, Midas, Georgie Boy and others. A surprisingly large number of full-time RVers also are using either dual-fuel carburetion or straight propane conversions on their trailer towing vehicles. There are, indeed, good reasons why RVers should consider dual-fuel systems. Foremost among those is the fact that there is a glut of propane in the marketplace, and an increasing supply of propane is likely as both foreign and domestic sources continue to hike production of it. A dual-fuel system offers the RVer the flexibility of two kinds of fuel on board, allowing him not only to lengthen his driving range, but also to choose whichever fuel—propane or gasoline—is the least expensive at the moment. Furthermore, in the event of a severe gasoline supply shortage, propane should still be widely available, and that availability can prevent the RVer from waiting in lines at service stations.

On the other hand, the initial cost of a dual-fuel conversion is rather high (up to $2,000), and unless the RVer expects to use propane for at least 12,000 miles a year, the conversion is not cost-effective. Noticeable loss in power and fuel economy can be expected with a dual-fuel system, primarily because an engine cannot be tuned to operate at peak efficiency with both types of fuel and because the fuel has less heat content than does gasoline. If the conversion system needs to be serviced, finding qualified mechanics to do the job can be difficult. Also, an RV such as a motorhome cannot be equipped with a propane tank large enough to provide the kind of driving range that is desirable with a fuel that is sometimes hard to find because LP-gas dealerships are not ordinarily at convenient, major intersections and at nearly every highway interchange, the way gasoline service stations are. Most LP-gas stations are closed on weekends and open only from 8 A.M. until 5 P.M. on weekdays, and there are not nearly enough LP-gas refueling stations in the country to make refueling a rather routine kind of process.

Alcohol

As for alcohol, there is little hope that fuel can be widely used in this country before the end of the century, if then. The U.S. Department of Energy had hopes in 1980 that several hundred alcohol fuel plants—300 of them in Indiana alone—would be built in America by 1985. But that project was being promoted by the National Alcohol Fuels Commission, and the commission suffered an unexpected setback in November of 1980 when its chairman, Senator Birch Bayh, was defeated in his bid for re-election. Even if the project realizes its goal, however, those new plants could produce only a maximum of 300 million gallons of alcohol a year—an amount not likely to have much impact on the 110 billion gallons of gasoline Americans consume annually—and it would have to be mixed with gasoline and marketed as higher-priced gasohol.

Pure alcohol already is being used in Brazil to operate several hundred thousand automobiles which have been converted to withstand the higher corrosiveness of the fuel. Alcohol-burning cars in that country cost about 3% more than gasoline-driven autos, while the alcohol there sold (in September, 1980) for $1.24 per gallon, compared to $2.61 per gallon for gasoline. In 1980, Brazil produced one billion gallons of sugar cane derived alcohol, and that output was expected to nearly triple by 1985. The Brazilian government encouraged the use of alcohol by cutting taxes on alcohol-burning cars, subsidizing refinement costs, and allowed alcohol pumps to be operated on Saturdays, when gasoline pumps had to be shut down. Expectations were that 45% of Brazil's one million new cars in 1981 would be alcohol-burners.

Solar Power

Obviously, no one believes that solar power can be used as motor fuel, but there are indications that it *can* be used some day to reduce the living costs of full-time RVers by powering appliances and light fixtures. As long ago as 1979, Roust-A-Bout of California, a travel trailer manufacturer, built a coach that ARCO Solar, Incorporated—a subsidiary of the Atlantic Richfield Company—outfitted with an experimental, rooftop solar unit that furnished power for lighting, air conditioning, a refrigerator, a color TV and a washer/dryer. The ARCO system featured photovoltaic panels that directly converted the sun's rays into electricity while mounted along the length of the roof at a 20-degree angle. An ARCO representative said in 1979 that the rooftop system "conceivably could be mass produced several years from now so that it would be within the financial reach of the average family."

About the same time, the Amfridge Division of American Formed Plastics Corporation in Elkhart, Indiana, built and exhibited a prototype for a portable solar refrigerator. Amfridge president Tom McLaughlin predicted that a similar solar refrigerator would be adapted to RV use sometime during the 1980s.

Hydrogen

The most exciting—and most controversial—source for motor fuel is hydrogen. It is exciting because the supply of hydrogen is limitless; it is controversial because its detractors claim it cannot be considered a practical motor fuel during this century. The Hudson Institute considered hydrogen power as an alternative source of fuel when it did its energy study for the American Recreation Coalition in 1980. It concluded: "Present methods of hydrogen production center on electrolysis of water. This is too expensive a process to permit its use as a fuel except in certain special applications—such as space vehicles—where its low density gives it special advantages. The few experimental automobiles operating on hydrogen today are very short ranged, since the problems of storing hydrogen are formidable. This, coupled with the high cost of production, makes hydrogen highly unlikely as a motor fuel in the near or mid-term future. It will not be a suitable fuel without a process to produce large volumes of hydrogen at very low cost, such as through use of nuclear or solar energy, and unless storage methods compatible with automotive use are developed. Such developments will probably not be seen in this century."

However, at least two American companies claim they have perfected methods of producing hydrogen at a low cost. Consumers Solar Electric Power Corporation of Culver City, California, contracted in 1979 to modify five hydrogen-powered vehicles for the U.S. Postal Service. The company claims that through a new technology, it is able to break down water into oxygen and hydrogen, using solar-produced electricity. The hydrogen is then combined with other elements to form a nonexplosive hydride costing only fifty cents a gallon to produce, according to Consumers Solar president Jerry Schflander. He said any conventional automobile's gasoline engine can be converted to run on the hydride fuel for about $300.

Roger Billings, the president of Billings Energy Corporation, has patented a system of storing hydrogen in powdery metal hydride form. Using the Billings system, a car is equipped with a tank containing the metal powder and, at a filling station, gaseous hydrogen is forced into the tank and absorbed by the hydride. When the automobile is operating, the powder gives off gaseous hydrogen, which is delivered to the engine and burns, leaving only clean water as a residue. Billings Energy already has converted several hydrogen-fueled vehicles for use by various businesses and the postal department.

CONSERVING ENERGY ON THE ROAD

Until the time when energy becomes inexpensive and abundant—*if* that time ever comes—full-time RVers will just have to continue their practice of conserving as much fuel as possible. Not that conservation is all that difficult; full-timers report that conservatism fits in with their lifestyle perfectly. Don and Audrey Klemczak are good examples of that. They live full-time in a Blue Bird Wanderlodge, towing a fuel-efficient Chevette behind them, and although they are surrounded by luxury in their big coach, they are very energy-conscious and hold down their living expenses by using the least amount of gasoline and propane possible.

Don reported that they spend less for propane in a year than they spent each month heating their home in Michigan before they hit the road full time. And, he said, by using their 30 mpg small car to run errands, they have cut their gasoline bills considerably from what they paid when he drove a full-size Mercury back and forth to work every day. A combination of high fuel prices and living on a limited budget does force them to plan their travels carefully, though. Audrey said, "We know how much we have to spend each month on gasoline, and that's it. This summer, we did quite a bit of traveling, so we have to cut back this fall."

Don added, "We worry a little bit about whether fuel will be rationed someday. That might frighten some people who want to travel a lot, but I don't think it should deter somebody from full-timing. I would hope that the government would consider full-timing people if rationing is implemented. People who are RVing don't use nearly the energy that people who have homes and go to work every day do. And we're still vital to the nation's economy because we spend money in all the ways other people do."

As a routine practice, full-timers with home bases leave their houses, apartments or mobile homes in the "down" position while they're following the sun to warmer climates. Home-base thermostats are set to seasonal minimums, just adequate to prevent pipes from freezing and to eliminate excessive humidity. Gas appliances are turned off.

Tips On Saving Energy

Although most full-timers already practice good conservation habits while traveling, here are some energy-saving tips from the Recreation Vehicle Industry Association: "Rid your RV of excess weight, such as eight-pound-per-gallon water; it's available at the campgrounds. Preserve the vehicle's aerodynamic shape by putting everything possible inside; externally carried chairs, grills and bikes cause extra wind drag. Don't speed; for each 5 mph over 50 mph, you lose one mile per gallon. Begin your trips early in the day; early morning departures reduce fuel-wasting stop-and-go driving in traffic and the need for air conditioning. Reduce the number of short runs you make for buying small items; use of a bike or moped for visiting the campground store is recommended. Use the campground's electrical hookup instead of the less efficient on-board generator, when possible."

There are other steps that can be taken to conserve energy. For example, propane can be saved by the use of candles, kerosene lamps, and charcoal for cooking occasionally. A candlelight dinner cooked over an open fire is a nice, romantic change of pace, too. When driving, avoid pedal-pumping, and try to maintain a light foot on the accelerator. Avoid jackrabbit starts. Roll to a stop at traffic lights rather than brake hard. Shut off your engine at blocked railroad crossings or when otherwise idling for more than one minute. Use a cruise control on level terrain, but override it manually on slopes to build up momentum and keep the engine from laboring on upgrades. Keep tires inflated to their maximum recommended pressures. Keep your engine well tuned by checking and recalibrating points and plugs every 5,000 miles and replacing them every 12,000 to 15,000 miles. Use radial tires on tow vehicles and travel trailers; they provide 2.8% better fuel efficiency than normal bias-ply tires.

Perry "Steamboat" Van Osdol, a former LP-gas dealer who now RVs full-time as a Good Sam Club Sambassador, emphasized that recreational vehicles are naturally energy-conservative units. "If I operated everything in my rig at once—the furnace, the refrigerator, the range, the water heater—I would use 50,000 btus of energy an hour. If we were in our mobile home—which is not large, but about average size—we'd use 250,000 btus an hour. So our trailer is five times more efficient than even a mobile home, and it's a lot more efficient to operate than a house. With all its efficiency, though, we are just as comfortable in it as we would be in either a house or our mobile home. We have all the facilities we need."

While representing the Good Sam Club all over the country, Steamboat frequently conducts seminars on the use of propane. Often, he tells RVers that if they are serious about conserving energy, they should use more propane and less electricity. He explained, "It seems to be automatic that, when campers pull into a site, they switch their refrigerator from propane to electricity right away. But really, that's not a good practice. There are 3,412 btus in a kilowatt hour of electricity, and that kilowatt hour costs about six cents. Propane, which provides 91,000 btus per gallon, would have to cost $1.65 a gallon to be the equivalent of a kilowatt hour of electricity."

THE GAS GUZZLER IMAGE

During the worst of the gasoline supply problems in 1979, my wife and I stopped in Fargo, North Dakota, to fill our motorhome with gasoline. Like the rest of the motorists who had been attracted by the lights of the lone service station open for business, we waited in line for our turn at the gas pumps. A young man looked over our coach as we stood side by side, filling our tanks. He replaced the gasoline hose on the pump, screwed on his fuel cap and then, before walking away to pay his bill, he glared at me and said, "You've got some nerve, driving around in a gas guzzler like that."

I was stunned and couldn't think of an immediate reply. Then, in spite of the fact that my very livelihood depended upon my working with and writing about RVs, I began to feel a twinge of guilt. Perhaps, I thought to myself, the fellow was right. Maybe the motorhome was a dinosaur and no longer a sensible product during these energy-conscious times. My doubt didn't last long because I quickly remembered that the value of an RV is far greater than any short-term fuel shortage. But the fact of my guilty feeling was brought home to me more than once during the next several months as RVer after RVer reported being the butt of similar criticisms by non-RVers. Some dedicated but misguided super-patriots even gave up RVing temporarily due to cruel criticisms.

The fact is, RVs are *not* gas guzzlers. True, they are not as fuel efficient on a per-mile basis as downsized automobiles, but they are not used in the same ways automobiles are used, either. And no full-time RVer should stand for charges that his RV—his home!—wastes energy. Because it doesn't. Full-timers have a whole battery of arguments they can use to refute such charges: the fact that the RV *is* a home, not just a highway vehicle; the fact that its water heater is operated only when needed, not all the time, and then just to heat a mere six gallons of water; the fact that the RV is used primarily in warm climates so that little energy is required for warmth; the fact that it burns no heating oil, and very little propane. Full-time RVers can point out they do not waste gasoline by commuting to work with one person driving and the rest of the automobile empty. They can argue that their RV carries two people wherever it goes and that, figured on a people-miles-per-gallon, it is probably a more ef- ficient motor vehicle than the average family car. They can explain that their RV achieves 8 mph—or 10 mpg, or whatever the fuel consumption rate is—whereas a transit bus gets only 4 mpg, yet no one would think of labeling a bus as "a gas guzzler."

The full-timers should point out to non-RVers at every opportunity that they do not travel constantly, that they park for long periods of time and, as a consequence, use far less gasoline while enjoying their lifestyle than the average working couple does on a day-to-day basis. If their motorhome or tow vehicle is equipped to conserve gasoline by operating at least part of the time on propane, they should make note of that fact.

They should explain that their RV is lighter and more aerodynamic—and therefore more fuel-efficient—today because of significant new advances in production techniques. They should report on some of the new types of RVs being developed that will be even more fuel-efficient.

As a final argument, they should point out that a 1979 study by a renowned economic consulting firm—Robert Nathan Associates—revealed that RVs use only 1.8% of all highway fuel consumed in the U.S. Not only that, but the Nathan study concluded that if all RVs were eliminated from America's highways, the fuel savings would *not* amount to 1.8% because people would continue to travel in something else. Nathan estimated that if the nation's six million RVs were replaced by medium size cars, the fuel savings would amount to only six-tenths of one percent each year.

It really is unfortunate that RVers—and especially full-timers—have been put into a position of having to justify their way of life to other people. Good Samer Hall Blair emphasized that point in October, 1980, when he wrote a guest editorial for his club's newspaper, "Hi-Way Herald." Blair pointed out, "There is a real case to be made for this segment of the public, and it doesn't need to be cheapened by excuses like 'saving energy by locking up the house and going off in the RV.'"

Blair wrote, "I think the only possible chance for RV survival is the hope that reasonable, plausible, constructive and positive arguments for it will be substituted for all this defensive nit-picking that's making us look ridiculous . . . We represent a very appreciable segment of the quiet, decent, friendly, retired family folk who are not exploiting their clout, but need a quiet recreation away from the congestion and higher cost of hostelries. It's one thing to lock up the motorhome because it's scary to think of twenty cents a mile for a 2,000-mile vacation, but who reckons with the alternative—$80 motels, $12 dinners, etc.? Inflation is everywhere! $1.25 gasoline takes some getting used to, but the question isn't, 'Will we ever?' Rather, it is 'When?' This thing [RVing] is too good to die of fright . . . There is absolutely no question about it. RVing's the *only* way to go!"

Chapter Seventeen

Avoiding Rip-Offs

or the most part, full-time RVers are honest, conscientious, forthright people who take a "live and let live" attitude toward most things. They are open, trustworthy and fiercely independent. Their biggest fault, as a group, is that they assume other people are as honest and trustworthy as they. Thus, they often become the natural prey—and victims—of thieves, cheats and con artists. A couple in Nashville, Tennessee, are good examples. I'll call them John and Mary Smith to protect them from embarrassment.

After John retired from his job of twenty-five years, they decided to follow the examples set by a couple of their close friends and become full-time RVers. Although they had never been RVers, they felt sure they knew what size trailer they needed and how it should be equipped. Their experienced RVing friends offered to help them select thir coach, but they declined, believing they would feel more self-satisfaction if they did the shopping by themselves. Following several weeks of looking at travel trailers in the 28- to 32-foot range, Mary announced to John that she had found their dream coach. It was a richly furnished, bright colored 32-foot Impala, being sold by a woman who said she had bought the trailer only a few weeks earlier. The woman, who was camped in the trailer at a Briley Parkway campground near the Grand Ol' Opry, told Mary she and her husband had purchased the trailer for $11,000, intending on traveling in it, but her husband had died suddenly, and she was being forced to give up the trailer in order to pay his medical expenses and funeral bills. She was willing to part with the trailer for only $7,000.

"It's the chance of a lifetime," Mary told John when she informed him of the trailer's availability. "Not only are we getting a bargain, but we can also help out that poor woman."

What Mary didn't realize was "that poor woman" was a member of a band of itinerant con artists who call themselves Irish Travelers. Each Irish Traveler tows his coach to an area where experience has taught him that the potential is good for a quick turnover. The coach is then advertised in a local newspaper, and buyers are told a hard-luck story such as the one the woman in Nashville told Mary Smith. The Irish Travelers and a clan of Scottish con artists widely known as "The Terrible Williamsons" also peddle inexpensive travel trailers made by a Wakarusa, Indiana, company that carry the brand names of Marauder, Lariet, Rogue and Buccaneer. A third northern Indiana company supplies them with Safari brand trailers. Workmanship and materials on all of the trailers is, at best, of low quality, and the units are not worth nearly the prices asked for them by the clans.

John went to the Briley Parkway campground with Mary to look at the Impala, and he agreed with her that the coach seemed to be a bargain. He gave the woman a check for $500 to serve as a deposit, and arrangements were made for Mary to meet the woman at a local bank in mid-morning so the rest of the money could be drawn out of the Smiths' account. The "widow," however, had her own plans. At 8 A.M. the next morning, she was at the bank alone when it opened. She cashed the Smiths' $500 check, returned to the campground, hooked up her trailer and left the state.

Typical Scams

The $500 was only a small part of the rich fortune the "Irish" and "Scottish Travelers" con out of trailer-buyers annually. In 1980 alone, the "clans" swindled trailerists out of a *minimum* of $32,760,000. RVers are the targets of more cheats and rip-off artists than just these so-called "clans," however. Several RVers have actually lost their entire rigs—mostly motorhomes—to fake rental operations. Thefts of RVs are increasing at an alarming rate throughout the country. RVers are being cheated out of their savings by sophisticated con artists selling condominium campsites that often are never developed. Violations of federal warranty laws frequently leave innocent RVers in the position of owning a worthless piece of equipment that either cannot be serviced or which would require a small fortune to repair. Unscrupulous mechanics prey on travelers in many sections of the country, overcharging for service work, performing work that is not needed and even charging people for work that has not been done.

Full-time RVers are often dupes of con artists who offer business opportunities and boast that retired people and travelers can earn extra money in their spare time with very little effort. Other schemes convince middle-aged and older people to shell out money for worthless medical exams, for unnecessary but expensive eye glasses and for "miracle cures" of diseases ranging from arthritis to cancer. Unfortunately, RVers of all types also are sometimes victimized by unscrupulous RV dealers.

While the vast majority of the nation's RV retailers are honest, trustworthy merchants dedicated to keeping their customers satisfied by providing them with quality products and good service, there are a few scattered dealers who are cheats and swindlers of the first magnitude and who look upon buyers as pawns to be victimized in every way possible. Within the RV industry, one of the best known crooks is a dealer in Indiana who has an annual advertising budget of well over a half million dollars and who is said to earn in excess of $20 million each year from sales to customers in three states. In late 1976, I wrote an article about some of his schemes for *Trailer Life*, and the article appeared in the May issue of the publication. Four years after my investigations, the dealer was operating out of a huge new lot and showroom and not only was continuing to bilk unsuspecting customers on a regular basis, but he had become the nation's top dealer for one of the largest RV manufacturers in the country.

He and his crew of high-pressure salesmen consistently use tactics such as "low-balling" and "bait-and-switch" in order to attract customers to the lot and consummate sales. He strips necessary standard-equipment accessories from his units and sells them back to customers as extra-cost options. He charges manufacturers for warranty work that he does not do, and he frequently collects twice on warranty work by charging the customer in addition to the manufacturer. He advertises service facilities and skills he does not have. He refuses to repair damaged merchandise, and he fleeces people in a large number of other ways.

It is common for a customer to be victimized by low-balling at the Indiana dealership. He buys an RV for an agreed-upon price, pays either the full price or a down payment for the unit and waits a couple of days for it to be serviced. When he returns to the dealership to pick up his new RV, he is told the salesman made a mistake on the contract, that the price of the product is higher—maybe even $1,000 or $2,000 higher—than was originally quoted. Fine print in the contract specifies that all deals must be approved by the dealer himself, and that stipulation is pointed out to the customer. Many times, the customer is so charged up about picking up his new RV that he consents to pay the additional charges.

Mr. and Mrs. Richard Pauley of Bruno, Minnesota, became victimized in 1980 by another kind of dishonest dealer. What happened to the Pauleys is evidence that experienced RVers can be victimized by con artists too. They were hoping to buy their twenty-eighth lifetime RV when they were attracted to a 1980 Midas mini motorhome with only 950 miles on it being sold by a dealership in nearby Anoka. They were promised warranty papers on the coach, but never received them. They discovered that the dealership was not an authorized Midas outlet and that warranties did not exist on some of the RVs sold there. Their hopes of getting warranty work done in several problem areas were crushed when, in late 1980, they learned that the dealership had been closed by the police and its operators charged with consumer fraud.

Mr. and Mrs. Pauley appealed to the crooks' attorney for help, "and he was very short with us and told us lots of people would not get titles or warranties or money for their coaches. You see, they took coaches in to sell for people and rented them out and put the money in their pockets." The dealer also sold individuals' consigned RVs and pocketed that money. The Pauleys finally considered themselves fortunate that they had a valid title on their mini.

RVers who do not use their vehicles all the time were victimized quite a lot during 1979 and 1980 by bogus rental operations that worked different sections of the country. RV owners were contracted by an alleged rental agent who advised them they could earn thousands of dollars each year if they would allow him to rent out their units for them, on consignment. Instead of receiving such income, though, the owners lost their RVs when the agent either rented out the units and pocketed the money or simply sold the units and disappeared.

CAMPSITE SALES SCHEMES

The desire of many full-timers for a home base has resulted in a boom in sales of condominum campsites both in the sunbelt and in the North. Some RVers even buy two sites—one in the North and one in the South—and then travel back and forth between the two locations seasonally, while taking side trips for sightseeing and adventure. Unscrupulous con artists quickly recognized the potential fortunes that could be made from selling small lots to RVers, and a variation of the old land-fraud scheme resulted. Thousands of RVers from coast to coast, but especially in the Midwest, Florida and Arizona, have been ripped off for millions of dollars by fraudulent condominium developers.

A typical scam involves advertising campsites at a yet-to-be-built park at bargain rates for the first couple of dozen buyers. Prospects are shown detailed plans for a huge complex that includes one or more swimming pools, a large clubhouse and recreation hall, wooded campsites with full hookups (including telephone and cable TV service), paved streets and regular, structured activities such as parties, dinners, festivals, religious programs and self-improvement classes. Potential buyers are taken on tours of the property and shown how the streets, while still unpaved, are laid out and the campsites are arranged. Over there will be the Olympic-size pool, and here will be the meeting room and rec hall. Tennis and racquet ball courts will be built in that corner, and those rolling fields will be landscaped for an 18-hole golf course. Laundry rooms, bath houses and security guards will be provided.

High-pressure salesmen emphasize that site costs are increasing rapidly, and a site not bought immediately will cost many thousands of dollars more within a few months. Convinced of the bargain they will get if they buy right away, the unsuspecting couple purchases a site, content with the knowledge that they will have a beautiful, quiet place to spend their time when they aren't traveling. Unfortunately, months pass before they realize that no additional work is being done on the property. Construction equipment seems to be doing little more than moving around piles of dirt. Suddenly, without warning, the sales office is closed, and the friendly, smiling developer who promised to build the campground is gone, hundreds of thousands of dollars richer, and his customers are left with titles to practically worthless pieces of land and no amenities of any kind.

In theory, consumers are protected against land fraud schemes by the U.S. Housing and Urban Development and by the Interstate Lands Sales Full Disclosure Act which prohibits the interstate sale of property to anyone not provided with a HUD-prepared "Property Report." But dishonest developers have learned they can either avoid HUD restrictions by limiting sales to residents of one state or, they can simply discourage prospects from examining their "Property Reports" in detail. A condominium campground developer in southeastern Indiana, for example, told potential buyers that copies of his HUD report were limited, that they could examine the report in his sales office, but they could not take copies home with them. Most buyers simply skimmed the report, considering it unimportant, or were told that some of the warnings in the report were no longer valid.

The report warned, in rather blunt terms, that the developer had not set aside funds for any of the street, sewer, water or electrical improvements that were promised and that no guarantee could be given that either those improvements or a proposed swimming pool/recreation complex would ever be built. Still, the developer was able to convince several dozen people to buy his campsites during the six-month period before he closed his sales office and left the state.

Certain other condominium developers are not crooked in the sense that the Indiana developer was, but they are frequently less than honest with their customers. Often, they sell "memberships" in the nonprofit corporation that operates the campground instead of selling land parcels complete with deeds and titles, but their salesmen are ordered to ignore that fact when dealing with buyers. In theory, most "memberships" may either remain within a family forever or may be disposed of in a manner similar to the sale of property. Usually, however, if the member fails to pay his annual dues, membership fee or special assessments, his membership may be terminated, and not only will he lose all rights to use the campground and campsite, but he also will have to continue paying for the membership until it is resold. The campsite holder also is in an awkward position if the entire project is ever acquired by anyone holding a lien on the development; there is no guarantee that a title free of liens will be turned over to the members' association when the developer finally relinquishes ownership of the campground and leaves for greener pastures. Also, an individual could lose access to his campsite simply because mineral, oil and gas rights have already been sold to companies engaged in exploration of those commodities.

Furthermore, some contracts at condo projects stipulate that anyone who wants to sell his membership must offer it first to the governing members' association at the then-current membership fee. That restriction could prevent the owner from selling his membership at a profit, but more importantly, the association (which is usually controlled by the developer until the campground is nearly completed) is not under any obligation to buy the offered membership.

Several years ago, a company called Western Growth Capital Corporation held a free dinner party for prospective buyers of its development in Arizona and, after showing an elaborate slide presentation, convinced 174 persons to invest a total of $350,000 in lots. Buyers subsequently discovered that the property had no utilities or paved roads, that the "PGA-approved nine-hole golf course" was a weed field, that the "well-equipped pro shop with the year-around pro" in attendance was an empty shack and the "beautiful blue lake" was a 40-acre, dried up mudhole. But by then, the company had gathered up its money and moved to Minnesota, where it ran the same scam. Next, land was sold in Pennsylvania before the company was shut down and declared bankrupt. Promissory notes for purchase of the sites were sold to various banks, and most of the buyers of those worthless pieces of ground are still making payments on them every month.

THOSE REPAIR CHEATS

In 1978, Cal and Evelyn Williams were on their way north after spending the winter in the Florida sun. They planned to tour New England for a couple of months before visiting relatives in Chicago and then heading back to Florida that fall. They were towing their 31-foot Carriage travel trailer with a two-year-old Chevrolet Suburban which needed a tuneup and a new seal in its transmission. In Washington, D.C., Cal noticed an ad in the newspaper that offered a reseal job for only $26, plus parts. The ad was placed by a local shop of a nationally known and widely advertised transmission repair company. The shop promised one-day service, so Cal called, made an appointment, and took the Suburban in for the routine seal job.

That afternoon, Cal returned to the shop by taxi, convinced he would be able to pick up his truck and leave for New England the next day. However, he was told shop workmen had discovered problems with his transmission; metal shavings were found, indicating more work would be required, and the pump was worn out. "I asked them how much the work would cost altogether, and they said about $90," Cal reported a couple of years later. "I told them to go ahead and fix it for that price."

The next morning, Cal telephoned to find out when he could pick up the Suburban, and he was told the bushings were shot and would have to be replaced. The cost: another $38. "When I picked up the truck that afternoon, the shop foreman tried to convince me to have some other work done, such as front-wheel alignment and things like that, but I refused. I was convinced I had been cheated, but I didn't know what to do about it. Then a couple of weeks later in New Hampshire, I got to know a small-town mechanic pretty well, and I told him what had happened. He said he wanted to look at my transmission, so he put the Suburban up on a hoist and took the transmission cover off. He said that shop in D.C. hadn't done anything except replace the transmission seal. The pump was an old one—the same one that had come with the truck—and there was nothing wrong with either it or the bushings."

The company that worked on Cal's car is notorious for "low-balling"—offering to do work for one price and then jacking up that price by finding other problems—and has been the subject of legal action in several states since the 1960s.

RVers are often the targets of highway repair swindles because the vehicles themselves and the out-of-state license plates on them are advertisements that the prospective victims are travelers and are in no position to haggle over the quality or cost of repairs. Unscrupulous but enterprising service station attendants have learned how to create repair work for themselves by cutting customers' fan belts, squirting brake fluid or oil in places it shouldn't be and then calling attention to it, poking holes in tires with icepicks or even cutting alternator wires.

The subject of repair swindles came up one day while I was discussing RVing with full-timers L. F. "Whitey" Whitesell and Dick March—the man Loners on Wheels club members refer to affectionately as "The Shadetree Mechanic." The two men emphasized that RVers should be wary of business places, and especially mechanical repair shops, that tend to cheat unsuspecting travelers. "Really, it's kind of a hazard for anyone traveling," Dick said. "Day-to-day, routine problems cause only minimum difficulties: problems such as 'where's a grocery store, which gasoline station should I choose, where should I spend the night?' If those are problems, let me have some more of them. The big problem is avoiding getting ripped off for repairs and maintenance."

Whitey added, "It doesn't matter whether you're a man or a woman; they're gonna get you unless you're careful!"

"And boy, do I hear complaints!" Dick said. He even conducts "shadetree seminars" at rallies and advises RVers how to avoid being cheated. "One of my first pieces of advice has to do with preventative, routine care and maintenance. The RVer should find someone he trusts and then preplan his service and maintenance around visits to that person. That includes oil and filter changes, flushing the radiator, servicing the transmission, inspecting front wheel bearings and the brakes and things of that nature. He should plan on stopping at that garage or whatever every six months. On the other hand, when the RVer breaks down away from that person he trusts, he should try to get the nearest small town of 5,000 or 10,000 people and find a good, independent garage. Ask the manager of an auto parts store for directions to the oldest independent garage in town—a place that the auto parts store has serviced for years. That's the guy that the auto parts store will consider a good customer; he's the guy who will be reliable because a neighborhood garage can't get away with much in a small town and survive. I'm not saying that the neighborhood garage is 100% faithful to good service, but if it's been there a long time, you can usually rely on its work. If that garage practiced ripping people off and didn't treat them right, the word would be all over town within twenty-four hours, and that guy's business would go downhill fast. Businessmen in small towns have to baby their customers, but they don't have to do that in the big cities."

MORE RIP-OFFS TO AVOID

Carla and Bill Baker (not their real names) wanted to earn extra money in order to supplement their retirement income and enable them to have more money for their RV travels. Bill found what he thought was the answer through an ad in a Miami, Florida, newspaper: "More Men Needed. You can earn $4 to $6 per hour in your spare time using revolutionary new equipment. No selling, no soliciting, no experience needed. Small investment which can be repaid quickly out of earnings." Bill answered the ad and was fast-talked into taking three days of training to learn how to use a floor buffing machine. Then, after being judged qualified to handle jobs referred to him, he was told he would be given floor buffing assignments as soon as he bought one of the machines. He was convinced to sign a judgment note with a finance company to pay $1,296 for the buffer, then was advised to wait in his travel trailer for the work to roll in. He never heard from the company again and, after a couple of weeks when he went to the company's offices to ask about jobs, he discovered that the company had gone out of business. A check with the local Better Business Bureau revealed that at least a dozen other people— most of them senior citizens—had been victimized in the same way. Bill also discovered that the buffing machine he bought sold elsewhere in the community for less than $300.

In Phoenix a few years ago, the word spread rapidly through a campground frequented by full-time RVers that a local clinic was providing free eye examinations to anyone over the age of fifty-five. Several way-of-lifers decided to take advantage of the exams. After the examinations, they were handed pairs of eyeglasses and bills for up to $100. When they objected to buying the glasses they were told, "You *have* to buy them. We made them especially for you, and we can't sell them to anyone else." Perhaps dozens of RVers paid for the glasses and wore them until bonafide optometrists in the community got wind of the scam and informed police. Personnel at the so-called clinic left town just before the police arrived, however, and subsequent investigations revealed that the lenses of the eyeglasses were simply clear, unground glass.

Medical quacks bilk arthritis sufferers out of between $300 and $500 million each year, according to the Arthritis and Rheumatism Foundation, and some of those who are cheated are undoubtedly full-time RVers in search of miracle cures. And RVers in the sunbelt are often the targets of fake weight-loss and cancer-cure clinics.

AVOID BEING CHEATED

Esther Peterson, who was Director of the U.S. Office of Consumer Affairs under President Carter, had a simple philosophy about avoiding rip-offs: "An ounce of prevention can save a pound of aggravation." She provided a "consumer checklist" that she advised people to consult before signing on the dotted line for anything and said, "If you are in doubt when answering any of these questions, it would be wise to look elsewhere in shopping for goods or services." Here's her checklist:

- Does the advertiser promise more than the product can reasonably deliver? Beware of claims that seem too good to be true.
- Have you comparison-shopped? A little time spent comparing prices and quality of goods and services can often save a lot of money and trouble.
- According to your local consumer protection agency or Better Business Bureau, does the company have a good track record for reliability?
- If you are seeking professional assistance, have you asked about fees, services, qualifications and licenses?
- Have you checked consumer product testing magazines and other informative sources to see how the experts rate the product you are considering?
- Do you feel you are being pushed too fast to buy or to sign a contract?
- Do you understand the contract and your full obligation—finance charges, total price, and what happens if you miss a payment or want to pay off in advance? If necessary, take the contract home or seek legal advice. Get any oral promises in writing.
- Is there a warranty? Does it cover parts and labor, and for how long? Where do you have to take the item for repair?
- What are the company's policies for complaint handling?
- Does the company give refunds?

To avoid being cheated by a dishonest RV dealer such as the one in Indiana mentioned earlier, be wary of RVs that are advertised for considerbly less than the market price; the dealer may be low-balling or using bait-and-switch tactics just to draw people to his lot. Give first consideration to dealers near your home; they are more likely to provide you with the best and most accessible service. While shopping, ask one dealer for his evaluation of another's reputation. Although you run the risk of getting a colored opinion, my experience is that most dealers are honest and will readily tell you if they believe another is not. If a dealer displays, prominently, the manufacturer's suggested retail prices on his units, there is a good chance he will not play dollar games with you. Ask to inspect the dealer's service facilities; even if you know nothing about such facilities, you will be able to determine if his shop is busy, if it seems well equipped and, most importantly, if there is a service facility. Ask to see the training certificates issued by manufacturers certifying that the dealer's service personnel have been trained to work on the unit you are considering buying.

Make sure you know, and have in writing, exactly which accessories you are buying as standard equipment and which ones you will have to buy as options; ask to see the manufacturer's list of options—usually prominently displayed on the company's literature—for your unit. If you are cheated, or think you have been, by all means complain to the manufacturer who supplies RVs to the dealer; most manufacturers do not want dealers who cheat the public and misrepresent their products. In comparison shopping, check back copies of consumer magazines such as *Trailer Life* and *Motorhome Life* in an effort to learn whether the magazines have ever done test reports on the units that interest you most.

Buying A Campsite

RVers who are considering buying condominium campsites need to take special care. They should insist that the developer has escrow accounts for road, utility and sewage improvements because, without those improvements, a campground is merely a parcel of land. The RVer also should learn how the roads will be maintained and who will pay for at least the initial maintenance. He should make sure potable water is available for every site in the campground—not just his own—since the availability of water will affect the project's value and that, in turn, will determine the value of his property. He should know whether permanent attachments to water lines are permitted or whether only detachable hose connections are allowed. He should learn who is responsible for installing electrical lines to the campsites and whether the installation cost will be assessed to property owners. The same kind of checks should be made for sewer lines, and the RVer also should learn what steps have been taken to build a sewage disposal system and whether that system will be large enough to handle the effluent channeled into it. Site drainage should be checked closely to determine not only if his own property is subject to flooding from nearby sites or higher terrain, but also whether he could be legally liable for drainage from his site to another site.

The availability of fire and police protection—not just security guard protection—should be checked out. If the campground will place an unexpected load on either the local police department or fire department, chances are that an increase in tax rates—over which the nonresident RVer has no control—will be necessary. The RVer should also make sure adequate trash pickup is provided, and he should determine whether the cost of pickup is included in his maintenance fee or whether he will have to pay for it separately. The RVer should review, closely, the rules of the campground and consider whether they are acceptable to him; he should make sure his RV conforms to the styles and types permitted in the park, and he should learn the extent of improvements to his site that he will be permitted to make.

If You Have Been Cheated

To avoid being ripped off by repair cheats, do not allow any service station attendant to look under your hood, check your oil or even your tires unless you are standing beside him. Better yet, check your own oil and tire pressure and fill your own gasoline tank at self-service pumps. Consider repairs for your vehicle the same way you should consider surgery on your own body; ask for a second opinion.

If you feel you have been cheated with defective products, shoddy repairs, poor workmanship or incompetent service, the U.S. Office of Consumer Affairs offers this advice: "Identify the problem and what you believe would be a fair settlement of your complaint (your money back, a repair, a replacement, etc.). Have documentation available to substantiate your complaint—a sales receipt, a repair order, warranties, canceled checks, etc. Go back to the person who sold you the item or performed the service and calmly state the problem and what action you would like taken. If the person is not helpful, ask to see the supervisor or manager. Repeat the complaint. If you are not satisfied with the response, don't

Although there are many reputable repair places such as this, full-time RVers should be wary of rip-offs.

give up. If the company operates nationally or the product is a national brand, write a letter to the president or the consumer official of the company. If you are not satisfied with the company's response to your letter or never receive a response, you should consider contacting outside sources for help. Those include Action Lines, AFL-CIO Community Services, Consumer Action Panels, consumer credit counseling, federal agencies, government services, legal services, media programs, an attorney, the police, private consumer organizations, public interest law centers, small claims courts, state licensing boards and bureaus and state or local consumer offices."

The Office of Consumer Affairs provides, free of charge, a "Consumer's Resource Handbook" that lists names, addresses and telephone numbers of assistance agencies and even tells how to write a complaint letter. The 80-page booklet is available through the Consumer Information Center, Department 38, Pueblo, Colorado 81009.

Chapter Eighteen

Boondock Camping

Boondocking—the art of camping in primitive areas without benefit of electricity, sewers or usually even fresh water—is not for everyone. Full-time RVers, however, often feel at least some boondocking is necessary for them to maintain their traveling lifestyles. Boondocking is the best way many full-timers have for trimming their expenses to the bone and waiting for their incomes to catch up with their previous months' expenses. They can park their rigs for long periods of time—many do it for as long as five months!—at little or no cost, eat a lot of fresh fish, fruit and vegetables and take part in activities that are free while they soak up the sun and plan their next travel adventures.

Boondocking has several forms, actually, ranging from overnight stops at places where there are no parking fees, to short-term campouts in national forests or along streamsides, to private escapes to secluded environments where birds and animals provide the only companionship. The rapidly escalating costs of travel, meals and campsites, however, have recently resulted in a phenomenal growth in the popularity of so-called "coyote" camps. Such primitive camps were once shunned by serious RVers because of their lack of desirable facilities and their remoteness from water, gasoline, electricity and food supplies. But the last decade's increase in the number of full-time RVers with self-contained rigs has made the coyote camps more attractive to budget-conscious way-of-lifers.

Desert Camping At The Slabs

The three coyote camps that full-timers talk about most are The Slabs and The Cedars of Southern California and a place in Arizona called Coyote Howls. The Slabs, in fact, is probably the most popular boon-docking area in America, drawing several thousand RVers into its strictly primitive desert terrain every winter. Full-timers camp free there in their self-contained rigs and spend their days socializing, relaxing or exploring nearby attractions. While no charges have ever been levied for camping at The Slabs, there were indications in early 1981 that the owner of the desert land was considering asking RVers to pay for camping.

Members of the Loners on Wheels organization gather at The Slabs annually and even set up share-a-ride programs so that RVers can hold down their gasoline costs while shopping and sightseeing in the nearby communities. Helen Duffessy, a Loner who researched the background of The Slabs while spending the winter there a few years ago, told me about the uniquely interesting camp as she considered whether to go there during the 1980-81 winter season.

"During World War II," she reported, "General Patton trained his North Africa corps out in the desert of Southern California. There was an army base near Niland, which is on the Salton Sea—a lake that is 285 feet below sea level. When the war was over, the base was closed by the army, and everything was removed except for the concrete slabs that the buildings were on. The army then deeded the property to a local board of education to prevent squatting and homesteading. There's still an active bombing range not far away, but the desert area where The Slabs is is just beautiful, with a magnificent view of the Chocolate Mountains to the east."

Helen sketched out the area of The Slabs on a map of southern California and said, "You take Route 111 out of Niland, then go out this little road here. When you come over the first rise, you see nothing ahead of you except desert, and you think to yourself, 'My God, where is this road going?' But it's a perfectly good blacktopped road. And all of a sudden, you come over another little rise, and there in front of you are thousands of travel trailers and motorhomes. It's the most breathtaking sight you can imagine! The first time I went there, I sent a cassette tape to my daughter, Rosemary, describing it. She got the impression that The Slabs was just a squatter's village with a lot of gypsies living there, and she immediately began to worry about her mama out there by herself with goodness knows what kind of dangers. But I told her later, 'Hey, my

General Patton trained his North Africa corps in the desert campground now known as The Slabs.

rig's one of the cheap ones. There are rigs here that make mine look like a squatter's shack.' "

But how can RVers keep busy and enjoy themselves living out in the desert without benefit of hookups or recreational facilities? Helen answered, "The days aren't long enough! In the first place, living out like that, the mere mechanics of living takes up a certain amount of time. The first thing in the morning, you have to go outside, get down on your hands and knees and look beneath your rig and up against your wheels to make sure no coyotes are resting there waiting for tender little tidbits—such as my two cats—to be put out. Those coyotes love to eat cats and dogs, and there have been some very regrettable incidents with RVers at The Slabs losing their loving pets to skulking coyotes.

"Next, you have to make sure your battery is charged up. I have a little Honda generator that can run for four hours on a half-gallon of gasoline, and I use it to charge my batteries. We have to run our lights a lot there because it gets pitch dark very suddenly, about 4 P.M., in December and January when the sun goes behind the mountains. As soon as a woman starts to check her battery, she can just figure a couple of retired men will come over and ask if she needs help. A lot of those fellows have accumulated an endless amount of knowledge about different things over the years, and they bring that knowledge and all kinds of fantastic tools with them to The Slabs. So they usually end up checking my input and output and recharging my battery for me, if it needs it.

"Then you have to make sure you have enough water to get through the day. If you need water, you can go into Niland and get it at one of the service stations. If the sewage tank on your rig has to be dumped, you can do that in Niland too. There's an RV service center in Brawley (about five miles south of The Slabs) in case you need maintenance work done that the shadetree mechanics can't handle. After I make all my checks, I usually go for a two or three-mile walk around the camp, then make some coffee and stand around and gab with friends. The minute you see two or three people together, you know something is cooking, so you've got to go over and find out what's up and if you're interested in doing whatever is being planned. Maybe someone is going somewhere interesting, and everyone else decides to double up and go together. Someone's always coming in with a load of lemons, oranges or vegetables that a farmer let them pick so it wouldn't go to waste."

Helen added, "The Loners on Wheels club always reserves one of the big slabs for its headquarters, and after about three o'clock every day, Loners start heading there from all directions with a drink in one hand and a lawn chair in the other. Suddenly, it's happy hour, with everybody sitting around chatting and having a few drinks. Maybe a few of them will decide to drive to Niland or Calipatria or Brawley for dinner. But because of the altitude, by nine o'clock, nearly everybody is in bed and out like a light."

The lifestyle is just as leisurely, while not exactly relaxing, at The Cedars—a coyote camp among old salt cedar trees not far from the American Canal along the Colorado River in Southern California—and at Coyote Howls, a less primitive campground west of Tucson where showers and fresh drinking water are available and sites cost senior citizens only $10 a month. Boondockers save their battery power by operating propane lights and catalytic heaters, and they save money by engaging in inexpensive or cost-free recreation: hiking, observing birds and wild animals, looking for wildflowers and wild cactus, bathing in mineral springs, fishing in lakes or rivers, attending square dances and card games, searching out flea markets, window shopping, attending matinee movies and free concerts, visiting libraries, and taking free industry tours.

Camping At K-Mart

Boondocking is not, by any means, limited to the coyote camps. To some RVers, boondocking simply means stopping overnight in a rest area or in a restaurant, church, school, supermarket or shopping center parking lot. Charles and Violetta Legler, a couple of full-timers from Waterloo, Iowa, make it a point to search out free and inexpensive campsites of those kinds. They frequently make use of shopping mall parking lots, and they have never been refused permission to park overnight in the parking lot of a K-Mart store; they always ask the manager for permission first. They utilize city campgrounds which offer either free or very inexpensive camping, and they park near police stations, in rest areas and alongside picturesque streams. My copilot and I have slept overnight in shopping center parking lots, beside the buildings of gasoline service stations, in rest areas, on the shores of wilderness lakes and even once—during a heavy storm—in the parking lot of a church, but we have never felt completely at ease doing that.

Other RVers apparently feel the same way. Full-timers Walt and Charlotte Consider, for example, reported they have never taken advantage of free camping of any kind except for occasional overnight stops at rest areas. "Even there, we won't do it unless we're with another couple and have room to park our rigs door-to-door next to each other," Walt said. "A lot of people get themselves into trouble just so they can save a few bucks. We carry campground directories with us that tell us where we can find inexpensive campsites that are quiet and safe because they're patrolled. Like the city park campground we stayed in at Beaumont, Texas, a couple of weeks ago; full hookups cost only $2.50 a night, and we felt safe because there was a ranger station right there."

Flo Cooper said she and her husband Ken rarely try boondock camping. "We have an electric freezer, and it keeps us from stopping at places where we can't plug in. But besides that, I would prefer to spend the extra money and be in a comfortable spot where we have water if we want to use it and where we have electricity for an electric blanket if the night turns cold. I don't sleep well if we're just sitting somewhere by ourselves, either. I'm always listening for unusual sounds outside."

Ken added, "One of the former Good Sam Club state directors traveled with us for a while, and he said he and his wife try to stay in a free place every night. They will frequently stop at a restaurant for dinner, and after dinner they'll ask the manager if he minds it if they stay in his parking lot all night. They'll also stay overnight sometimes in shopping center parking lots. And they said they're never bothered.

WILDERNESS AREA CAMPING

Full-time RVers can find safe, inexpensive boondock camping in nearly every part of the U.S. due to recreational programs of the state, local and federal governments, the U.S. Army Corps of Engineers, hydroelectric power companies and lumber, paper and mining companies. Many of the privately owned camping areas, in fact, are open to anyone on a first-come, first-served basis with no fees of any kind charged, even though the areas are patrolled regularly by corporate security forces.

The best example I can recall of a free, privately owned camping area is the Ohio Power Recreation Area southeast of Zanesville in southern Ohio. Known by many of the people who use it as "Little Canada" because of its wilderness terrain and its abundance of lakes, the recreation area is essentially a reclaimed complex of strip-mines owned by the Ohio Power Company. Since 1944, the company has planted more than 34 million trees, and some 400 small lakes have been stocked with twelve kinds of game fish by the Ohio Division of Wildlife. Hundreds of free campsites are available, many of them on the edges of ponds; no utility hookups are provided, but fresh drinking water is pumped from cold wells on the property. Picnic tables and free firewood are furnished for every campsite. Wildlife is plentiful, and even the beaver, which was once almost extinct in Ohio, can be seen at many of the ponds. The recreation area also is a bird-watcher's paradise, with species ranging from warblers to wild turkeys. Although entry to the area is free, a permit from the Ohio Power Company (Post Office Box 328, McConnelsville, Ohio 43756) or the Ohio Division of Wildlife is required.

Free camping is permitted in hundreds of other recreation areas operated by the nation's utility companies due to requirements by the Federal Energy Regulatory Commission. Few of the recreation areas have formal hookups at the campsites, but most of the rather primitive sites are well maintained and regularly patrolled. A list of more than 2,000 free and inexpensive sites is published in an ERC directory titled "Recreational Opportunities at Hydroelectric Projects Licensed by the Federal Energy Regulatory Commission." Copies of the directory cost $3 each and are available through the Superintendent of Documents, U.S. Government Printing Office, Washington, D.C. 20402; ask for directory number 061-002-00014-6.

A list of paper, lumber and mining companies that allow RVers to use their campgrounds—usually free—is available through the Snowbird Newsletter, Post Office Box 1059, San Jacinto, California 92383 by sending a large, self-addressed, stamped envelope. My favorite campground

Minnesota's Echo Lake offers rustic camping and some of the best walleye fishing in the state.

among those is a small, 26-site recreation area owned by Boise Cascade on Minnesota's Bass Lake. Like most other campgrounds of its kind, it does not have utility hookups, and facilities are limited to picnic tables, pit toilets and a dump station, but the fishing at Bass Lake is marvelous, and the scenery is spectacular. The campground is about ten miles east of Effie on State Route 1, only a short drive from the Chippewa National Forest.

Minnesota also is the site of a truly beautiful, inexpensive campground operated by the National Forest Service. The park is on Echo Lake east of the small town of Orr and not far from the thriving community of Ely. Camping costs only $2 a night, and while facilities are strictly rustic, Echo Lake has some of the best walleye fishing in the northeastern part of the state. Excellent free and inexpensive camping is available, too, around North Dakota's Lake Sakakawea and Oklahoma's Tenkiller Lake, according to full-timers who travel those sections of the country a lot in the summer. Good, quiet and enjoyable low-cost or free camping can be discovered nearly anywhere, though, and most of the parks are listed in books such as the annual *Trailer Life's RV Campground and Services Directory.*

RVers who enjoy boondocking seem able to find plenty of things to keep them busy at wilderness camps. A woman writing to *Trailer Life* magazine a few years ago advised readers not to think that full-timers do not have enough to do to keep them busy. She said that although she was then camped in a public park that had no planned activities, no rec hall and no bulletin board, "Each day is a different surprise, and boredom is nonexistent. There are constant games of lawn bowling and horseshoes. A card game over a cup of coffee is a great way to spend an evening. A picnic lunch taken to a nearby town and enjoyed at a small park is topped off with a visit to a flea market on the way home. Christmas Eve here was spent around a huge bonfire singing carols. On New Year's Eve, a dance was organized around taped music and Guy Lombardo on the TV. What do we full-timers do with our time? We stay here a few months, go on to another park, another state and meet new, interesting people. We talk, we listen, we play, we visit, we plan. But most of all, we just have fun!"

Chapter Nineteen

Full-Timing
With Pets

When Helen Duffessy hit the road as a full-time trailerist in May, 1977, she took two companions with her: a pair of beautiful cats—an Abysinnian and a Himalayan. Three years later, when I met Helen at the Eby Pines Campground in Indiana, the two playful felines were still with her. "They've been all over the U.S.—as much of it as I've gone through—from border to border and coast to coast," she said. "They travel either in the car or in the trailer, and as far as they know, that trailer is theirs—it's where they live."

Helen, a part-time writer, told about her travels with her pets in an article published a year earlier by a leading cat lover's magazine. "You'd be surprised how many cats there are on the road, traveling with people," she said later. "Everyone sort of takes it for granted that people are going to take their dogs camping with them, but it used to be rare to see RVers with cats. Now, it seems, more and more people are traveling with cats. And it *should* be that way. Cats travel just as well as dogs, and they're a heck of a lot less trouble. You don't have to take a cat out for a walk at 6:00 in the morning in the rain. Cats are friendly, they're compatible with each other, and they're good company to have along. My cats love all the people they meet, and they just lap up the attention they get."

One of her cats, Nicki, sometimes protests, though, when his mistress decides to leave one familiar spot for another. "Nicki and I had a fight coming up here from Florida," she reported. "I started to put his leash on him and carry him to the car, but he did not want to go. He insisted on staying in the trailer. So I let him stay there and took the other cat in the car with me. But cats are wonderful traveling companions. No matter

Helen Duffessy's only travel companions are her two exotic but friendly cats.

how fussy they are about eating, you can find cat food anywhere. My cats weren't traveling cats in the beginning, either. But they've sure settled into traveling now, and they're good travelers."

It is not unusual for full-timers to travel with pets, but interestingly enough, most of the way-of-lifers I interviewed while researching this book said that pets are too much trouble; former owners said they would never have another pet while they're full-timing, and nearly all present owners admitted their current pets would be their last. In Minnesota, I met dog-owners Glenda and Sam Beaideme and their friends, Doris and John Lockwood, who traveled full time with a cat. Both couples said their pets were companionable, but troublesome. "Our dog's a barker," Sam said. "We try to keep her quiet, but we can't. And then, of course, there's the daily routine of walking her and picking up after her. Also, in Florida, where we like to spend our winters, all of the state parks and a lot of the private parks prohibit pets."

Doris interjected, "No pets of any kind are allowed in Maryland state parks, either. That includes cats; a pet's a pet. I'm sure we could get away with taking ours into one of those parks easier than a dog owner could because a cat's quieter and we could keep it inside the trailer. Ours has a loud meow, but he only meows when he hears us coming. Pets of any kind are a lot of bother, though, and when ours is gone, I don't think we'll get another."

Kentuckians Mickey and Laila Rutledge have coped with the problems of traveling with a dog since they began full-timing in 1974. "Our dog has been with us sixteen years, and we're really attached to her; she's like part of the family. But she'll be the last dog we'll own. Her medical bills are as high as ours, and keeping a dog and cleaning up after her and keeping her from bothering other people—all of that—is a problem in a condominium-type campground. And a lot of other people—especially the state parks—won't allow dogs at all. Our dog's a good traveler, but she's got to be on medication for her heart and for allergies all the time."

A DOG FOR FULL-TIMING

RVers who insist on full-timing with a dog for the companionship, love and even protection it provides probably should heed the advice of trainer Rudy Drexler in selecting a dog for the road and then training and caring for it. Drexler, an RVer himself and a man who trains a lot of animals for RV owners because his Orchard Kennels is on the edge of the nation's travel trailer capital—Elkhart, Indiana—was asked for his recommendations on pets for full-timers. He responded, "I think the most suitable all-around dog is the German shepherd, if you can get a good one. When I tell people that, they say, 'But a shepherd sheds a lot, and I don't want dog hair all over my RV.' Well, that's a misconception. A shepherd won't shed a lot if he's given the proper food and a proper diet is followed. The doberman, if he's a nice, gentle animal, is an excellent choice for a full-timer's pet. He has a thinner coat, but he also sheds. I'd prefer the German shepherd, though, because he's not as restless and he's easier to maintain. A hyperactive dog can be even more hyper on the road if he doesn't get a lot of room to run and a lot of exercise. A shepherd doesn't need an awful lot of exercise, but dobermans do. I'd even consider a standard poodle as a good dog for traveling with in an RV. But I always urge RV owners not to own guard dogs. Rather, they should consider a command dog or an image dog or even a good, big dog that's obedience-trained if they're worried about protection. An RVer doesn't need—and shouldn't have—a dog that's attack-trained."

There are four basic kinds of personal dogs: a command dog, which is obedience-trained and will attack on its owner's command, can be taught to protect a house, car or RV and even to search through a house or RV for intruders; a guard dog is taught to protect property when unattended, attacking without command, but it is not recommended as a pet for individuals; the image dog is fully obedience-trained and is trained to bark an alarm when strangers approach, but not bite; a basic obedience dog will work on and off a leash and by hand signals and can be protection-trained against poisoning and theft. RVers who want a pet strictly for companionship, should own a gentle breed that is taught to obey simple commands; an image dog is a good animal for RVers who want a friendly pet that can also raise an alarm and threaten prowlers and intruders by barking and growling. When trained, the image dog is taught to stand his ground, but generally not to attack. Owners of image dogs often report, though, that their pets *will* attack anyone who seems to be threatening physical violence to their owners; most image dogs become very protective of their families, and they are especially protective of their owners' children and grandchildren.

When RVers ask Drexler for a pet that can be used for personal protection, he sometimes recommends either purchase of a command dog or training that will convert an image or standard obedient dog into a command animal. "The command dog is fully obedience-trained; he's good with children and adults in general, but he is trained to attack when ordered to do so or, in some cases, automatically if his owner is being hurt. The command dog is taught to attack on a five-foot leash, on a 30-foot leash and off-leash, but he's also trained to break off an attack on command. Good command dogs are animals 65 pounds and heavier that have the right temperament. They are usually German shepherds, dobermans and Rottweilers, but Irish setters and Labrador retrievers also are suitable."

Guard dogs are not recommended for RVers because they are taught very little obedience and are trained to hate anyone other than their handlers, and it is difficult, if not impossible, for anyone to reverse the education of an attack dog and convert it into a safe, friendly command or image dog.

Training For The Traveling Dog

Without any question, dogs traveling with full-time RVers should be obedience-trained, both for their own protection and for the convenience and protection of their owners. Untrained dogs are more likely to cause their owners legal difficulties because chances are better they will bite someone or injure another animal—possibly even a very valuable one—in a fight. Drexler, who is Indiana Regional Director of the United States Professional Dog Trainers Association, said most owners can teach their own dogs basic obedience, but such training should be intense and repeated often over a short period of time. To teach a dog to come on command, Drexler advised tying the animal to a 30-foot lunge line—or even a simple clothesline. "Let him drag it around the yard a while and then tell him to come. Sound like you mean it. If he doesn't, give the line a sharp jerk, draw the dog to you and make him sit in front of you. When he finally does come, praise him in a happy, excited voice. Repeat the training about 150 times a week until there's no question in your mind that the dog will come when you call him."

Drexler added, "Another thing you might consider teaching him is to obey a 'sit-stay' command because that way you can keep him from jumping out of a car, motorhome or trailer into the path of another vehicle. Actually, it's best to put the dog on a leash before you even get out of a car or motorhome. Give him the 'sit-stay' command, get out of the vehicle yourself first, then give him a 'come-heel' command. Don't allow a dog to jump into a car or RV either unless you have given him an 'in' command because he might have muddy feet. I do not like to allow a dog to sit on the upholstery, not only because of animal hair, but because he can be thrown from the seat if you should come to a sudden stop. It's best to put the dog on a 'down-stay' command on the floor and maybe even put him in a harness that can be tied to a secure object in the vehicle."

While an RVer should make certain his dog is fully obedience-trained, he should not assume that other dogs are as well trained. If your dog and another one get into a fight, you should grab the other dog by the back legs and hold him and, at the same time, shout "No!" or "Stay!" to your own dog. By exerting voice control over your dog and grabbing the other dog's hind legs, you lessen the chances that you'll be bitten. Dog trainers recommend that owners be able to exert at least voice-obedience control over their own pets so that they can be called back to heel instantly under any situation. RVers who either cannot train their own pets in obedience or do not wish to do so can hire the work done by Professional Dog Trainers Association members.

According to Drexler, most members of the association will obedience-train all breeds, from the smallest Chihuahua to the biggest St. Bernard. Drexler, for example, offers two types of obedience courses. One is a general $95 course of three lessons in which the pet is taught to come, heel, sit, stay, and respond to other similar commands. The owner is provided with an instruction sheet outlining how to train his own dog to work off-leash in about seven weeks, and the owner himself is given a free lesson if he is not sure how to handle the trained dog. The other obedience course is a military-type program in which the dog is taught, for $145, how to work both on and off a leash; he's taught obstacle work such as going up and down stairs and leaping over obstacles on command; he's poison-proofed so no one can poison him, and he's theft-proofed so no one can steal him. A more intense training program under which the animal is kept at the kennel for two weeks and the owner is given a fully schooled pet costs $325. An even more advanced course costs $425 and takes three or four weeks.

Professional trainers also work with dog owners on what they call "problem consultation" and try to show owners how to correct bad habits such as digging up yards, chewing on furniture, chasing cars, jumping on people or biting. To train a command dog, experts such as Drexler charge around $700; to buy a fully trained dog, a new owner would have to expect to pay between $750 and $2,700, depending upon the species.

Protection For You And Your Dog

RVers should not, of course, take pets on the road with them until the animals are immunized against common diseases, distemper, heartworm and rabies. Drexler emphasized that heartworm is an especially deadly danger to traveling dogs; it is a worm-type egg that is transmitted to canines by mosquitos. "If your dog gets heartworm, he can die a very painful death," the Indiana trainer said. "All dogs that are taken to mosquito areas should be on heartworm preventatives. Heartworm is a very expensive disease to try to cure, and it is easy to kill a dog when trying to cure it."

Pet owners also should make sure they are themselves properly protected—with adequate liability insurance. An RVer's travel insurance or vehicle insurance should contain a liability rider in case the dog bites someone or chews up someone else's pet so badly that the services of a veterinarian are needed. A dog owner also is legally responsible if his male dog impregnates someone else's female dog—especially if the other animal is a valuable one. In addition, if your dog is bitten by another RVer's pet, make sure its owner has proof the dog has been immunized against rabies. Don't rely on the owner's word, either; write down his veterinarian's name and telephone number so that you can verify the immunization.

Loose dogs in a campground or rest area are more than a nuisance;

they are illegal. Most states and communities have leash laws requiring dogs either to be on a five-foot leash or secured with a 30-foot line, and in many locales, a dog is considered dangerous—and therefore could be destroyed by authorities—if he bites someone just once. If a dog must be left at an RV while his owners are sightseeing or having a picnic, he should be tied to a 30-foot line attached to the curbside, and preferably the shaded side, of the unit. Periodic checks should be made to ensure the dog is all right and no one is teasing him. Drexler warned: "It's seldom a good idea to tie a dog to an RV unless absolutely necessary, though. Especially if you're in a campground. There's a chance that he could get into a fight with a dog that isn't leashed, or someone might walk up to him and get bitten. Also, he can get tangled up in his leash around the tank area and around the wheels."

On a long trip, a large container of water—at least five gallons—should be taken from the water supply the dog has been using to prevent urinary tract infections caused by different strains of bacteria in strange water. Unfortunately, such infections are risks dog-owning RVers must take if they are constantly on the move because it is not likely that one permanent water supply can ever be found.

A traveling dog should be fed lightly, preferably when he is not inside a moving vehicle because many dogs get motion sickness very easily. And don't switch foods on your pet. Take along enough of his favorite food to last until you are sure it can be replenished; switching food can cause diarrhea. It's even a good idea to take along anti-diarrhetics because dogs sometimes get very nervous in unfamiliar surroundings, and that nervousness can cause diarrhea. Try to feed and water the dog on a regular schedule. If it's extremely hot, give him water three times a day, but do not allow him to have water at all times. Not only could that ruin his housebreaking, but a constant supply of water, coupled with the motion of the vehicle, will irritate his bladder and make him urinate more often. During cold weather, a traveling dog will eat more than during hot weather. And if the combination of heat and travel excitement causes the pet to lose his appetite, a food stimulant or a B-12 complex vitamin given orally will improve his appetite and relax him. Dog experts also encourage stirring canned meat into dry dog food to encourage a pet to eat.

Dog waste is one of the most aggravating problems in campgrounds, but it also presents possible problems to the canine. Drexler advised: "You should never allow your dog even to sniff a pile of defecation. Sniffing the odor is not going to infest the dog, but if he brushes his lip against it, he could infest himself with worms." Full-time RVers should check their dogs regularly for worm infestations.

It is safe to leave a pet alone overnight in an RV, but if the air temperature is warm, open the windows at least two inches so he can get air but can't poke his head through and choke to death. Windows with screens, of course, can be opened completely if the dog is trained both to repel intruders and not leave the unit if the screen is poked out. We once left our small but fiercely protective dog in a motorhome all day with all the windows and the entry door open (the screen and screen door were, of course, closed). We asked a friend, whom our dog knew and had even played with a few times, to freshen his water, check his food and take him for a walk during the day. But when she approached the motorhome, he growled and threatened to attack her. She opened the screen door, hoping he would jump out, but he stood his ground at the edge of the entrance and refused, all day until our return, to either leave or allow anyone near the coach.

Traveling dogs often suffer from heat stroke in the summer, Drexler warned. "Symptoms you can watch for include extreme, heavy panting and excessive slobbering. A dog with those symptoms can pass out and either go into convulsions or a state of collapse." If your dog does suffer from heat stroke, immerse him completely, except for his head, in a bath-tub full of water. Or, if no tub is available, wet him down thoroughly with a garden hose, then fan the water off him. If you're traveling and can't get to a large water supply, put as much water on him as possible—even a pint of it if that's all there is—and lay him near a window or air vent so that the water will evaporate off him. On the other hand, if a dog is hit by a car or struck a heavy blow, his body temperature should be kept high—as near his normal temperature of 101 or 102 degrees as possible—to prevent shock. Full-time RVers with pets should carry a book on treating poisons and a first-aid kit, both for their own use as well as for use on the animal in emergencies. Drexler warned, "One of the most serious poisonings a dog can have comes from drinking radiator coolant that leaks from a car or motorhome. That antifreeze will kill a dog quicker than anything else." Ingested antifreeze can be diluted by a combination of water and bicarbonate of soda, however.

Pets should not be allowed to ride with their heads out the car or motorhome windows because they could get hit in an eye or the nostrils with a hard insect and injured seriously, and they can also get severe sinus infections. If your dog encounters a skunk and is sprayed, bathe him liberally with tomato juice and then wash him in a stream or rinse him off with a hose. If your dog has porcupine quills in his face or nose, they should be pulled out before they become infected, but before they're removed, the dog should be muzzled by tying a rag or handkerchief around his jaws. The quills should be pulled out with pliers and the wounds treated with peroxide. Pets not accustomed to boating should be left on shore, Drexler advised. "A lot of dogs get scared in a boat, and they sometimes jump overboard and try to swim to shore. Now, say you're out a half mile from land and you've got an English sheepdog or another heavy-haired dog who panics and jumps over the side. His coat will soak up a lot of water, and he'll panic even more and could even cause the boat to overturn." Anyone considering taking a dog boating should also make sure, by a few short trips first, whether the animal gets seasick easily.

If you have to board out your dog, inspect the facilities before leaving your pet. If the manager says he can't permit inspections because it upsets the animals, be wary of the place because it probably is dirty and infested. The rule dog trainers follow is, "if it's clean enough that I'd sleep there, it's clean enough for my dog." Be sure the kennel has insurance in case something happens to your pet. Tell the kennel manager you do not want tranquilizers given to your dog and that you want the animal fed only the food you have provided. Check out the reputation of the kennel with a local veterinarian.

Protection Without A Pet

Professional trainers such as Drexler realize there are many reasons why RVers—and particularly full-timers—do not want to travel with a pet but feel they should keep a dog anyway for the protection it provides. For those people, Drexler has a couple of solutions. One is a little sign that can be attached to the screen door that states, "Property protected by command dog." Another solution is a tape recording of a barking dog. One such tape mimics the sound of a vicious dog barking for 80 seconds, and it is attached to a device that repeats the bark at intervals. Called the "Sound Guard," it sells for $9.95, but that is quite a lot less expensive than an $800 guard dog. The device can be turned on instantly if an RVer hears a sound outside his rig at night. While the "dog" is barking, the RVer can shout, "King, be quiet! Nothing's out there!" but the "dog" continues barking ferociously.

RVers also can simulate the presence of a dog by laying a piece of carpet outside the RV for a few days until it kills the grass in a shape similar to a dog's body, and then a leash or lunge line can be tied to the unit's grab handle and just allowed to hang there.

Like most full-time RVers, Helen Duffessy keeps her pets with her not for protection, but for the companionship they provide. Curious as to how much she actually valued their presence, I asked her: "If something would happen to those cats, do you like traveling with pets enough that you'd replace them, or are they enough of a bother that you wouldn't?"

She hesitated a moment, then replied, "I have thought about that many times, but I can't answer that question. I spent quite a lot of time finding them a proper boarding kennel before I went to Europe, and when I leave here, I'm going to fly to Yellow Knife for ten days, so I'll put them in a boarding kennel again. So taking care of them sometimes is difficult. But it is a responsibility I have accepted. Knowing myself as well as I do, if something happened to the cats, I would say to myself, 'Helen, you're spending more time on airplanes now than you used to, and you always had problems finding good places to leave the cats, so now that they're gone, you've got to be sensible and not replace them.' But then, somewhere, I'd see a scrawny little stray cat that needed a home . . . I guess what it comes down to is this: the cats are good company, and I'm willing to put up with the problems of having them because of the companionship they provide. They're lovable, people enjoy watching them, and they do all sorts of amusing things. If gasoline prices get so high I can't afford to drive my car and tow my trailer, I'll park it at LoWzark (the Loners on Wheels campground) and take airplanes wherever I want to go. But I won't give up my cats even if I do that. They learned how to ride in a car and camp in a trailer; they can learn to fly!"

Chapter Twenty

Getting Along With Each Other

How many times have you heard someone say, "Marriage is a 50/50 proposition"? It might be that while a couple is living together in a normal, workday environment, with at least one of them leaving home every morning for a job—with meals, child-rearing, recreation, house-cleaning, vacations and even TV viewing structured around those jobs. But once a couple joins the full-time RVing lifestyle, their marriage is *not* a "50/50 proposition" any more. It's more of a 70/30 arrangement, with the wife giving her husband all the attention he can soak up and rearranging her life to fit his erratic new schedule.

Eleanor Ratliff, the wife of a retired lawyer, told me in Texas one winter: "The first few months we were full-timing, I thought Paul was going to drive me crazy. He followed me everywhere; he wouldn't let me out of his sight. He insisted that I talk to him constantly. Even if I went to the bathroom, he'd wait for me outside and talk to me through the door. He wouldn't let me do my work in the trailer, he wouldn't let me sit quietly with my needlepoint or a good book, and he really got upset if I sneaked off to the rec hall without him. I was about ready to chuck the whole full-timing thing and go back to an apartment in New York. I even thought of leaving Paul with our daughter for a few months and traveling around the country in a trailer by myself. I was practically a nervous wreck."

She added, "Finally, a fellow whose trailer was parked next to ours—now imagine, we'd been living side by side for three months, and Paul hadn't even spoken to him yet—took pity on me after I told his wife I was going crazy. They had apparently gone through the same sort of thing. He invited Paul to go out into the lagoon fishing with a bunch of guys. Paul at first said he would go because he always liked fishing, but then he said he wouldn't because he didn't want to leave me alone. Alone? Hah! There I was, surrounded by a couple of dozen full-time RVers, all of them nice and friendly, and he was afraid of leaving me alone! He just didn't want me out of his sight: that's what it was. But I told him he'd better go fishing with those men because I was planning a shopping trip to McAllen with a couple of other ladies, and he wasn't welcome to come along!"

She continued, "Well, that fishing trip did it. The men caught a whole lot of fish and had a fish fry that night for everyone in the campground at the rec hall. Paul spent the whole evening laughing and joking with the men, allowing me to be free to do whatever I wanted for the first time in three months. A few of the fellows from the fishing trip invited him to join them the next night for a poker party. Then they got him into a billiard tournament—which he won, by the way! Then they went fishing again. Now, Paul and I see each other in the morning when we get up, at noon for lunch and in the evening for dinner and television, and the rest of the time we're doing our own things, sometimes together and sometimes with other people. I even get a chance to read a book or do needlepoint without interruptions from my darling husband. We're having a blast, all because of that fishing trip. If it hadn't been for that, I'd probably be back in New York right now, bored out of my skull. But that was a year ago, and since then we've traveled over about one-third of the country, and we've got friends everywhere. I have to chuckle when I think back on everything now, because when we pull into a new campground, Paul is the first one outside talking to people and looking for things to do."

Together: Twenty-Four Hours A Day

Like the Ratliffs, many new full-timing couples find difficulty adjusting to the close proximity of their mates and their own lack of outside interests during the first weeks of living in an RV. In their preretirement days, each of them had his or her favorite diversions, hobbies and friends. The husband probably worked at least five days a week at his job, and the wife had her own routine around the house. The husband had special friends at work that he shared common interests with, and the wife had different friends in the neighborhood where they lived. Even while both of them were at home together, they were able to keep out of each other's way

Tom Burrier, Oak Harbor, Washington

What person could resist the lure of a fishing spot like this one on the Buffalo River in Newton County, Arkansas?

and pursue separate interests in different parts of the house. Suddenly, as full-time RVers, they were thrown together, within elbow's distance of each other, in a relatively small recreational vehicle and, nearly always, on a small campsite in the middle of a bunch of strangers. Quickly, they begin to get on each other's nerves, and they discover many opportunities to argue: over destinations, over recreation, over parking the RV, and even over meals and what programs they will watch on TV. They realize for the first time, even though they've been married for thirty years, that the sound of each other's voices grates on their sensitivities. He also plays the radio too loudly, and her sewing machine makes a terrible racket.

More importantly, he's now on her turf! She's always had the house to herself during the daytime and could do whatever she wanted. Now, he's there all the time, getting in her way, insisting that she talk with him and entertain him. He wants to take a nap in the afternoon at the same time she watches her favorite afternoon TV show, and he says he can't sleep with the TV operating. She misses her friends, her family, her neighborhood, her favorite supermarket, her yard, but she's willing to find new interests; her husband, though, doesn't seem to want to leave the trailer, and he wants her with him all the time.

"The wife usually has the biggest adjustment to make when a couple begins full-timing," suggested Laila Rutledge, who began full-timing in 1974 with her husband, Mickey. "There is a certain amount of adjustment required for the husband because he was in the habit of going to work every day, but the wife needs to get away too, and it's usually up to her to adjust to him, rather than him to her. I think each person should have a hobby, such as golf, that allows him or her to get away from the RV for a certain amount of time. A lot of the wives I know have taken up crafts just so they can get away from their husbands and force their husbands to find new interests."

Mickey said he believes it is important for full-timers to buy rigs that are sectionalized so that the couple can escape from each other during periods when weather confines them to the RV. "We've got a TV in our trailer, and if Laila wants to watch soap operas in the afternoon, she can take it into the bedroom and lie down and watch it while I'm in the other end of the trailer working on bookkeeping, taking a nap or doing whatever else I want to."

A few weeks after I interviewed Mickey and Laila, I talked with full-timer Bert Dean at an Outdoor Resorts of America park in south Texas. I asked him if his wife, Greta, had a difficult time adjusting to his being around all the time when they hit the road together in 1975. "Let me tell you something," he said. "The very fact of being together all the time is a key item too many people overlook when they go RVing full-time. This June, Greta and I will celebrate our fortieth anniversary, but before I retired, our lives were almost completely separate. You think that when you're married, you're close to each other. But really, you don't do much together. Then all of a sudden you get popped into an RV, and you're able to reach out and touch your spouse twenty-four hours a day. That is a whole new ball game. You get to know your spouse fully for the first time."

Bert continued, "My wife is the kind of person who never complains. She's a very congenial person; everyone who has ever known her loves her. If there were any problems when we began full-timing, I'm certain I caused them, but she adjusted her life to mine. We started doing a lot of things together, for the first time. Greta loves to play golf, so we started playing more golf than we ever did before. We also took up square dancing and got very involved with the Texas square dancing scene. We just have a great time with each other."

Sam and Glenda Beaideme of Southern California admitted they had some adjustments to make to each other when they began their full-timing lifestyle—but primarily because they both worked at jobs and were accustomed to living independently. "Every now and then, we tend to get on each other's nerves because we live in such a small area, but one of us can always walk outside, get on a bike and go for a ride. Either that, or go for a walk. That's what we do to relieve tension if it ever develops between us," Glenda reported.

Sam said, "Our kids can't believe we get along as well as we do. One of them said, 'Are you telling me you live in that trailer twenty-four hours a day and you don't get at each other's throats?' But we had more arguments when we were at home and both of us were working."

Glenda added, "I think when you're working, there's more tension. Full-timing, you don't have the pressure of jobs, and you're meeting new people all the time."

"The main thing is, we both like the way we live."

"We've both got gypsy blood in us!" Glenda added.

She said, "Our family is all spread out. We can travel from now on just visiting family members all over the country. We always go back to California because Sam's mother is in a convalescent home there, and she's not very well. So that's where we spend most of our stay-put time—maybe a month or two months. The rest of the year, we're on the road."

The Beaidemes' friends, Doris and John Lockwood of Maryland, reported that their adjustment to each other while full-timing was made easier because they worked together in a business for seven years before retiring. "But some adjustment is still required," John emphasized. "You have to be willing to go off and do something by yourself once in awhile because you can't stay together twenty-four hours a day, seven days a week in the trailer. That's why, at rallies we attend she goes to the shows by herself or with some other people, and I stay back at the trailer and relax."

Doris added, "We spent most of last winter in Florida, and while I went to the craft classes and exhibits, he either went fishing or played shuffleboard or did other things. I'm sure that getting away from each other and having separate interests is a problem for most new full-timers, especially if they never worked together the way we did."

John said, "This is a lot more relaxing lifestyle, though, so adjustments are easier to make. When I was working and took a month's vacation, it took me two weeks to settle down to the point where I was really comfortable. Now, I'm comfortable all the time. We don't fight, either. We argued more when we were at home. Now, the only time we fight is when Doris sees me looking at some pretty girls." She laughed and poked him in the ribs.

Ken and Flo Cooper also worked together several years before they became full-timers. "We've always done everything together," Flo reported. "I could see how a couple that had not been together as much as we have—maybe because they both worked and were used to leading separate lives—might have quite an adjustment to make. The women full-timers I've known have tended to get heavily into crafts activities of some kind, and the reason they do that is that they're looking for their own identities and their own diversions apart from their husbands. Just about every woman I've run into on the road does some kind of crafts, whether it's knitting, crocheting, or macrame—*everyone* is doing *something*."

Marriage: "A Job You Work At Every Day"

Separate interests and diversions are, indeed, necessary for full-timers, according to Audrey Klemczak, who joined that lifestyle in 1977 with her husband, Don. "I do think that people need to be away from each other and be by themselves from time to time. You've got to know one another well and recognize each other's moods. I know that Don gets crotchety at times, and when he's like that, I should get away from the motorhome and do something by myself for an hour or so. And if I'm having one of my rotten days, Don should be able to get involved in something that interests him, such as playing golf or walking around. Full-timers should have separate hobbies so that they don't have to be together constantly."

Don said, "My recreation is my motorhome. I could spend most of my time fooling around with it and with our car. I'll give you an example. When we had our Airstream, I wanted to find out if it was really built the way I was told it was. I took one entire section of wall off the inside and looked behind the wall to see what the insulation was like. Then I put the rivets back in and closed it up. I was satisfied with the construction; it was built the way the factory said it was.

"I also like to talk to people. I'll go outside in the morning and start talking to someone for what I think is five minutes, but before I know it, an hour has passed. A lot of people in this park play tennis every day,

Full-time togetherness is one of the joys but also one of the challenges of the RVing way of life.

and they'll play golf once or twice a day. A lot of the people just go for long walks, though, and that's what we do for our exercise."

"The big climax of the day around here is when the mail comes in," Don said. "That sounds dull, but it isn't. Our mail is forwarded to us once a week, but we never know which day it will arrive."

"Don and I get along so well because we're very compatible," Audrey said. "We've been with each other three years now, twenty-four hours a day, but being together all that time has never bothered us. We enjoy each other very much."

One of the happiest full-timing couples I met while researching this book were Jerry and Betty Campbell, who had begun their life on the road together in 1974 and were financing their adventures by working in the offices of campgrounds. I asked them about compatibility on the road, and Betty responded, "For the most part, we get along well together. I read, I sew, and I find other ways to occupy my time. Jerry likes to get on the CB radio and talk with people. He philosophizes at them a little too much sometimes, though."

Jerry added, "I think people should recognize that if they can't get along with each other in an eight-room house, there ain't no way they're going to get along in an eight-foot-wide recreational vehicle."

"I think if there's compatibility in a home," Betty continued, "it should carry over into RVing. I don't care who you are, marriage is a job you work at every day. If you're content in the marriage, it grows and, as you get older, the couple should grow more compatible, not less. Jerry and I live together; we work together, and there is no problem too big for the two of us to overcome together. I think everyone should have interests and do things to make themselves useful, and I also think that a woman should get away from the notion that her retired husband is invading her home. That can never be true, you know, because it's his home too!"

Chapter Twenty-One

When You're Healthy

Alice and Mac McGinleys' fathers both died before reaching retirement age, and the Mississippi couple decided they would prevent that from happening to them by enjoying themselves as much as possible while they were young. They had begun camping as a family in 1960 when Alice was twenty-nine and Mac was thirty-one. They progressed from a folding camper to travel trailers and, along the way, formulated plans to take an early retirement in the mid-1980s after Mac completed twenty years of teaching at Mississippi Junior College. He had already retired in 1966 from the Air Force, so the McGinleys expected to be able to live well on the two retirement incomes and travel widely while still in their fifties.

They spent their 1978 winter vacation in Florida before heading north toward Indiana for a rally of the Holiday Rambler RV Club. On the way, they stopped in Mississippi to visit their daughter briefly. It was fortunate they did. "My daughter is an X-ray technician," Mac explained, "and she had been nagging me for five years to let her take some pictures of me. While we were there, I agreed to let her do it; then we left for Indiana right away without waiting for the results. I guess the good Lord was watching out for us because that night our daughter chased us down and told me not to do *anything*, not even strain myself a little, because I had an aneurysm. So we didn't make it to the rally. I had open-heart surgery instead and, afterward, was medically retired from teaching."

With Mac's teaching career cut shorter than they had planned, the McGinleys faced a decision of how to spend the coming years. After some discussion, they agreed to move up their retirement plans several years and hit the road in their 1978 Holiday travel trailer. For the first few months they traveled, Alice had to do everything—park the trailer, block the wheels, hitch up, unhitch and do all the towing. Frustrated both by the tough job of handling the load equalizer bars and by their trailer's lack of closet space, the McGinleys switched to a 34-foot Holiday fifth-wheel following their first winter as full-timers. When I talked with them during the summer of 1979, Mac said, "Alice still does most of the driving, but I can do some of it now—maybe an hour or two at a time—especially if I use the cruise control."

A year later, I saw Mac in Minnesota at the Holiday club's annual rally. Not only had he recovered satisfactorily from his surgery, but he had also volunteered to help direct rally traffic at the Bemidji fairground. He admitted to enjoying a type of lifestyle that most RVers only aspire to. He was fifty-two years old.

I asked him how he planned his travels, and he said, "We don't go more than 300 miles a day because it's too hard on us and our rig. Unless we are on a specific trip such as going to a rally or on a caravan, we just wing it. We plan ahead, but not very far ahead, because we've discovered that we might just change our minds and go in a different direction. Most of our traveling, though, is geared to Holiday Rambler club activities. Nearly everyone we are with, no matter where we go, has something to do with that club."

Because of Mac's health, the McGinleys traveled most of the first year with other RVers, but occasionally they got off on their own. Once, they were traveling alone when they ran into some unexpected trouble. "We were on our way to a rally, and Alice was doing the driving while I played with the CB radio. I heard a bleep on the CB and, since I knew we were too far from an interstate highway to hear the truckers, I flipped the channels until I caught the tail end of someone telling us we either had a flat tire or our trailer was on fire. Alice pulled over right away and stopped. We had had our trailer serviced about 3,000 miles earlier, but apparently it hadn't been done right, and the bearings and spindle had burned out. There we were on a country road that was about as wide as our trailer, and we had stopped in front of a truck carrying a load of caskets. Of course, I couldn't do anything because of my surgery, and I didn't know what to tell Alice to do. The driver of the truck asked us if he could help, and he took the wheel off the trailer for us. Then, up the road came a trailering friend who had already gone to the campground twenty-six miles away and parked his trailer. He drove back up the mountain, got some able-bodied men and brought them back. They chained up my axle and followed us all the way up to the top of the mountain and helped us set up our rig in the campground. I called my Holiday dealer and then the factory, and a new axle was sent to us. Those other Holidayers installed the axle for me right there on top of the mountain."

Living For Today

Mac and Alice are part of a rather large contingent of couples who are RVing full time both because of and in spite of health setbacks. A fifty-four-year-old man from Iowa who admitted he was dying of cancer told me, "When you're healthy, you feel as if you have your whole life ahead of you, that you can do whatever you want to and earn as much money as you are able to before the time comes when you have to retire. But when your good health is gone, you suddenly realize that all that hard work, all those future years, mean nothing. The word 'today' takes on new meaning, and you have to face the fact that each 'today' might be your last. My wife and I planned to retire and travel full time in our trailer when I reached sixty-two, and we started saving money five years ago to do that; we figured that by the time I retired, we would have such a huge nest egg that we could live comfortably on just the interest income. But last year, when doctors discovered I had cancer, every bit of money we had saved during those five years disappeared in a matter of weeks. The way I look at it, we wasted those five years; we should have taken an early retirement then and done what we wanted to do while we were better able to enjoy ourselves."

He continued, "Now, we're living on the money we got when we sold our home, plus a few minor investments, and whatever occasional work we can pick up. But we're content with the way we're living; we're enjoying each other more than we ever did before, and each day is an adventure for us."

Later, I talked with the man's wife, Kathleen. She asked me not to use her husband's last name because most of their RVing friends did not know that her husband's health was as bad as it was. Tears welled in her eyes and then trickled down her cheeks. "This has been the best year of my life," she said, referring to their months on the road. "I only wish we could have known, years ago, how economically people can live while they're full-timing so that we could have done this earlier. We literally could not have afforded to stay in Iowa and live the way we were, with the doctor and drug bills we have and with the mortgage payments on our house and operating two cars and the heating bills. Even if full-timing weren't as economical as it is, it would have been worth it for us. I don't think I'll ever go back into a house. My husband and I have discussed it, and the way things stand now, after he's gone, I'll keep our Coachmen and our van and stay on the road alone."

She paused, then sobbed quietly for a few minutes while I sat there helplessly, not knowing what to say or do. She brushed the tears away at last and smiled through the sadness. "It's been great! It really has. The doctors gave my husband three months to live, and that's when we decided to sell everything and live in our trailer. That was nine months ago. I think sometimes my husband is stronger now than he was then, but I suppose he really isn't. Remember when he said each 'today' could be his last? Well, to us, each 'today' is a bonus. A gift of life. And I'm ever so thankful for each one."

Almost a year has passed since I talked with the Iowa couple as they paused in their travels at a KOA campground on the outskirts of McAllen, Texas. Kathleen promised to call me when her husband's "todays" ended. I haven't heard from her yet.

STAYING HEALTHY

While full-time RVing obviously has great therapeutic value, there are things way-of-lifers can do to improve their own chances of staying healthy. Like any other lifestyle, full-timing has its built-in disadvantages, and some of those are health-related. Beginning full-timers, especially, tend to have poor eating habits and become too sedentary. They drive long hours behind the wheel of a tow vehicle or motorhome, and that can lead to blood clotting and circulatory problems. They should exercise more regularly, and make a point of stopping about every two hours while they're driving in order to walk around. Middle aged and older full-timers tend to increase their salt intakes too much and maintain too high a level of fats and cholesterol in their diets.

A poor diet can cut antibody levels and lower an RVer's resistance, thus making him an easier target for influenza, common colds, pneumonia and communicable diseases. Dieticians recommend that people the age of most full-timers should eat less red meat, poultry skins, whole milk and cheese, and consume more fiber by eating whole grain cereals and breads, fresh fruits and vegetables. RVers also should eat a light breakfast and lunch and limit their caloric intakes at evening meals. They should be aware that they are more susceptible to heat exhaustion, especially in temperatures above 98 degrees, which can be very debilitating. They should wear loose-fitting clothes in warm climates to allow heat to escape from their bodies, and they should shade their faces with headgear. Older RVers should know that in cold climates, their appetites will increase, they will need more oxygen, they can expect to have a higher incidence of arthritis and that their resistance to disease will be lowered. They should not only keep fully stocked first-aid kits in their rigs with them, but they also should carry copies of their own medical records in case of emergencies.

One health-related problem that faces many full-timers, and for which there does not seem to be an easy solution, is filling drug prescriptions. Don Klemczak, who began full-timing at the age of forty-three when a heart condition forced him to retire early, said prescriptions can sometimes be a tough problem to solve because a prescription issued by a doctor in one state often cannot be filled by a druggist in another state, and many druggists will not accept prescriptions from physicians that are unfamiliar to them. Fortunately for Don, he spends his winters in a popular retirement area of Florida where pharmacists are so accustomed to seeing out-of-state prescriptions that they usually will fill a drug order after calling his physician in Michigan for verification.

Walt Consider, an Ohio full-timer who must take high blood pressure medication twice a day, has another solution. "Being that we're from a small town where we knew everybody, the druggist there is a friend of ours, so I'll just go to him and tell him in advance that I want a large quantity of my medication, and, when I make my annual visit to my hometown doctor, he'll give me a prescription for enough medication to last six or seven months. He'll also give me a prescription for a thirty or forty-day supply of medication in case something happens to my regular supply. In an emergency, I can find a place that will fill that prescription until I can get some more medication. Then too, I can always call my hometown druggist, give him my prescription number and ask him to mail the medication to me."

Many full-timers fifty-five years of age or older have joined the American Association of Retired Persons because of the unique drug service the organization offers. Members can purchase drugs by mail at about half the cost charged by local pharmacies, and the AARP will mail the medication for pickup at whatever mail drop is stipulated.

Planning For Adventure

Charles Mogg, a Michigan full-timer with a heart problem, tries to keep a six-month supply of prescription drugs with him at all times because he and his wife Helen travel extensively. "I also try to make it back to Michigan every three to five months for my checkups, but if anything goes wrong while we're on the road, no matter whether we're in Michigan or Alaska, the first thing I do is head for the local hospital. I know that if I'm going to live, the hospital may be the only chance I've got. If we're in any town a couple of days, we'll make sure we know the fastest way to get to the hospital."

Chuck retired from set-up work at the Chevrolet Engine Plant in Michigan when he was only forty-five years old. "That was 4½ years ago," he told me when I met him at a Midwest Good Sam Club rally in the spring of 1980. "I had open heart surgery, and the doctors took a 2½-pound aneurysm off the side of my heart, and I wasn't allowed to go back to work. We started full-timing as soon after my surgery as we could. The Lord must have been looking out for us, and He gave us the opportunity to do this. So I'm looking forward to tomorrow, now, but I don't worry about next year. I'm living every day one at a time, and I'm living each day the same as the last.

"I really believe people who want to become full-time RVers should quit what they're doing and hit the road while they're young and can do it instead of saying, 'My God, I've got to make it financially. I've got three jobs, and I've got to earn extra money because the kids need shoes and the wife needs a new house.' I think our kids thought we were kind of foolish when we told them what we were going to do. They figured we'd never do it. We've been doin' it for more than a year now, though, so I think they've figured out we were committed to it."

Chuck added, "When the doctors told me I couldn't do any kind of work—I figured there was no use staying at home; we might as well go on the road. I knew that way, I could work with the Good Sam Club and maybe help other people because of what I know about camping and rallies and RVs. We go to a lot of Samborees, and I can't tell you how fast the time flies. There's something new every day. We're curious about what's over the next hill, I guess."

The Moggs sold their farm in Michigan and bought a mobile home. They lived in it for a short while before deciding it was too restricting; then they bought a 40-foot Kountry Aire fifth-wheel trailer and turned their mobile home over to their daughter. While they lived in the mobile home only a couple of years, they now feel, in retrospect, that it allowed them to adjust from moving out of a large house into smaller quarters and was kind of a step toward their move into an RV.

"We moved into the trailer a year ago in February [1979], and the first month we were in Michigan, we almost froze to death. We decided to get out of there and head for Florida. The trailer was so buried in the snow, however, that we couldn't get it out, so we got into the car and drove to Florida and stayed in motels. I told Helen that was the last time

I'd ever do that! The people just aren't friendly, and I can understand why. You have to start looking for a motel room at three o'clock in the afternoon. If you're lucky, you'll find something by seven o'clock, but it'll probably be some kind of flophouse that you'll be charged $49.50 a night for. Everybody else who is staying there kind of grunts at you because they went through the same thing and they're upset. Then you go to a restaurant to eat. We went into one that had a sign out front saying, 'Pancakes, all you can eat, for $1.50.' They brought out a 12- or 14-inch platter, and in the middle of it were three pancakes about four inches in diameter, and they were as thin as a sheet of paper.

"When we came home from Florida, we stayed in our trailer three weeks until we could get it out of the snow, and then we left for Texas. We went to the Texas International Samboree, the Pennsylvania rally, caravaned to Ohio for the state Samboree, then to the Michigan Samboree at Coldwater, down to Indiana for the state Samboree there and back to Michigan again. I suppose you could say that Samborees are our hobby!

"Last fall, at the Florida state Samboree, we met some Florida Good Sam members named Louis and Bonnie Parker. Before we left, they said, 'Why don't you come back down and park in our yard? See if you like it, and if you don't you can leave. If you do like it, you can stay as long as you want.' Well, we went down there again about the first of December, and we stayed there for 6½ months—so you could say we kind of liked it! And those people—if they weren't the best I've ever met—they certainly were in the top five. It's that way with all the Good Samers, though; everyone I've ever met at the Samborees has been as friendly as if he'd known me all his life."

When I talked with the Moggs, they were making plans for a big adventure, determined not to let Chuck's health problems hamper them too much. Chuck was shopping for a pickup camper he could put on the bed of his Ford truck so that they could travel from Michigan to California more economically. "Now, I realize that going from a 40-foot fifth-wheel to an 11-foot camper will be a big adjustment," Chuck said, "but we're on a fixed income, and we've got to cut our gasoline expenses as much as we can in order to be able to afford that trip. I don't feel that it's worth it to go to California if we can't afford to take side trips to see what's in that part of the country. We don't want to limit ourselves to what we can see from the expressways."

Although Chuck receives a disability pension from General Motors, it is not enough money to allow them to travel extensively and live extravagantly. Therefore, he limits his driving to 400 miles a day, and he and Helen cut expenses any ways they can. "While we're traveling, we sleep in rest areas or truck stops, and we eat strictly in the unit. We don't need any facilities because we've got all of our own. When we traveled to Texas last year, we were on the road five days, but the only thing we bought was gasoline. With our rig, I know I'm going to use thirteen gallons of gasoline for every 100 miles we drive. We carry a big gas tank in the back of our pickup because we know we can't pull into just every little service station with a truck and forty feet of trailer. But we never fill up our gas tank because I feel it costs us too much to haul it around; 150 gallons of gas adds 1,200 pounds to the weight of our rig. So I buy just enough gas to allow us to travel 300 or 400 miles."

EYE STRAIN, HEART STRAIN

In my younger days as a newspaperman, I would work all day Friday, through half the night and then hit the road for a weekend camping/fishing trip. Sometimes, I'd drive all night, fish frantically for two days with very little time out for sleep and then drive back home Sunday night in time to catch a few winks before going to work Monday morning. Over the years, I was astounded to discover that I was less able to judge distances at night while driving, especially if I were not well rested. By the time I was forty years old, I had all but given up nighttime driving, partly because I didn't enjoy it any more and partly because the natural aging process had taken a noticeable toll of my night vision.

In recent years, vision experts have learned a great deal about the aging process of people's eyes. They've discovered that eyes do not "wear out," as was once believed, but that eyes do undergo natural changes that place limitations on older persons, especially older drivers. With aging, for example, the eye's focusing ability decreases, and changing focus from distant to near objects and vice versa becomes more difficult. After age forty-five, most people need glasses to see well either at a distance or near, or both, according to the American Optometric Association. One vision change common with aging is when the pupils of the eyes become smaller and the crystalline lenses inside the eyes become less clear, causing a need for more light than before in order to see well. The optometric association also reported, "As the crystalline lenses age, they scatter light entering the eye, sometimes producing a fogging of vision. Bright headlight glare may then cause discomfort and make night driving more difficult." Reaction time tends to slow with age, too, so the association advises older drivers not to impair their reactions further with alcohol, carbon monoxide, drugs or an overly full stomach. Further, "The ability to see to the side while looking straight ahead (peripheral vision) may diminish with age. Loss of peripheral vision, with loss of visual sharpness, can handicap a driver." In addition, older drivers may find it more difficult to distinguish quickly and accurately between the colors of traffic signals because the lights appear to be dimmer.

In an October, 1980, background report to the news media about the vision problems of older adults, the American Optometric Association warned that virtually everyone over the age of fifty suffers from a vision disability called presbyopia. "Presbyopia," the report said, "is a gradual decline in the eyes' ability to focus sharply and clearly on near objects, particularly at a normal reading distance. It is not an eye disease, nor is farsightedness, with which it is sometimes confused. Although presbyopia seems to develop suddenly, it actually starts at about age ten but usually is not noticeable until between age forty and forty-five. Then, changes may appear to be more rapid but, in reality, they are not. The most common sign of presbyopia is blurred vision at a normal reading distance, with a tendency to hold reading material farther away. Eye fatigue and headaches are common when attempting to do close work. To compensate for the effects of presbyopia, doctors of optometry prescribe reading glasses, bifocals, trifocals or contact lenses. Presbyopia cannot be stopped, and periodic lens changes are necessary as it progresses. At about age sixty-five or seventy, however, vision sometimes stabilizes and the need for lens changes may be less frequent."

As for nearsightedness, the association said about 30% of all older adults have that condition. Nearsighted people in their early forties often think their vision is improving because they may be able to see better for reading and other close work without glasses than with them, but the association said, "This is caused by the onset of presbyopia and is temporary." Farsighted persons are usually the first to notice the early effects of presbyopia and think their farsightedness is getting worse; such persons may eventually need bifocals containing one prescription for distance vision and a stronger one for near vision, the association reported.

Older adults with good vision can help maintain it through diet, since it is known that Vitamin A deficiencies can cause night blindness, and vision experts believe there may be other ties between vitamins and eye problems. "Proper nutrition is also important in the control of diabetes and high blood pressure, both of which contribute to potentially blinding retinal disorders," the optometrists said.

The association's report revealed that the most common traffic violations of older drivers are associated with failure to yield right-of-way, improper lane changes, passing, turning and expressway driving. "Since about 90% of driving decisions are based on what drivers see or think they see, changes in vision due to aging are often to blame," the association stated. The organization urged older drivers to compensate for such changes by seeking regular vision examinations to maintain proper day and night driving vision; taking time to adjust to new eyeglass or contact lens prescriptions before driving; avoiding frames with wide side pieces that may block side vision; wearing quality sunglasses on sunny or bright days; refusing to wear sunglasses or tinted lenses when driving at night; avoiding driving at dusk; reducing speeds at night; keeping head and eyes moving while driving, checking rearview mirrors and the sides of the road frequently; keeping pace with the average traffic flow; avoiding, if possible, stopping alongside a highway; choosing a car with a clear rather than tinted windshield, and knowing the effects on vision of any drugs taken before driving.

The optometric association pointed out that drugs of all types have physiological effects on driving ability but that certain prescribed medications used to combat diseases, nervous tension and fatigue may interfere with both muscular coordination and clearness of vision, and possibly judgments related to contrast, distance and color. "Some drugs that directly affect vision are barbituates, narcotics, tranquilizers, patent medicines used to assist or resist sleep, and bromides used for sedative purposes. Antihistamines used to combat allergies and colds can cause sufficient drowsiness to render the driver unsafe, but common colds or hay fever can also blur vision dangerously. Even aspirin, when extensively used, can adversely affect vision."

To save money on eyeglasses, keep these facts in mind: Large lenses usually cost more than smaller ones. Tinted lenses cost more than clear lenses. Cataract lenses and special lenses such as "invisible bifocals" are more expensive. Designer signature frames are higher priced than equally fashionable frames without such signatures. Discontinued frame models, while not always the most fashionable, can be a good buy for reading glasses or spares, but replacement parts may be impossible to find. Also remember that Medicare limits vision care coverage to the diagnosis and treatment of eye diseases and the providing of glasses following cataract surgery.

Campaigning For Health Care

While vision problems certainly should be of concern to full-timers, at least they are usually not, in themselves, life-threatening. Heart attacks, however, are another matter.

When the Connecticut Good Sam Club held its state rally at Salem during the summer of 1980, full-timers Hal and Penny Gaynor put on a show with their Trailering Safety Clinic. The next day, the Gaynors donated a resuscitation training machine to a local volunteer fire department so that firemen could be taught how to revive heart attack and drowning victims. I found out later that Hal and Penny had paid for the machine, which cost a couple of hundred dollars, themselves even though they, like most full-timers, were living on a limited income. I didn't know Hal and Penny at the time, and I wondered if they had an ulterior motive for making such an unselfish donation. It turned out, they did; they are waging a personal campaign to make RVers more aware of the need everywhere for special health treatment equipment.

Here's the story Hal told me later:

"A fellow who was parked next to us a year or so ago was getting ready to break camp and leave for Canada. He was having trouble with his hitch, so I said, 'Don't worry about it. I'll hook it up for you after dinner.' He thanked me and said he wanted to go swimming first anyway. It was about six o'clock, and Penny and I were sitting in our trailer eating dinner, when we heard a commotion outside. I looked out, and there was a whole mob of people behind our trailer. That fellow had tried to hook up his trailer by himself, and he had a heart attack. No one knew what to do. We sure didn't. Someone called the rescue squad, but by the time the ambulance arrived, it was too late. We started talking to one of the men from the rescue squad and asked him if there was anything we could have done that we didn't do. He said, 'Well, possibly if someone had known CPR [cardio-pulmonary resuscitation], that might have helped, but we can't be sure. There's a four-minute period after a heart attack that sometimes can make all the difference if CPR is administered.' "

Hal continued, "That bothered us for a long time. And when we came back the following fall, we looked up the local Red Cross and said we were interested in learning about CPR. The Red Cross people were delighted and said, 'We're going to give you a course second to none. They put us through a first aid program, then they sent us to a different part of the county every night so we could learn a different part of the course. Now, as we travel around the country, we talk about CPR and encourage people to take the course, and gradually we've also begun promoting equipment such as the resuscitation machine. This rally represents the tenth anniversary of the Connecticut Good Sam Club, so we thought it would be an appropriate time for us to give the local firemen that equipment in the name of the club. Next season, we're going to start pushing blood pressure equipment, and we'll donate a few of those to trailer clubs so RVers can take their own blood pressure and become more aware of their own physical health. We also push oxygen kits, and we carry one ourselves."

Penny recalled, "We were on a caravan to Wyoming once, and a man traveling with us had a heart attack because he tried to change a flat tire on his trailer by himself without asking anybody to help him." Hal and another RVer loaded the man into a truck and headed for the nearest hospital.

"We had to go fourteen miles down a dirt road, then twenty-eight miles on the interstate to the town with a hospital. Of course, we kept calling on the CB to keep the road ahead of us clear, and we kept him alive with that little oxygen kit that I had."

Hal added, "The same thing happened once in Michigan. That time it was a woman who had a heart attack. We keep trying to convince all the Rving clubs to carry oxygen kits to rallies with them. But I don't know . . . here we are at a big rally where, just yesterday, a man we know very well had a heart attack and had to be rushed to the hospital. And the club doesn't have an oxygen kit. I've got the only one in the whole campground."

Chapter Twenty-Two

Time To Stop
And Smell The Flowers

The full-time RVers of this world are truly blessed! As I am writing these words, it is mid-October. The cold north winds are blowing toward us from the vast expanse of Lake Michigan, reminding us that summer is long gone and winter is near at hand. Our Holiday Rambler motorhome is parked out in the driveway, stocked with supplies and ready to go but, alas, our four children have school tomorrow, and I have several magazine article deadlines drawing near. We know that most of our full-timing friends are already on their way south toward the snow-belt—and we won't see them again until next spring—while we await the first snowfall.

If only we had the time . . .

Time, after all, is the key to leading The Good Life. Full-time RVers have learned to put aside all those things that keep time from working against them, that keep them tied to a house and a job and a climate they don't like. They're making time for adventure. For travel. For relaxation. For meeting new people and seeing new sights and talking with old friends. For enjoying a special, unique lifestyle.

A Composite Couple

Let's create a composite of all the full-time RVing couples in America. Their names are Robert and Wanda Able, and he retired about a year ago, at age sixty, from a middle-management level job with an automobile manufacturing company. Wanda is fifty-seven and four times a grandmother. They were active RVers for seven years before Robert's retirement, members of the Good Sam Club and once were joint chapter presidents of an RV factory-sponsored owner's club. Their three children—two sons and a daughter—are scattered around the country, and only one made his home in the Midwest where the Ables have lived all their lives. The Ables own a 32-foot travel trailer—their third—that was two years old when they joined the ranks of the full-time RVers; they tow it with a pickup truck that Robert bought just before he retired.

Income from Robert's pension fund and interest on investments totaled just over $700 a month when he and Wanda began full-timing. They decided against selling their family home in Indianapolis because they thought they would use it as a home base, and they also wanted a place to return to if their full-timing efforts did not work out. They left home in June, two months after Robert's retirement party, and traveled east through New England, south through the Smoky Mountains and then to South Carolina, where they spent the winter in two different campgrounds. They had already decided to try full-timing for one year and, if they didn't like it, return home and consider starting a small business. The year passed far more quickly than they expected it would, but in June, they reluctantly drove back to Indianapolis.

As they approached the outskirts of their neighborhood, they were suddenly glad to be home. They looked forward to seeing their house once again, to sleeping in their familiar beds, to puttering in their back yard. But they were shocked when they saw their house. Paint was peeling from all the trim, and a heavy wind had blown several shingles off the roof. A downspout was hanging from the gutter, swaying in the breeze. The neighbor boy they had paid to care for the lawn had not done a very good job. Weeds were growing in Wanda's flower beds, and the grass looked as if it had not been cut for three weeks. A heavy limb had fallen from a large tree in front of the house, and it was blocking the driveway, seemingly announcing to the world that the Able house was empty and fair game for vandals and burglars. Inside everything was as they left it except for the stale, musty odor and the cave-like darkness and cold. Robert turned on the furnace, but discovered that the water heater was out of commission and would have to be replaced. The back yard looked like a jungle, and the patio cover had fallen down. Wanda shouted for Robert, and when he rushed to see what was the matter, she showed him evidence that mice had spent the winter inside the mattress of their double bed.

For the next month, the Ables worked around the house, repairing damages, replacing the water heater, mattress and patio cover and man-

Full-timers explore the solitude of a redwood forest at an unhurried pace.

icuring their front and back yards. Friends and relatives called and stopped by and asked about their travels, and the Ables found themselves reliving their adventures of the last year one by one. Every conversation included the same question: "Where are you off to next?" One afternoon Robert realized he was spending more and more time making improvements on his trailer and less and less time puttering around in the yard. Then came the day when the camera shop called and said the Ables' color slides were ready to be picked up. Wanda and Robert went through the slides three times that night, recalling their year on the road more vividly than ever as the images flashed on the screen in color. When the last slide had been viewed for the third time, Robert shut off the projector and sat there silently. Then he and Wanda looked at each other covertly, and they both laughed.

Two months later, they were on the road again. They had sold their house on a land contract basis, and the 10% interest they would receive from the sale would increase their monthly income to more than $1,000 a month—an amount the Ables knew would allow them to travel quite comfortably on a year-around basis. Most of their furniture also had been disposed of during a gigantic garage sale/auction, although they put some favorite pieces in storage, along with some other belongings, and gave the rest to their youngest son and his wife.

Now, the Ables follow the sun. They plan to spend one winter in Florida, another in Texas and a third in Arizona so they will have a basis for comparison when they shop for a lot on which to park the mobile home that they intend to buy and use as a home base. They've learned that they don't spend all of the income they receive every month, so they're also considering buying a condominium campsite where they can park their trailer whenever the mood strikes them. They enjoy camping at KOA parks and Safari campgrounds, but they also like to experience the solitude of a forested state or federal park occasionally, and they camp in parks without hookups sometimes in order to save a few extra dollars for their condominium kitty. In Florida, they pick beans, tomatoes, squash and peppers for ten cents a pound, and in Texas they glean free onions, potatoes and carrots after asking farmers for permission to do so. They eat a lot of fresh fish these days because Robert has discovered he had a lot of hidden fishing talent. They also like to take part in campground bingo contests and craft classes. Wanda lost nine pounds last winter by attending morning exercise sessions at Florida KOA park. Next summer, the Ables plan to drive to California to visit their oldest son, his wife and the two grandchildren they've never seen.

They have only one regret about full-time RVing: they wish they had begun doing it sooner. And they offer this advice to anyone who is contemplating joining the ranks of the full-time RVers: "Do it as soon as you can. Don't put it off. If you can swing it, do it now!"

FINDING THE TIME

I have been an active RVer since the mid-1960s, and today, as a staff member of the *Trailer Life* family of publications, I probably travel more in various kinds of RVs than most full-timers do in their private rigs. I drive the same highways the full-timers do; I camp in the same parks; I meet a lot of the same people. I even attend RV rallies on occasion. But full-time RVers do something I don't do; something I *can't* do, but wish I could. They take time to stop and smell the flowers.

If I only had the time . . .

Edith Lane, another *Trailer Life* writer, said it best back in 1977 in one of her monthly "Lady Alone" columns: "A few times I have managed to slow myself down and to amble along a backroad just looking at things. There is much to be said for ambling. It takes less gas, is more relaxing and along the way are many odd and curious things to be observed. Even the people going about their daily tasks seem relaxed and unhurried. One can find roadside stands where produce or souvenirs are displayed, rock shops or bait stores or little restaurants featuring home-cooked specialties of the region. These places frequently have much to offer besides the things they sell. Often the proprietors are friendly, gregarious people, with much local knowledge, and are eager to pass it on to an interested traveler who expresses curiosity."

Full-time RVers have time to do things like that. As full-timer Jerry Campbell told me, "I don't have anything *but* time."

Edith, founder of the nationwide Loners on Wheels organization, wrote, "Even exploring a great city can be fascinating, when you can do it leisurely. Many of us have lived our lives in cities and were eager to get away from them. But how different it can be when one stops to visit a city when there are no deadlines to meet—especially during a Sunday or holiday when all the workers are at home and everything is uncrowded and quiet! Have you ever walked down Wall Street in New York, or Montgomery Street in San Francisco, on a weekend? The stillness, the emptiness of the streets between the empty, towering buildings is like a different world from the one I knew when I spent a third of every weekday of my life there! Recently . . . I dawdled along from one fishing village to another along the Gulf coast, then followed the spring up through the lovely wooded section of eastern Texas and Arkansas, watching the leafing-out of the trees and the blooming of the dogwoods and wildflowers, as each hundred miles showed a different stage of the season unfolding. I took my cue from the way nature phases in spring; I avoided hurrying and absorbed nature's offerings leisurely."

Full-time RVers can do things like that every day . . . Gene and Luisa Woods are two of the best known full-timers in America, due in part to their extremely popular monthly column in *Trailer Life* called "Full Time On the Go." In the September, 1979 issue, Gene told about a relaxing campout in the Feather River country near Oroville, California. "The mood here is peaceful. It is quiet and serene, just the sort of place to recharge the batteries . . . I have slung Luisa's hammock in a shady spot where she reads, watches the birds and squirrels and takes afternoon naps . . . I have had a book on the back burner for some time now, and if it is ever to be finished, I must have lots of quiet and a 'happy' place to write. This is it. They have a good library in the town of Oroville, and I have already spent many hours of research . . . there is a time to live and a time to die, and there are a certain unknown number of years for each of us in our retirement days, if we live that long. One cannot postpone these years for a better time in America. You must live them right after the work days are over. For us, that is now. We are living the final years of the Great American Dream."

THE LIFESTYLE

Walt and Charlotte Consider, formerly of Ohio, are among the thousands of other full-timers who are living that dream. I talked to them in Minnesota exactly one year after they had joined the RVing lifestyle. "What made you decide to do it?" I asked 60-year-old Walt.

He answered simply, "I just wanted to get out while I could still enjoy myself."

"But you started full-timing during the summer of 1979 in the middle of a gasoline availability crisis. Didn't that frighten you?"

"Yes, and no," Walt answered. "Shortly after we retired, we left for Nova Scotia. It's only a 5½-hour drive from home to Ontario, and since we knew we wouldn't have trouble finding gasoline in Canada, we drove to Nova Scotia through Ontario and Quebec. When we came back down into the U.S., we found that there weren't enough people in New Hampshire, Vermont and Maine buying gas, and the service stations there were really hurting. I drove into one gas station and asked the owner if he'd take Master Charge or Visa, and he said, 'I'll take anything I can get my hands on.' Tourism there was down about 60% because people were afraid they wouldn't be able to buy gas."

"Since then, of course, the price of gasoline has increased quite a lot," I pointed out. "Has it affected your travels?"

"No," he said. "I converted my tow vehicle to run on propane, which is thirty or forty cents a gallon cheaper than gasoline. And, I'm certain propane will still be available if our President and Congress ever decide to ration gasoline."

Walt retired early from the installation department of the Bell System's Western Electric Company in order to fulfill his and Charlotte's dream of traveling throughout the country. "We did a lot of preplanning," Charlotte said, "but we haven't carried through with most of those plans because we've gotten sidetracked."

Walt said, "What we were going to do was travel the rally circuit the first year and camp with friends down the East Coast to Florida, and we haven't done that. But being on the road full-time is better than we thought it would be."

I asked why it was better, and Walt said he and Charlotte meet more new friends, as well as some old ones, than they expected they would, especially among the ranks of the Holiday Rambler Club, the Good Sam Club and among former Bell Systems employees. "There are a lot of Bell Systems employees around the country that have little Pioneer emblems on their RVs. The Pioneer emblem means that person has at least eighteen years with the Bell System. No matter where we are, if we see a Pioneer emblem, we'll stop and talk."

Both Walt and Charlotte tow their 32-foot trailer. "I made a good deal," Walt explained. "Our marriage is a 50/50 proposition. I tow half the time, and she tows half the time. As long as I don't have to cook a meal now and then, that's okay. But I think I found my calling anyway—I take out the garbage."

Charlotte said, "We like to cook out on our portable gas grill where we can't have an open fire, but otherwise we try to cook over a campfire."

The Considers reported that they follow "a very strict budget." Walt explained: "When I was working, we were in a position where, if we saw something we wanted, we'd just buy it. Now that we're on a fixed income, we have to give up some of those extra goodies we'd been accustomed to buying."

"There's No Competition"

Don and Audrey Klemczak also experienced quite a change in their life-style when they began RVing full-time in 1977. They had camped actively for 4½ years, but the idea of full-timing was something they rather hoped to consider in the distant future. Severe health problems changed all that, though, by forcing Don to retire from his engineering job at the age of forty-three. "We didn't really know what to do," Don recalled. "We had a motorhome at the time, so we had to decide whether to keep our house or start RVing full-time. My wife was working, but we knew we couldn't maintain the house on what she was earning, and I was unable to do any repair work, so we decided to try full-timing for a while. We listed our house, sold it and moved out in twelve days. We found ourselves sitting in a 29-foot motorhome with a car in tow behind us."

Audrey said, "We probably could have kept the house and lived there, but it would have been difficult for us to keep the motorhome too. And if we had, we wouldn't have had any money to travel."

"We thought we'd try full-timing a year and, if we didn't like it, we'd buy another house," Don said. "But now thirty-seven months have rolled by, and we haven't even entertained the thought of buying another house."

"It was the best decision we ever made," Audrey stated. "Don has never felt better in his life."

And if Audrey ever gets bored, she knows she can always find a temporary job because of her accounting background. "When you're not making a career out of what you're doing, you can do anything," Audrey emphasized. "It's a lot of fun working at various jobs, too. There's no competition involved. It's a whole different—and better—attitude toward working."

Audrey and Don were in their Blue Bird Wanderlodge, parked on a condominium campsite they had bought a year earlier at the Outdoor Resorts of America complex near Orlando. "I already know Orlando like the back of my hand," said Don, "so now it's time for us to go someplace else. We'll put our lot up for rent while we're gone and get some income from it. Most of the people in this park, though, are people who like to spend their whole winter here and see friends they made from years before."

I asked, "Did you ever consider that you might have difficulty selling this lot if you decide to relocate?"

Don answered, "Well, no, we never thought that because the need for these lots is so great. There are more people around looking for them than there are vacancies. We didn't think about buying this strictly because we felt we could make money from selling it, but because we wanted a guaranteed spot to park near Orlando."

Audrey said, "It's no different than buying a home. If you want to sell it eventually, you have to run the risk that the market might be down."

Don added, "We bought our first lot [in Michigan] just so we'd have someplace to go for three holidays before I retired. We could never find a place where we liked to camp, so I decided we should buy a place that would provide that, plus possibly bring in enough rent to take care of its maintenance. As luck would have it, I was forced into retirement that same year, so that lot became a summer haven for us. We didn't buy a lot in Florida right away because we weren't sure what area we liked best. Then last year we decided we liked central Florida, so we bought this lot."

"Have you figured how much rental income you receive from the Florida lot?" I asked.

"The maintenance fee here is $35 a month," said Audrey, "and we have to pay for the electricity used. Last year we used this lot all winter and rented it out the rest of the year, and it cost us only $20 for the entire year."

Don said, "Ours is a very relaxing type of full-timing. We'll go someplace and play bingo one night and then go to dinner another place the next night. We're going to a rally of the Blue Bird club next week at Lake

Okeechobee. It's great to be a member of a club like that because then you can plan your winter or summer travels around the rallies. If the club has its national rally in Nevada this summer, for example, we'll start out there in February even though we won't have to be there until July. We've got all the time we need to get there. People can't really appreciate the meaning of freedom until they've been full-time RVers."

He added, "What a person does every month depends upon his income; that's what gauges the kind of full-timer he is. There are people living on everything from $200 a month to $2,000 a month, but they're all enjoying themselves, each in his own way. Full-timing is a state of mind. You can make it as bad as you want it to be or as good as you want it to be. There are days we sit around and get bored; I'm hesitant to believe anyone who says he never gets bored. The day we're bored is the day we take advantage of the $1.50 matinee at the movie theater."

The Klemczaks began full-timing in a Sportscoach motorhome, switched to an Airstream travel trailer and then to their used Blue Bird Wanderlodge. Although the huge gasoline tank on their coach provides them with a 600-mile driving range, Don said, "The longest distance we've traveled in the last couple of years has been about 400 miles in one day. Generally speaking, we cover 250 to 300 miles a day when we're traveling. We drive right at 55 mph, and we find that distance and speed are very comfortable for us."

"We love the way we live," Audrey added. "I wouldn't change it for anything else. There are drawbacks, of course, as with any other style of life, and I can appreciate it when people hesitate going into full-timing. People have often asked me if I think they should do it, and I've always said, 'If you possibly can, lease your home out for a year and try it, and then make the decision.'"

ASPIRANTS TO THE GOOD LIFE

At the annual Mini Samboree of the Michigan Good Sam Club, vacationers Carl and Elsa Smith of Georgia parked their new Travco motorhome next to the Jayco fifth-wheel trailer owned by Jerry and Helen Garrett of Michigan. The two couples struck up an acquaintance and discovered they had more in common than being Good Sam members: they were all aspiring full-time RVers. The five of us gathered in the Garretts' trailer for a chat about full-timing, and I asked Jerry, "Are you looking forward to it very much?"

Jerry responded, "I've got one daughter still at home. She's nineteen, and she's getting married this fall. The minute she says 'I do' we're leaving! By the first of November, we'll be full-timers. We're not going to sell our house; our daughter and her husband will live in it. I was a supervisor at General Motors, and I figured on retiring this month when I'm sixty, but they offered me an early retirement opportunity, so I got out six months sooner. Now we're counting on being in California in November, and we'll be in Pasadena for the Rose Parade."

I asked, "What have you done to prepare for full-timing?"

"A year ago Helen and I took a course on retirement at Lansing Community College. A stockbroker, a lawyer, a nurse and people from Social Security came in to talk to us about different aspects of retiring. One of the questions I was asked was, 'What are you going to do if there's gas rationing?' I said, 'No problem. I'll just sit at the campsite until I can get enough gas to move on.' The same thing with the price of gasoline. I know how much income I'll have, and just so much of that will go toward gasoline. Also, I'm in the process of setting up a trailer pad at the house. I'll put in a sewer line and a water line and electricity. Then, if I'm running short of money, I can pull in there and park, with full hookups, and it won't cost me anything until I can build up my finances." He said he and Helen planned to live on $856 a month while full-timing.

I asked Carl and Elsa if they had estimated how high their expenses would be when they began full-timing, and Elsa answered, "We'll be able to spend $100 a day [$3,000 a month]. That includes medical expenses and a fund for vehicle breakdowns and replacements. I'm going to make sure we have something in reserve in case something happens. All that's holding us back is my ninety-year-old mother, who is bedridden."

Carl added with a grin, "That and convincing ourselves to walk away and leave all our property."

Elsa agreed. "It's quite hard to think about leaving a home you've had for thirty-nine years and deciding what you're going to take with you that you might use full-timing. This is what I'm going through right now. I'm getting ready for a rummage sale. I told both my daughters to take whatever they wanted. One daughter just bought a new house, so she took everything she could get to furnish that house, and then she had to bring some of it back because she took too much!"

I asked Elsa, "Where do you want to go, and what do you expect to see after you're full-timing?"

"I want to see all of the U.S.—every corner of it," she said. "That's all I care about seeing, though. We have a friend who retired and went to Africa; they've also made three or four trips to Alaska. But I don't want to travel that way. When we drove to Michigan, we cut off the highway and traveled the backroads. We took it slowly and saw some beautiful country. And in doing that, we met people like these people—the Garretts—that we feel now like we've known all our lives. We camped in northern Georgia, where we didn't know a soul, and someone built a bonfire so we went out and said hello. We talked and played cards until one o'clock in the morning, and they invited us to join their group."

Helen suggested, "There's something else to consider when you go full time, and that's your duties at church or with organizations. I'm going to have to give those up, and face the fact that I'm going to be away from my children and my friends."

THE WINTER TEXANS

Like many Midwesterners, when Frank Salerno retired from his government job at Chicago's O'Hare Field in 1976, he and his wife, Agnes, went to Florida for the winter. But they kept hearing stories about the warm breezes and the white sand beaches of south Texas, so the following year they checked out the Rio Grande Valley. They were so enthralled with life there that they bought a condominium campground lot and joined the ranks of the Winter Texans. The Texas communities of Harlingen, Brownsville and McAllen attract an estimated 100,000 out-of-staters into the Rio Grande Valley each year, and businesses have geared their whole economy to the people they call Winter Texans. Northern tourists respond by pouring as much as a half billion dollars annually into the valley's economy between September and May. Thousands of full-time RVers, like Frank and Agnes Salerno, bear the Winter Texan label proudly. "It's quiet, peaceful, here; not hectic," said Salerno. "I like the fishing and the good weather, and the food is excellent. I like to eat fresh fish and Mexican food, and it's in abundance here. The valley is very uncluttered; it's still undeveloped. It will get that way eventually, of course, but it has a long way to go."

Wintering On South Padre Island

When the Salernos bought their campground lot in 1978, their familiarity with the developer, Outdoor Resorts of America, prompted their decision to buy it. "We'd been to a couple of other ORA parks, and they are first-class places—clean, well kept with nice pads and good roads and good activities. And it was important to us, too, that the park was so close to South Padre Island. The first year we were in the valley, we stopped in

Harlingen, and we found we were driving down to the island three times a week, thirty miles each way. We figured, 'If we're going to the island so much, let's stay near the island.'

For Frank, the big draw of the Padre Island area is the Laguna Madre—the lagoon between South Padre and the mainland. "It has good fishing, three-feet-deep water with a good channel through it, and there's 100 miles of protected water," Frank said. He motors into the lagoon with his lightweight aluminum boat and catches speckled trout. Seven to eight pounders are not unusual, he said, "and two, three or four-pounders are run of the mill."

Frank found other outlets for his energies at the park. He works part-time cleaning the pools, changing light bulbs, maintaining the recreation building and keeping activity areas clean. An experienced electrician, he rewired the rec hall for a PA system, and then he donated his own tape recorder, tapes and records so that music could be piped into the activity rooms.

Agnes, meanwhile, joins the park's morning exercise classes, takes swimming and tennis lessons and goes fishing with Frank. "She just learned how to drive and got her license," her husband boasted. For the Salernos, full-time RVing in south Texas is an active life. "Our first year here, we didn't do hardly anything in the park," Frank reported. "We mainly spent our time walking the beaches, fishing and visiting all the towns in the valley and just across the border in Mexico. But during the last year, most of our activity has been here in the park."

The Salernos look forward to the special winter festivals held by the border towns, and they also like to shop in Mexican neighborhoods. "In Mexico, I like to walk around, look at the people, eat the food and just enjoy the atmosphere," Frank said. "I like to take a mini bus into one of the towns and then walk around, but I always take a map with me because I always get lost. I run into some very nice things that way. The people are all very nice, and I've never had any problems. In the valley, there is plenty to keep full-timers active if they want to run around. But we've cut down on our running tremendously; our driving has shrunk to practically nothing."

The Salernos live in a 31-foot Royals International travel trailer towed by a 1978 GMC Suburban. The first year they were full-timing, they kept a mobile home in Kenosha, Wisconsin, for a home base, "but we were in it two months out of twelve, and we did nothing but work the two months we were there to clean up the yard and maintain the property. So we figured we didn't need that, and we saved a heck of a lot of money by getting rid of it." They prepared for full-timing by subscribing to

South Padre Island's uncrowded beaches attract winter Texans from across the country.

Trailer Life magazine and joining the Good Sam Club even before they owned an RV. "Originally, we thought we'd buy a lot in Texas, keep it five years and then sell it and move on to Arizona. Now I figure we'll keep the lot here indefinitely because wherever we go, I think we'll always want to come back to the valley."

Unlike many full-timers, the Salernos did not postpone their retirement until they were in their sixties. Frank was fifty, Agnes forty-eight, when they hit the road. "One thing I would tell anybody who is contemplating RVing full time is, 'Go the first day you have the opportunity. Don't lose your chance to do it early because every day lost is just that—a day lost.' I've talked with a lot of people who say, 'I'm thinking about retirement, but I hate to leave my job because I don't know what I'd do.' Believe me, when you're full-timing, there aren't enough hours in the day to do the things you want to do."

The Rio Grande Valley

Bert and Greta Dean also are Winter Texans, and they own three campsites—two for investment purposes and one for themselves—near the Rio Grande Valley. "I retired April 1, 1975, and I planned to build a house, do a couple of other things I had in mind and then buy an RV to take off traveling in. But I had an opportunity to buy an RV and an old Cadillac to tow it with, so we left home in December of 1975, and we've been full-timing ever since. The first year, we covered the whole coast of Florida. Then we spent one summer in the Maritime Provinces of Canada. We were going to go west across Canada and then down into the Southwest to see a friend in Arizona, but . . . we headed directly for Arizona . . . and got side-tracked into south Texas. Here, we found ourselves getting into square dancing, so for the last three years, we've spent every winter here and go home to New York in the summer."

The Deans were inexperienced RVers when they began their full-timing life in 1975. "We had gone through the business of camping with our kids in a tent, but we'd never had an RV. The fact of the matter is, this is the only way of life that a retired person can have for the price he can afford to pay. Full-time RVing is like being on a full-time vacation. We're here, right now, in a resort area that cannot be equaled anywhere else in the world. What they don't have here, they'll provide if you need it, and we live here for practically nothing. It amazes me that more people haven't gotten wise to this way of life. I have no desire to get back into a house again. In fact, I feel sorry for people who have to put up with that burden."

Greta said, "We enjoy living in our trailer, it's much easier than keeping a home."

Bert added, "I retired when I was fifty-seven years old, but I should have done it sooner. I would recommend that people retire as early as they can—just as soon as they can work it out financially."

Greta said, "When we started trailering, we thought we'd stay in a motel one or two nights a week. We never thought we could live like this. But we have never stayed in a motel. The very thought of pulling up in front of a motel and carrying our stuff inside is almost repulsive."

Bert added, "If I were single and just getting out of college, I wouldn't even think of having anything but an RV . . . I'd never even think of owning any real estate except as an investment."

Condominium Camping In South Texas

Another pair of Winter Texans, Maurice and Evelyn Parker, began their RVing experiences early, unlike the Deans. "We started with a tent at my urging when our children were small," Evelyn reported. "I prodded him to rent one, but he said no at first and told me, 'I know you won't like a tent. One weekend in a tent will be enough for you.' Well, I surprised him.

Bastrop State Park, on the Texas Brazos Trail, is just one of the many camping areas along the Texas Travel Trails.

I liked it. So we bought a tent of our own. Next we built a truck camper, and we had a lot of fun with that. We bought various kinds of trailers over the years, then, until we got the one we have now—a 29-foot, 1973 Holiday Rambler."

Maurice retired from the welding business in 1977 at the age of sixty-two, and they traveled in their rig full time, using a mobile home in Wisconsin as a home base, until they began spending their winters in a south Texas condominium campground, where they bought a lot. There, they've found their niche, and they enjoy taking part in all the activities the campground offers its Winter Texans. But not everyone is as fortunate, they reported. "Evelyn meets women all the time who say they're unhappy with full-time RVing, and they've just started it," Maurice said. "The trouble is, when they go into a campground, they spend too much time in their trailers. They don't use the activities and facilities that are available to them. Nearly every campground has some activities. I don't know how people can live together and hole up in a trailer all the time."

Evelyn added, "And you can't sit and watch the boob tube all day long."

Maurice, an expert pool player, was recruited by the park manager to teach a group of women campers how to shoot pool so they could schedule an all-woman tournament. Evelyn joined the class too, and Maurice, with a twinkle in his eyes, said, "I never have figured out whether she comes up here to shoot pool or whether she wants to watch how I behave with all those other ladies."

His wife poked him in the ribs and said, "Just keep trying to figure it out, dear."

Each summer, the Parkers spend several weeks in their mobile home. It's quiet there, on their wooded lot in Wisconsin. "But by November, we're starting to get sick of being alone, and we look forward to the day we can go back to Texas and meet our old friends again," Maurice said. A few weeks before I met the Parkers, their children and grandchildren had visited them in Texas for the Christmas holidays. "We went over on Padre Island to the beach, and we had a Christmas Day lunch on the sand dunes," Evelyn reported. "The kids really had a ball."

The Parkers keep an electric freezer with them in Texas so they can buy large supplies of meat and vegetables and save money on food bills. The freezer enables them to buy a large roast, cut it into three sections and eat it over a period of weeks. Maurice also carries two large, fully equipped toolboxes with him on his travels. "There are enough tools in those boxes to tear either one of my rigs apart," he said. "And I carry an extra coil and an extra condenser for my truck because those are the main things that will stop us along the road." He said he figures the 1973 truck would last at least until 1983 before it would have to be replaced. "I do my own work on it, and I know what shape it's in."

Maurice also prepared for the possibility of financial emergencies by buying an electric welder and a complete cutting outfit. "I could go out and make a lot of money, but we don't need it right now. With that equipment, though, I could supplement our income rather easily if I had to."

ANYWHERE, USA

It doesn't really matter whether you call most full-timing couples Winter Texans or Summer Iowans, Snowbirds or RV gypsies; they regard the entire nation as their home. And even though they might still own a house or keep a mobile home as a base camp, their real residence is that trailer or motorhome that travels with them. Their address: Anywhere, USA.

Perry "Steamboat" and Hazel Van Osdol have regarded the whole nation as their home for several years—first, while he was a traveling wholesaler of propane gas equipment and then, since 1979, as "Sambassadors" for the Good Sam Club. "In the backs of our minds, we'd planned to go into full-time RVing for years," reported Steamboat, "I had a Scout troop for about thirty years, and Hazel was involved with the Girl Scouts. We loved camping of all kinds and traveled as much as possible. What kept us from doing it for so many years, though, was that I was a propane gas dealer, and that took a lot of time. We were just riding the middle road between being successful in business and not being successful in it, and we kept thinking that we ought to get into the business more heavily. We had three other stockholders, and we decided to borrow enough money through the Small Business Administration to pay them off and put a little more into the business to expand. But when we applied to the SBA, we learned that although our credit was good, we didn't fit into their categories properly, so we couldn't get any money. The SBA did us a favor, really. We began traveling in our trailer and putting on propane safety demonstrations at Good Sam rallies."

They sold their house in Kansas to their oldest son and put a mobile home on a lot in Hutchinson, Kansas, to serve as a home base. When I talked with the Van Osdols in the spring of 1980, they were towing a 28-foot Silver Streak trailer with a Chevrolet Suburban powered, of course, by LP-gas. They live on about $1,000 a month—not including some of the expenses paid by the Good Sam Club—on income from a military pension fund and Social Security. And although they watch how much they spend rather carefully, they agree with the philosophy behind the familiar full-time RVers' bumper sticker: "We're spending our children's inheritance!"

Steamboat said, "Everyone knows you can't take it with you, and we figure that if we leave it behind, someone's going to fight over it. So we spend as we go, up to a point of not putting ourselves into a bind. We see our children and grandchildren as often as possible—at least four times a year, in fact—but we keep remembering the way we grew up. We were raised in Kansas during the dustbowl days when we were lucky to have anything to eat on the table. And we feel like someone up there is taking real good care of us. He has, through the years, and He is still continuing to do so. We feel very fortunate, and we're really thankful we can live the way we do."

Another full-timer once wrote to *Trailer Life* magazine expressing the same attitude of thankfulness. "We see the country at an easy pace and get enough exercise sightseeing and riding our bikes around parks to keep fit. There may be a hidden blessing in having to do with less refrigerator space and having a low food budget; we eat more fresh foods produced in the localities in which we are; simultaneously, we get acquainted with people of the countryside, experiencing accents and mannerisms, but also learning that there are good people all over the country. And no matter where we go, we eventually find someone who knows someone we know or who lives so close to our home that we feel we know them. So we never lose our own accents. Nice, isn't it?"

Alberta M. Torgeson did a good job of summing up The Good Life of full-time RVing in her *Trailer Life* article, "We Vacation Every Day!" (November 1979). She wrote, "Our children ask us, 'Don't you get bored with all this free time?' I can truthfully say no. We keep so busy that I have not found the free time to do the needlework which I had thought I would do. My domain is the kitchen. I enjoy cooking, and now that we are just two, I have been making gourmet dishes that were too impractical to make for a family. My husband takes over the rear section to paint his watercolors, which he plans to exhibit somewhere. We always take a walk each day for exercise and sometimes walk two or three miles in the woods on nature trails. We do not know how long we can keep going with this style of living, but we plan to do it as long as possible. When we reach the time that we can no longer travel, we will decide then, where and in what we will live. However, we now feel that we have many miles to go before we sleep."

And I'd be willing to bet that, along the way, she and her husband will always take time to stop and smell the flowers.